CICERO AND THE EARLY LATIN POETS

The writings of Cicero contain hundreds of quotations of Latin poetry. This book examines his citations of Latin poets writing in diverse poetic genres and demonstrates the importance of poetry as an ethical, historical, and linguistic resource in the late Roman Republic. Hannah Čulík-Baird studies Cicero's use of poetry in his letters, speeches, and philosophical works, contextualizing his practice within the broader intellectual trends of contemporary Rome. Cicero's quotations of the "classic" Latin poets, such as Ennius, Pacuvius, Accius, and Lucilius, are responsible for preserving the most significant fragments of verse from the second century BCE. The book also therefore examines the process of fragmentation in classical antiquity, with particular attention to the relationship between quotation and fragmentation. The Appendices collect perceptible instances of poetic citation (Greek as well as Latin) in the Ciceronian corpus.

HANNAH ČULÍK-BAIRD is an Assistant Professor of Classical Studies at Boston University.

T0382454

CICERO AND THE EARLY LATIN POETS

HANNAH ČULÍK-BAIRD

Boston University

CAMBRIDGE
UNIVERSITY PRESS

CAMBRIDGE
UNIVERSITY PRESS

Shaftesbury Road, Cambridge CB2 8EA, United Kingdom

One Liberty Plaza, 20th Floor, New York, NY 10006, USA

477 Williamstown Road, Port Melbourne, VIC 3207, Australia

314–321, 3rd Floor, Plot 3, Splendor Forum, Jasola District Centre, New Delhi – 110025, India

103 Penang Road, #05–06/07, Visioncrest Commercial, Singapore 238467

Cambridge University Press is part of Cambridge University Press & Assessment,
a department of the University of Cambridge.

We share the University's mission to contribute to society through the pursuit of
education, learning and research at the highest international levels of excellence.

www.cambridge.org
Information on this title: www.cambridge.org/9781009013703

DOI: 10.1017/9781009031820

First published 2022
First paperback edition 2023

A catalogue record for this publication is available from the British Library

Library of Congress Cataloging-in-Publication data
NAMES: Čulík-Baird, Hannah, 1989– author.
TITLE: Cicero and the early Latin poets / Hannah Čulík-Baird.
DESCRIPTION: Cambridge, United Kingdom ; New York, NY : Cambridge University
Press, 2022. | Based on author's thesis (doctoral) – University of Southern California. |
Includes bibliographical references and index.
IDENTIFIERS: LCCN 2021049226 (print) | LCCN 2021049227 (ebook) | ISBN 9781316516089
(hardback) | ISBN 9781009031820 (ebook)
SUBJECTS: LCSH: Cicero, Marcus Tullius – Criticism and interpretation. | Latin poetry –
Appreciation. | Poets, Latin – Quotations. | Quotations, Latin, in literature. | BISAC: HISTORY
/ Ancient / General | LCGFT: Literary criticism.
CLASSIFICATION: LCC PA6350 .C85 2022 (print) | LCC PA6350 (ebook) | DDC 871/.0109–dc23
/eng/20211214
LC record available at https://lccn.loc.gov/2021049226
LC ebook record available at https://lccn.loc.gov/2021049227

ISBN   978-1-316-51608-9   Hardback
ISBN   978-1-009-01370-3   Paperback

"All minds quote. Old and new make the warp and woof of every moment. There is no thread that is not a twist of these two strands."

Ralph Waldo Emerson

uetustas pauca non deprauat, multa tollit
"There is little that time does not distort, much it obliterates completely."

Varro

To Austin

Contents

Acknowledgements

The book that you hold in your hands started its life as a PhD dissertation supervised by Tom Habinek at the University of Southern California. Tom, a challenging and fiercely influential figure in my life, as in so many others, passed away at the beginning of 2019. Tom's iconoclasm and intense intellectual curiosity had a profound impact on my own thinking – I thank him for providing a model of courage and creativity. I thank Tony Boyle, whose own work on Roman tragic fragments first inspired this project, for his stern guidance, incisive critique, devoted friendship – and for welcoming me so warmly into the Pac Rim community.

To John Dugan I owe the deepest gratitude for years of counsel and support.

I express enormous appreciation and esteem to my students and colleagues at Boston University. In particular, I thank James Uden for his enthusiastic support, helpful advice, and thoughtful feedback. I am deeply grateful to the BU Center of Humanities whose Junior Fellowship provided me the time and space to complete this manuscript. I would also like to thank a number of scholars who have supported my work and well-being in innumerable ways: Afroditi Angelopoulou, Sarah Bond, Hamish Cameron, Joel Christensen, Kayla Dang, Stephanie Frampton, Nicole Giannella, Joe Howley, Sharon James, Christian Lehmann, Scott Lepisto, Suzanne Lye, Elke Nash, Nandini Pandey, Dan-el Padilla Peralta, Joe Romero, Tom Sapsford, Enrica Sciarrino, Debby Sneed, Lisl Walsh, Christina Wilson. I also thank Sander Goldberg, who read a draft of the manuscript shortly before its publication and offered useful critique. I thank the two anonymous reviewers whose insightful feedback immeasurably improved the project. And I thank Michael Sharp and Liz Davey at Cambridge University Press for their work on this book.

Thank you to my parents, Lesley Keen and Jan Čulík, for instilling in me the strength, stubbornness, and creative fire I needed to complete this project. I thank my sister, Ema Sibikina, the living, sparkling embodiment of inspiration, my role model from the beginning; and Alesha Sibikin for his friendship and inexhaustible good humour. To Olya, my young nibling, born in Scotland under the COVID-19 lockdown: I look forward to meeting you, my lovely one. I would like to thank my husband's family as well as my own for their care and support all these years. Our stalwart friend, GT, passed away during the composition of this text – we miss him every day. I thank him and Max, his brilliant and naughty successor, for the love and wisdom that only dogs can bring.

I thank Classics Twitter for being a welcoming home to me and so many others.

I thank Austin Baird, love of my life, for his patience, kindness, and incredible (so he thinks) sense of humour.

Note on Editions of Fragments

Since the editions of Latin fragments cited in the present work each have different goals and therefore function slightly differently, it would be helpful here to clarify a number of conventions and idiosyncrasies. Several Latin poets discussed in this book have standalone editions which treat their author's extant fragments together as a totality: Pacuvius is served by Petra Schierl's *Die Tragödien des Pacuvius* (2006); Accius by Jacqueline Dangel's *Accius: Oeuvres, Fragments* (2002). While newer editions of Lucilius have appeared since Eric Herbert Warmington's Loebs, it is still conventional to refer to his fragments by their numeration in Warmington (*Remains of Old Latin*, Vol. III, 1938); where fragments of (or references to) Lucilius are omitted by Warmington, I use the edition of Friedrich Marx (1904–1905). Fragments of Ennius are numerous enough to be served by standalone editions defined by genre (*Annales*: Skutsch 1985; tragedies: Jocelyn 1969), but also appear in other editorial series: the new *Tragicorum Romanorum Fragmenta* (*TrRF*) collects all of the fragments of Ennian tragedy in Volume II (ed. Gesine Manuwald, 2012); and the new Ennius Loebs in the *Fragmentary Republican Latin* series, edited by Sander Goldberg and Gesine Manuwald (2018), contain fragments from all of Ennius' works. The fragments of unknown tragic poets are referenced by their numeration in *TrRF* Volume I (ed. Markus Schauer, 2012). The fragments of comedy, mime, and Atellan farce – those attributed to a known author (e.g. Caecilius Statius) as well as fragments which are unattributable (*incerta*) – are referenced by their numeration in Otto Ribbeck's (1855) edition of comic fragments. Other kinds of Latin verse quoted (but mostly alluded to) by Cicero, such as the epitaph of A. Atilius Calatinus (cos. 258 BCE) or the *carmina conuiualia,* are referenced by their numeration in the *Fragmenta Poetarum Latinorum* (*FPL*) most recently edited by Willy Morel (2011). Fragments of more "contemporary" Latin poets quoted (or alluded to) by Cicero, such as the epigram of Q. Catulus (cos. 102 BCE) for Roscius the actor or the tragedies of Quintus Cicero, are

referenced by their numeration in Edward Courtney's *The Fragmentary
Latin Poets* (2003). Fragments of Cicero's poetry and Latin translations of
Greek poetry are served by Jean Soubiran (1972). Many fragments discussed in this book have either no secure attribution – we do not know who
wrote them, or to what text they belonged – or a contested attribution. In
the latter case, I have tried to record degrees of doubt rather than to
adjudicate the attributions. The already complex question of attribution
has been further complexified by the recent *TrRF*, which is more conservative than its forebears: several of the fragments discussed in this volume
which were once attributed to Latin poets have been downgraded by the
editors and listed among the fragments of unknown tragic poets in *TrRF*
Vol. I. Since the study of fragments requires a sense of imagination as well
as the reflex of scepticism, I have noted prior attributions as well as the
downgrading: e.g. a fragment at *Fin.* 5.63 appears as Pacuvius' *Chryses*
(fr. 69) in Schierl's edition but among the fragments of unknown poets in
the *TrRF* (= *TrRF* I 48); in the text and the Appendices, I give both. For
a full list of editions of fragments employed in this book, including editions
of fragmentary Greek poetry, see the list of Abbreviations.

Texts and Abbreviations

The texts of Cicero reproduced in this book derive from the editions contained within the Classical Latin Texts prepared by The Packard Humanities Institute (*latin.packhum.org*). The texts of Latin fragments follow what is printed in each fragmentary edition (Skutsch, *TrRF*, Warmington, etc.). Significant differences between the text of Cicero and the text of the fragment (made via editorial intervention) are noted in the pertinent passages.

Courtney	*The Fragmentary Latin Poets* (2003).
CPG	*Corpus Paroemiographorum Graecorum*, ed. E. von Leutsch, F. W. Schneidewin (1839).
Dangel	*Accius. Oeuvres, Fragments* (2002).
Diehl	*Anthologia Lyrica Graeca*, ed. E. Diehl, 2 vols (1936/1942).
FPL	*Fragmenta Poetarum Latinorum*, eds. W. Morel, K. Büchner, J. Blänsdorf (2011).
Goldberg-Manuwald	*Fragmentary Republican Latin, Volume I: Ennius, Testimonia. Epic Fragments*, eds. S. Goldberg and G. Manuwald (2018).
GRF	*Grammaticae Romanae Fragmenta*, ed. G. Funaioli (1907).
Jocelyn	*The Tragedies of Ennius* (1969).
Kock	*Comicorum Atticorum Fragmenta* (1880–1888).
Marx	*C. Lucili Carminum Reliquiae*, ed. F. Marx (1904–1905).
Nauck	*Tragicorum Graecorum Fragmenta. Supplementum adiecit Bruno Snell*, ed. A. Nauck (1964).[1]

---

[1] Nauck's *TGFr* has now been substantially revised by B. Snell, R. Kannicht, and S. L. Radt. Yet the new edition for the most part retains Nauck's numeration.

Pfeiffer	*Callimachus*, ed. R. Pfeiffer 2 vols (1949–1953).
Ribbeck	*Scaenicae Romanorum poesis fragmenta: Vol. II. Comicorum Romanorum praeter Plautum et Terentium fragmenta*, ed. O. Ribbeck (1855).
Schierl	*Die Tragödien des Pacuvius: ein Kommentar zu den Fragmenten mit Einleitung, Text und Übersetzung* (2006).
Skutsch	*The Annals of Q. Ennius* (1985).
Snell	*Pindari Carmina cum Fragmentis*, ed. B. Snell (1953).
Soubiran	*Aratea: fragments poétiques* (1972).
TrRF	*Tragicorum Romanorum Fragmenta. I: Livius Andronicus, Naevius, Tragici Minores, Fragmenta Adespota*, ed. M. Schauer (2012); II: *Ennius*, ed. G. Manuwald (2012).
Warmington	*Remains of Old Latin Vol. III: Lucilius, The Twelve Tables*, ed. E. H. Warmington (1938).
Zillinger	*Cicero Und Die Altrömischen Dichter* (1911).

"All Minds Quote"

In 1991, the American novelist Nicholson Baker, author of works such as *The Mezzanine* (1988) and *Vox* (1992), published a short, non-fiction, and first-person exploration of his own relationship with a preeminent literary precursor, John Updike. This work is called *U and I: A True Story*, and in it, Baker discusses literary influence.[1]

In *U and I*, Baker explores the phenomenon of greatly admiring and being greatly influenced by John Updike by engaging in a citational experiment. As he writes the essay on the first pass, he quotes phrases of John Updike from memory. On the second pass, he checks these citations from memory with how they appear in print, leaving the "errors" in his essay but marking them with square brackets and comment. As Baker (1991: 37) corrects his misquotations, he is surprised to find that several of Updike's phrases originally appeared in different works than the ones he remembered:

> ... when I finished the entire essay I assembled all my Updike books, and I took out from the library the ones I lacked, and I tried to locate each phrase I had used. In most cases I regretfully corrected my misquotations – regretfully because my errors of memory were themselves of mild scientific interest to me. A surprising number of phrases weren't where I remembered them as being – for example, I was sure that "vast dying sea," which I encountered in 1982, was in "Who Made Yellow Roses Yellow," but I finally found it in "Incest." And I *knew* that his sentence about reading "what they told me" in college was in *Esquire*'s 1989 summer reading issue – it isn't.

In cases where Baker (*ibid.*) could not find the original Updike passage, he rephrased his citation to indicate that the quotation was a paraphrase:

> Where my argument depends in some way on my misquotation, I have left the error intact and simply corrected myself between brackets: []. If the

---

[1] I owe my thanks to Christian Lehmann, who first introduced me to Baker's *U and I.*

phrase was not to be found anywhere in a week of flipping and skimming, I resorted to "Updike says something like" and kindred fudgings to indicate that what I'm remembering is only a paraphrase, and may not even exist.

Baker's (1991: 81) citational self-correction allows the reader to compare the impression of Updike's words upon him alongside the original:

> ... in one of his early poems he talks about the view from shipboard:
>
> > The blue below
> > Is Aquamarine
> > Sometimes the blue below
> > Is green
>
> [The real lines, from "Shipbored," are:
>
> > That line is the horizon line.
> > The blue above it is divine.
> > The blue below it is marine.
> > Sometimes the blue below is green.]

In this case, Baker's misremembering of the verses has the feel of exposing a mental imprint: instead of producing a facsimile, Baker has presented a memory artefact of his own cognition, his process of understanding (and retaining) the poem. Updike's "The blue below it is marine" is turned into Baker's "The blue below is Aquamarine." The change of "marine" into "aquamarine" is an artefact of Baker's interpretation and understanding of the poem, and it is *this* understanding that has implanted itself into his memory. And as Baker the novelist wrote his own works, it is this alchemical mix of the original and his own mind which influences his compositional techniques and his own writing. Baker's citational experiment reveals that the material effects of literary influence require two parts: both the text of the literary icon, *and* the mind of the individual who invokes it. While memory may distort text even in the act of citation, this distorted text nonetheless influences the very mind which created the distortion. Citation takes text on a deviating path – but such deviations enshrine the power of the original literary object.

When Baker contemplated the idea that Updike had had so great an influence on him and for so long, he quoted a passage from the Australian-born Classicist, Gilbert Murray, who published *A History of Ancient Greek Literature* in 1897. In *U and I*, Baker (1991: 28) quotes part of Murray's preface to this work:

> Writing this reminds me of a touching fritter from the preface to Gilbert Murray's *Ancient Greek Literature* [1897: xi–xii]: " . . . for the past ten years at

least, hardly a day has passed on which Greek poetry has not occupied a large part of my thoughts, hardly one deep or valuable emotion has come into my life which has not been either caused, or interpreted, or bettered by Greek poetry." Hardly a day has passed over the last thirteen years in which Updike has not occupied at least a thought or two.

Quoting Murray's insistence that Greek poetry has always loomed large in his mind (and thereby influenced both his emotional experiences of life and motivated his scholarship), Baker presents the idea of his own persistent mental vision of Updike. After the direct citation of Murray, Baker also paraphrases Murray to describe his own relationship to Updike:

MURRAY: . . . for the past ten years at least, hardly a day has passed on which Greek poetry has not occupied a large part of my thoughts, hardly one deep or valuable emotion has come into my life which has not been either caused, or interpreted, or bettered by Greek poetry.

BAKER: Hardly a day has passed over the last thirteen years in which Updike has not occupied at least a thought or two.

The paraphrase includes several exact snippets, such as "hardly a day has passed" and "has not occupied," but there are also changes: "*for* the past ten years" has turned into "*over* the last *thirteen* years,"[2] "*on* which" has turned into "*in* which," and "a large part of my thoughts" into "a thought or two." With this paraphrase or quotation, however it ought to be categorized, of Gilbert Murray, Baker deepens his claim of Updike's influence, while also demonstrating the transference of ideas which citation can achieve. There are two quotations of Murray: one is explicit, i.e. *marked as a quotation* – with quotation marks, the name of the author, the title of the work, *where* in the work the quotation appears (the preface), and activates Murray's sentiment that constantly thinking about Greek poetry indelibly influenced his life; the repeated sentiment is a paraphrase rather than a word-for-word quotation – it is looser, and fitted to Baker's own use. But this paraphrasing echo allows Murray's relationship with Greek literature to be folded into and reenacted by Baker's relationship to Updike.

There is a negative side to the persistent mental imprint of a literary icon. In the beginning of *U and I*, Baker (1991: 3) reflects on preparing to

---

[2] Murray 1897: xii in fact reads "over the *last* ten years," not past; another artefact of Baker's citational memory, or else a typographical error: Baker's "paraphrase" of Murray uses last, not past.

write in the morning, and having his creativity stymied by the looming spectre of Updike:

> ... but before I could move my fingers, I recalled that Updike had said something similar in *Self-Consciousness*: "In the morning light one can write breezily, without the slightest acceleration of one's pulse, about what one cannot contemplate in the dark without turning in panic to God." A memorable sentence for me (though I only remembered the first half) not only because it seemed simple and true, but because I had read it twice, first quoted in a book review and then in the book itself. And with this memory of Updike I hesitated; I didn't type what I was going to type; I shifted course.

A memorable sentence, even one whose power is such that it apparently destroys originality of thought, is only "half-remembered"; a literary precursor can be powerful even if it cannot be fully called to mind. The power of the quotation is its "simplicity and truth"; its proverbial, gnomic character. Baker had read the memorable sentence twice; however, the first time was not in the book itself, but in a *book review*, demonstrating that a canon focalization had led his attention to it in the first place. Finally, the looming of Updike stopped Baker from writing what he was going to write, and he wrote something else. Yet the destruction of Baker's originality by the spectre of Updike is only partial; the sensation of Updike's influence upon him led Baker to formulate his own theory of influence, allowing Baker's reader to contemplate the broader phenomenon of literary debt and originality, the very literary amalgam which *U and I* presents itself to be.

In his essay, "Quotation and Originality," the American transcendentalist, Ralph Waldo Emerson, highlighted quotation as an essential structural feature of human society, while simultaneously criticizing it for a 'stymieing' effect (§2):

> Our debt to tradition through reading and conversation is so massive, our protest or private addition so rare and insignificant, – and that commonly on the ground of other reading or hearing, – that, in a large sense, one would say, there is no pure originality. All minds quote. Old and new make the warp and woof of every moment. There is no thread that is not a twist of these two strands. By necessity, by proclivity, and by delight, we all quote. We quote not only books and proverbs, but arts, sciences, religion, customs, and laws; nay, we quote temples and houses, tables and chairs.[3]

---

[3] On a different view of the "architecture" of the ancient in modern thought, see duBois 1995: 2–3: "I want to think about classical antiquity, and not just as the source of quotation for postmodern architecture but as an unstable object in our construction of a relationship to the past."

In the same essay, Emerson (§11) compares the "admirable mimic" who has "nothing of their own" to parasites of the natural world such as the vampire bat or the *teredo navalis*, the naval shipworm which wreaks havoc upon any submerged timber. The impulse to quote is thereby figured as a destructive one fit only to feed the life-force of parasitical entities. Emerson also looks upon the instinct to situate oneself within a tradition as a kind of economics – a "mental indebtedness" like "pecuniary debt" (§13), an ineffective economic system that does not reward innovation and which is prone to bankruptcy. Perceiving influence, Emerson writes (§4), also reveals an infinitely recursive chain of allusion: "read Tasso, and you think of Virgil, read Virgil, and you think of Homer; and Milton forces you to reflect how narrow are the limits of human invention."

In his infamous (and itself influential) work, *The Anxiety of Influence* (1973), Harold Bloom discussed citationality and allusion in terms which are in some ways reminiscent of Emerson's comments, in that both writers considered quotation and originality to be essentially antithetical.[4] For Bloom, every generation of (post-enlightenment) poets fights against their poetic precursors in a struggle which he figures as a manifestation of Freud's Oedipal complex; the struggle for primacy and authority between fathers and sons. To idealize the poetic precursor is to be "weak," in Bloom's view; the "strong" poet is the one who fights for immortality, which means killing not only death, but the surviving images of the old poets.[5] In the twentieth century, Wallace Stevens claimed to have been influenced by no other poet; indeed, Stevens claimed deliberately not to read T. S. Eliot and Ezra Pound so as "not to absorb anything, even unconsciously."[6] According to Bloom, however, the poet can never entirely escape the influence of precursors, but achieves supremacy over them via a series of mechanisms whereby poetry of the past is reconstituted and made new.[7] The brutal spiritualism of Bloom's poetic theory insists that, even when the modern poet "defeats" his precursors, such a victory can only be achieved where reference to the prior poet is an absolute constant.

---

[4] While Bloom's work was deeply influential upon both academic and public thought, his "strong man" theory of literature and his insistence upon the supremacy of a "Western Canon" (1994) has itself had a destructive, fragmenting effect.

[5] Bloom 1973: 10: "Oedipus, blind, was on the path to oracular godhood, and the strong poets have followed him by transforming their blindness towards their precursors into the revisionary insights of their own work."

[6] In a letter to Richard Eberhart, written January 15, 1954.

[7] Bloom 1973: 14–15. The poet does this by: swerving away from the original (*clinamen*); by completing the precursor (*tessera*); the hollowing out from the self of internalized images (*kenosis*); adoption of a latent aspect of the precursor (*daemonization*); shutting off certain imaginative avenues (*askesis*); holding a poem open to assert dominant authority over prior exempla (*apophrades*).

The anxiety of originality has a different character in the context of the culture of Republican Rome. While certainly the extant writers of Republican literature each make a deliberate claim to their own authorial voice and creative prowess, literary production at Rome is also deeply rooted in a broader cultural conservatism and an overt respect for exemplary forebears. Textual artefacts from Rome, whether oratorical, poetic, or historiographical, all draw from a deeply ingrained conservatism rooted in the understanding that ancestors and ancestral values permeated and gave measure to Roman life. Bloom's impulse to "defeat" his precursors and take their place is, to some extent, a counter-cultural maneuvre; an attempt to upturn the past while simultaneously reabsorbing it. However, if this literary Oedipal instinct was operative in Republican culture, it was latent. Writers during the Republican period *extended* the literary past with their development of its ideas; they wanted to embody and vivify it to give it new potency, not destroy it with their own originality. Recursiveness and self-replication was a key aspect of Roman culture, with repetition and iteration as an ostensible index of stability. Examples of a Roman interest in cultural recursiveness are plentiful: the statue of a patrician carrying the busts of two male relatives known as the Barberini Togatus is a famous *mise en abyme* of ancestral veneration; Cicero invokes the ancient Appius Claudius in the *Pro Caelio* (33–34) to chastise Clodia's break from ancestral models, and similarly criticized L. Calpurnius Piso's inability to live up to the *imagines* of his household in the *In Pisonem* (1).[8]

Citationality as a cultural mechanism is deeply instinctual. The notion of imitation implicit in the citational impulse is noted by the anthropologist, Paul Connerton, who, in *How Societies Remember*, discussed Thomas Mann's understanding of the Freudian ego:[9]

> We are to envisage the ego, less sharply defined and less exclusive than we commonly conceive of it, as being so to speak "open behind": open to the resources of myth which are to be understood as existing for the individual not just as a grid of categories, but as a set of possibilities which can become subjective, which can be lived consciously. In this archaising attitude the life of the individual is consciously lived as a "sacred repetition," as the explicit reanimation of prototypes.

In *The World of Roman Song* (2005), Thomas Habinek argued that icons of Roman memory such as the aristocratic *imagines* or the *ancilia* of the Salian

---

[8] On the Barberini Togatus, see Marlowe 2013: 71–75. On Appius Claudius in the *Pro Caelio*: Dufallo 2007: 13–35. On *imagines*: Flower 1996, Dufallo 2001, Højte 2002.
[9] Connerton 1989: 62.

priests could be explained with Mann's theory of the "explicit reanimation of prototypes."[10] In Habinek's (2005: 130) view, "the archaic miniatures, as likely marks of initiation, would seem to invite reanimation of ancestral prototypes on the part of their bearers while alive." Such ritual repetition and performative "citational practice" was key to gender theorist Judith Butler's explanation of how culture propagates by repetition, constructing the human idea of the body:[11]

> ... regulatory norms materialize "sex" and achieve this materialization through a forcible reiteration of those norms. That this reiteration is necessary is a sign that materialization is never quite complete, that bodies never quite comply with the norms by which their materialization is impelled. Indeed, it is the instabilities, the possibilities for rematerialization, opened up by this process that mark one domain in which the force of the regulatory law can be turned against itself to spawn rearticulations that call into question the hegemonic force of that very regulatory law.

Butler's understanding of citationality as replication makes clear that an attempt to rematerialize (or "reanimate") a prototype is not an immediate instantiation, or copy, of the cited referent. Indeed, as Amy Hollywood (2002: 94), commenting on Butler, notes: "the gaps and fissures in that citational process – the ways in which repetition both repeats the same and differs and defers from it – mark the multiple sites on/in which the contestation of regulatory norms occurs." The impossibility of creating a faithful copy of the cited referent *necessarily* introduces variations and distortions, *even if* the quoting individual intends to be faithful to their precursor. To some extent, we here arrive back at Bloom's essential theory of the "strong" poet's conflict with his precursor; in the process of *apophrades*: "the later poet ... holds his own poem so open again to the precursor's work that at first we might believe the wheel has come full circle."[12] We also arrive back at Nicholson Baker and his unconscious, yet transformative, citations of John Updike.

 Citationality has many manifestations which are interconnected yet also distinct from one another. Citationality is a constellation which includes but is not limited to: quotation, reference, imitation, iteration, substantiation, invocation, intertext, allusion, replication, renunciation.[13] Verbal quotation, which is the topic of this book (indeed, the topic is even

---

[10] Habinek 2005: 129, drawing on Connerton 1989: 62. Tronzo (2009: 1) remarks that fragments "have the resonance of archetypes."

[11] Butler 1993: xii.   [12] Bloom 1973: 16.

[13] While citation is very often used to express assent (i.e. approval of the contents of the quotation), citation is also an underlying mechanism of criticism. Recently, Henriette van der Blom (2016: 191–194) has

narrower than the quotation of "words," the quotation of poetry; even
more specifically, Latin poetry), is just one part of a much larger process.
While citation and intertextuality share many similarities, quotation has
a slightly different character. In the context of Latin poetry, intertextuality
consciously (and unconsciously) embeds elements of precursor poetry into
the new poem's body, elements which can be activated by an alert reader.[14]
While quotations can certainly be "inert" – in that they can be so entangled
with the body of the text in which they are embedded that they are
rendered either invisible, or very difficult to delineate – the majority of
the quotations which this book studies were intended to be explicit, overt,
unavoidably detectable.

Quotations, then, actively engage their referent via a substantial representation, whether word-for-word, in paraphrase, or in other truncated
form. In the context of theoretical reflections regarding the individual's
relationship to their forebears, it becomes clear that quotation is itself an
iteration of the mechanism of cultural replication. Yet, if we return again to
Baker's representation of Updike's influence upon him, we can see that the
relationship between the cited and the citer is not to be understood as
either simple or one dimensional. Baker's "misrememberings" of Updike
may have been distortions of the original text, but their changed form also
demonstrates the essential creativity of citation. As Butler shows, replication can *never* achieve a completely "faithful" reinstantiation (i.e.
a "copy"); via accidental error, accretion, or deliberate adjustment, citation
always introduces a new archaeological layer of meaning. As a result,
citation as an iteration of an original creates something inherently new.

Fragmentation

Citationality and fragmentation have an intimate relationship. While the
vast majority of classical texts have been preserved because they were
transmitted via a manuscript tradition which, in its own complicated
way, allowed some ancient texts to survive via medieval and renaissance
intermediaries, many extant texts today exist in a fragmentary state. Some
texts have become fragmented because of material causes, such as the
fragments of Sappho which are solely preserved in papyrus shards (rather

---

demonstrated that Cicero's negative "citation" of L. Calpurnius Piso in the *In Pisonem* resulted in
oratorical fragments skewed against their ostensible author.
[14] Hinds 1998: 23: "One of the reasons for the durability and continuing usefulness of 'allusion' as
a description of this kind of gesture is precisely the teasing play which it defines between revelation
and concealment."

than via quotation); or the text of Cicero's *De Republica*, parts of which were preserved in a palimpsest.[15] However, a large number of literary fragments survive because they were embedded as quotations in the works of later authors. When these later writers quoted their literary precursors, in many cases the full text (or at least, a fuller text) of the cited work was available;[16] e.g. when Cicero quoted Ennius' *Annales*, book copies of this text were still circulating at Rome.[17] Over time, however, these earlier works stopped circulating and were not included in the canon of ancient authors subsequently transmitted to modernity. Yet since the works of the *citing* authors survive, we are still able to read the excerpts of the *cited* authors embedded within.

For a time, it was enough for modern readers of ancient texts to see these fragmentary precursors through the eyes of the ancient writers who cited them. This was certainly the case for Petrarch, who famously encountered Ennius when he read Cicero's *De Officiis*.[18] While Petrarch could only be exposed to Ennius via intermediaries, this did not stop him from wholeheartedly embracing the poet as a spiritual forebear and reanimating him as a prototype. Indeed, as Nora Goldschmidt (2012: 2) has remarked, Ennius in fragments has greater appeal: "like the 'touch of Sappho' in Victorian England, Ennius exerts a fascination that exceeds that which he would have generated had his text survived complete." Petrarch's Latin epic, the *Africa* (left unfinished

---

[15] Much of what survives of Cicero's *De Republica* (excluding the *Somnium Scipionis*, see Zetzel 1995: 34, Dionisotti 1997: 1) derives from the seventh-century manuscript, Vaticanus Latinus 5757, a copy of Augustine's commentary on the Psalms written over the text of Cicero's *De Republica*. On the palimpsest and Angelo Mai, the discoverer of the Ciceronian layer, see Zetzel 1995: 33. In the case of both Sappho and Cicero's *De Republica*, whose texts are fragmented via material degradation (papyrological disintegration and manuscript reuse), fragments of the same works are also created via literary quotation. Two of Sappho's most famous poems, fragments 1 and 31, were also quoted by Greek writers of the Roman era. Fragment 1, a small scrap of which appears on P. Oxy. 2288, was quoted and preserved more fully by Dionysius of Halicarnassus (*De Compositione Verborum* 23); fragment 31, which appears on P.S.I. 15 1470, was quoted by the author of Περὶ Ὕψους (10.1–3). Fragments of Cicero's *De Republica* were also preserved by grammarians and as well as by the church fathers, in particular Augustine; see Zetzel 1995: 34.

[16] Many citing authors (including Cicero in certain cases) did not quote material from the original text, but from an intermediary; i.e. they quoted a quotation. In particular, grammarians often quoted literary material from other grammatical works, rather than from the full text.

[17] In the *Orator* (160), Cicero mentions that an archaic form of a Latin word can be found in the "old manuscripts" (*antiqui libri*) of Ennius. In the Antonine period, Aulus Gellius was able to consult a book containing Ennius' *Iphigenia* (19.10.12), and he writes that a contemporary scholar "rented" (*conducere*) a copy of Ennius' *Annales* (18.5.11) said to have been edited by Octavius Lampadio. On the circulation of Ennius' scripts and the point at which they vanished, see Jocelyn 1969b.

[18] *Fam.* 3.18.4: *Ennii nomen in Officiorum libris audivi*, "I heard Ennius' name in the *De Officiis*." On this passage, see Dionisotti 1997: 18.

at his death in 1374) told the story of the Second Punic War, a narrative which once made up Books 7–9 of Ennius' *Annales*.[19] Ennius appears in Petrarch's *Africa* as a character and is depicted telling Scipio the dream he had on the eve of battle. In this dream, Homer appeared to Ennius and foretold the future coming of another poet, a young man of Florence, i.e. Petrarch (*Africa* 9.229–239).

Ennius presented himself as Homer reincarnate; recursively, Petrarch became "a second Ennius" (*uelut Ennius alter, Africa* 2.443).[20] Given that Cicero's *Somnium Scipionis* explicitly took Ennius' dream of Homer as an inspiration for its contents, the appearance of "Ennius" in Petrarch's *Africa* is not a straightforward reception of the poet, but rather a reception of Cicero's invocation of Ennius.[21] Indeed, Petrarch explicitly drew from Cicero for his own understanding of poetry: in the *Coronation Oration* (*Collatio laureationis*), delivered on 8 April 1341 at Rome upon his crowning as poet laureate, Petrarch meditated on the power of poetic inspiration with a paraphrase of Cicero's *Pro Archia* (18).[22] Petrarch's invocation of Cicero included a word (*sancti*, "sacred") which may be a fragment of Ennius' *Annales*:[23]

> Non mihi sed Ciceroni credite qui in oratione pro Aulo Licinio Archia de poetis loquens verbis talibus utitur. Ab eruditissimis viris atque doctissimis accepimus, ceterarum rerum studia et ingenio et doctrina et arte constare, poetam natura ipsa valere et mentis viribus excitari et quasi divino quodam spiritu afflari ut non inmerito noster ille Hennius suo quodam iure "sanctos" appellet poetas quod deorum munere nobis commendati esse videantur, hec Cicero.[24]

---

[19] On Ennius' treatment of the Punic Wars in Books 7–9, see Skutsch 1985: 5, Elliott 2013: 300. Cicero (*Brut.* 76) remarks that Ennius, manifesting a Bloomian anxiety, treated the First Punic War less extensively because it had already been dramatized by Naevius; see Hinds 1998: 57–58, 63–70; Goldschmidt 2013: 38.

[20] On Ennius as Petrarch's *alter ego* in the *Africa*, see Dionisotti 1997: 18, Goldschmidt 2013: 193, 2012: 10–11.

[21] In Cicero's *Somnium Scipionis* (*Rep.* 6.10), Scipio Aemilianus says that Scipio Africanus appeared to him in a dream while he slept because he had been thinking and talking of him during the day, just as Ennius often thought and subsequently dreamt of Homer (Skutsch 1985: 151). Ennius' dream of Homer was more explicitly referenced by Cicero in the *Academica* (2.51; 2.88) producing what is considered a fragment of the *Annales* (Skutsch 3): *uisus Homerus adesse poeta*, "Homer the poet appeared in a dream." Ennius' dream of Homer was invoked by Lucretius (1.112–126; see Nethercut 2021: 14) to discuss the nature of the soul, and was referenced (and parodied) a number of times by subsequent writers: Horace *Epistle* 2.1.50–52 (with Porphyrio); Virgil *Aen.* 6.686; Persius 6.10 (with Cornutus); Fronto *Ep.* 1.4.5; Lucian *Ver. Hist.* 2.21.

[22] Petrarch (*Sen.* 16.1) famously describes having rediscovered the *Pro Archia* at Liège in 1333 and copying it in his own hand with yellow ink "like saffron" (*id croco simillimum*).

[23] Skutsch 1985: 131; xvi.   [24] Hostis 1874: 312–313.

Take not my word for this, but Cicero's who in his oration for Aulus Licinius Archias has this to say of poets: "We have it upon the authority of the most learned men that whereas attainment in other activities depends upon talent, learning, and skill, the poet attains through his very nature, is moved by the energy that is within his mind, and is as it were inspired by a divine inbreathing – so that Ennius fairly calls poets 'sacred' in their own right, since they appear to be commended to us by the possession of a divine gift." So says Cicero.

Since Petrarch was fundamentally interested in the recursiveness of poetic identity which Ennius, enshrined in Cicero, represented, the fact that Ennius was solely accessible via his installation in the text of Cicero was only further evidence of the poetic aspect which so deeply interested Petrarch; namely, an immortality achieved precisely through citationality. Put another way, Cicero's interest in Ennius is itself evidence of the poet's enduring influence, and, to some extent, the proof that Ennius was powerful enough to outlast his lifetime. Indeed, a fragment of Ennius preserved by Cicero's *Tusculan Disputations* (1.34) testifies to the poet's power to escape death: *uolito uiuos per ora uirum,* "alive, I fly upon the lips of men."[25] In the *Annales*, Ennius presented himself as a reinscription of the epic spirit; for Petrarch, Cicero's appreciation of Ennian power was an invitation to present himself as Ennius reanimated. Since Petrarch so deeply admired Cicero, Cicero's vision of Ennius was, to some extent, of greater cultural value to Petrarch than an independent transmission. Petrarch never attempts to break Ennius apart from Cicero; their entanglement was itself of great interest to Petrarch.

The modern term "fragment," deriving as it does from the Latin *frangere,* calls to mind something that is "broken."[26] Yet, while fragments of Ennius and the other Latin poets preserved in the Ciceronian corpus may have been "broken" off from the fullness of the poems which originally contained them, the process by which these verses were embedded into Cicero's works should be figured as a kind of textual embrace rather than an act of shattering. The idea of the "fragment" *qua* "the broken" most naturally lends itself to examples of material destruction: damaged papyri, inscriptions, or works of art.[27] In some cases, the ambiguity of the modern term "fragment" introduces further interpretative challenges: in the sixteenth century, Alessandro Guarino reported that he had seen a "large

---

[25] Epigram of Ennius = Goldberg-Manuwald F2a.
[26] Dionisotti 1997: 1. Tronzo (2009: 1), invoking the image of the severed head of King Louis XVI in Villeneuve's 1793 engraving, reflects that some fragments are "a thing created, not simply received."
[27] Zinn 1959: 161–166, Dionisotti 1997: 15.

fragment" after line 10 of Catullus poem 2 in an "ancient manuscript" (*in codice antiquissimo*), leading some to believe that he had seen Catullan verse which had since vanished; but Guarino's *ingens fragmentum* meant "a large gap" not "a large piece of text."[28]

The term "fragment" circumscribes both emptiness and substance simultaneously. For Petrarch, the *fragmentum* did not mean the excerpt of text which had become dislodged from the rest of its body, but instead evoked imagination in the face of loss. For example, Petrarch describes the ruins of Rome as *fragmenta* (*Fam.* 6.2):

> *et euntibus per moenia fractae urbis et illic sedentibus, ruinarum fragmenta sub oculis erant. quid ergo? multus de historiis sermo erat.*

> And as we walked around the walls of the broken city and sat there, the fragments of its ruins were before our eyes. So, of course, we talked long of its past.[29]

Petrarch's longing for a world which signified its absent presence via broken ruins dramatizes the power of fragmentation to evoke some degree of substance while echoing its lost substantiality. In *The Writing of Disaster*, Maurice Blanchot described this effect as the tendency of the fragment "to dissolve the totality which it presupposes" and to "maintain itself as the energy of disappearing."[30] While Walter Benjamin in *Einbahnstraße* used the image of the static ruins of Heidelberg Castle against the backdrop of passing clouds to convey the idea of "eternity" via fragmentation, Hans Ulrich Gumbrecht questioned Benjamin's interpretation of the symbolism of ruins, instead reframing the quality of "eternity" as the "almost visceral feeling of lack":[31]

> Quite irresistibly, the ruins of a building make us think of the building in the state of its no longer existing wholeness. And what kind of a lack does the spectacle of the passing clouds evoke? It is the frustration coming from a process that is nothing but a continuous emerging and continuous vanishing of forms, an ongoing transition in which these forms never gain any stability.

That the fragment urgently calls out for stability (i.e. intervention of some kind) explains the development of certain scholarly techniques as an attempted remedy for its continuously emerging and vanishing form. While Petrarch accepted Ennius in Cicero, others were not content with

[28] Reeve 1996: 22.   [29] Translation by Dionisotti 1997: 17.   [30] Blanchot 1995: 60.
[31] Gumbrecht 2003: 10.

textual fusion, but attempted to mine out *bona fide* excerpts of ancient authors for examination in isolation from the texts which preserved them. The English book collector and Benedictine monk, William of Malmesbury (c. 1095–1143), read in Cicero's *De Divinatione* (2.1) that the orator had written a protreptic towards philosophy called *Hortensius*, as well as the six books of *De Republica*:[32]

> Dicit idem Cicero in principio secundi libri *De Divinatione* se composuisse librum in quo introduxit Hortensium hortantem ad studium philosophiae. Dicit etiam ibidem se sex libros *De Republica* edidisse. Qui libri quia in Anglia non reperiuntur, ego Willelmus Malmesburgensis more meo hic apposui quicquid de materia et intentione in beato Augustino invenire potui.

> Cicero also says at the beginning of *De Divinatione II* that he composed a book in which he makes Hortensius deliver a protreptic for the study of philosophy. And in the same passage he says he has produced six books *De Republica*. Since these books are not to be found in England, I, William of Malmesbury, have appended here, as is my custom, everything I could find about their content and purport in the works of Augustine.

William collected everything he could find "on the content and purpose" (*de materia et intentione*) of these Ciceronian texts in the works of Augustine, and presented this material between the *Academica* and the *Timaeus*.[33] William's effort to find evidence of the *Hortensius* and *De Republica* was motivated by the fact that those books could not be found in England (*in Anglia non reperiuntur*). By reading Cicero, William was able to discover that he lacked some of Cicero's works; this lack, from William's perspective, had the possibility of being remedied, i.e. these books might exist outside of England. Although Angelo Mai did discover some remains of the *De Republica* in 1819, no full (or fuller) text of Cicero's *Hortensius* has ever been found. William's collection of Ciceronian fragments, mined from Augustine, was an early attempt to display what could be known of texts when their originals were not at hand.[34] For William, the collection of Ciceronian fragments was therefore an extension of his book collecting as scholar and librarian. Against the "inevitable vagaries of

---

[32] Cambridge University Library Dd. 13.2 is a fifteenth-century manuscript containing a massive corpus of Ciceroniana deriving from the work (although perhaps not solely) of William of Malmesbury; see Thomson 1987: 51. Text and translation of William from Dionisotti 1997: 6.

[33] William presents excerpts from Augustine's *Confessiones, De Trinitate,* and *De Civitate Dei*; on which see Dionisotti 1997: 6, Thomson 1987: 50–55. On William's *Polyhistor* and the perception of Cicero in the 12th century, see Ward 2015: 318–321.

[34] The first collection of fragments preserved exclusively by quotation may have been Carlo Sigonio's *Fragmenta Ciceronis variis in locis dispersa* (1559); see Dionisotti 1997: 24.

tralaticious information,"[35] William sought to know which books were at
his disposal and which were not; in the face of lack, William curated what
he *did* have as a synecdoche for lost wholes.

While William's approach to the "lost" works of Cicero can be figured as
an attempt to remedy lack, textual fullness was not the guiding principle in
his more famous *Polyhistor*. This work collected wisdom from classical and
patristic writings for a different kind of fullness. As a digest, it gave its
reader a broad overview of ancient and Christian thought, guided, of
course, by William's hand. Such collections aim at notional completion
by separating wheat from chaff; a reader could theoretically reach a certain
level of understanding without being subjected to textual totalities.[36]
William told the *Polyhistor's* addressee, a certain Guthlac, that he had
selected materials which were "enjoyable to read and profitable to remember" (*lectioni iocunda et memorie fructuosa*).[37] William's *Polyhistor* is therefore a spiritual precursor to later collections of literary excerpts, famous
examples of which include Thomas of Ireland's *Manipulus florum* (1306)
and Erasmus' *Adagia* (first edition 1500).[38] *Florilegia* such as these collected
anecdotes, *bon mots*, and proverbial wisdom organized by theme, and as
a result opened up an immense world of literature to a broad audience via
the means of quotation. Of course, the quotation of a pithy turn of phrase,
and its presentation in aggregate has the effect of flattening out richness;
a quotation of Cicero is no longer connected to the rest of the original via
the organic fibres of connection, but is made to be in dialogue with
quotations of other authors from different times and places. In such
works, totality or fullness is figured as the human experience in abstract,
rather than the specific meaning of an author's words in their own cultural
context.

Cicero's works are synthetic; a textile woven from different parts of contemporary intellectual and cultural life.[39] As a result, the body of Cicero's text
contains many elements which were originally non-Ciceronian. Yet Cicero's

---

[35] Dionisotti 1997: 5.
[36] Or weighed down by cultural context. Ward 2015: 320: "it is difficult to conclude from any survey of
the *Polyhistor* that his attitude towards Cicero smacked of anything other than the cursory and the
anecdotal. William missed completely the value of Cicero's philosophical writings as an index of
ancient philosophical systems and as a reasonable guide to many important philosophical questions
both of his own and of Cicero's day. William did not display any urge to learn from Cicero, let alone
of him."
[37] Ward 2015: 318.
[38] On Thomas of Ireland's *Manipulus florum*, see Rouse and Rouse 1979, Dionisotti 1997: 10.
[39] While the Ciceronian corpus, with its immense size and breadth, presents itself as a unique testing
ground for the continued influence of the "classic" Roman poets in the late Republic, Cicero is not
alone among his contemporaries in his synthetic use of poetry. Catullus drew heavily from the

own literary elevation and canonization meant that excerpts of his work quickly became the wisdom of "Cicero," even if the fabric of his words was woven from composite parts. The eighteenth-century Italian adventurer, Casanova, began his autobiography with a Latin quotation which he attributed to Cicero:

> *Histoire de ma vie jusqu'a l'an 1797.*
> *Nequicquam*[40] *sapit qui sibi non sapit*
> *Cic. ad Treb.*

> History of my life until the year 1797.
> "No one is wise who is not wise for his own sake."
> Cicero, to Trebatius

Indeed, the "Ciceronian" quotation Casanova presents as an epigraph, and therefore to some extent summation, of his own life is a paraphrase of a sentiment which does appear in a letter from Cicero to the jurist Gaius Trebatius Testa (*Fam.* 7.6.2; May 54 BCE); however, the words are not Cicero's own:

> . . . quoniam Medeam coepi agere, illud semper memento:
> *qui ipse sibi sapiens prodesse non quit, nequiquam sapit.*   [*TrRF* II 90]

> . . . since I have begun to play the *Medea*, always remember this:
> "*the man who cannot be wise for his own sake, is wise in vain.*"

Here, Cicero attributes the "phrase" (*illud*) to Medea, and in the *De Officiis* (3.62) he would present it in prose paraphrase, adding that the sentiment belonged to Ennius (*ex quo Ennius*); as a result, the verse from *Fam.* 7.6.2 has been assigned to Ennius' *Medea* (*TrRF* II 90).[41] Casanova attributed to Cicero a piece of wisdom which Cicero took from (or attributed to) the poet Ennius. Casanova's use of this *bon mot* was made possible by the fact that Erasmus included the phrase in his *Adagia*; the text of Casanova's

---

Roman stage in ways which are both explicit and implicit, see Uden 2006, Polt 2021; and Lucretius drew heavily on Ennius, see Elliott 2013: 115–117, Gellar-Goad 2018, Nethercut 2021.

[40] Erasmus (*Adagia* 520: I, VI, 20) writes *nequicquam* in the heading but *nequidquam* in the body of the entry. *Nequicquam/nequidquam* means "not at all" (*ne* + *quisquam* = "not anything"), but *nequiquam* also appears as a variant of *nequiquam* ("in vain"); see OLD *ad loc.* In the autograph ms. of *Histoire de ma vie* in the Bibliothèque nationale (NAF 28604), Casanova writes *nequicquam*. While some Ciceronian mss. do have *nequicquam* (see *TrRF* II p199), editors of Ennius (Jocelyn 221; *TrRF* II 90) print *nequiquam*.

[41] Angelo Poliziano's *Miscellanea* (1489) recognized that *Fam.* 7.6 contained Ennius, not Euripides: *verba in Ciceronis epistola ex Enni Medea, de graeca Euripidi,* "The words in Cicero's letter come from Ennius' *Medea,* from the Greek *Medea* of Euripides" (first century, 27th chapter); see Jocelyn 1969b: 183.

quotation of "Cicero" does not correspond to the text of Cicero's letter, but it does match an entry in Erasmus. In the Aldine edition of the *Adagia* (1508; 520: I, VI, 20), Erasmus noted that while the sentiment of this phrase was "today commonly thrown about" (*hodie vulgo frequentissime iactata*), Cicero "took it from Ennius' tragedy, the *Medea*" (*Cicero usurpat ... ex tragoedia Medea sumptam*). Casanova therefore had the opportunity to appreciate that these words were not Cicero's own, but nonetheless attributed them to him because Cicero was an authority figure worth citing. The sentiment that being wise is useless unless you profit from your wisdom is, of course, a proverbial statement, as Erasmus notes.[42] It was important to Cicero to attribute this particular expression of gnomic knowledge by yoking it to the authority, Ennius; for Casanova it was important to yoke the wisdom to Cicero.

Over time, it became apparent that the words of the poets embedded in Cicero's own textual body needed to be mined out somehow if they were to be studied. The sixteenth-century Spanish humanist, Juan Luis Vives, a student of Erasmus, remarked in his commentary on Augustine's *De Civitate Dei* (2.21) that there was a need for a collection of Ennian fragments.[43] In 1564, Henri Estienne, drawing on the work of his father, published a collection of the remains of the "old Latin poets."[44] Estienne's edition presented the poetic verses under alphabetical headings of author and title; i.e. the first entry is Accius' *Achilles*, with its three extant fragments.[45]

Over time many new collections of the fragmentary poets appeared, refining the text of the fragments and, in some cases, furnishing them with commentaries. Each collection had a slightly different focus.[46] The

---

[42] Indeed, Erasmus goes on to cite Cicero's letter to Caesar (*Fam.* 13.15.2; summer 45 BCE?), where Cicero quotes a similar sentiment from Euripides: *itaque ab Homeri magniloquentia confero me ad uera praecepta* Εὐριπίδου: μισῶ σοφιστήν, ὅστις οὐχ αὑτῷ σοφός, "And so I turn from the elevated style of Homer to Euripides' true maxim: 'I hate the sophist who cannot be wise for his own sake.'" Cicero here preserves a fragment of Euripides (Nauck fr. 905).

[43] *Ennii poetae. Huius praeter fragmenta quaedam, quae ex variis antiquis scriptoribus colligere et in unum velut corpus dispersa redigere, in animo habeo, nihil extat.* "Ennius the Poet. Nothing remains of his work except for certain fragments which I intend to collect into one body, as it were, from the various ancient authors among which they are dispersed." On Vives and Ennius, see Jocelyn 1969b: 184. The passage of *De Civitate Dei* (2.21) upon which Vives was here commenting contains Augustine's remarks on Cicero's *De Republica* (5.1); here Cicero commented that Ennius' *moribus antiquis res stat Romana uirisque* ("the Roman state stands fast on its ancient customs, and its men," Skutsch 156) had the quality of an oracular utterance.

[44] H. Estienne, *Fragmenta Poetarum Veterum Latinorum* (1564). On Estienne and Ennius, see Jocelyn 1969a: 184–186, Dionisotti 1997: 24, Goldschmidt 2012: 14.

[45] Estienne 1564: 5; cf. Dangel 2002: 129–130.

[46] For the sake of brevity, I here focus primarily on the major standalone collections of Latin fragments. As a result, I have omitted many of the important contributions to scholarship on the Latin fragment which appeared in other publications, such as commentaries on complete texts

fragments of Ennius were collected and edited by the Italian Girolamo Colonna, brought to press by his son in 1590.[47] In 1593, the Spanish Jesuit, Martin Anton del Rio, prefixed his edition of Senecan tragedy with the fragments of the Republican tragedies, thereby initiating an idea of a dramatic continuum at Rome.[48] The Dutch historian and jurist Paul van Merle issued a new edition of Ennius' *Annales* in 1595; such was Merle's longing for the lost Ennius that he fabricated a number of fragments.[49] In 1597, another Dutchman, Frans van der Does, issued the *editio princeps* of Lucilius' *Satires*.[50] In 1620, yet another Dutch scholar, Peter Schrijver, issued a collection of Latin tragic fragments which drew on del Rio's edition, with notes by G. J. Voss.[51]

In the nineteenth century, Otto Ribbeck grappled with the fragments of the Roman stage, issuing separate editions of the tragic fragments (1852) and the comic fragments (1855), revising each of these twice (1871, 1897; 1873, 1898).[52] Ribbeck's narrative study of Roman tragedy (1857) also remains authoritative.[53] Shortly after Ribbeck's first volume was issued, Johannes Vahlen produced another complete Ennius collection in 1854, which he revised and reissued in 1903.[54] In 1886, Emil Baehrens produced a new edition of the fragmentary Latin poets.[55] At the end of the nineteenth and beginning of the twentieth centuries, a number of new Lucilius

---

(especially the grammarians) or critical miscellanies. For a fuller account of such issues, see Jocelyn 1969b (focusing on Ennius). On the history of editing Ennius' *Annales*, see Elliott 2013: 1–8; Goldschmidt 2013: 1–5. For a bibliography of the editions of Ennius, see *TrRF* II pp383–386. For a full bibliography of the editions of Latin tragic fragments, see *TrRF* I, ppXXXVIII–XLIII, pp323–326. For a bibliography of Roman scenic fragments, see Manuwald 2011: 353–356.

[47] H. Colonna, *Q. Ennii poetae vetustissimi quae supersunt fragmenta* (1590). An earlier edition of just Ennius' *Annales* and "minor" works had been completed by 1585, see Skutsch 1968: 59n2. Colonna's commentary was originally appended to each book; F. Hesselio's reprint (1707) placed Colonna's commentary underneath the text itself. On Colonna and Ennius, see Jocelyn 1969b: 185; Skutsch 1985: xi, 256, 488, 788, 791, 767n3.

[48] M. A. Delrius, *Syntagma Tragoediae Latinae* (1593). However, del Rio seems not to have been aware of Colonna's recent work on Ennius; see Jocelyn 1969b: 186.

[49] P. Merula, *Q. Enni, poetae cum primis censendi, annalium libb. XIIX : quae apud varios Auctores superant, fragmenta* (1595). On Merle's forgery of 15 fragments of Ennius' *Annales*, detected by Joseph Lawicki in 1852, see Goldschmidt 2012: 14–16.

[50] F. Dousa, *Satyrarum quae supersunt reliquiae* (1597).

[51] P. Scriverius, *Collectanea veterum tragicorum fragmenta cum notis G. I. Vossii* (1620); see Jocelyn 1969b: 187. On F. H. Bothe's "hasty and unsystematic revision" of Schrijver in 1823, see Jocelyn 1969b: 189.

[52] On the influence of Friedrich Ritschl upon Otto Ribbeck, see Jocelyn 1969b: 190–191. Alfred Klotz's *Scaenicorum Romanorum Fragmenta* (1953) relitigated Ribbeck but, as Beare (1955: 170) predicted, did not supplant Ribbeck's editions.

[53] O. Ribbeck, *Die römische Tragödie im Zeitalter der Republik* (1875).

[54] J. Vahlen, *Ennianae Poesis Reliquiae* (1854). On Vahlen, see Knapp 1911, Jocelyn 1969b: 192.

[55] E. Baehrens, *Fragmenta poetarum Romanorum* (1886).

collections appeared; of these Friedrich Marx's edition (1904–1905) became the standard.[56] New collections of the fragmentary Latin poets by Ernst Diehl and Alfred Ernout appeared in the early 1900s.[57]

Before the Second World War, Willy Morel reedited Emil Baehrens' collection (1927).[58] Shortly afterwards, the fragments of the Latin poets were opened up to a broader audience with Eric Herbert Warmington's three volumes of the *Remains of Old Latin* in the Loeb Classical Library (1935–1940).[59] Ennius received renewed attention in the form of Henry Jocelyn's *The Tragedies of Ennius* (1967; reissued 1969) and Otto Skutsch's *The* Annals *of Quintus Ennius* (1985).[60] Around this time, fragmentary Latin poets who had generally not been studied individually received their own collections: editions of Pacuvius and Accius appeared from the 1960s onwards.[61] In 1982, Karl Büchner made a second revision of Baehrens' collection of fragmentary Latin epic and lyric.[62] In 1986, Antonio Traglia issued an edition of "archaic" Latin poets.[63] Edward Courtney's *The Fragmentary Latin Poets* (1993, reissued 2003) selected a series of fragmentary Roman poets and presented them as part of a coherent intellectual continuum. Shortly afterwards, Jürgen Blänsdorf (1995) produced a fourth edition of Baehrens' collection.[64]

[56] E. F. Corpet, *Satires de C. Lucilius* (1845); F. D. Gerlach, *C. Lucili Saturarum Reliquiae* (1846); L. Müller, *C. Lucili Saturarum Reliquiae* (1872); C. Lachmann, suppl. by M. Haupt, ed. by J. Vahlen, *C. Lucili Saturarum Reliquiae* (1876), with F. Harder *Index Lucilianus* (1878); F. Marx, *C. Lucili Carminum Reliquiae* (1904–5). While a number of newer editions of Lucilius have since appeared – Terzaghi (1934; 1966), Krenkel (1970), Charpin (1978–91), Christes and Garbugino (2015) – the fragments of Lucilius are still generally cited according to the numbering of Marx, or Warmington's Loeb.

[57] E. Diehl, *Poetarum romanorum veterum reliquiae* (1911; 6th ed.: 1967); A. Ernout, *Recueil de textes latins archaïques* (1916; 4th ed.: 1973).

[58] W. Morel, *Fragmenta poetarum Latinorum epicorum et lyricorum praeter Ennium et Lucilium, post Aemilium Baehrens iterum* (1927).

[59] Vol. I: *Ennius and Caecilius* (1935, revised 1956); Vol. II: *Livius Andronicus, Naevius, Pacuvius, and Accius* (1936); Vol. III: *Lucilius and the Twelve Tables* (1940; 1967). While Warmington's Loebs were critiqued for their overimagination (e.g. Skutsch 1985: xii), they remained the most accessible (and perhaps therefore influential) edition of the fragments until the appearance of the new fragmentary Latin Loebs in 2018.

[60] Otto Skutsch acknowledged the influence of his own scholarly precursors, with his *Annales* dedicated to his own father, Franz Skutsch, Eduard Fraenkel, W. Lindsay, and A. E. Housman. Skutsch was also in conversation with Sebastiano Timpanaro whose dissertation laid a groundwork for a new edition of Ennius (1946, 1947, 1948). Although Timpanaro did not produce the edition itself, he continued to publish on Ennius and to correspond with Skutsch. On their relationship, see Goldschmidt 2013: 2.

[61] Pacuvius: G. D'Anna (1967); Accius: Q. Franchella (1968), A. R. Barrile (1969), V. D'Antò (1980), A. Pociña (1984), J. Dangel (1995; reprint 2002); Accius' *praetextae*: Pedroli (1953), Durante (1966).

[62] K. Büchner, *Fragmenta poetarum Latinorum epicorum et lyricorum praeter Ennium et Lucilium* (1982).

[63] A. Traglia, *Poeti latini arcaici* (1986).

[64] J. Blänsdorf, *Fragmenta poetarum Latinorum epicorum et lyricorum praeter Ennium et Lucilium. Post W. Morel novis curis adhibitis ed. Carolus Büchner* (1995).

In the twenty-first century, Latin verse fragments received renewed attention: understudied authors were given fuller standalone commentaries, and editorial collections were revised with great care. Livius Andronicus received a new edition by François Spaltenstein (2008);[65] Pacuvius new editions by Petra Schierl (2006) and Esther Artigas (2009).[66] At this time, a new edition of Ennius' *Annales* appeared under the editorship of Enrico Flores (2000–2009).[67] In 2012, a new edition of the Latin tragedians appeared, the *Tragicorum Romanorum Fragmenta*.[68] And, finally, new Loebs of the early Latin poets are now appearing in the new *Fragmentary Republican Latin* series.

From this brief survey of collecting and editing the Latin poetic fragment a number of trends emerge. Since Ennius was a poet of great importance to the Romans and, as a result, more substantial quotations of his poetry were embedded into the works of subsequent Latin writers than other fragmentary poets, there was simply more material to work with. As a result, greater scholarly attention was paid to Ennius over the history of the curation of Latin verse fragments. A consequence of Ennius' importance to the editors of fragmentary Latin is that Ennius gained a further level of canonicity beyond even his poetic reputation. Since the most famous scholars of Latin fragments were the editors of Ennius, a new Ennian edition was an invitation to engage in a scholarly tradition with an illustrious pedigree.

In the history of editing Latin fragments, tragedy also has a tendency to be of greater interest to classical scholars. In addition to the fact that many more Latin tragic fragments survive than comic ones, scholarly interest in tragic fragments can further be explained by the perception that tragedy is of greater cultural value than comedy due to its relative seriousness, psychological complexity, and relationship to the sublime. The Latin tragic fragments were also, for a time, the object of scholarly interest principally because of their relationship to Greek tragic precursors; i.e. because Greek tragedy enjoyed a powerful position in the classical curriculum, Roman tragedy was studied as a supplement to its understanding.[69] Yet despite the fact that Roman tragedy evidently drew on Greek tragedy, the Roman use

[65] F. Spaltenstein, *Commentaire des fragments dramatiques de Livius Andronicus* (2008).
[66] P. Schierl, *Die Tragödien des Pacuvius* (2006); E. Artigas, *Marc Pacuvi, Tragèdies. Fragments* (2009).
[67] E. Flores et al., *Quinto Ennio. Annali* (2000–09).
[68] Vol. I, edited by Markus Schauer, containing the fragments of Livius Andronicus, Naevius, the "minor" poets, and the unattributable fragments ("*adespota*"); Vol. II, edited by Gesine Manuwald, containing the fragments of Ennius.
[69] Jocelyn 1969b: 189–190.

of Greek tragic precursors is most fruitfully understood as an act of reception rather than a straight line of influence.[70]

A consequence of this scholarly preference is a tendency to classify Latin fragments which cannot be attributed to a particular author or genre as fragments of tragedy. Preceding the list of Latin fragments which cannot be assigned to a specific author in the new *TrRF*, the editors present a list of *incerta* along with the prior attempts to assign them.[71] Tellingly, this list of "tragic" fragments includes verses which some editors had previously assigned to a variety of non-tragic genres, such as satire, comedy, or *fabula praetexta*. By presenting such a list, the editors of the *TrRF* recognize the essential instability of fragments, particularly "anonymous" fragments. Otto Ribbeck had also recognized this instability, sometimes remarking that he did not know whether he ought to categorize a fragment as tragedy or comedy.[72] In general, fragments whose authorship or genre is not certain will find their way into collections of tragic fragments because these often function, *de facto* if not *de iure*, as a collection of many different kinds of fragments.

The history of the study of Latin fragments reveals one further issue, a problem which almost all collections of literary fragments must deal with. Collecting Latin verse fragments means mining out discrete parts from the body which transmitted and contains them; i.e. excerpting what is Ennian from its Ciceronian embrace. Out of their longing to reconstitute and partially reconstruct lost wholes, the collectors of Latin fragments were initially less interested in the citing authors than the cited ones, and, as a result, presented the fragment as a text in a void: verse surrounded by blank space. While this technique served to represent the text as an artefact of the fragmentary poet rather than the citing one, the image of a verse surrounded by void constitutes another phase of fragmentation. How to present the fragment on the page is as much a philosophical problem as a typographical one.[73] Over time, textual editions have made greater efforts to

---

[70] Boyle 2006: 112: "Where a dramatic precedent exists . . . a substantially different dramatisation may result; even a play with a famous title, such as *Medea* may have been an essentially original dramatisation."

[71] *TrRF* I, p173. The list is preceded by the following note: *viri docti etiam atque etiam temptaverunt singula fragmenta incerta certis auctoribus vel fabulis vel generibus tribuere*, "Learned men again and again have attempted to attribute uncertain fragments to certain authors, plays, or genres." On the "anonymous" Latin verse fragments in the Ciceronian corpus, see Čulík-Baird 2021.

[72] On the fragment of verse in a letter to Atticus (*Att.* 6.9.5; *TrRF* I 36), Ribbeck (1871: 274) remarked: *Dubito utrum tragoediae an comoediae tribuam,* "I do not know whether to attribute it to tragedy or comedy." Ribbeck had similar hesitations over the fragments in *De Or.* 3.166 (*TrRF* I 23a) and a verse repeated by Cicero three times (*Att.* 4.1.8, 4.2.1, *Ep. ad Brut.* 1.10.2; *TrRF* I 160), see Ribbeck 1871: 255, 274.

[73] On the typographical challenge of a deeply entangled text, see Carson 1992: 112.

present the text of the fragment *within* the frame of the text which preserved it, providing citational context.[74] Such context very rarely has much to add regarding the original meaning of the fragment, which is one of the reasons why the earlier editors did not include this information. Nonetheless, studying these verses in their cited context *does* tell us about the reception of Republican poetry in the intellectual climate of the first century BCE.

Identifying the Fragment

In 1911, Wilhelm Zillinger collected the fragments of the Latin poets in Cicero, cross-listing them with the author and genre assignments in the editions of Latin fragments which were current at the time.[75] While the standalone editions of the fragmentary Latin poets were edited over and over again, Zillinger's work has never been updated, despite the fact that so many fragments derive from Cicero. Zillinger identified around seven hundred fragments of Latin verse in the Ciceronian corpus. While these Latin verses are fragments now, they were not fragments when Cicero quoted them. In his philosophical works, rhetorical treatises, letters, and speeches, Cicero drew from the "classic" Latin poets of the previous century who had entered the common cultural consciousness at Rome via the variety of mechanisms which are discussed over the course of this book.

Yet Cicero's very familiarity with the poetry which he embedded into his own corpus presents a number of interpretative obstacles to us now. While Cicero often preceded his poetic citations with an explicit indication that the quotation was imminent – such as the name of the poet, the title of the work, the name of a character,[76] a verb of speech, or some other signpost[77] – he also

---

[74] Jocelyn's edition of the Ennian fragments presents large swathes of the transmitting text; the *TrRF* presents the text of every transmitting author; the new Loebs gives a minimalistic but significant contextual frame to the fragment.

[75] E.g. Johannes Vahlen's (1903) edition of the works of Ennius; Otto Ribbeck's (1897, 1898) collection of fragments from the Roman theatre. The Appendix to this book is based on Zillinger's work, with updated cross-references to modern editions.

[76] On titles and names of poets or characters, see n92.

[77] Cicero introduces or marks quotations with verbs: *ait* (*Rep.* 1.49, *Leg.* 1.33, *TD* 1.31; cf. Varro *LL* 6.50, 7.41), *dico* (*Sest.* 102, *TD* 4.52, 4.55), *inquit* (*Mur.* 30, *Sest.* 102, *TD* 1.117), *narro* (*Div.* 1.40), *loquor* (*ND* 3.68, *Div.* 1.43, *Fin.* 2.106); prepositions and adverbs: *apud* (*Fin.* 1.13, *TD* 1.107, *Fam.* 15.6.1); *praeclare* (*Fin.* 2.24, 2.106, *TD* 3.20); *ut* (*TD* 3.63, *Fam.* 7.33, *De Or.* 2.253); with *illud* (*ND* 2.60, *Fin.* 2.22, *Fam.* 9.22.1); with *uersus* (*Or.* 147, 163, *Div.* 1.132); with identification of metre: *anapaestus* (*Fin.* 2.18, *TD* 3.57), *creticus* (*De Or.* 3.183), *spondalia* (*De Or.* 2.193); with an indication of genre: *comoedia* (*TD* 4.69, *Fam.* 9.22.1), *tragoedia* (*TD* 4.69, *Fam.* 9.22.1). Cicero also occasionally remarks that verses cited together come from different parts of the same poem: verses from Ennius' *Andromacha* (*TrRF* II 23) quoted in the *Pro Sestio* 121 appear *paulo post in eadem fabula* "a little later in the same play" (cf. *Div.* 1.132: *paucis ante uersibus*, "a few lines before"); verses from Pacuvius' *Niptra* (Schierl fr. 200) quoted in

quoted poetry with no prior warning: for example, a short quotation of Ennius' *Achilles* (*TrRF* II 1) which appears in the *Verrines* (2.1.46):

> tum subito tempestates coortae sunt maximae, iudices, ut non modo proficisci cum cuperet Dolabella non posset, sed uix in oppido consisteret *ita magni fluctus eiciebantur.*   [*TrRF* II 1]

> Suddenly so great a storm arose, judges, that Dolabella not only was unable to set off, as he wanted, but he could hardly remain in town *"such great waves were being cast ashore."*

That the italicized phrase is a citation of Ennius is only known to us because it was marked as such by the Gronovian scholiast.[78] The presence of verse fragments in Ciceronian prose is also occasionally intuited by modern scholars where there is unusual diction, metre, or repetition, despite no explicit signpost.[79] Yet, since Cicero used prose rhythms in his work, the appearance of metrical rhythm in his prose is not a guarantee that a passage contains a verse fragment.[80] Additionally, Cicero often makes prose paraphrases of poetic material, removing its underlying rhythm. An (apparently) verbatim poetic citation may appear in one part of the corpus, such as a verse of Lucilius' *Satires* in a letter to Atticus (*Att.* 13.21.3):[81]

> nec est melius quicquam quam ut Lucilius:
> *sustineas currum, ut bonus saepe agitator equosque*   [Warmington 1249]

> For nothing is better than what Lucilius says:
> *"Hold back your chariot and horses as a good driver often does."*

---

the *Tusculans* (2.50) appear *in extremis* "at the end of the play" (cf. *Fam.* 7.16: *in Equo Troiano . . . in extremo*, "at the end of *Trojan Horse*"); verses *ab eodem poeta* "from the same poet" (i.e. Ennius, *TrRF* II 157) are quoted *ex altera parte* ("from a different part of the play") at *TD* 3.44.

[78] Zetzel 2007: 2; cf. *TrRF* II pp34–35.

[79] Such inferences are marked in collections of fragments, e.g. *TrRF* I p253's remark on the unknown verse (*TrRF* I 83) repeated five times by Cicero (*Att.* 14.12.2, 15.11.3; *Fam.* 7.30.1, 7.28.2; *Phil.* 13.49; see Čulík-Baird 2021): *uerba poetae intellexit Muret.*, "Muretus noticed that these are poetic words."

[80] The phrase *terram fumare calentem* was marked as a quotation of an unknown poet by Mayor (1883: 112), who stated that it did not seem "at all likely that Cicero could inadvertently have fallen into the hexameter"; cf. *De Or.* 3.191, where Cicero remarked that some metres could occur unintentionally (including the hexameter). Palmer (1883: 446) thought that *Att.* 15.1.4 contained a quotation of Latin comedy; Shackleton Bailey (1967: 243) believed the iambic senarius to be accidental. A reference to Pacuvius' *Medus* at *Rep.* 3.14 was taken as a literal quotation of cretic canticum by Nosarti (1993: 39, 1999: 68), but Schierl (2006: 352) took it only as a *testimonium* because there was no other evidence of a reference to a "snake-chariot" (*currus anguium*) outside of iambic senarii.

[81] Cf. *ND* 2.151, paraphrasing an unknown verse (*TrRF* I 81) which is quoted at *De Off.* 2.13; *Fin.* 1.7 and *Brut.* 99 paraphrase a verse of Lucilius' *Satires* (Warmington 635) quoted at *De Or.* 2.25; *Ac.* 2.88 paraphrases a verse of Ennius' *Annales* (Skutsch 3) quoted at *Ac.* 2.51.

Yet appear in a paraphrased form in another (*Ac.* 2.94):[82]

> nihil me laedit, inquit, ego enim *ut agitator* callidus priusquam adfinem
> ueniam *equos sustinebo*

> "It doesn't hurt me at all," he said. "For just *as* the clever *driver I will hold
> back my horses* before I come to the finish line."

Cicero also quotes poetry expecting his audience to recognize the verses or,
at least, to feel the pressure of recognizing them. In several instances,
Cicero cuts off a quotation after a few lines and says *nosti quae sequuntur*
("you know what follows"), or a similar phrase.[83] This is the case when
Cicero quotes extremely famous passages, such as in the *Pro Plancio* (59),
where Cicero gives two verses from Accius' *Atreus* (Dangel 45; 62), followed
by *nosti cetera* ("you know the rest"); or in the *Tusculans* (4.77) where
a different section of the *Atreus* (Dangel 58–59) is followed by *nosti quae
sequuntur*. In a letter to L. Papirius Paetus (*Fam.* 9.22.1), Cicero quotes
a verse from a comedy with the remark: *nosti canticum* ("you know the
song").[84] And in one instance, Cicero represents an imagined interlocutor
failing to recognize the poetic source: to Cicero's lengthy citation of
Aeschylus (translated into Latin), the younger dialogue partner of the
Tusculans (2.26) responds *unde isti uersus? non agnosco* ("where are these
verses from? I don't recognize them").[85]

Due to this assumed familiarity, Cicero often quotes a verse or verses
with the expectation of recognition but *without* naming the author or the

---

[82] And even more loosely "quoted" in *De Amicitia* (63), where it would not now be picked up at all as
a reference to Lucilius unless Cicero had quoted it elsewhere.

[83] In a letter to Atticus (*Att.* 4.16.1), Cicero writes *sed nosti genus dialogorum meorum*, "You know the
form of my dialogues"; evidently *nosti* in this context means, "you know well." As Halliwell (2000:
96n7) notes, discussing Plato's use of poetry, "the citation of poetry would be, of course, precisely
one way of sharing it and giving others an opportunity to acquire or renew familiarity with it."

[84] The song comes from Turpilius' *Demiurgus* (Ribbeck 43–44). Cicero adds (*Fam.* 9.22.1) that it was
performed by Roscius; see Fantham 2002: 366n19, Hanses 2020: 49, 53.

[85] In this case, the inability of the younger interlocutor to recognize the originally Greek verses may
be intended to demonstrate the incompleteness of his education. Ironically, Cicero has complicated the matter by making a mistake in his own attribution. At *TD* 2.23, Cicero quotes four
anapaestic verses which he attributes to Aeschylus: *ueniat Aeschylus*, "let Aeschylus come forward."
However, part of this same passage was quoted by Varro (*LL* 7.11), who attributed it to Accius'
Philocteta (= Dangel 208–211). The 28 lines of verse which Cicero cites at *TD* 2.23–24 (Soubiran fr.
i) seem to be Cicero's own Latin translation of Aeschylus. However, the Aeschylean tragedy which
Cicero here claims to translate, *Prometheus Unbound*, is no longer extant, so we cannot confirm
that this is the case; cf. *TD* 2.20–22 (Soubiran fr. ii) where Cicero translates Sophocles' *Trachiniae*
(1046–1102), which is extant. Cicero's Latin translation of Aeschylus at *TD* 2.23–25 (Soubiran fr.
ii) appears as a fragment of the *Prometheus Unbound* (Προμηθεὺς Λυόμενος) in editions of
Aeschylean fragments (Nauck fr. 193).

title of the work. As a result, even though the cited verses were evidently famous in antiquity, in many cases we no longer know which works they originally belonged to. Such is the case with the "oft-quoted verse" (*peruolgatissimus ille uersus*) in the *Orator* (147), which cannot be confidently assigned to a poet or even a genre.[86] In the *De Finibus* (2.71), Cicero quotes a "famous phrase" (*illud*),[87] which he expects his interlocutor to recognize (*nosti, credo*, "I think you know this"), which now ironically must be placed among the *incerta*.[88] Cicero also quotes verses from an uncertain play in the *De Oratore* (3.219) which he partially repeats in the *Orator* (164); in the latter passage, Cicero marks the end of his (incomplete) quotation with *et quae sequuntur*.[89] Cicero quotes one verse (*TrRF* I 83) from another unknown source five times over a three year span.[90] Cicero's deployment of the verse does not include an indication of its source, but repetition suggests that it was famous and recognizable.[91]

There are, however, a number of cases where Cicero does explicitly name the author or the title of the poetic work cited.[92] In some cases, Cicero referred to titles in order to make a pun rather than to refer to the actual content of that work: e.g. a remark upon Atilius' *Misogynus* (*TD* 4.25) is a reference to the *concept* of "hating women" rather than

---

[86] Ribbeck (1852: xix) initially categorized this as a fragment of an unknown tragedy, but later (1873: xxii) placed it among the fragments of unknown comic authors. When he reassigned the fragment to comedy, he noted that it could come from mime: *fortasse mimicus est* (1873: 117).

[87] Cicero frequently refers to the content of verses with *illud*: *ex quo illud Terentii* (Terence's *Eunuchus* 732; *ND* 2.60), *ex hoc illud etiam* (Ennius' *Thyestes*, *TrRF* II 134; *ND* 3.10), *atque illud* (between two *incerta*: *TrRF* I 23 and *TrRF* I 24; *De Or.* 3.166); cf. *Fam.* 9.21.1, 9.22.1; *De Or.* 2.253; *Fin.* 2.22, 2.24; *TD* 2.13, 3.56, 4.45, 5.52.

[88] *TrRF* I 47.

[89] Cicero does not give any explicit indication of the author or the title of this work, but several editors have assigned it to Pacuvius' *Iliona*; see Schierl 2006: 319, 330.

[90] Twice in letters to his friend, Manius Curius (*Fam.* 7.28.2, 7.30.1; 46 BCE, 44 BCE); twice to Atticus (*Att.* 14.12.2, 15.11.3; both 44 BCE); and once as part of his humiliation of Antony in the *Philippics* (13.49; 43 BCE). In one of these instances (*Fam.* 7.28.2), Cicero quotes the verse partially, followed by *nostis cetera*, a variation on *et quae sequuntur*; see p23.

[91] For a discussion of Cicero's use of *TrRF* I 83, see Čulík-Baird 2021.

[92] Author, title, book number: *Q. Ennius ... in nono ut opinor Annali* (*Brut.* 57–58). Author, title: *Plautinus pater in Trinummo* (*Ad Brut.* 1.2.3(2a.1)), *ille Pacuuianus, qui in Chryse* (*Div.* 1.131); *in Cresphonte usus Euripides* (*TD* 1.115); *in Naeui poetae Ludo* (*De Sen.* 20, on the alternatives: *Lupus, Lydus*, see Powell 1988: 145–146). Title, no author: *Equus Troianus* (*Fam.* 7.1.2; 7.16.1); *Iphigenia* (*TD* 1.116). Author, named character: *Hector ille Naeuianus* (*TD* 5.12.7), *uersibus apud Ennium Thyestes* (*TD* 1.107), *ut est in Melanippo . . . praeclare Accius* (*TD* 3.20), *ut Terentianus Chremes* (*Fin.* 1.3), *ut ait Philoctetes apud Accium* (*Fam.* 7.33), *apud Ennium Vestalis illa* (*Div.* 1.40), *apud Euripiden a Theseo* (*TD* 3.29), *Prometheus ille Aeschyli* (*TD* 3.76). Just author: *ut Naeuius* (*Or.* 152), *apud Ennium* (*TD* 3.63), *Pacuuius hoc melius quam Sophocles* (*TD* 2.48), *quem Caecilius* (*TD* 4.68), *falsumque illud Accii* (*TD* 2.13), *apud Trabeam* (*TD* 4.67), *dixit Afranius* (*TD* 4.55), *ut ait Lucilius* (*ND* 1.63). Just title: *in Equo Troiano scis esse in extremo* (*Fam.* 7.16.1), *ut ille in Demiurgo* (*Fam.* 9.22.1), *in Chryse* (*Or.* 155), *itaque in extremis Niptris* (*TD* 2.50), *qualis in Leucadia* (*TD* 4.72), *ex Hymnide* (*Fin.* 2.22).

a literary allusion.[93] Cicero tends to name poetic sources in works which were intended to be read privately, such as treatises and letters, while the orations, which reflect or simulate live performance, tend to attribute verses to a "poet" (*poeta*).[94] There are, of course, exceptions. Given that Cicero was usually quoting very famous passages of literature, he was able to omit the name of the poet even in the treatises. In the *De Legibus* (1.33), for example, Cicero paraphrases the famous verse from Terence – *homo sum: humani nil a me alienum puto* ("I am human: I consider nothing human alien to me," *Heaut.* 77) – accompanied by the tag, *ut ait poeta* ("as the poet says").[95] In other circumstances, Cicero does not even need to call the author a poet but refers to him simply as a "famous man": *ut ait ille* ("as he says").[96]

Cicero may also acknowledge the dramatic context of the verses he cites. In certain cases, Cicero includes notes akin to "stage directions" which give background to the verses quoted, such as his annotation of Ennius' *Alcmeo* in the *Academica* (2.89):

incedunt, incedunt;[97] *adsunt, me expetunt.*	[*TrRF* II 13, 3]
quid cum uirginis fidem implorat	
fer mi auxilium, *pestem abige a me . . .*	[*TrRF* II 13, 4]

"They are coming, they are coming; they are here, they're looking for me."
What then, when he begs the loyalty of the young woman:
"Bring me help, drive this contagion from me . . . "

Occasionally, Cicero will quote a dialogue between two different characters, such as the quarrel in "interchanging verses" (*alternis uersibus*) between Thyestes and Atreus from Accius' *Atreus* (Dangel 58–59) in the *Tusculans* (4.77), or the exchange between Orestes and Pylades from (perhaps[98]) Pacuvius' *Chryses* in *De Finibus* (5.63):[99]

---

[93] Similarly, a reference to Terence's *Heautontimoroumenos* at *TD* 3.65 is really a reflection upon "self-punishment"; cf. *Fam.* 15.6.1 (pun on Naevius' *Hector Proficiscens*); Quint. *Inst.* 6.3.96 (pun on Book 6 of Ennius' *Annales*); see p100.

[94] "*Poeta*" in oratory: *ut ait ingeniosus poeta* (*Mur.* 30), *scripsit grauis et ingeniosus poeta* (*Planc.* 59), *ut ait poeta* (*Scaur.* 3), *ut ait poeta ille noster* (*Rab. Post.* 28), *ut est apud poetam nescio quem* (*Phil.* 2.65), *ut ait poeta nescio quis* (*Phil.* 13.49). "*Poeta*" in treatises: *appellatus a summo poeta* (*De Or.* 1.198), *quae recte a bono poeta dicta est* (*De Or.* 2.187), *ut ait poeta* (*De Leg.* 1.33).

[95] In the *De Officiis* (1.30) Cicero quotes part of this same verse verbatim – *humani nihil a se alienum putat* – attributing it to the "Terentian" character, Chremes (*Terentianus ille Chremes*). On Terence *Heaut.* 77, see Jocelyn 1973b, Henderson 2004: 60.

[96] *Att.* 9.15.4 (*Od.* 3.26–27).

[97] On the text of this fragment, see *TrRF* II p57. Jocelyn (1969a: 74) prints †*incede incede*†.

[98] Several editors have attributed this fragment to Pacuvius' *Chryses* (including Schierl = fr. 69); the *TrRF*, however, categorizes it as unknown verses from an unknown poet (= *TrRF* I 48; pp217–218).

[99] Cf. *De Am.* 24 where the interchange between Orestes and Pylades is paraphrased.

> qui clamores uulgi atque imperitorum excitantur in theatris, cum illa
> dicuntur:
> *ego sum Orestes*   [Schierl fr. 69]
> contraque ab altero:
> *immo enimuero ego sum, inquam, Orestes!*
> cum autem etiam exitus ab utroque datur conturbato errantique regi,
> *ambo ergo †sunaneganum† precamur.*

> What great shouts of the crowd and of the uneducated are aroused in the
> theatre, when these words are said:
> *"I am Orestes"*
> and these words in response, by the other character:
> *"No, no, I am Orestes, I say!"*
> But when a solution is offered by each of them to the confused and mistaken
> king:
> *"Therefore both of us (?)*[100] *we pray."*

Every now and then, Cicero speaks apostrophically to a dramatic character,
such as in the *Tusculans* (3.26), where Cicero follows a poetic quotation
(*TrRF* I 57[101]) with a direct address to the speaker: *haec mala, o stultissime
Aeëta, ipse tibi addidisti* ("oh foolish Aeëta, you have added these troubles
yourself"); or later in the *Tusculans* (3.44) where Cicero behaves like the
chorus, urging aid to the wretched heroine of Ennius' *Andromacha*:

> ecce tibi ex altera parte ab eodem poeta
> *ex opibus summis opis egens Hector tuae*   [*TrRF* II 23, 3]
> huic subuenire debemus; quaerit enim auxilium.

> Take another example from the same poet:
> *"From the heights of power, now without your protection, Hector –"*
> We ought to help her, she's asking for aid.

In addition to naming (or not naming) the poet, Cicero also names
dramatic characters to introduce quotations.[102] In the *Tusculans* (1.107),
the insertion that "Thyestes in Ennius" (*apud Ennium Thyestes*) utters the
curse identifies the passage as a fragment of Ennius' *Thyestes* (*TrRF* II
132).[103] Similarly, verses spoken by the "leader of the Argonauts in

---

[100] On the textual issue, see Schierl 2006: 218.

[101] The majority of editors assign this fragment to Pacuvius' *Medus* (= Schierl fr. 181); the fragment has
recently been downgraded by the *TrRF* (= *TrRF* I 57; p228).

[102] In addition to explicitly naming characters, Cicero also refers to stock character types: the libertine
son in Afranius (*TD* 4.45, 4.55); the severe father in Afranius (*TD* 4.45) and Caecilius Statius (*Cael.*
37–38); the parasite in Terence's *Eunuchus* (*Fam.* 1.9.19, *Am.* 93).

[103] Cf. *Fam.* 7.33.1, *ut ait Philoctetes apud Accium* = Accius' *Philocteta* (Dangel 221–222).

a tragedy" (*ex tragoedia princeps ille Argonautarum, TD* 4.69), i.e. Jason, are "virtually certain"[104] to come from Ennius' *Medea* (*TrRF* II 92). Agamemnon "speaks" (*loquitur*[105]) in a passage of Homer's *Iliad* which Cicero translated (*Div.* 2.63); Ulixes "wails in pain" (*lamentatur in uulnere, TD* 2.49) in Pacuvius' *Niptra*; and Ilia "tells the story" (*narrat . . . Vestalis illa, Div.* 1.40) in Ennius' *Annales.*[106]

Yet, the technique of naming the character rather than the work also creates a number of fragments which cannot now be attributed to a specific play: we hear the voices of exiled Telamo, furious Ajax, and doomed Amphiaraus,[107] but we do not know their author.[108] When Cicero does not present verse with contextual information, editorial judgement regarding where the fragment belongs results in diverse interpretations.[109] Cicero, for example, quotes a phrase in a letter to Atticus (*Att.* 5.15.3):

> *clitellae boui sunt impositae; plane non est nostrum onus.* sed feremus, modo, si me amas . . .

> "*The saddle-bags are on the ox; certainly, it's not my burden.*" But I will put up with it, only, if you love me . . .

The similarity of the phrase to utterances made on the comic stage (slaves would regularly complain about the imposition of burdens, e.g. Plaut. *Poen.* 857) persuaded Ribbeck to include the line among the fragments of Roman comedy.[110] But Latin writers called this saddle-bag phrase a "proverb," and so Otto later included it in his collection of Roman proverbs.[111] A verse by

---

[104] Goldberg-Manuwald 2018: 99.
[105] Atreus "speaks" (*loquitur, ND* 3.68) in Accius' *Atreus* (Dangel 31–32); Tarquinius Superbus "himself speaks" (*loquitur ipse, Div.* 1.43) in Accius' *Brutus* (Dangel 657–662); Scipio Africanus "speaks" (*loquens, Fin.* 2.106) in Ennius' *Scipio* (Goldberg-Manuwald F1).
[106] *Div.* 2.63–64 = *Iliad* 2.299–330; *TD* 2.49 = Schierl fr. 199; *Div.* 1.40 = Skutsch 34–50.
[107] Telamo: *TD* 3.39–40, *Fam.* 9.26.2 (*TrRF* I 59); Ajax: *TD* 4.52 (*TrRF* I 61), *De Off.* 3.98 (*TrRF* I 82); Amphiaraus: *Fam.* 6.6.6 (*TrRF* I 44).
[108] That the character is the same does not guarantee that the poetic source is the same: e.g., Cicero quotes speeches of Achilles composed by three different poets – Ennius (*Rep.* 1.30), Accius (*TD* 1.105), and Homer (*TD* 3.18).
[109] E.g. a letter to Varro (*Fam.* 9.7.2) contains the Greek proverb πολλοὶ μαθηταὶ κρείσσονες διδασκάλων, "many students are better than their teachers," which appears among the fragments of the Greek tragedians (Nauck fr. 107); the same phrase occurs identically in an epigram by the Neronian-era poet, Lucillius, in the *Greek Anthology* (11.176). Certainly this phrase could have appeared in a Greek tragedy, but it may simply be a well-known saying.
[110] Ribbeck *com. inc.* 66–67.
[111] Quintilian (*Inst.* 5.11.21) uses this saddle-bag phrase as an example of a proverb (παροιμίας *genus illud*), a type of utterance which is an abbreviated tale (*fabella breuior*) understood allegorically (*per allegorian*). Ammianus Marcellinus (16.5.10) had the emperor Julian cry out this phrase, which he called an "old proverb" (*uetus illud prouerbium*), during military conditioning. See Otto 1890: 57.

"some poet" (*nescio poetam quem, Phil.* 2.65) quoted by Cicero was considered by Zillinger (1911: 94) to be a comic fragment because of its gnomic tone.[112] But, of course, wise sayings appear in all genres, with tragedy and comedy alike containing sentiments drawn from popular usage.

Judging the provenance of a fragment which Cicero preserves without contextualizing information on the basis of style alone is a very difficult task, and ambiguities in attribution necessarily remain. In the *Tusculans* (1.10), Cicero quotes a verse which has been attributed to either Ennius or Lucilius.[113] A verse quoted in the *De Divinatione* (2.133) has been identified either as a verse of Lucilius or as a Latin translation of Greek poetry by Cicero.[114] Finally, Cicero's own verse style drew so heavily on the Latin precursors that there is occasionally ambiguity as to whether a verse belongs to Cicero or, for example, Ennius. A verse quoted in a letter to Atticus (*Att.* 2.15.3) referring to "the mountains of my fatherland" (*montes patrios*) and "my birthplace" (*incunabula nostra*) was suspected to be Ennian by nineteenth-century scholars.[115] Skutsch (1985: 770) instead suggested that it could have been spoken by Marius in Cicero's epic, referring the verses to Marius' (and Cicero's) hometown, Arpinum.[116]

While Cicero's citational technique does introduce difficulties for the study of the poets whom he quotes, it nonetheless demonstrates great intimacy with Latin verse, as well as a significant entanglement between his prose and the poetry of others. Cicero was deeply familiar with the Latin poets, and could assume the same familiarity in his audience. While it may be difficult to determine the origin of a verse fragment which is preserved due to Cicero's inclusion of it in his own work, there can be no doubt about the significance of poetry to Cicero's intellectual project, nor about the perceived potency of Latin poetry in the late Republic.

Indeed, the large number of verse quotations embedded within the Ciceronian corpus, combined with the variety of ways in which Cicero put them to use, presents something of a challenge to the scholar who

---

[112] Naevius (*TrRF* I 46): *male parta male dilabuntur*, "things got badly will turn out badly." When Cicero (*Phil.* 2.66) quotes this phrase he does not name the author; Paulus attributes the phrase to Naevius (see *TrRF* I p119). A similar sentiment appears at Plautus *Poen.* 834.

[113] Ennius' *Annales* (Skutsch *dubia* 3–4); Lucilius' *Satires* (Marx 1375–1376). The issue is discussed by Skutsch (1985: 769–770) who weighs the arguments on each side but does not make a decision himself.

[114] Lucilius' *Satires* (Marx 1377); Cicero translation (Soubiran fr. ii).

[115] Skutsch (1985: 770) rejected this hypothesis on the grounds that the poet's home, Rudiae, was not mountainous (!).

[116] While Soubiran (1972: 300) assigns the verse to Cicero, he notes the possibility that it may be a fragment of a different poet.

might wish to make sense of Cicero's engagement with poetry. In the present work, I have attempted to document Cicero's citational practices as a larger system, while also paying close attention to its finer details. It is clear that Cicero found Latin poetry to be deeply meaningful as a moral, historical, linguistic, and aesthetic resource, and his quotation of the "classic" Latin poets reveals a network of intellectual practices which might otherwise remain difficult to detect, or see the significance of, when encountered in isolation – i.e. the philosophical, rhetorical, and commemorative practices which grounded themselves in the authority of poetry. In order to document the various layers and nodes of Cicero's engagement with the Latin poets, I begin in Chapter 1 by discussing Cicero's use of poetry on the theoretical level: how did Cicero conceptualize poetry as a mirror of reality, and how did he interconnect Latin poetry with his own intellectual output? Next, in Chapter 2, I move through more formal concerns: how did the genre of Ciceronian writing impact his citational method? Finally, in Chapters 3–5 I conduct test cases with Cicero's use of poetic genres: comedy (Chapter 3), tragedy (Chapter 4), satire and epic (Chapter 5), demonstrating their distinct operations within the Ciceronian corpus, and highlighting the unique intellectual contexts which informed Cicero's approach in each case.

CHAPTER I

Cicero and the Poets

1.1   The Mirror of Poetry

O Tite, si quid ego adiuero curamue leuasso   [Skutsch 337–339]
quae nunc te coquit et uersat in pectore fixa
ecquid erit praemi?
licet enim mihi uersibus eisdem affari te, Attice, quibus affatur Flamininum
ille uir haud magna cum re sed plenus fidei   [Skutsch 335]
quamquam certo scio non ut Flamininum
sollicitari te, Tite, sic noctesque diesque   [Skutsch 336]
noui enim moderationem animi tui et aequitatem teque cognomen non
solum Athenis deportasse, sed humanitatem et prudentiam intellego.

"O Titus, if I could help or lighten the care
fixed in your chest which now boils and twists you,
what will be my reward?"
I can address you, Atticus, with the same verses that he used to address
Flamininus,
"the man not high in stature, yet full of faith"
although certainly I know that it is not, like Flamininus,
"that you are tortured in this way, Titus, night and day."
I know the moderation of your mind and your evenness, and I understand
that you brought back not just your name from Athens, but also your
humanity, your practical judgement.

Cicero's quotation of Quintus Ennius' *Annales* at the beginning of the *De
Senectute* immediately sets up a number of parallels. The first words – *O Tite*,
"O Titus" – refer simultaneously to the dedicatee of the work, Cicero's
friend, Atticus (whose full name was, of course, *Titus* Pomponius) and to
Titus Quinctius Flamininus (cos. 198 BCE).[1] Ennius' words are thought to

---

[1] Skutsch 1985: 511. Cicero played a similar name game in a letter to Atticus (*Att.* 12.5.1), where he used
a verse of Ennius' *Annales* (Skutsch 290), applying a reference to a historical "Quintus" (Quintus
Fabius, see Skutsch 1985: 469) to his own brother, Quintus.

30

refer to an abortive attempt at diplomacy between Flamininus and Philip of Macedon, which had taken place in a narrow gorge on the River Aous. Fighting ensued, but the steep terrain made it difficult for Roman soldiers to follow the king's army as it withdrew into the rugged landscape.[2] A shepherd who pastured his sheep in the woods and who was familiar with the narrow, winding paths of the mountains, was sent to help Flamininus' troops reach the king's camp.[3] Flamininus, suspecting betrayal, did not immediately trust the shepherd. But this man – "not high in stature, yet full of faith" (*ille uir haud magna cum re sed plenus fidei*) – promised to relieve Flamininus of his anxiety and be his guide, for a price.

The parallelism set up by the citation of Ennius' *Annales* casts Atticus in the role of Flamininus, with Cicero as the shepherd guide. But just as Cicero sets up the parallel, he shatters it. Flamininus and Atticus may share the same name, but they do not share the same capacity for withstanding anxiety. Ennius' verses depict Flamininus cooked alive by apprehension, while Atticus, famously Epicurean, has learned to be even-keeled. Having connected Atticus and Flamininus via their *praenomen*, Cicero uses his friend's adopted name as index of their difference. It is not just the name "Atticus" that Titus Pomponius brought back from Athens (*De Sen.* 1), but the *humanitas* ("humanity") and *prudentia* ("practical judgement") which protect Cicero's Titus from anxiety. Cicero's treatise will offer advice, but Cicero makes clear that he knows Atticus is not in need of it.

I here begin with the beginning of Cicero's *De Senectute* and its invocation of Ennius' *Annales* because this is an exemplary instance of Cicero's poetic citational technique.[4] Cicero initiates his treatise on old age with a quotation of poetry which allows him to model the conventional relationship between the writer and his literary dedicatee. Further, the invocation of Ennius also situates Cicero's own work within the Roman literary

---

[2] Livy 32.10.10. For a detailed account of the fighting on the River Aous in 198 BCE, as well as photographs from modern Albania, see Hammond 1966.

[3] Livy 32.11.1. In Plutarch (*Flam.* 4.3), several shepherds come of their own volition to Flamininus, but refer him to the Epirote elite, Charops, as a character witness.

[4] Cicero evidently felt that there was no difficulty beginning his own work with someone else's verse: in a letter to Atticus (*Att.* 16.3.1), Cicero refers to the *De Senectute* not by its title but by the first, Ennian words, i.e. *O Tite, si quid* (Skutsch 337). Cicero regularly begins a work with a poetic quotation: according to Pliny (*NH* pf. 7), *De Rep.* 1 began with Lucilius' *Satires* (Warmington 632–634); according to Augustine (*CD* 2.21), *De Rep.* 5 began with Ennius' *Annales* (Skutsch 156); *De Fin.* (1.3) begins with Terence's *Heaut.* (69); *ND* (1.13) with Caecilius Statius' *Synephebi* (Ribbeck 211–213); *De Leg.* (1.2) with Cicero's *Marius* (Soubiran fr. i and ii). Several letters begin with a verse quotation (on which, see Hutchinson 1998: 14): *Fam.* 5.12.7 (Naevius' *Hector Proficiscens TrRF* I 14), *Att.* 9.13.1 (Stesichorus Diehl fr. 11), *Att.* 12.5.1 (Ennius' *Annales* Skutsch 290), *Att.* 13.11.1 (Euripides' *Ion* 585), *Att.* 13.47.1 (unknown tragedy *TrRF* I 68a). Quotations could also be used as signoffs: *Fam.* 7.10.4 ends with Terence's *Heaut.* 86; *Q. fr.* 2.14.5 ends with Euripides' *Suppliants* 119.

tradition: just as Ennius left behind a record of moral instruction via his depiction of Roman history in verse, Cicero may do the same via his philosophical revivification of Cato the Elder. There is, of course, special significance to the fact that Cicero's *Cato* in particular begins with a citation of Ennius. Cicero has "Cato" name Ennius as a "personal friend" (*familiaris noster*) when he quotes another passage of the *Annales* (Skutsch 363–365), verses which praise Q. Fabius Maximus Cunctator (*De Sen.* 10):

> quaestor deinde quadriennio post factus sum, quem magistratum gessi consulibus Tuditano et Cethego, cum quidem ille admodum senex suasor legis Cinciae de donis et muneribus fuit. hic et bella gerebat ut adulescens, cum plane grandis esset, et Hannibalem iuueniliter exsultantem patientia sua molliebat; de quo praeclare familiaris noster Ennius:
> *unus homo nobis cunctando restituit rem.*   [Skutsch 363–365]
> *noenum rumores ponebat ante salutem.*
> *ergo postque magisque uiri nunc gloria claret.*

> After that, I was made quaestor four years later, holding that office when P. Sempronius Tuditanus and M. Cornelius Cethegus were consuls (204 BCE). At that time, Q. Fabius Maximus was a very old man, yet he advocated for the *Lex Cincia* on gifts and reciprocities. Fabius was waging war like a youth despite the fact that he was advanced in years, and he tamed Hannibal's puerile pride with his own patience. Our friend, Ennius, excellently says of Fabius:
> *"One man by delaying restored the republic for us.*
> *He did not put his reputation before our safety.*
> *More and more, therefore, glory now brings him renown as a man."*

Ennius here is represented (possibly fictively) as an acquaintance of Cato the Elder, whereby Cicero creates a romantic network of Roman wisdom figures.[5] Additionally, the value of the Ennian verse lies in the fact that the poet speaks "excellently" (*praeclare*).[6] Elsewhere, it is important aristocratic

---

[5] Cato the Elder is credited with bringing Ennius from Sardinia to Rome in 204 BCE by Cornelius Nepos (*Cato* 1.4). If Cicero knew this tradition, he does not explicitly say so, despite referring to events of 204 BCE via citations of Ennius here in the *De Senectute* and in the *Brutus* (60). Since Cicero describes Cato's frustration with M. Fulvius Nobilior's patronage of Ennius (*TD* 1.3), and since Cato's hostility to cultural pursuits is well-documented (and suggested by Cicero himself in *De Sen.* 3), some scholars doubt the historicity of their association. See Badian 1972: 155–156, Zetzel 2007: 11. On Cicero's romantic imagination of second century BCE intellectual networks, see Zetzel 1972.

[6] That an idea expressed in verse form represents a worthy ideal is often marked by Cicero with adverbs such as *praeclare* ("excellently"), *bene* ("well"), or *commode* ("aptly"): Ennius speaks *praeclare* in three gnomic phrases cited in the *De Officiis* (2.23 = *TrRF* II 163; 2.62 = *TrRF* II 164; 3.104 = *TrRF* II 165), and the aria of the *Andromacha* (*TD* 3.44–46 = *TrRF* II 23; see p191) is described as a *praeclarum carmen* ("an excellent song"); Accius writes "bad Latin" (*male Latine*) "but the sentiment is good" (*sed praeclare Accius*, *TD* 3.20) in a passage of the *Melanippus* (Dangel 536); Afranius spoke "aptly" (*commode*, *TD* 4.55) on pain (in an unknown comedy, Ribbeck 411); Ennius "correctly" (*bene*, *TD* 4.52) defined anger as the beginning of insanity (in an uncertain work, Goldberg-Manuwald F4); and

figures such as Q. Mucius Scaevola (*Fin.* 1.9) and Gaius Laelius (*Fin.* 2.24) who are said to speak *praeclare*, so evidently Ennius' words hold tremendous moral and cultural weight.[7] Despite the fact that Q. Fabius Maximus Cunctator was advanced in age, Cicero has Cato argue, he was still capable of the feat of heroism for which he is remembered, and which Ennius immortalized in the *Annales*. That Ennius' gift of immortality is a vital part of Cicero's interest in him is made clear in a subsequent passage, where "Cato" refers to the speech of Appius Claudius (censor 312 BCE) concerning peace with Pyrrhus of Epirus, and, instead of citing the extant oration, quotes the Ennian version (*De Sen.* 16):[8]

> ... non dubitauit dicere illa, quae uersibus persecutus est Ennius:
> *quo uobis mentes, rectae quae stare solebant*   [Skutsch 199–200]
> *antehac, dementis sese flexere †uia?*
> ceteraque grauissime;[9] notum enim uobis carmen est, et tamen ipsius Appi exstat oratio.

> ... Appius Claudius did not hesitate to speak these words which Ennius rendered in verse:
> *"down what road (?) have your senses, which before used to*
> *stand upright, wandered off senseless."*[10]
> And the rest, so impressively put; for you know this poem well,[11] and, anyway, Appius' speech still survives.

While Appius Claudius' speech reportedly survived until the Ciceronian era (*Brut.* 61) and beyond (Sen. *Ep.* 114.13, Tac. *Dial.* 18.4, 21.7), it is Ennius' version which Cicero reaches for. Appius' speech may be a "historical document" (at least, of a kind), but Ennius' rendering of the event into poetic form elevated it beyond historical datum to an artefact of cultural significance in the broader Roman consciousness.[12] Yet Ennius was

---

Ennius spoke "correctly" (*bene*, *TD* 4.70) about Roman morals in an unknown tragedy (*TrRF* II 158). In the *De Oratore* (3.101), Cicero says that *bene* and *praeclare* are the positive reactions which all poets and orators hope to receive from their audience.

[7] Scaevola and Laelius speak *praeclare* via Lucilius' *Satires*: *Fin.* 1.9 = Warmington 87–93; *Fin.* 2.24 = Warmington 200–205.

[8] On Ennius' version of Appius Claudius' oration, see Skutsch 1985: 360–362, Powell 1988: 136–138, Flores *et al.* 2002: 152, Elliott 161–163, 220–222.

[9] *Cetera* here acts as an equivalent for *nosti quae sequuntur*; see p23.

[10] I here give the translation of Goldberg-Manuwald (2018: 211) for Skutsch 199–200. On the textual issue surrounding *uia*, see Skutsch (1985: 361–362), who thought that Lambinus' genitive "*uiai*" is "the easiest correction imaginable" but "senseless and ungrammatical."

[11] A variation on *nosti quae sequuntur*; see p23.

[12] The discussion of Cicero's attitude towards the "historicity" or "historical distortion" of Ennius' version of Appius' speech by Elliott (2013: 163) misses, I think, the fact that for Cicero it was not the content of the speech which was particularly significant, but its moral impact.

important to Cicero not only because he bestowed canonicity and narrative coherence upon figures and events from the Roman past. In the *De Senectute* (14), Ennius is also praised for what he says of himself:

> sua enim uitia insipientes et suam culpam in senectutem conferunt, quod non faciebat is, cuius modo mentionem feci, Ennius:
> *sicuti fortis equus, spatio qui saepe supremo*   [Skutsch 522–523]
> *uicit Olympia, nunc senio confectus quiescit.*
> equi fortis et uictoris senectuti comparat suam. quem quidem probe meminisse potestis.

> Fools attribute their own faults and defects to old age,[13] but not Ennius, whom I mentioned just a moment ago:[14]
> *"Just as the vigorous horse, who often, in the final lap,*
> *came first at Olympia, now, worn out by old age, rests."*
> He compares his own old age to that of a vigorous and victorious horse; indeed, you yourselves might well remember Ennius.[15]

Like other wisdom figures who traditionally continued their intellectual pursuits well into old age (*De Sen.* 13: Plato, Isocrates, Gorgias), Ennius expresses both pride in a life of literary achievement and an acceptance of the quiet rest which old age brings.[16] Ennius is therefore not solely invoked as a conduit to the past, its heroes, and its values, but as a figure of wisdom himself, one worthy of citation and emulation. Ennius' prominence as an authority who validated the prestige of others with his song but whose

[13] Cf. *De Sen.* 36, where Cicero quotes an unknown play by the comic playwright, Caecilius Statius (Ribbeck 243), for its example of "foolish old men from the comedies" (*comicos stultos senes*) who are stupid but not because they are old. A fuller citation of this passage appears in the *De Amicitia* (99).

[14] I.e. *De Sen.* 10. Cicero regularly returns to characters, plays, or poets previously cited in this way: e.g. *Medea modo et Atreus commemorabatur a nobis*, "I called to mind Medea and Atreus just now" (*ND* 3.71, referring to *ND* 3.65–68); *Aeëtam, de quo paulo ante dixi*, "Aeëta, about whom I spoke a little while ago" (*TD* 3.39, referring to *TD* 3.26).

[15] "You" being Cato's younger interlocutors, Gaius Laelius and Scipio (*De Sen.* 4). Cicero here (*De Sen.* 14) uses the dramatic technique of addressing the dialogue participants to introduce some historical details which are not exactly pertinent, but do contribute to the impression that he has researched the personages depicted. The dramatic date of the *De Senectute* is 150 BCE (Powell 1988: 16–17); Ennius died "only nineteen years ago" (*anno enim undeuicesimo post*, *Sen.* 14), i.e. in 169 BCE (cf. *Brut.* 78), when Cato himself was "sixty-five" (*quinque et sexaginta annos*, *Sen.* 14), and the interlocutors would have been teenagers. The heaping up and interlinking of historical information also here resembles Cicero's resumé of L. Licinius Crassus' oratorical career (*Brut.* 159–164), which centres around a passage of Lucilius' *Satires* (*Brut.* 160; Marx 1180).

[16] Ennius is not alone among the Latin poets in receiving praise for taking pride in his literary accomplishments in his old age. *De Sen.* 50 also cites the geriatric pride of Naevius in the *Bellum Punicum*, Plautus in the *Truculentus* and the *Pseudolus*. Cicero has Cato add that although Livius Andronicus reportedly produced a play six years before Cato was born, i.e. in 240 BCE (cf. *TD* 1.3), he saw the poet as an old man because he was so long-lived (*uidi etiam senem Liuium*, *De Sen.* 50). On the disagreement over Livius' dates in the Republican era, see Welsh 2011.

achievements also made him worthy of praise naturally suggests an intentional parallelism between the poet and Cicero himself. Further, Cicero hooks himself into the recursive, generative system of Roman memory via his citation of Ennius: the values of Cicero's "Cato" are consciously built from those monumentalized by Ennius' poetry, and Cicero, by giving voice to these values, himself authorizes a traditional, literary view of Roman cultural practice.

Such a vision of recursive regeneration via poetic invocation is, in fact, seeded in the *De Senectute* itself, which praises the foresight of elders who cultivate resources which they themselves will not benefit from via an invocation of the comic poet, Caecilius Statius (*De Sen.* 24–25):

> ... nemo est tam senex qui se annum non putet posse uiuere; sed idem in eis elaborant, quae sciunt nihil ad se omnino pertinere:
> *serit arbores quae alteri saeclo prosint,*   [Ribbeck 210]
> [25] ut ait Statius noster in Synephebis.

> ... no one is so old that he does not think he can live another year, yet these same men engage in labours which they know will not benefit them in any way:
> *"he sows trees to benefit another age,"*
> [25] as our Caecilius Statius says in the *Synephebi.*[17]

Roman wisdom planted for the benefit of future generations flourishes in the gnomic utterances of the old poets whose words remain long past their own lifetimes, repurposed to breathe new life and gain greater significance than they did in the context of the poems which originally framed them. Old Latin poetry is figured metaphorically not only as cyclical, agricultural growth, but as the funerary inscription of a culture.[18] Cicero has Cato quote the inscription on the tombstone of Aulus Atilius Calatinus (cos. 258 BCE), composed in Saturnian verse (*De Sen.* 60–61):

> apex est autem senectutis auctoritas ... [61] quanta in A. Atilio Calatino, in quem illud elogium:
> *hunc unum plurimae consentiunt gentes*   [*FPL* pp13–14]

[17] Cicero follows this citation of Caecilius Statius with quotations from the same author which do not live up to the moral standard of the passage of the *Synephebi*: *De Sen.* 25 = Caecilius Statius' *Plocium* (Ribbeck 173–175); *De Sen.* 25 = Caecilius Statius' *Ephesio* (Ribbeck 28–29).

[18] Cicero explicitly connects these two ideas in the *Tusculans*. After citing the same verse from Caecilius Statius' *Synephebi* (*TD* 1.13; Ribbeck 210), Cicero asks: *quid procreatio liberorum, quid propagatio nominis, quid adoptationes filiorum, quid testamentorum diligentia, quid ipsa sepulcrorum monumenta, elogia significant nisi nos futura etiam cogitare?* "What is the point in having children, cultivating a name, adopting sons, preparing a will carefully, monuments of tombs, or funerary inscriptions, unless it is about thinking of the future?"

populi primarium fuisse uirum.
notum est totum carmen incisum in sepulcro.

But the pinnacle of old age is authority. What great authority Aulus Atilius
Calatinus had, for whom this famous inscription was written:
"Him alone[19] many families agree
to have been the foremost man among the people."
The whole poem, cut into the tomb, is well known.[20]

Shortly afterwards, "Cato" quotes the funerary epitaph which Ennius
wrote for himself (*De Sen.* 73):

Solonis quidem sapientis est elogium, quo se negat uelle suam mortem
dolore amicorum et lamentis uacare. uolt, credo, se esse carum suis. sed
haud scio an melius Ennius:
nemo me lacrimis decoret nec funera fletu   [Goldberg-Manuwald F2b]
faxit.
non censet lugendam esse mortem, quam immortalitas consequatur.

There is indeed the epitaph of wise Solon in which he says that he does not
wish his own death to lack the pain and grief of his friends.[21] (He wants,
I think, to be dear to his own). But Ennius may have put it better:
"Let none embellish me with their tears nor a funeral
with their weeping make."
He does not think that death followed by immortality is a cause for grief.

Both verse citations are referred to as *elogia*, a term which regularly refers to
words inscribed into physical materials: writing on tombstones, alongside
imagines, on votive tablets, etc.[22] The lives and achievements of the Roman
statesman and the poet are thereby aligned.[23] While the tomb of the
Calatini is placed by Cicero (*TD* 1.13) on the Via Appia, it is not clear

---

[19] Compare *hunc unum* ("him alone") of Calatinus' epitaph with Ennius' praise of Q. Fabius Maximus Cunctator (*De Sen.* 10; Skutsch 363): *unus homo* ("one man"). Evidently, Ennius' verses coopted the traditional language of praise as reflected in inscriptional practice at Rome.

[20] In the *Tusculans* (1.13), Cicero says that the tomb of the Calatini could be seen on the Via Appia alongside the tomb of the Scipios, the Servilii, and the Metelli after exiting Rome via the Porta Capena.

[21] In the *Tusculans* (1.117) Cicero gives a Latin translation of the Greek fragment of Solon (Campbell fr. 22) here only paraphrased. There, Cicero more forcefully says that "Ennius' sentiment is better than Solon's" (*melior Enni quam Solonis oratio, TD* 1.117).

[22] Tombstones: *De Sen.* 16, *Fin.* 2.35 (both of A. Atilius Calatinus); *Pis.* 29 (of the Republic!); *TD* 1.31 (epitaphs as a general practice); Suet. *Claud.* 5 (Augustus' verses inscribed into the tomb); Suet. *Galba* 3 (*imagines* and *elogia* as the history of a family). Public notice: Suet. *Gaius* 24 (*elogia* to accused sisters placed in public). Honorary inscription: Cato the Elder *ap.* Gellius 3.7.19.

[23] Indeed, Cicero says that both Calatinus (*Leg.* 2.64) and Ennius (*De Sen.*) endured poverty in their old age; a *topos* of wisdom through suffering.

that Ennius' epitaph stood in any physical location at Rome.[24] Nonetheless, in the tradition of Hellenistic epigram, the verses themselves create an imagined funerary context and their own sense of place.[25] Yet the power of the Ennian verses lies in their very immateriality: Ennius does not want embellishment beyond the memory of his own poetic prowess – no tears, no grief. Cicero tells us why: immortality is enough. Indeed Cicero's citation of Ennius' *elogium* validates the poet's thesis: Ennius continues to live on without body, without inscribed stone. In the *De Senectute* (73), Cicero only gave the first part of Ennius' *elogium*; in the *Tusculans* (1.34), he finished it:

> *nemo me lacrimis decoret nec funera fletu*   [Goldberg-Manuwald F2a, 3–4]
> *faxit. cur? uolito uiuos per ora uirum*

> "Let none embellish me with their tears nor a funeral
> with their weeping make. Why? I fly, alive, on the lips of men."

The gallery of poetic citations in the *De Senectute* presents a set of framed images which together convey a coherent moral message. Old age, approached with the right exemplars in mind, is not to be feared. Almost all of the verse quotations of the *De Senectute* appear again in other Ciceronian works, often more than once.[26] If Cicero's repetitious return to the same excerpts of Latin poetry suggests that they were famous and well known to his contemporaries, then the *De Senectute* is not simply a neutral selection of thematically pertinent verse, but a culturally charged anthology of the best examples of Roman wisdom.[27]

---

[24] In the *Pro Archia* (22), Cicero says that a marble image of Ennius "is thought" (*putatur*) to be part of the family tomb of the Scipios (cf. Livy 38.56.4; Ov. *Ars* 3. 409–410) on the Via Appia, but he does not say in this speech that there was an accompanying inscription. Scholars have generally been sceptical of Cicero's claim at *Arch.* 22: Suerbaum 1968: 208–210, Badian 1972: 154, Gruen 1990: 110–111, Zetzel 2007: 9; Goldberg 1989: 258 is agnostic; Skutsch 1985: 2n7 is willing to accept it. Another Ennian epigram quoted by Cicero (*TD* 1.34; Goldberg-Manwald F2a) asks the reader to "look on the form of the image of old Ennius" (*aspicite . . . senis Enni imaginis formam*).

[25] Gutzwiller 1998: 2.

[26] Ennius' *Annales* (Skutsch 363–365): *De Sen.* 10: *De Off.* 1.84, *Att.* 2.19.2; Caecilius Statius' *Synephebi* (Ribbeck 210): *De Sen.* 24: *TD* 1.31; unknown comedy of Caecilius Statius (Ribbeck 243): *De Sen.* 36: *De Am.* 99; Ennius' *Annales* (Skutsch 308): *De Sen.* 50: *Brut.* 59; epitaph of A. Atilius Calatinus (*FPL* pp13–14): *De Sen.* 61: *Fin.* 2.116; epitaph of Ennius (Goldberg-Manuwald F2b): *De Sen.* 73: *TD* 1.34, *TD* 1.117.

[27] Collins (1998: 23) suggests that it is specifically the ritual return to certain acts or objects by a community which "charges" them with their cultural significance: "The survival of symbols, and the creation of new ones, depends on the extent to which groups reassemble periodically. Symbols which are sufficiently charged with feelings of membership carry the individual along certain courses of action even when the group is not present."

Examining the citational technique of the *De Senectute* reveals the fact that Cicero's quotation of poetry was a way to introduce authorizing evidence. In the *De Inventione* (1.67), Cicero, following the contemporary orthodoxy of rhetorical theory, described the dependence of a premise upon substantiating proofs.[28] Such proofs naturally could take the form of narrative (Cicero himself relied heavily on *narratio* when the "facts" were not in his favour); but the Roman court system also required material evidence for the proof of a case.[29] Citation as a practice is grounded in the need to present evidence which supports an argument, and this is true of poetic citation as much as any other kind. In a context where a well-told story (i.e. *narratio*) might stand in place of a material proof, poetry is cited for its own ability to "tell a story" or structurally reflect the proposition in some other way.

For Cicero, poetry had an evidential value.[30] The category of "evidential value" is, of course, one which itself contains several subcategories; i.e. while the citation of verse may generally function to provide confirmation or proof of a premise, the nature of the premise affects the persuasive outcome of the verse's use. In the *De Senectute*, given the purpose of the work, the evidence of poetry is primarily that of an ethical or moral nature: e.g. Caecilius Statius' old men planting trees for future generations, or Ennius celebrating rest after a life of achievement with the image of the racehorse. Many of *De Senectute*'s citations can also be categorized as evidence of cultural or social values as carefully circumscribed within the Roman conception of elite status, values which Cicero wished to endorse and perpetuate: e.g. the authority of the old man in Roman society as typified by Appius Claudius (via Ennius) and Aulus Atilius Calatinus (via inscriptional Saturnians).[31] Poetry is cited as "proof" of various other kinds throughout the Ciceronian corpus: proof of historicity, proof of language, proof of philosophical precept.

---

[28] *Inv.* 1.67: *approbatio, per quam id quod breuiter expositum est rationibus affirmatum probabilius et apertius fit,* "proof by which the briefly stated premise is corroborated with reasoning and made more credible and more demonstrable." Such a relationship between a proposition and its proof is reflected in the epistemological theory that knowledge is justified true belief.

[29] *De Or.* 2.100, 116, Quint. *Inst.* 5.1.2; cf. May 2002, Butler 2002: 35–60.

[30] Likewise, Aristotle (*Metaphysics* 2.995a7–8) remarked that there are those who do not accept a proposition unless a poet is cited as a "witness" (μάρτυς); see Halliwell 2000: 94.

[31] The element of "perpetuation" is an important one. Collins (1998: 28) notes that in the formation of intellectual groups, the consciousness of predecessors in intellectual or cultural work is a vital ingredient; individuals within a circumscribed group "will go on to incorporate these ideas in their own future creations and discourses – at least, they are sifting through them to see whether materials are worthy to take on for this purpose." Ennius is an authorizing figure for Cicero, but Cicero also authorizes Ennius via his repeated invocation.

Yet, the expressive capability of verse citation goes far beyond the fact that poetry provides evidence of various kinds. Since there are several genres of poetry with which Cicero engages – i.e. epic, tragedy, comedy, satire – and since each genre has its own expressive, performative, and social significations, we find a wide variety of use when it comes to the citation of verse. The fact that the poet himself as a literary and historical figure is often the referent, rather than the content of his verses, further complicates the generic schema; Cicero recognizes a difference between the author and his work (while often eliding the two), but occasionally he will also depict the poet as a historical character.[32] And although Cicero does turn to specific poetic genres for particular intellectual tasks – e.g. Cicero regularly quotes comic verse to define Roman words, defend grammatical usage, or otherwise establish "Latinity" – Cicero generally finds communicative value in each of these genres. While Cicero acknowledges their formal differences (e.g. *Inv.* 1.27), he is also comfortable using different poetic genres, sometimes interchangeably.

The communicative capability of the poetic citation is an important aspect of its functionality. Poetic citation was one of the ways in which Cicero could convey (and construct) the nature of his interpersonal relationships: we have seen already that Cicero (*De Sen.* 1) used a passage of Ennius' *Annales* to cast *Titus* Pomponius Atticus as *Titus* Quinctius Flamininus and himself as the shepherd guide through the hills of philosophy. Elsewhere, Cicero cited poetry to demonstrate his respect to others: on two occasions (*Fam.* 5.12.7; 15.6.1) he quotes a verse from Naevius' *Hector Proficiscens* (*TrRF* I 14), in order to communicate the impact of having received praise from praiseworthy men: L. Lucceius the historian and Cato the Younger respectively.[33] Enmities and jealousies could also be expressed through verse. Asked by Lentulus Spinther (*Fam.* 1.9.19) why he had defended Publius Vatinius, whom he had previously repudiated, Cicero responds with a quotation of Terence's *Eunuchus* (440–445):[34]

> sed tamen defendendi Vatini fuit etiam ille stimulus de quo in iudicio, cum illum defenderem, dixi me facere quiddam quod in Eunucho parasitus suaderet militi:
> *ubi nominabit Phaedriam, tu Pamphilam*   [Terence, *Eunuchus* 440–445]

[32] Ennius (*Arch.* 22, 27; *De Or.* 2.276; *Brut.* 79; *TD* 1.3; *Ac.* 2.51); Lucilius (*De Or.* 3.171, *Or.* 149, *Brut.* 274); Accius (*Arch.* 27, *Leg.* 2.54, *Brut.* 107).

[33] Since Naevius is not a poet whom Cicero regularly quotes (see Appendix II), the austerity of the author lent extra solemnity to the correspondence; on Cicero's engagement with Naevius, see Malcovati 1943: 92–94. Cicero also quotes the same verse of Naevius' *Hector Proficiscens* (*TrRF* I 14) in the *Tusculans* as part of a definition of honourable joy (*gaudium*, *TD* 4.67), in contrast to hedonistic pleasure.

[34] On Cicero's use of *Eunuchus* 440–445, see Goldberg 2005: 87–88.

continuo. si quando illa dicet "Phaedriam
intro mittamus comissatum." "Pamphilam
cantatum prouocemus." si laudabit haec
illius formam, tu huius contra. denique
par pro pari referto, quod eam mordeat.
... quoniamque illi haberent suum Publium, darent mihi ipsi alium Publium
in quo possem illorum animos mediocriter lacessitus leuiter repungere.

But nonetheless, I had an incentive to defend Vatinius, which I explicitly
stated in the trial while I was defending him: I said that I was doing what the
parasite advises the soldier to do in the *Eunuchus*:
"Whenever she names Phaedria, you name Pamphila
in response. If she should want Phaedria to come
to dinner, you should say: "Why not bring Pamphila
to sing?" If she praises his good looks, you praise
the girl's. In short: pay back what hurts."
... since they had *their* Publius, I looked for my own Publius, to sting them
back a little in return for the mild provocation.

In each of these cases there is a certain parallelism between the content of
the verses and communicated reality. Poetic excerpts stand as a symbol or
metaphor for Cicero's own experiences; they are structurally reflective of
the philosophical, social, or political circumstances as Cicero understands
them. Poetry's ability to reflect a mirror image of reality and to be
excerpted as a communication of that image suggests that verse citation
is more than simply the selection of wise ideas from culturally enshrined
authors. Indeed, the quotation of verse takes an idea beyond the context of
its original utterance and presents it as an artefact of experience and truth,
i.e. a truism beyond the literary constraints of the initial poetic context. If
poetry stands as a model of human experience, and can therefore power-
fully convey it when excerpted and redeployed, then verse is not a purely
"fictive" category of utterance (in contrast to the putative realism of, e.g.,
oratory or history), *even if* it depicts fictional or mythological characters or
elements of fantasy. Put another way, the evidential value of poetry extends
not only to philosophical, historical, or linguistic "proofs," but to social
and emotional ones. While Cicero regularly points out the ahistoricity or
fictionality of poetry (e.g. *Div.* 2.115–116; *Inv.* 1.27), he nonetheless treats it
as a repository of deeper wisdom, and as a structural mechanism for
understanding everyday life.

While such parallelism is generally operative among the poetic citations,
Cicero's engagement with verse from the Roman stage is a particularly
pointed example of the mirroring between the real world and the poetic

world. According to Donatus (*De com.* 5.1), Cicero in the *Hortensius* called comedy an "emulation of life, the mirror of experience, the image of truth" (*imitationem uitae, speculum consuetudinis, imaginem ueritatis*).[35] In the *De Senectute* (65), Cicero remarks that faults of old age can be improved "in real life just as on stage" (*cum in uita tum in scaena*), in reference to the moral lessons taught by Terence's *Adelphoe*. Likewise, in the *Tusculans* (4.45), a verse from a comedy by Afranius "is drawn straight from real life" (*illud e uita ductum*). While theatrical verisimilitude is sometimes rather literal – as in the *Pro Roscio Amerino* (47), where, as I discuss in Chapter 2, there is apparently little difference between the Caecilian *adulescens* and some young man from Veii – many of Cicero's invocations of the Roman stage are more symbolic, indicating the impact of theatre as an institution on the structure of Roman thought.[36] Public life is metaphorically referenced as "the stage," and political scandals are figured as "dramas."[37] Cicero's philosophical treatises may open like a stage production with an invocation of Roman theatre, as is the case with the quotation of Caecilius Statius' *Synephebi* in the *De Natura Deorum* (1.13–14):

> sed iam, ut omni me inuidia liberem, ponam in medio sententias philosophorum de natura deorum. quo quidem loco conuocandi omnes uidentur, qui, quae sit earum uera, iudicent; tum demum mihi procax Academia uidebitur, si aut consenserint omnes aut erit inuentus aliquis, qui, quid uerum sit, inuenerit. itaque mihi libet exclamare ut in Synephebis:
> *pro deum, popularium omnium, omnium adulescentium*　　[Ribbeck 211–212]
> *clamo, postulo, obsecro, oro, ploro atque inploro fidem*
> non leuissuma de re, ut queritur ille
> *... in ciuitate fieri facinora capitalia:*　　　　　　　　　[Ribbeck 213–214]
> *ab amico amante argentum accipere meretrix non uult,*
> [14] sed ut adsint, cognoscant, animaduertant, quid de religione, pietate, sanctitate, caerimoniis, fide, iure iurando, quid de templis, delubris sacrificiisque sollemnibus, quid de ipsis auspiciis, quibus nos praesumus, existimandum sit.

> But now, to free myself from criticism, I will place in the open the opinions of philosophers concerning the nature of the gods. Indeed, everyone ought to be called to this place to judge which of these opinions is true. If it turn

---

[35] Hanses 2020: 57.

[36] As Mathias Hanses (2020: 34) has recently noted, the lasting appeal of Roman comedy at Rome seems to have derived at least partially from the fact that comedy "invited moral contemplation regarding *typical* human behaviour" (my emphasis).

[37] *De Or.* 3.177: *neque ex alio ... ad scaenam pompamque sumuntur*, "we do not use a different kind of diction for the public stage and the parade of political life"; see Mankin 2011: 269. Cicero refers to the Bona Dea scandal as a "Clodian drama" (*fabulae Clodianae, Att.* 1.18.2); see Geffcken 1973: 63.

out that all the schools agree, or if any one philosopher can be found who
has discovered the truth, then but not before will I consider the Academy to
be impudent. And so I am free to cry out like the character in the *Synephebi*:

"*Oh gods, all people, all young men,*
I cry, I demand, I beseech, I beg, I plead, and I seek your faith,"
not in the trifling matter that he complains about:
"*that a capital crime has taken place in the city:*
a prostitute does not want to accept money from her loverboy!"
[14] but to be present in court, to examine the case, to pay close attention to
what ought to be the verdict, from those of us who are present, concerning
religion, piety, sanctity, sacred rites, faith, oaths; concerning temples,
shrines, and solemn sacrifices; about the very auguries themselves.

Cicero uses Caecilius Statius' parody of Roman court proceedings to turn his
philosophical readership into a forensic audience: while Caecilius tries the
case of a *meretrix* who will not accept her lover's money, Cicero tries the case
of the nature of the gods.[38] Verse citation allows Cicero to bring his own
works to life by imbuing them with the drama of the Roman stage.

Just as the theatre was a mirror of Roman social and intellectual life, so
too were its poets and actors taken as avatars of the Roman elite.[39] Cicero's
Brutus (2–3) begins by mourning for the recent death of Hortensius,
a preeminent oratorical rival whom Cicero figures as forefather by invoking
poetic genealogy:[40]

> dolebamque quod non, ut plerique putabant, aduersarium aut obtrecta-
> torem laudum mearum sed socium potius et consortem gloriosi laboris
> amiseram. [3] etenim si in leuiorum artium studio memoriae proditum est
> poetas nobilis poetarum aequalium morte doluisse, quo tandem animo eius
> interitum ferre debui, cum quo certare erat gloriosius quam omnino aduer-
> sarium non habere?

> I was grieving not, as many people thought, because I had lost an adversary
> or a detractor of my own great deeds, but rather because I lost a comrade and
> even a partner in a glorious work. [3] If living tradition relates that noble
> poets, in their pursuit of a less serious discipline, grieved at the death of their

---

[38] On Caecilius Statius (Ribbeck 211–214) as a parody of Latin formula, see Christenson 2000: 212.
Cicero's (*ND* 1.13) use of *procax* ("impudent," "wanton") to describe the Academy is also an echo of
comedy, where it is used to describe the pimps and prostitutes: Plaut. *Persa* (406–410); cf. *Pro Caelio*
49: *non solum meretrix, sed etiam procax,* "not only a prostitute, but a wanton one."

[39] In addition to the metaphorical ways in which the theatre reflected Roman society, it also did so in
a literal sense. In the *Philippics* (2.44), Cicero criticizes Antony for sitting in the wrong area of the
theatre under the *Lex Roscia* since his family had declared bankruptcy. On the *Lex Roscia* (67 BCE),
see Manuwald 2011: 107.

[40] On Hortensius' death in 50 BCE as Cicero was returning from Cilicia: *Att.* 6.6.2, *Brut.* 1; cf. Dugan
2005: 218, 248.

contemporaries, with what spirit, then, ought I to bear the death of a man with whom it was more glorious to compete than to have as complete adversary?

Just as poets mourn their own, so too does Cicero regret the loss of a fellow orator.[41] Cicero (*Brut.* 6) adds that if Hortensius were still alive to see the contemporary state of Roman oratory, he would feel pain at the sight of the Roman forum "which was, so to speak, the theatre of his genius" (*quasi theatrum illius ingeni*). Later in the work (*Brut.* 229), Cicero makes the comparison between notable orators and notable poets even more explicit:

> ut Accius isdem aedilibus ait se et Pacuuium docuisse fabulam, cum ille octoginta, ipse triginta annos natus esset, sic Hortensius non cum suis aequalibus solum sed et mea cum aetate et cum tua, Brute, et cum aliquanto superiore coniungitur . . .

> Just as Accius says that he and Pacuvius each put on a play for the same aediles when Pacuvius was eighty and Accius was thirty, so too Hortensius was not only associated with his own contemporaries but with my age, and yours, Brutus, as well as an earlier time . . .

Hortensius is here presented as the Pacuvius to Cicero's Accius: just as the elder and younger dramatic poets produced plays in 140 BCE,[42] so too did Hortensius and Cicero overlap for a time, even though Hortensius' most illustrious period (like Pacuvius') belonged to the past.[43] Cicero found parallels between the lives of Rome's classic poets, and his own relationship to the Roman oratorical canon.

Actors, too, were viewed as reflections of the orator.[44] Acting and oratory shared certain techniques, and Cicero drew upon the actor's performance of Latin verse to exemplify a number of vocal tones. In the

---

[41] The image of poets mourning the death of their contemporaries was part of the traditional biography of Euripides (*Vita* 45–49) who is said to have been mourned by Sophocles.

[42] Boyle 2006: 88, Manuwald 2011: 209, 216. Aulus Gellius (13.1.2; cf. Jer. *Chron. ad Ol.* 160.2) relates a story (disbelieved by D'Anna 1967: 11–13) that Accius recited his *Atreus* to Pacuvius at Tarentum on his way to Asia.

[43] Hortensius' first known speech is the defense of Africans in the senate in 95 BCE (*De Or.* 3.229, *Brut.* 229). In 86 BCE, Hortensius defended Pompey (*Brut.* 230), charged with the theft of public property following his father's siege of Asculum (89 BCE; Plut. *Pomp.* 4). The first confrontation between Cicero and Hortensius came in the *Pro Quinctio* (81 BCE), Cicero's earliest extant speech; see Vasaly 2002: 72–76, Lintott 2008: 43–59. When Cicero successfully prosecuted Verres in 70 BCE, he unseated Hortensius, who had defended Verres, as Rome's most prominent orator (*Brut.* 319, cf. Dugan 2005: 221). By Cicero's consular year, Cicero and Hortensius were able to cooperate, acting on the same side in several defenses; see Dyck 2008: 155.

[44] Fantham 2002.

De Oratore (3.217), Cicero quotes from Accius' *Atreus* to demonstrate how the actor modulates his voice to convey anger:[45]

> hi sunt actori, ut pictori, expositi ad uariandum colores. aliud enim uocis genus iracundia sibi sumat, acutum, incitatum, crebro incidens:
> *ipsus hortatur me frater, ut meos malis miser*   [Dangel 58–59]
> *mandarem natos*
> . . . et
> *ecquis hoc animaduertit? uincite . . .*   [Dangel 64]
> et Atreus fere totus.

> These are the colours available to the actor to add variety, just like the painter. Anger takes up one kind of voice for itself, one which is sharp, rapid, thick falling:
> "My very own brother urges me, wretch that I am, with my jaws
> to masticate my own children."
> . . . and:
> "Does no one punish this? Put in chains . . . "
> and almost the entire *Atreus*.

While the focus here is upon the vocal quality used to convey anger during the performance of verse, in the *Tusculans* (*TD* 4.55) Cicero quotes the same verses as part of an ethical argument:[46]

> oratorem uero irasci minime decet, simulare non dedecet. an tibi irasci tum uidemur, cum quid in causis acrius et uehementius dicimus? quid? cum iam rebus transactis et praeteritis orationes scribimus, num irati scribimus?
> *ecquis hoc animaduertit? uincite . . .*   [Dangel 64]
> num aut egisse umquam iratum Aesopum aut scripsisse existimas iratum Accium? aguntur ista praeclare et ab oratore quidem melius, si modo est orator, quam ab ullo histrione, sed aguntur leniter et mente tranquilla.

> While it is especially inappropriate for an orator to become angry, it is not inappropriate to simulate anger. Do you think I am really angry when I am speaking in court with a sharper and more passionate tone? What? Do you think that, after the matter is done and over with, when I am writing down the orations, that I'm angry as I write?
> "Does no one punish this? Put in chains . . . "
> Surely you don't think that Aesopus was angry when he played this part, or Accius angry when he wrote it? Such things are excellently acted, and,

---

[45] *De Or.* 3.217–219 is a heavily citational passage, where Cicero draws from the Roman stage in order to demonstrate how to convey a number of different emotions; see Moore 2012: 91.

[46] Cicero's discussion of anger from two different angles in the *De Oratore* and the *Tusculans* depend on the same verses of Accius' *Atreus*: Dangel 64 (*De Or.* 3.217; *TD* 4.55); Dangel 58–59 (*De Or.* 3.217; *TD* 4.77). See Manuwald 2011: 221 on Cicero's use of Accius' *Atreus*.

indeed, even better acted by an orator, if he really is one, than by any actor. But they are acted gently, and with a peaceful mind.

In the context of a Stoic condemnation of "anger" (*irasci, TD* 4.54), Cicero emphasizes a moral consonance between the actor, orator (and poet),[47] who are each capable of simulating the anger needed for performance, but do not, Cicero says, actually feel the emotion they are displaying.[48] In the *De Officiis* (1.114), Cicero makes another gesture towards acting when he argues that it is necessary for every individual to assess themselves honestly and to embrace their own strengths and weaknesses, just as actors do when they are choosing a role:

> suum quisque igitur noscat ingenium acremque se et bonorum et uitiorum suorum iudicem praebeat, ne scaenici plus quam nos uideantur habere prudentiae. illi enim non optumas, sed sibi accomodatissimas fabulas eligunt; qui uoce freti sunt, Epigonos Medumque, qui gestu Melanippam, Clytemestram, semper Rupilius, quem ego memini, Antiopam, non saepe Aesopus Aiacem. ergo histrio hoc uidebit in scena, non uidebit sapiens uir in uita?

> Everyone should therefore get to know their own particular talents and present themselves as a critical judge of their own strengths and weaknesses, lest we let the theatricals show more wisdom than we ourselves do. For they pick not the best plays, but the ones which are the best fit for themselves. Those who rely on their voice pick *Epigoni* and *Medus*, those who rely on gesture pick *Melanippa, Clytemestra*. Rupilius, whom I remember, always picked *Antiopa*; and Aesopus did not often pick *Ajax*. Will an actor have this degree of consideration on stage, but not a wise man in real life?

Referring here to plays by Ennius, Pacuvius, and Accius,[49] Cicero notes that actors pick their roles based upon critical self-assessment of their own particular strengths. Again, everyday life is figured as a kind of stage play in which every Roman is an actor who must decide how to put on their own performance. An alignment between the Roman stage and "real life" is therefore a persistent figure of thought for Cicero, who threads his understanding of political, oratorical, and philosophical concerns with theatrical parallels. The poet and the actor, poetry and performance; each of these presented a reflection of Roman life. Cicero viewed Latin poetry as a mirror of the Roman world.

---

[47] Cf. *Sest.* 122 where Accius the poet and Aesopus the actor are each figured as acting "on behalf of" (*pro*) Cicero.
[48] Cicero makes the opposite argument in the *De Divinatione* (1.80), where Aesopus is inspired with Platonic "divine frenzy" when he performs in Pacuvius' *Teucer*.
[49] *Off.* 1.114: Accius' *Epigoni*, Pacuvius' *Medus*, Ennius' *Melanippa*, Accius' *Clytemestra*, Pacuvius' *Antiopa*, Ennius' *Ajax*.

1.2 Cicero and the Latin Poets

nihil est enim simul et inuentum et perfectum; nec dubitari debet quin
fuerint ante Homerum poetae, quod ex eis carminibus intellegi potest, quae
apud illum et in Phaeacum et in procorum epulis canuntur. quid, nostri
ueteres uersus ubi sunt?

quos olim Faunei uatesque canebant,						[Skutsch 207–209]
cum neque Musarum scopulos . . .[50]
nec dicti studiosus quisquam erat ante hunc

ait ipse de se nec mentitur in gloriando: sic enim sese res habet. nam et
Odyssia Latina est sic tamquam opus aliquod Daedali et Liuianae
fabulae non satis dignae quae iterum legantur.

Nothing is fully developed at the moment of its invention. We don't doubt
that there were poets before Homer, in fact, we can tell that there were from
Homer himself, who depicts songs sung both among the Phaeacians and at
the banquets of the suitors. Where are our old verses
"which once the Fauns and the prophets sang,
since not yet the craggy heights of the Muses . . .
nor was there anyone learned in the word, before him"
as he says about himself? He is not false in his boast, for this is really how it
was. The Latin *Odyssey* is like some work of Daedalus, and Livius
Andronicus' plays are not worth reading more than once.

In this famous and much discussed passage of the *Brutus* (71), Cicero
traces the trajectory of oratory by introducing Latin poetry as its developmental parallel. In the *Annales*, Ennius made a formal departure from
the Roman poetic tradition by adopting the hexameter for his epic
instead of the Saturnian which had been used by his poetic forebears.
In this passage, Ennius consciously figured his epic as a point of rupture
in Roman literary history, and, indeed, Cicero and subsequent Romans
accepted Ennius' claim.[51] By invoking the songs of the Homeric bards
who appear in the *Odyssey*, Cicero imagines a parallel point of priority in
the development of Latin verse.[52] Just as the songs of Phemius and
Demodocus imply pre-Homeric song, so too, Cicero argues, does
Ennius' rejection of the song of the "Fauns and prophets" (*Faunei
uatesque*) suggest a prior tradition. While Ennius, Cicero says (*Brut.*
75), counted his precursor, Naevius, among the Fauns and prophets,

[50] Cicero gives only a partial quotation of the passage; see Skutsch 1985: 374.
[51] Goldberg 1995: 90, Hinds 1998: 64–69.
[52] In addition to the mention of two anonymous singers (3.267–71, 4.17–18), the *Odyssey* depicts two
bards: Phemius in Ithaca (Books 1, 17, and 22) and Demodocus among the Phaeacians (Books 8
and 13).

Cicero interpreted Ennius' poetic self-presentation as a piece of posturing:

> tamen illius, quem in uatibus et Faunis adnumerat Ennius, bellum Punicum quasi Myronis opus delectat. [76] sit Ennius sane, ut est certe, perfectior: qui si illum, ut simulat, contemneret, non omnia bella persequens primum illud Punicum acerrimum bellum reliquisset. sed ipse dicit cur id faciat:
> *scripsere* inquit *alii rem*   [Skutsch 206–207]
> *uorsibus*
> et luculente quidem scripserunt, etiam si minus quam tu polite. nec uero tibi aliter uideri debet, qui a Naeuio uel sumpsisti multa, si fateris, uel, si negas, surripuisti.

> Despite the fact that Ennius numbers Naevius among the prophets and the Fauns, his *Punic War*, like a work of Myron, still delights. [76] Say that Ennius is more developed, as he certainly is. But if Ennius really valued Naevius so little, as he claims to, he would not, in seeking to treat all wars, have left out that first Punic War, so bitterly fought. But he himself says why he does so:
> *"Others,"* he says, *"have written the matter*
> *in verse."*
> And indeed, they wrote brilliantly, even if they did so with less polish than you, Ennius. It should not seem otherwise to you, who have taken so much from Naevius, or, rather, stolen so much, whether you admit it or not.

Cicero represents the relationship between Ennius and Naevius in terms reminiscent of Harold Bloom: Ennius, even while making a departure from Naevius, could not help but reference him, and, indeed, carried Naevian influence in his work via poetic borrowings or, as Cicero puts it, thefts.[53] As a result, neither Naevius, nor even Livius Andronicus, whose work Cicero describes as primordially "Daedalic" (*Brut.* 71), truly belongs to the precursor age figured as vatic, woodland song. While Cicero recognizes that the recursivity of influence allowed old songs to echo through the works of new poets, he nonetheless felt that the prior age of Roman verse was difficult to access. Cicero says (*Brut.* 75) that he had read in Cato's *Origines* of an ancient epainetic tradition at Rome, but he adds that these songs, the *carmina conuiualia*, no longer survived:[54]

---

[53] Goldberg 1995: 46, Hinds 1998: 57–58, Habinek 2005: 39.
[54] Cicero also refers to the *carmina conuiualia* in the *Tusculans* (1.3; 4.4 = *FPL* p2), where he again cites them via Cato's *Origines*. On the scholarly controversy surrounding the *carmina conuiualia*, see Sciarrino 2011: 21–28, who summarizes the evolution of the debate. Whatever the significance of the *carmina* in the history of Latin literature, let it here suffice to say that, as Habinek (2005: 36) notes, the Romans believed they had a song culture prior to the third century BCE from which "literature" could emerge.

atque utinam exstarent illa carmina, quae multis saeculis ante suam aetatem
in epulis esse cantitata a singulis conuiuis de clarorum uirorum laudibus in
Originibus scriptum reliquit Cato!

If only those songs, which Cato leaves a record of in his *Origines*, were
extant. He writes that, many generations before his own age, these songs
were sung by guests at banquets who took turns to celebrate the deeds of
famous men.

In addition to these *carmina,* Cicero was aware of other elements of ritual
song or authoritative verse from Rome's precursor period which did persist
in various ways.[55] Yet it is a point of significance that Cicero did not engage
with these traditions citationally as he did with poets like Ennius. Cicero's
consciousness of early Roman verse did not translate into an explicit
engagement in his own texts. Given that such songs and authoritative
utterances were so deeply connected with Roman rituals, cult practices,
and commemoration, they had evidently worked their influence upon
Cicero in profound but more subtle ways. Traditional songs such as
these were part of Cicero's unconscious linguistic and cultural inheritance,
and as a result could not be disembodied or made distinct via citation.

In the context of Cicero's broader consciousness of Roman literary
history, his focus upon Ennius becomes even more significant. Cicero
knew, of course, that Ennius was not Rome's first poet. Even discounting
Rome's "pre-poetic" era, Cicero was aware that Livius Andronicus,
Naevius, and Plautus preceded Ennius. Yet Cicero shows very little interest
in these poets. Livius Andronicus' *Odyssey* was, according to Cicero,
"primitive," and his plays not worth reading twice (*Brut.* 71).[56] While
Cicero several times referred to Livius' role at the "beginning" of Latin
literature in 240 BCE, he seems never to have quoted Livius directly.[57] Even
though Cicero in the *Brutus* (71) defended Naevius against Ennius'

---

[55] Funeral dirges (*neniae, Leg.* 2.62; cf. Habinek 2005 *passim*); songs at ceremonial banquets (*epulae
solemnes, De Or.* 3.197) such as the public feasts at the *Ludi Romani* (cf. *Leg.* 2.22, 2.38; *Har.* 21); the
Hymn of the Salii (*De Or.* 3.197 = *FPL* p3), Appius Claudius' *carmen* (*TD* 4.4 = *FPL* p12), and the
pronouncements of the *vates*, Marcii and Publicius (*Div.* 1.89, 1.115, 2.113 =*FPL* p15).

[56] Hanses 2020: 27.

[57] Livius Andronicus in 240 BCE: *TD* 1.3, *De Sen.* 50, *Brut.* 72; cf. Welsh 2011. In the *De Legibus* (2.39),
Cicero says he had heard the austere melodies which accompanied Livius Andronicus' (and
Naevius') plays in the theatre, and observed their effect on audiences. Aside from the possibility
that one of the many now unattributable fragments in Cicero's corpus came from Livius, there is
only one potential instance of citation. Cicero writes (*Fam.* 7.2.1) that *Equus Troianus* was
performed as part of the inaugural games for Pompey's theatre in 55 BCE. A play of this name was
attributed to Naevius as well as Livius (see *TrRF* I p85), but Cicero does not name its author. In 54
BCE, Cicero quotes from an *Equus Troianus* (*TrRF* I *adesp.* 29a) in a letter to Trebatius Testa (*Fam.*
7.16.1), but likewise gives no author.

apparent criticism, he only explicitly quoted Naevius a handful of times.[58] Likewise Plautus, whom Cicero regularly pairs with Naevius as a contemporary, was only quoted by Cicero five times in the extant corpus.[59] In contrast, Cicero's engagement with Ennius is immense: over sixty discrete citations of the *Annales*, over a hundred citations of the tragedies, as well as quotations of other "minor" works.[60]

For Cicero, then, Ennius was the event horizon of Latin poetry. While Ennius was not the first, he was the first to matter: he was era-defining, epoch making. Ennius' poetry was, for Cicero, proof of authoritative order in the universe: golden letters of the alphabet thrown randomly together could never produce the beauty and order of the *Annales* (*ND* 2.93); nor could the pig, who might accidentally be able to produce the letter A with his snout, write Ennius' *Andromacha* (*Div.* 1.23). Additionally, Ennius' work was the window through which Cicero could glimpse famous and venerated Romans from generations past: Scipio Nasica (*De Or.* 2.276), Servius Sulpicius Galba (*Ac.* 2.51), M. Fulvius Nobilior (*Arch.* 27, *Brut.* 79, *TD* 1.3), Scipio Africanus (*Arch.* 22).[61] Ennius was a trusted witness of contemporary Roman culture, as well as an aesthetic and moral model.

From Cicero's perspective, then, Ennius opened the flood gates of Latin poetry. After Ennius, Cicero engaged most extensively with the Roman tragedians: Pacuvius, with fifty discrete quotations in the Ciceronian corpus; and Accius, with another fifty.[62] Across the corpus, Cicero consistently quotes tragedy more than any other poetic genre.[63] As with Ennius, the tragedies of Pacuvius and Accius, originally produced in the mid to late second century BCE, were revived during the Ciceronian period; indeed, Cicero often speaks of these works in the context of their live performance.[64] While Cicero sometimes described Ennius as a living, breathing person (e.g. walking with Servius Sulpicius Galba, *Ac.* 2.51), his remarks on the lives of Accius and especially Pacuvius are very light

---

[58] Quotations of Naevius' *Hector Proficiscens*: *TD* 4.67, *Fam.* 5.12.7, *Fam.* 5.16.1 (*TrRF* I 14); quotations from unknown Naevian tragedies: *Or.* 152 (*TrRF* I 41), *Or.* 152 (*TrRF* I 42), *De Sen.* 20 (Warmington 107); *Phil.* 2.65 (*TrRF* I 46).

[59] Naevius and Plautus as contemporaries: *Rep.* 4.11, *TD* 1.3, *De Or.* 3.45, *Brut.* 60, 73. Quotations of Plautus: *Div.* 1.65 = *Aulularia* 178; *De Inv.* 1.95 = *Trinummus* 23–26; *ad Brut.* 1.2.3 (2a.1) = *Trinummus* 319; *Pis.* 61 = *Trinummus* 419; *De Or.* 2.39 = *Trinummus* 705.

[60] See Appendix II.

[61] On the social network of Ennius' poetry, and the extent of its historicity, see Badian 1972.

[62] See Appendix II.

[63] Tragedy makes up approximately 50 percent of the citations in Cicero's speeches, 40 percent in the letters, 35 percent in the philosophical works, and 35 percent in the rhetorical works.

[64] On the revival of the "classic" Latin tragedies, see Manuwald 2011: 108–119, 340–341; on the revival of comedies, see Hanses 2020: 33–122.

indeed.[65] Aside from asserting that Pacuvius produced a play in the
same year as Accius (*Brut.* 229), Cicero gives no "biographical" details for
Pacuvius.[66] Accius, however, Cicero knew as both a scholar and a poet
(*Brut.* 72–73). Cicero also claims (*Brut.* 107) to have met Accius in person
and through him heard about great men such as Decimus Brutus Callaicus
(cos. 138 BCE) and Quintus Fabius Maximus (cos. 121 BCE); and so, like
Ennius, Accius was a conduit for the memory of Romans whom Cicero
could never have met.[67]

Reflecting a contemporary impulse to align Roman literary history with
the developmental model of Greece, Cicero referred to the trio of tragedians, Ennius, Pacuvius, and Accius, as the Roman Aeschylus, Sophocles,
and Euripides.[68] While Cicero's sustained engagement with Ennius betrays
his own opinion, he nonetheless discusses the fact that poetic preference is
subjective (*Or.* 36):[69]

> sed in omni re difficillimum est formam, qui χαρακτήρ Graece dicitur,
> exponere optumi, quod aliud aliis uidetur optimum. Ennio delector, ait
> quispiam, quod non discedit a communi more uerborum. Pacuuio, inquit
> alius; omnes apud hunc ornati elaboratique sunt uersus, multa apud alterum
> neglegentius. fac alium Accio. uaria enim sunt iudicia ut in Graecis nec
> facilis explicatio, quae forma maxume excellat.

> But in all things it's very difficult to explain the best "form" ("stamp" in
> Greek), since what's best is a matter of taste. "I like Ennius," one person
> says, "because he uses everyday language." "Pacuvius," another says. "All his
> verses are ornate and highly wrought. Many things are expressed more
> carelessly in Ennius." Imagine another likes Accius. There are such varied
> judgements (it's not easy to make a definite judgement about Greek litera-
> ture either) about what makes the best "form."

---

[65] Cicero evidently inferred biographical details about Ennius' life from the poet's own verse testimony, as we have seen, for example, in Cicero's treatment of the Ennian *elogia*. Poets who did not
include themselves as characters in their own works, or who did so only obliquely, do not appear in
Cicero as fully fleshed individuals.

[66] Cicero's references to Pacuvius are limited to: his place in the Latin tragic canon alongside Ennius
and Accius (*Ac.* 1.10, *De Or.* 3.27, *Or.* 36); his producing a play in the same *ludi* as Accius in 140 BCE
(*Brut.* 229); and his "bad" Latin (*Brut.* 258).

[67] Cicero also associates Accius with D. Brutus Callaicus (cos. 138 BCE) in the *Pro Archia* (27) and in
the *De Legibus* (2.54).

[68] *De Or.* 3.27, *Ac.* 1.10. Despite their shared canonicity, each poet, Cicero says, has a very different
style: *quam sint inter sese Ennius, Pacuuius, Acciusque dissimiles* (*De Or.* 3.27). The framing of Ennius,
Pacuvius, and Accius as the new Aeschylus, Sophocles, and Euripides is an artificial alignment
principally intended to canonize the former, rather than to reflect their style; see Skutsch 1985: 26.

[69] Cf. Horace *Epistle* 2.1.50–55, Quintilian *Inst.* 10.1.97; see Hanses 2020: 64–65.

Cicero goes on (*Or.* 36) to say that an "expert" (*eius rei gnarus*) could make such a judgement, but he does not explicitly give his own opinion. Likewise, in the *De Optimo Genere Oratorum* (2), where Ennius is described as the best epic poet, Pacuvius the best tragedian, and Caecilius Statius the best comic playwright, Cicero suggests these rankings tentatively: "one might say" (*licet dicere*) that Ennius is the best epic poet, "if he thinks so" (*si cui ita uidetur*); and Caecilius is the best comic, "perhaps" (*fortasse*). While Cicero's expression of canonicity names famous poets, it also insists upon the subjectivity of such a judgement and the openness of the matter to debate.[70]

Of the comic playwrights, Cicero engaged most extensively with Terence, with forty discrete quotations.[71] Caecilius Statius, despite his apparent rank as best comic poet (*Opt. Gen.* 2), receives twenty; and Plautus only five.[72] Cicero quotes comedy about half as much as he quotes tragedy, with the majority of the comic citations appearing in the philosophical works.[73] By the Ciceronian era, Plautus had become a point of focus for Roman scholarship, as I discuss in Chapter 3, yet Cicero did not mirror that interest. Nonetheless, Cicero did consider the language of Plautus both venerable and austere: in the *De Oratore* (3.45), Cicero has Crassus compare the "undeviated" (*rectus*) and "pure" (*simplex*) language of

---

[70] Indeed, in the Republican era we see a number of different judgements and rankings regarding poetic quality. Volcacius Sedigitus promised to resolve debate over at least the comic poets with his own expertise (Courtney fr. 1), ranking Caecilius Statius first, Plautus second, Naevius third; Terence sixth. Ennius, who comes in tenth and last place, is only included out of respect for his "ancientness." The larger scope of Sedigitus' list grants us a glimpse into a richer world of Roman comedy beyond the binary of Plautus and Terence to which we are limited by the fact that they alone survive in full. Several of the lesser known comic poets on Sedigitus' list (Atilius, Turpilius, Trabea) are indeed quoted by Cicero (see n72), though Cicero does not confer upon them the same level of significance.

[71] See Appendix II. In his extant writings Cicero did not explicitly rank the comic poets, but he did praise Terence in his youthful poem, *Limon* (Suet. *Vit. Ter.* 7 = Courtney fr. 2). Transmitted alongside Cicero's *Limon* in Suetonius' *Life of Terence* (7) is a slightly different perspective on the poet composed by Julius Caesar (Courtney fr. 1), who, broadly speaking, praised Terence but criticized him for lack of "force" (*uis*). On the Terence poems as a school exercise set by M. Antonius Gnipho, see Casali 2018: 211 with bibliography. On Antonius Gnipho's philological activities, see Zetzel 2018: 27, 36, 83.

[72] In addition to the *fabulae palliatae* of Plautus, Caecilius Statius, and Terence, Cicero also quotes or refers to *palliatae* of Trabea (*TD* 4.35, 4.67; *Fin.* 2.13; *Fam.* 2.9.2, 9.21.1), Atilius (*TD* 4.25; *Att.* 14.20.3), Turpilius (*TD* 4.72–73; *Fam.* 9.22.1), and the *togatae* of L. Afranius (*TD* 4.45, 4.55; *Fin.* 1.7; *Sest.* 118; *Att.* 16.2.3).

[73] The highest number of discrete citations of Roman comedy occurs in Cicero's philosophical works (approximately 60 altogether, compared to 130 of tragedy). Yet Cicero's correspondence contains the greatest *frequency* of comic quotations: 30 percent of the quotations in the letters come from comedy, compared with only 20 percent in the speeches, and 10 percent each in the philosophical and rhetorical works respectively.

his mother-in-law, Laelia, to the comedies of Plautus.[74] This anecdote emblematizes Cicero's consistent belief that poetry has the power to reflect the qualities and values of the age which produced it and thereby to stand as an artefact of its cultural moment. To Cicero, Terence reflected the noble and refined Latinity of the mid second century BCE: he proclaims Terentian comedy to be so fine that it could have been composed by none other than Gaius Laelius, confidant to Scipio Aemilianus (*Att.* 7.3.10).[75]

Although other Roman poets are known to have composed satire, such as Ennius and Pacuvius, Cicero engaged almost exclusively with Lucilius, its most famous practitioner.[76] Citations of Lucilius' *Satires* are comparable to engagements with Terence, with around forty discrete quotations.[77] Significantly, the majority of Cicero's citations of Lucilius occur in the *De Oratore*. As I discuss in Chapter 5, this is due to Cicero's dependence upon Lucilius' *Satires* for the worldbuilding of this dialogue, particularly regarding the character of L. Licinius Crassus (cos. 95 BCE). Given that Lucilius often spoke in the first person, Cicero was able to infer a number of biographical details from his work, and, furthermore, it was Lucilius' *persona* as an individual operating in elite Roman society which drew Cicero to him. Cicero, too, used vignettes of Lucilius to reflect aspects of real life and society at Rome: Lucilius' observations of contemporary spectacles were picked up by Cicero as metaphors for his own experiences;[78] dinner parties attended by Cicero resembled those criticized in Lucilius.[79] And as with Terence, Lucilius' poetry preserved, from Cicero's perspective, a certain linguistic "purity." Cicero wrote (*Fam.* 9.15.2.), that the language used by his friend, L. Papirius Paetus, resembled that of Lucilius, whose own Latinity mirrored that of famous elites.[80]

---

[74] And Naevius (*De Or.* 3.45). But, as far as we know, Cicero never quoted Naevius' comedy.

[75] Not all poets are good reflections of their age. In the *Brutus* (258), Cicero contrasts the "integrity" (*innocentia*) of Gaius Laelius' and Scipio Aemilianus' Latinity with their contemporaries, Caeilius Statius and Pacuvius, who both "used bad Latin" (*male locuti*).

[76] Lucilius' primacy is reflected in Horace's detailed criticism of the poet in three satires (1.4, 1.10, 2.1, cf. Poccetti 2018: 81). Cicero on one occasion cites Ennian satire (*ND* 1.97 = Goldberg-ManuwaldF17).

[77] See Appendix II.

[78] Cicero repeatedly quotes Lucilius' portrait of the gladiator, Pacideianus (Warmington 172–183) to describe real fighting (*De Or.* 3.86, *TD* 2.41, *Ph.* 13.15), oratorical competition (*De Opt. Gen.* 17), and the expression of anger (*TD* 4.48). In a letter to his brother (*Q. fr.* 3.4.2) Cicero also used a phrase from this passage of Lucilius to discuss Latin style (*Or.* 161).

[79] Cicero quoted Lucilius (Warmington 206–207) in a letter to Atticus (*Att.* 13.52.1; Dec. 45 BCE) after witnessing a banquet during the Saturnalia where Julius Caesar was on an emetic diet and therefore able to eat and drink to excess. See Goh 2018: 259–260.

[80] Cicero's insistence upon the confluence of Latinity and Roman identity led him to make some xenophobic remarks: e.g. *Fam.* 9.15.2 where old Roman wit typified by Lucilius is threatened by the language of "trousered" (*bracatis*) Gauls. The *Rhet. ad Her.* (4.17) likewise expressly forbids "barbarism" (*barbarismus*) from the purity of Latinity; see Zetzel 2018: 52–53.

There were, additionally, other genres of Latin poetry which Cicero engaged with only very minimally. Cicero quotes Roman mime directly only once, in the *De Oratore* (2.274), as part of an excursus on humour.[81] Cicero's discussion of mime in the context of *subabsurda* – i.e. jokes so silly that they are "discordant"[82] – suggests that mime was a genre considered beneath the dignity of most Roman elites, even if its style of humour could be used by the orator every now and then (*De Or.* 2.275). Given that mime was considered by ancient critics to be an especially obscene genre, it is perhaps not a surprise that Cicero does not engage with it beyond the casual remark here and there.[83] However, it was mime's very qualities of frivolity and obscenity which Cicero harnessed when he referenced the genre in his speeches (*Cael.* 65; *Phil.* 2.65, 11.13).[84] Cicero's engagement with Atellan farce (*fabula Atellana*) is also very minimal.[85] Cicero quotes *Atellanae* by Novius in the *De Oratore* (2.255, 279, 285), again as part of the excursus on humour, and by Pomponius in a letter to Manius Curius (*Fam.* 7.31.2) where it is used as an example of the "old Roman wit" (*ueterem urbanitatem*).[86] Otherwise, Cicero only makes two small references to Atellan farce.[87]

Cicero's extensive quotation of the Latin poets was evidently an engagement with an already established literary canon. Cicero's citation of the old poets reiteratively authorized their canonicity, and by lending him the weight of their cultural significance the poets in turn authorized Cicero. Within this context, Cicero's minimal engagement with contemporary poets does not come as a surprise. Cicero was interested in the fact that the earlier poets stood as a reflection of the age which produced them. Contemporary poets, in

---

[81] *De Or.* 2.274 = Ribbeck 1–2, 3–4, 5. On two occasions Cicero apparently refers to the titles of mimes, *Faba* (*Att.* 1.16.13) and *Tutor* (*De Or.* 2.259); on which see Panayotakis 2010: 15, 28, Manuwald 2011: 178.

[82] Cicero uses "*absurdus*" to describe vocal inconcinnity, i.e. ugly sounds: the croaking of frogs (*Div.* 1.15), a musician singing out of tune (*TD* 2.12, cf. *De Or.* 3.41).

[83] Mime was associated with the *Ludi Florales*, at which particularly lewd performances were allowed, and women were involved in mime as well – often naked; see Manuwald 2011: 178–179, Hanses 2020: 55. Although Cicero only quoted mime on one occasion, he did remark upon its ability to parody contemporary politics (*Fam.* 7.11.2), and he did refer several times to mime performances at Rome. A fragment (Crawford fr. 2) of Cicero's oration in defense of Quintus Gallius (64 BCE) seems to refer to a recent mime performance; see Crawford 1994: 154–155. Cicero angrily endured performances by D. Laberius and Publilius Syrus at Caesar's *ludi* in 46 BCE (*Fam.* 12.18.2; cf. Edwards 1993: 120); Atticus saw a mime by Publilius Syrus which conveyed the will of the people in 44 BCE (*Att.* 14.2.1).

[84] On Cicero's references to mime as expressions of contempt, see Panayotakis 2010: 15.

[85] On Atellan farce, see Manuwald 2011: 169–177.

[86] Novius: *De Or.* 2.255 (Ribbeck 115), *De Or.* 2.279 (Ribbeck 113–114), *De Or.* 2.285 (Ribbeck 116). Pomponius: *Fam.* 7.31.2 (Ribbeck 191).

[87] *Div.* 2.25, where a subject of derision belongs in an Atellan farce; *Fam.* 9.16.7, where L. Papirius Paetus' jests are likened to Atellan farce.

contrast, were entangled in a present moment whose significance was yet to be determined. As Virginia Woolf wrote in *A Room of One's Own*:[88]

> But the living poets express a feeling that is actually being made and torn out of us at the moment. One does not recognize it in the first place; often for some reason one fears it; one watches it with keenness and compares it jealously and suspiciously with the old feeling that one knew. Hence the difficulty of modern poetry; and it is because of this difficulty that one cannot remember more than two consecutive lines of any good modern poet.

While Cicero acknowledged the poetry of (some) contemporaries with casual references – Lucretius' *De Rerum Natura* (*Q. fr.* 2.10.3),[89] Varro's *Menippean Satires* (*Ac.* 1.8–9), his brother's tragedies (*Q. fr.* 3.1.13; *Q. fr.* 3.5.7) – he was apparently not interested in quoting them or enshrining them in his own work.[90] To cite a living poet was evidently to make too strong an endorsement.[91] In his literary treatises, however, Cicero did ventriloquize contemporaries quoting *his own* poetry.[92] While this practice is evidence that Romans like Cicero did discuss each other's verses, it also quite clearly demonstrates that Cicero himself was more interested in enshrining and discussing his own poetry than that of his contemporaries.[93]

Of the previous generation, Cicero knew Roman elites who had composed verse and referred to a number of them in passing, even if he did not (as far as

[88] Woolf 1929/1989: 14.
[89] On the casualness of the reference to Lucretius in the letter to Quintus, see Henderson 2016: 453. According to Jerome's *Chronicle* (*Ol.* 171.3 = 94 BCE), Cicero "edited" (*emendauit*) the *De Rerum Natura* after Lucretius' suicide. On Cicero and Lucretius, see Goldberg 2005: 38–39, Gee 2013: 90–96, Volk 2013: 98–99, Bishop 2018: 144.
[90] Assuming that the Latin verses quoted by Cicero which we cannot now attribute to any poet come from second century BCE poets and not contemporary ones. Given Cicero's citational practices, it seems likely that the majority of the *incerta* in the Ciceronian corpus do come from older poets, but of course we cannot know for certain. Like Cicero, Varro also avoids contemporaries; see Piras 2015: 60.
[91] Cf. Pliny *Ep.* 5.3.5: *neminem uiuentium, ne quam in speciem adulationis incidam, nominabo,* "I will not name any among the living, in case I fall into a kind of cringing flattery."
[92] Q. Lucilius Balbus extensively quotes Cicero's translation of Aratus' *Phaenomena* in the *De Natura Deorum* (2.104–214). Quintus Cicero in the *De Divinatione* quotes Cicero's *Aratea* (*Div.* 1.13–15), *De Consulatu Suo* (*Div.* 1.17–22; cf. 2.45), *Marius* (*Div.* 1.106); Quintus also quotes Cicero's *Marius* in the *De Legibus* (1.2). In one case, Cicero has a historical character anachronistically reference his *Aratea*: Scipio in *De Republica* (1.56) alludes to the beginning of Cicero's *Aratea*, which Cicero himself quotes in *De Legibus* (2.7). It is significant that the majority of Cicero's poetic self-citations were placed in the mouths of other figures; evidently, the embarrassment of self-quotation needed to be mitigated by displacement. When "Cicero" as a character in his own dialogues self-cites, the poetic quotations are short (e.g. the *Aratea*: *Leg.* 2.7, *Ac.* 2.66, *Or.* 152). Cicero also cites his own poetry in orations to defend it and to defend the actions which it represents (*De Consulatu Suo*: *Pis.* 72–74; *Ph.* 2.20). On the afterlife of Cicero's poetry, see Bishop 2018.
[93] Cf. *Q. fr.* 2.10.3, where Cicero says that he and Quintus will discuss Lucretius' poem more when Quintus arrives.

we know) quote them explicitly.[94] For these individuals, the composition of poetry was part of a rich intellectual life which included various other literary pursuits. For example, Q. Lutatius Catulus (cos. 102 BCE) wrote an account of his own consulship, in the style of Xenophon, which he dedicated to his friend, the poet, A. Furius Antias (*Brut.* 132), as well as Latin epigrams in the Hellenistic tradition.[95] Although Catulus was a figure of significance to Cicero, who had revivified him in the *De Oratore* and in the first edition of the *Academica*, Cicero seemingly only quoted Catulus' poetry on one occasion.[96] In the *De Natura Deorum* (1.79), Cicero has the Academic Cotta quote an erotic epigram composed by Catulus on the actor, Q. Roscius:

> Q. Catulus, huius collegae et familiaris nostri pater, dilexit municipem tuum Roscium, in quem etiam illud est eius:
> *constiteram exorientem Auroram forte salutans,*   [Courtney fr. 2]
> *cum subito a laeua Roscius exoritur,*
> *pace mihi liceat, caelestes, dicere uestra*
> *mortalis uisus pulchrior esse deo.*

> Q. Catulus, the father of our colleague and friend, loved your fellow townsman, Roscius. This famous poem was written by Catulus for him:
> *"I stood to greet the rising Dawn by chance,*
> *when suddenly Roscius rose on the left –*
> *(gods, forgive me speaking of your affairs)*
> *a mortal appeared more beautiful than god."*

Catulus' epigram with its *pulchrior deo* ("more beautiful than god") invoked Sappho half a century before Catullus 51; the elder statesman thereby stands as a precursor to the neoteric movement of the mid first century BCE.[97] Yet Catulus also spoke with Ennian lips. It was at dawn (Skutsch 84–85) that Romulus and Remus sought their divine sign of kingship in Ennius' *Annales*;

---

[94] A. Furius Antias (fl. late second century BCE), a poet to whom Q. Catulus (cos. 102 BCE) dedicated a work on his own consulship (*Brut.* 132). C. Titius (fl. late second century BCE), an orator whose tragedies were, according to Cicero, "incisive but hardly tragic" (*acute sed parum tragice, Brut.* 167). C. Julius Caesar Strabo Vopiscus (d. 87 BCE), whose orations and tragedies were extant in the Ciceronian period (*Brut.* 177); Caesar Strabo appeared as a character in Cicero's *De Oratore* (see Fantham 2004: 72). Q. Valerius Soranus (d. 82 BCE), known as a poet to Cicero's contemporaries (e.g. Varro, see *FPL* pp116–118); while Cicero does not explicitly discuss Soranus' poetry, he does call him *litteratissimus* (*De Or.* 3.43) and *doctus* (*Brut.* 169).

[95] On Catulus' epigrams, see Courtney 2003: 75–78. On Catulus' possible composition of an antiquarian "history," see Wiseman 1974: 33. A deep interest in literature is suggested by Cicero's repeated association of Catulus with a number of contemporary poets: A. Furius Antias (*Brut.* 132), Archias (*Arch.* 6), and Antipater of Sidon (*De Or.* 3.194). Catulus' epigram on the actor, Q. Roscius, also suggests an interest in the contemporary Roman stage; see Hanses 2020: 51–52.

[96] On Catulus in the *De Oratore*, see Fantham 2004: 72; in the *Academica Priora*, Stroup 2010: 289.

[97] Stark 1957: 330; Courtney 2003: 77.

and it was also "on the left that a most beautiful, sacred sign flew" (*pulcerrima praepes laeua uolauit*, Skutsch 86–87). Catulus greeted the dawn – and where the Ennian founder saw his power confirmed, the Roman epigrammatist saw the divine face of his love.[98]

Around the time of Catulus' death (87 BCE), Cicero was a young man and he too was composing short Latin poems in the Hellenistic style which was evidently already in vogue.[99] Of Cicero's poetic juvenalia, several titles and some fragments are attested: *Pontius Glaucus*,[100] *Alcyones*, *Uxorius*, *Nilus*, *Limon*, *Thalia Maesta*.[101] As a youth, too, Cicero translated Aratus' *Phaenomena*, a Greek astronomical epic, into Latin.[102] Cicero's interest in the *Aratea* persisted – he seems to have edited the poem later in life (c. 60 BCE), and he enshrined parts of it in the *De Natura Deorum*.[103] As Cicero's political career brought him to new heights, his relationship with poetry changed. Once a vehicle for engaging with Hellenistic traditions (and thereby with other Roman elites with such interests), over time, Cicero used poetry to create cultural artefacts of historical events to insist upon their significance. As I discuss below, Cicero considered the epic on his own consulship, *De Consulatu Suo* (60 BCE), a record of his service to the state and evidence of his legacy. The *Marius* (of uncertain date) argued the significance of a historical icon and claimed to establish a canonicity more persistent than the reality which inspired it.[104] Just as Ennius' depiction of the impact of Appius Claudius' oratory was more significant to Cicero than the extant speech itself, composing poetry was a way to ground the events of his life in narrative and imbue them with greater cultural power.

It is in the context of this theory of *poesis* as evidentiary and augmenting category that Cicero's passing comments on the "neoterics," the young contemporary poets, arise.[105] Cicero's youthful interest in Hellenistic forms and themes hints at the fact that he was not completely hostile to

---

[98] Ennius uses *"pulcer"* to describe divinity: e.g. in Ilia's dream, the god Mars "appeared as a handsome man" (*uisus homo pulcer*, Skutsch 38).

[99] Knox 2011: 193.   [100] Shackleton Bailey 1983: 239.

[101] On Cicero's early poetry, see Malcovati 1943: 233–252, Soubiran 1972: 4–27, Knox 2011. Given that Cicero enshrined his hexameter poetry in his corpus via self-citation, it is significant that it is not Cicero himself who transmits the notices or fragments of these poems.

[102] On Cicero's *Aratea*, see Gee 2001, 2013a, 2013b, Čulík-Baird 2018, Bishop 2019: 41–84.

[103] On Cicero's return to the *Aratea* c. 60 BCE, see Gee 2001: 521.

[104] *Leg.* 1.2; discussed in Chapter 5. In addition to the epics, *De Consulatu Suo* and *Marius*, Cicero composed an epic on his exile, *De Temporibus Suis* (56–54 BCE); while Cicero referred to the poem in several letters (*Q.fr.* 2.7.1, *Q. fr.* 3.1.24, *Fam.* 1.9.23), no fragments of the poem itself survive; see Malcovati 1943: 252–265, Harrison 1990.

[105] Spondaic line ends by οἱ νεώτεροι (*Att.* 7.2.1); stylistic departures of *poetae noui* (*Or.* 161); criticisms of *cantores Euphorionis* (*TD* 3.45). See Knox 2011: 192 and works there cited.

the neoteric aesthetic *per se*. Yet his sustained engagement with older poetry – both the extensive quotation as well as his own poetic emulation – argues that Cicero deliberately distanced himself from the neoteric movement. Instead, Cicero committed to the earlier poets both in form and in style. In the *Orator* (161), Cicero noted that the "new poets" (*poetae noui*) departed from the style of older poets, such as Ennius and Lucilius.[106] In the same work (*Or.* 152), Cicero had already presented himself as a poetic example alongside Naevius and Ennius to exemplify austere Roman style:

> sed Graeci uiderint. nobis ne si cupiamus quidem distrahere uoces conceditur. indicant orationes illae ipsae horridulae Catonis, indicant omnes poetae praeter eos qui, ut uersum facerent, saepe hiabant, ut Naeuius
>
> | *uos, qui adcolitis Histrum fluuium atque algidam . . .* | [Naevius |
> | et ibidem | *TrRF* I 41] |
> | *quam numquam uobis Grai atque barbari . . .* | [Naevius |
> | et Ennius semel | *TrRF* I 42] |
> | *Scipio inuicte . . .* | [Ennius' *Scipio* |
> | et quidem nos | Goldberg-Manuwald F3] |
> | *hoc motu radiantis Etesiae in uada ponti . . .* | [Cicero's *Aratea* |
> | | Soubiran fr. xxiii] |

> But let the Greeks see to their own business. We cannot separate our breaths even if we should wish to. Those rough little speeches of Cato demonstrate this; all poets demonstrate this except those who often use hiatus to make a verse, like Naevius:
> "*you, who live on the cold River Hister and the icy . . .* "
> and Naevius again:
> "*which never to you the Greeks and barbarians . . .* "
> and Ennius once:
> "*Scipio, unconquered . . .* "
> and indeed I do it too:
> "*By this movement the Etesians into the shallows of the shining sea . . .* "

While Cicero did in fact introduce innovations into the Latin hexameter, he nonetheless took great pride in emulating earlier Latin poetry and presented himself as an heir to their poesis, even while he himself departed from them in several ways.[107] Indeed, we might interpret Cicero's use of, for example,

---

[106] Dropping the final *s* in words which end in *-us*. *Or.* 161 = Ennius' *Annales* (Skutsch 61) and Lucilius' *Satires* (Warmington 173).
[107] On Cicero's innovations in the hexameter, see Ewbank: 1933: 40–71, Goldberg 1995: 135–157, Courtney 2003: 150–151.

Ennianism in his own poetry as an attempt to extend the values of the Ennian age into the present day. As we have seen, in at least one instance, it is impossible to tell whether a Latin verse quoted by Cicero was written by Ennius or Cicero himself.[108] Cicero's versification is therefore another kind of citational practice: if quoting poetry was a way to reanimate prototypes, then giving new flesh to old forms was even more so.

1.3 Cicero and the Greek Poets

Cicero quoted Greek poetry as well as Latin, though to a significantly lesser extent. It is only in Cicero's letters that we find quotations of Greek verse in the Greek language, and the vast majority of the letters containing verbatim citations of Greek poets are addressed to Atticus.[109] The function of these quotations is largely the same as the citations of the Latin poets, with the added layer of conspicuous display of Greek learning. The citation of verse elevates tone, and can be used to express emotion, to convey humour,[110] and to present poetic parallels to express and clarify real life situations. In the wake of Caesar's assassination, for example, Atticus had asked Cicero whether he enjoyed the hills or the seaside at Puteoli more, to which Cicero responded (*Att.* 14.13.1) with Odysseus' words to Achilles in the *Iliad* (9.228–230); namely, that immediate circumstances may be pleasant but that there were larger concerns to think of:[111]

> est mehercule, ut dicis, utriusque loci tanta amoenitas ut
> dubitem utra anteponenda sit.
> ... ἀλλ᾿ οὐ δαιτὸς ἐπηράτου ἔργα μέμηλεν,   [*Il.* 9.228–230]
> ἀλλὰ λίην μέγα πῆμα διοτρεφὲς εἰσορόωντες
> δείδιμεν· ἐν δοιῇ δὲ σαωσέμεν ἢ ἀπολέσθαι[112]
> ... quid nobis faciendum sit ignoro.

My god, it is as you say and it is so pleasant in each place that I hesitate which to put first.

---

[108] See p28.

[109] Jocelyn 1973a: 61, White 2010: 105. Cicero also quotes Greek poetry to his brother (*Q. fr.* 1.2, 2.14.5, 2.9.2, 3.5, 3.7), Tiro (*Fam.* 16.8.2), Q. Lepta (*Fam.* 6.18.5), Lentulus Spinther (*Fam.* 12.14.7); Appius Claudius Pulcher (*Fam.* 3.7.6), Varro (*Fam.* 9.7), and Caesar (*Fam.* 13.15). Cicero's use of Greek is an expression of complicated feeling towards the latter three individuals, see Behrendt 2013: 61, Hutchinson 1998: 15.

[110] E.g.: *Q. fr.* 1.2.1 where Cicero uses *Od.* 9.513 to mock the stature of a freedman whom Cicero believes to be acting beyond his station.

[111] Later in this letter (*Att.* 14.13.2), Cicero quotes verses of Zeus telling Aphrodite that she was not made for war (*Il.* 5.428–429), applying them to himself.

[112] Cicero breaks off the quotation here, but in the *Iliad* (9.230) the thought is grammatically completed with νῆας ἐϋσσέλμους; i.e. "it is in doubt whether we can save or lose | the benched ships."

" . . . *But our minds are not focused on the details of this lovely banquet,*
but, Zeus-cherished one, we look upon a great calamity
and are afraid; for it is in doubt whether we can save or lose"
. . . I don't know what we should do.

Odysseus' refocusing of attention from the immediacy of the moment towards dread of future outcomes allows Cicero to reframe doubt (*ut dubitem*) regarding the relative "pleasantness" (*amoenitas*; picked up by ἐπήρατος, *Il.* 9.229) of Puteoli into doubt regarding what will happen in the civil war to come. Cicero and his contemporaries were so steeped in Homeric epic that they used it as a prism through which to view their lives and express their own thoughts.

In addition to the use of poetry to model and express Cicero's thinking, we also find that Cicero deploys verse citations to charge up his letters with extra cultural cachet. Given that verse quotation was part of elite display, it is not surprising that we find citations of Greek verse carefully deployed in letters to men of power and status as a sign of respect. An infamous letter to Caesar (*Fam.* 13.15) containing seven conspicuous and elaborately intertwined quotations of Greek poetry conveys respect towards the dictator while retaining a certain ambiguity regarding Cicero's own attitude towards him.[113] Similarly, a letter to Varro (*Fam.* 9.7) which contains a rich mix of Greek and Latin verse expresses Cicero's esteem, yet also his uneasiness.[114] In addition to quoting verse in his correspondence with the individuals towards whom Cicero had ambiguous feelings, he also used verse in his letters *about* them, as in this letter to Atticus about Varro (*Att.* 13.12.3):[115]

> postea autem quam haec coepi φιλολογώτερα, iam Varro mihi denun
> tiauerat magnam sane et grauem προσφώνησιν. biennium praeteriit cum
> ille Καλλιππίδης adsiduo cursu cubitum nullum processerit. ego autem me
> parabam ad id quod ille mihi misisset ut
>
> αὐτῷ τῷ μέτρῳ καὶ λώϊον   [Hesiod *Op.* 350]
>
> si modo potuissem; nam hoc etiam Hesiodus ascribit,
>
> αἴ κε δύνηαι.   [Hesiod *Op.* 350]

But after I began these more learned compositions, Varro had already announced that he would make a great and serious dedication to me. Two

---

[113] *Fam.* 13.15.1 (*Od.* 7.258, *Od.* 1.302/3.200, *Il.* 17.591/*Od.* 24.315), 13.15.2 (*Il.* 22.304–305, Euripides Nauck fr. 905, *Il.* 1.343, *Il.* 6.208/11.784); see Hutchinson 1998: 15, Hall 2009: 33, Behrendt 2013: 183–194.

[114] *Fam.* 9.7.1 (*Il.* 10.224, Terence's *Andria* 112), *Fam.* 9.7.2 (Ennius' *Annales* Skutsch 309, Unknown Greek verse Nauck fr. 107); see Behrendt 2013: 149–155.

[115] Cf. *Att.* 2.25, where Cicero uses verses of Euripides (*Andr.* 448; *Phoen.* 393) to describe Varro as untrustworthy; see Kronenberg 2009: 88.

years have passed, during which this Callippides,[116] despite running hard,
hasn't made any progress. But I was myself preparing to repay him for what
he sent me
"in measure alike, and better too" –
that is, if I actually could. For even Hesiod adds this bit –
"if you can."

Here, Cicero uses a verse from Hesiod's *Works and Days* (350) to model the
ideal of literary reciprocity which he seeks from Varro.[117] Of interest, too, is
the fact that Cicero returned to this passage of Hesiod several times – once
in Greek, twice in Latin. Cicero quotes the verse to Atticus in Greek during
the summer of 45 BCE (*Att.* 13.2.3), but he had already rendered it into
Latin the year before, in the *Brutus* (15):

> ... ipsa mihi tractatio litterarum salutaris fuit admonuitque, Pomponi, ut a te
> ipso sumerem aliquid ad me reficiendum teque remunerandum si non pari, at
> grato tamen munere: quamquam illud Hesiodium laudatur a doctis, quod
> *eadem mensura reddere iubet qua acceperis aut etiam cumulatiore, si possis.*

> ... that learned treatment was helpful to me and it encouraged me,
> Pomponius, to take something from you to rework, and to pay back to
> you, hopefully with something equal, but if not, with at least a worthy gift.
> Although that Hesiodic saying is praised by learned men, because *"it
> commands you to repay in the same measure as you have received, or with an
> even greater measure, if you can."*

Cicero's use of the Hesiodic maxim to substantiate a code of literary
reciprocity fits into the broader citational phenomenon of quoting Greek
verse in letters which discuss Cicero's own literary endeavours.[118] Cicero
would repeat the Hesiodic maxim a third time in the *De Officiis* (1.48), where
he applied it more widely to the ideal of reciprocal, aristocratic generosity,
rather than to the specific mutual debt of literary composition. That Cicero

---

[116] Callippides is a proverbial figure who runs hard yet travels no distance. The proverb appears here
(*Att.* 13.12.3) and in Suetonius (*Tib.* 38); see Otto 1890: 66.

[117] Repayment is a consistent motif in how Cicero relates to Varro. The letter (*Fam.* 9.8) which
dedicates the *Academica* to Varro characterizes Cicero's intellectual labour as a *munus* ("duty") that
ought to be repaid; an extension of the Hesiodic maxim Cicero uses in the letter to Atticus (*Att.*
13.12.3). On *munus* as literary "debt-exchange," see Stroup 2010: 93–99.

[118] Quotations of Greek verse regularly appear in letters where Cicero discusses his own literary works,
e.g.: Hesiod (*Op.* 289) is quoted in a letter (*Fam.* 6.18.5) which also discusses Cicero's *Orator* (*Fam.*
6.18.4); Cicero quotes his favourite verse of the *Iliad* (22.105/6.442; see p62) to express anxiety to
Atticus about Varro and the *Academica* (*Att.* 13.24.1; cf. *Att.* 13.25.3 with *Il.* 11.654 to express this same
anxiety, see Kronenberg 2009: 88); Cicero quotes Pindar (Snell fr. 213; *Att.* 13.38.2) in a letter which
begins with a description of his current composition of something "against Epicureanism" (*contra
Epicureos, Att.* 13.38.1).

quoted Greek verse in both Greek *and* translated Latin is also a point of significance; such a citational technique bridges the gap between Greek and Latin poetry, and allows Cicero to present Greek and Latin verse in tandem.

The majority of the Greek poetic citations in Cicero's letters come from Homer, with sixty discrete quotations.[119] The remainder consist of short quotations attributable to the following Greek poets in order of frequency: Euripides (15); Sophocles (4); Leonidas of Tarentum (3); Aeschylus, Callimachus, Hesiod, Menander, Pindar (2); Archilochus, and Stesichorus (1).[120] A number of these are very short quotations indeed, between one and three words.[121] Several of Cicero's quotations of Greek poets can be traced to his engagement with Greek philosophers. Additionally, there are a number of Greek "literary" quotations which seem to belong to a proverb tradition.[122] Cicero is also aware of the fact that gnomic verses can be falsely attributed: in a letter to Atticus (*Att.* 7.18.4), Cicero quotes a well known Greek line which, he says, is "falsely attributed

---

[119] See Appendix III.

[120] Euripides: fifteen discrete citations, many of which are gnomic in character (see Appendix III). Sophocles: a fragment of *Tympanistai* (Nauck fr. 759; *Att.* 2.7.4), a fragment of *Tyro* (Nauck fr. 601; *Att.* 4.8.1), and two different fragments of unknown tragedies: Nauck fr. 601, *Att.* 2.16.2; Nauck fr. 877, *Q. fr.* 2.9.2. Cicero names Sophocles' *Syndeipnoi* in a letter to his brother (*Q. fr.* 2.16.3), but does not quote from it there. Leonidas: three letters to Atticus (*Att.* 9.7.5, 9.18.3, 10.2.1) quote small pieces of Leonidas' epigram on the twittering swallow as a sign for sailing (*Ath. Pal.* 10.1.1–2). Aeschylus: two very short quotations of *Prometheus Vinctus*. Callimachus: a letter to Atticus (*Att.* 6.9.3) contains three words which also appear in Callimachus (*Epigr.* 32.2) but are likely proverbial; another letter (*Att.* 8.5.1) contains a longer quotation which has been attributed to Callimachus (Pfeiffer fr. 732). Hesiod: the *bon mot* (*Op.* 350) on reciprocity (*Att.* 13.12.3; cf. *Brut.* 15, *Off.* 1.48); an aphorism from Hesiod (*Op.* 289) is quoted to Q. Lepta (*Fam.* 6.18.5). Menander: a fragment of the *Epitrepontes* (fr. 2; *Att.* 4.11.2), and part of a maxim which also appears in the later collection known as the *Gnomai Monostichoi* (*Mon.* 726; *Att.* 1.12.1). Pindar: a short quotation of *Nemean Ode* 1; and a fragment (Snell fr. 213; *Att.* 13.38.2). Archilochus: a short quotation (Diehl fr. 56.2; *Att.* 5.12.1). Stesichorus: a fragment of the Helen Palinode (Diehl fr. 11; *Att.* 9.13.1).

[121] E.g., *Att.* 9.18.3: λαλαγεῦσαν, "twitterer" (Leon. *Ath Pal.* 10.1.1); *Att.* 4.11.2: *Att.* 5.12.1: ἄκρα Γυρέων, "heights of Gyrae" (Arch. Diehl fr. 56.2); *Q. fr.* 1.2.13: ἅπαξ θανεῖν, "to die once and for all" (Aesch. *PV* 750); *Att.* 14.10.1: ταὐτόματον ἡμῶν, "chance [has better advisors] than us" (Menandr. *Mon.* 726); γῆν πρὸ γῆς, "land for land" (Aesch. *PV* 682); *Att.* 6.9.3: τοὐμὸν ὄνειρον ἐμοί, "my own dream to me" (Callim. *Epigr.* 32.2); *Att.* 12.5.1: ἄμπνευμα σεμνὸν Ἀλφειοῦ, "sacred place where Alpheus breathed again" (Pind. *Nem.* 1.1).

[122] *Att.* 1.19.10 (*CPG* I p314), *Att.* 5.11.5 (*CPG* II p44), *Att.* 7.18.4 (*CPG* II p759), *Att.* 10.5.2 (*CPG* I p207), *Att.* 13.21a.1 (*CPG* I p116). However, the distinction between a proverb and literary citation is not always easy to make; indeed, several of these "proverbs" appear in earlier Greek literature: e.g. *Att.* 5.11.5 quotes a proverb which had already appeared in Plato's *Republic* (563c). Should a Greek fragment attributed by editors to comedy (Kock fr. 189; *Att.* 4.8a.2) but which has a gnomic tone instead be categorized as a proverb? Does Cicero's use of a Greek aphorism derive from Euripides' *Telephus* (Nauck fr. 723; *Att.* 1.20.3, *Att.* 4.6.2) or should it simply be considered a deployment of the proverb (*CPG* I p307)? Is the beginning of a Greek aphorism (ἔρδοι τις . . ., "Let each man do . . . ") that appears in a letter (*Att.* 5.10.3) just a proverb, or a citation of Aristophanes' *Wasps* (1431)?

to Hesiod" (ψευδησιόδειος).[123] And, as with a significant number of the
Latin verse fragments, there are a number of Greek verses in the Ciceronian
corpus which cannot be attributed to any particular author with certainty.[124]
It is worth noting that Cicero is not only responsible for transmitting Latin
fragments, but, indeed, he is also the *sole* source for a number of Greek
fragments.[125] Given Cicero's significant role in transmitting both Greek and
Latin poetry, Cicero's interests deeply influence what we now see of classical
antiquity.

Just as Cicero repeated parts of his favourite Latin poems, so too did
Cicero repeat Homeric verse.[126] Indeed, Cicero quotes one line from the
Iliad (22.105/6.442[127]) six times in total.[128] Many of Cicero's letters contain
more than one quotation of Homer.[129] Quotations of Homer also appear
together with verses from other Greek and Latin poets in the letters.[130] In

[123] *Att.* 7.18.4: *ego autem etsi illud* ψευδησιόδειον (*ita enim putatur*) *obseruo* μηδὲ δίκην; "But I observe
that pseudo-Hesiodic maxim (it is thought to be his): '*Judge not . . .*'"
[124] Greek verses which cannot now be attributed to a specific author appear in several letters: *Att.*
14.22.2, 15.11.3, 16.6.2; *Fam.* 9.7.2, *Fam.* 12.14.7; *Att.* 4.8a.2. Cicero (*Att.* 1.20.3) seems to ascribe
a verse to Rhinthon, the third century BCE composer of "tragic *phlyakes*." However, the text here is
in question (*Rhinthon* is an emendation of *phi(n)ton*, cf. Shackleton Bailey 1965, Vol I.: 342); Kaibel
(1899: 189) attributed Cicero's verse not to Rhinthon but to Euripides based on a similarity to
Nauck fr. 565.
[125] A striking example of this appears in a letter to Atticus (*Att.* 8.5.1), where Cicero quotes a Greek
verse whose origin we do not know for certain. Without Cicero's preservation of the verse, which
some editors have attributed to Callimachus' *Hecale* (see Wheeler 1974: 139), we would not know
that Catullus 64.111 is a Latin translation of a Greek precursor. On Cicero's role in preserving this
fragment, see Young 2015: 41–43.
[126] Appendix III.
[127] *Il.* 22.105 is identical to *Il.* 6.442. Both are spoken by Hector. Cicero regularly quotes Homeric doublets:
Att. 4.15.7 (*Il.* 23.326/*Od.* 11.126); *Att.* 4.7.3 (*Od.* 17.488/20.384); *Att.* 7.1.2 (*Od.* 7.258/9.33), 7.1.9 (*Il.* 18.112/
19.65); *Att.* 10.12a.1 (*Il.* 18.112/19.65); *Fam.* 13.15.1 (*Od.* 1.302/3.200), *Fam.* 13.15.1 (*Il.* 17.591/*Od.* 24.315),
Fam. 13.15.2 (*Il.* 6.208/11.784); *Q. fr.* 3.5.4 (*Il.* 6.208/11.784); *Q. fr.* 3.7.1 (*Il.* 4.182/8.150).
[128] *Att.* 2.5.1, 7.1.4, 7.12.3, 8.16.2, 13.13(14).2, 13.24.1. Cicero gives the full verse (αἰδέομαι Τρῶας καὶ
Τρῳάδας ἑλκεσιπέπλους, "I feel shame before the Trojans, and the Trojans' wives with trailing
robes") only in *Att.* 2.5.1. The other letters contain only the two words αἰδέομαι Τρῶας, except for
Att. 7.1.4, which has αἰδέομαι . . . Τρῶας καὶ Τρῳάδας. Cicero also pairs *Il.* 22.105/6.442 with *Il.*
22.100 in two letters (*Att.* 2.5.1; 7.1.4).
[129] Letters containing more than one quotation of Homer: *Att.* 4.7.2 (*Od.* 22.412), 4.7.3 (*Od.* 17.488/
20.384); *Att.* 6.1.22 (*Il.* 6.236), 6.1.23 (*Il.* 7.93); *Att.* 7.1.4 (*Il.* 22.105/6.442, *Il.* 22.100), 7.1.9 (*Il.* 18.112/
19.65); *Att.* 9.6.4 (10.93–94), 9.6.6 (10.224); *Att.* 9.15.3 (*Od.* 20.18), 9.15.4 (*Od.* 3.26–27); *Att.* 14.13.1
(*Il.* 9.228–230), 14.13.2 (*Il.* 5.428–429); *Att.* 16.11.1 (*Il.* 20.308), 16.11.6 (*Il.* 7.93); *Fam.* 13.15.1 (*Od.*
7.258, *Od.* 1.302/3.200, *Il.* 17.591/*Od.* 24.315), 13.15.2 (*Il.* 22.304–305, *Il.* 1.343, *Il.* 6.208/11.784); *Q. fr.*
3.5.4 (*Il.* 6.208/11.784), 3.5.8 (*Il.* 16.385–386, 387–388); *Q. fr.* 3.7.1 (*Il.* 4.182/8.150), 3.7.2 (*Il.* 8.355)
[130] Homer with other Greek verse quotations: *Att.* 2.16.2 (Soph. Nauck fr. 701), 2.16.4 (*Il.* 6.181); *Att.*
6.1.8 (Eur. Nauck fr. 918.3), 6.1.22 (*Il.* 6.236), 6.1.23 (*Il.* 7.93); *Att.* 7.11.1 (Eur. *Phoen.* 506), 7.11.3 (*Il.*
9.524); *Att.* 9.7.3 (*Ody.* 11.634), 9.7.5 (Leonidas *Ath. Pal.* 10.1.1); *Att.* 16.6.1 (*Ody.* 3.169), 16.6.2
(unknown Greek tragedy Nauck fr. 106); *Fam.* 13.15.1 (*Ody.* 7.258), 13.15.1 (*Ody.* 1.302/3.200), 13.15.1
(*Il.* 17.591/*Ody.* 24.315), 13.15.2 (Eur. Nauck fr. 905), 13.15.2 (*Il.* 1.343), 13.15.2

certain cases, Cicero makes deliberate changes to the Greek verses, adjusting their content to fit his own syntax and tone, or adapting them for the sake of wit.[131] In a letter (*Att.* 16.13.1–2) which describes a journey to Arpinum in late 44 BCE, Cicero adjusts verses from the *Odyssey* (3.169–172) to describe a fortuitous meeting with a letter carrier:

> . . . ad pontem Tirenum, qui est Menturnis, in quo flexus est ad iter Arpinas, obuiam mihi fit tabellarius;
> qui me *offendit* δολιχὸν πλόον ὁρμαίνοντα.   [*Odyssey* 3.169]
> ego statim, cedo, inquam, si quid ab Attico? nondum legere poteramus; nam et lumina dimiseramus nec satis lucebat . . . [16.13.2] ecce tibi altera, qua hortaris
> παρ᾿ ἠνεμόεντα Μίμαντα,   [*Odyssey* 3.172]
> νήσου ἐπὶ Ψυρίης Appiam scilicet ἐπ᾿ ἀριστέρ᾿ ἔχοντα.   [*Odyssey* 3.171]
> itaque eo die mansi Aquini.

> . . . near the Tirenian bridge at Minturnae I met a letter carrier where the road branches off towards Arpinum.
> He "*happened upon*" me "*deliberating the long voyage.*"
> I immediately asked him, "Here, anything from Atticus?" I could not read it yet, since I had already sent on the torches and it wasn't light enough . . .
> [16.13.2] Behold! The second letter, in which you encourage me to go
> "*by windy Mimas*"
> "*towards the island of Psyria*" "*keeping it,*" i.e. the Appian Way, "*on the left.*"
> So I stayed that night at Aquinum.

In the original passage of the *Odyssey*, Nestor describes the homeward journeys of the Greeks after the sack of Troy. Menelaus had come upon Nestor and his crew late, finding them debating which route home to take (*Ody.* 3.168–172):

> ὀψὲ δὲ δὴ μετὰ νῶϊ κίε ξανθὸς Μενέλαος,
> ἐν Λέσβῳ δ᾿ ἔκιχεν δολιχὸν πλόον ὁρμαίνοντας,   3.169

(*Il.* 6.208/11.784). Homer with Latin verse quotations: *Att.* 1.16.1 (unknown Latin comedy Ribbeck 63), 1.16.5 (*Il.* 16.112–113); *Att.* 2.3.4 (Cic. *De Consulatu Suo* Soubiran fr. viii), 2.3.4 (*Il.* 12.243); *Att.* 9.6.4 (*Il.* 10.93–94), 9.6.5 (Ter. *Heaut.* 86), 9.6.6 (*Il.* 10.244); *Att.* 15.11.3 (unknown Greek tragedy Nauck fr. 105), 15.11.3 (unknown Latin tragedy *TrRF* I 83b); *Fam.* 9.7.1 (*Il.* 10.224), 9.7.1 (Ter. *Andr.* 112), 9.7.2 (Enn. *Ann.* Skutsch 309), *Fam.* 9.7.2 (unknown Greek tragedy Nauck fr. 107).

[131] *Att.* 4.7.2 (*Od.* 22.412): κταμένοισιν ("slain men") is changed to φθιμένοισιν ("perished men") in order to be respectful towards the recently deceased Metellus; *Att.* 7.1.2 (*Od.* 7.258 or 9.33): ἔπειθεν ("she persuaded") or ἔπειθον ("they persuaded") to ἔπειθες ("you persuaded"); *Att.* 7.3.5 (Eur. *Troad.* 455): τοῦ στρατηγοῦ ("the general") to τῶν Ἀτρειδῶν ("the Atreides"); *Att.* 7.6.2. (*Od.* 12.209): μὲν ("surely") to γὰρ ("for"); *Att.* 7.11.3 (*Il.* 9.524): καὶ ("and") to an ironic που ("how would it not?") to emphasize the line; *Att.* 14.13.2 (*Il.* 5.429): γάμοιο ("marriage") is changed to λόγοιο ("speech"); see Behrendt 2013: 70; 304–306, 87–93, 302–304, 286–288, 306–308, 294–296.

ἢ καθύπερθε Χίοιο νεοίμεθα παιπαλοέσσης,
νήσου ἔπι Ψυρίης, αὐτὴν ἐπ᾽ ἀριστέρ᾽ ἔχοντες,   3.171
ἢ ὑπένερθε Χίοιο, παρ᾽ ἠνεμόεντα Μίμαντα.   3.172

and late behind us came red-haired Menelaus,
who came upon us at Lesbos, as we were debating the long voyage:
whether we should sail north of rugged Chios,
toward the island of Psyria, keeping Chios on our left,
or should we sail south of Chios, by windy Mimas.

Cicero adjusts Homer's plurals (ὁρμαίνοντας, 3.169; ἔχοντες, 3.171) to singulars (ὁρμαίνοντα; ἔχοντα) so that they apply to himself alone.[132] Cicero's citational frame also shows his awareness of the original context of the verse: Cicero's *offendit* ("happened upon") translates the Greek word ἔκιχεν (*Od.* 3.169) which precedes the part of the verse which Cicero has cited.[133] Cicero also has a clear understanding of the geography which the Homeric lines describe, which he applies to his own immediate spatial landscape. Cicero's location (Minturnae) is made to take the place of the location of Nestor's fleet at Lesbos (ἐν Λέσβῳ, *Od.* 3.169).[134] Via this citation, the map of the *Odyssey* is laid over the map of Italy: the forked path of the Greek voyage – i.e. whether to sail around Chios on the left or on the right – is mapped onto the western region of Italy, with the landmark of Chios (αὐτὴν, *Ody.* 3.171) represented by the Appian Way (*Appiam*, *Att.* 16.13.2). Cicero's own homecoming to Arpinum is thereby transformed into a Homeric *nostos*.[135]

Cicero also used Homeric narrative to reflect his own political experiences. In a letter from the winter of 54 BCE (*Q. fr.* 3.5.8), Zeus' use of rain to punish the unjust (*Il.* 16.385–388) is inserted into a description of the heavy rain at Rome before the trial of Gabinius. Cicero's use of Homer to express political concerns also often included an emotional component. In a letter (*Att.* 9.5.3) from March 49 BCE, Cicero contemplated the struggle between

---

[132] When Cicero quotes *Od.* 3.169 in *Att.* 16.6.1 he retains the plural, but makes it nominative (ὁρμαίνοντες); see Behrendt 2013: 94.

[133] Cf. *Att.* 10.2.1 where Cicero follows one Greek word from Leonidas of Tarentum with a partial Latin translation: λαλαγεῦσα *iam adest*, "the twitterer is already here" renders *Ath. Pal.* 10.1.1–2: λαλαγεῦσα ... ἤδη μέμβλωκεν.

[134] Cicero also uses a citation of Archilochus (*Att.* 5.12.1; Diehl fr. 56.2) in order to describe moving through space; see Behrendt 2013: 63–69.

[135] Indeed, Cicero figured Arpinum as Odysseus' beloved, rugged Ithaca in another letter (*Att.* 2.11.2; *Od.* 9.27–28), and Formiae as the land of the Laestrygonians (*Att.* 2.13.2; *Od.* 10.82); see Behrendt 2013: 243. Cf. *Att.* 7.11.3 where Cicero quotes *Il.* 9.524 to make the κλέα ἀνδρῶν ("brave tales of men") refer to Roman history.

Caesar and Pompey and used Homeric verse to express his own role in the conflict:

> . . . sed uideo plane nihil aliud agi, nihil actum ab initio, <nisi> ut hunc occideret. ego igitur, sicut apud Homerum cui et mater et dea dixisset
> αὐτίκα γάρ τοι ἔπειτα μεθ᾽ Ἕκτορα πότμος ἑτοῖμος   [*Iliad* 18.96]
> *matri ipse respondit*[136]
> αὐτίκα τεθναίην, ἐπεὶ οὐκ ἄρ᾽ ἔμελλον ἑταίρῳ   [*Iliad* 18.98–99]
> κτεινομένῳ ἐπαμῦναι
> quid si non ἑταίρῳ solum sed etiam εὐεργέτῃ, adde tali uiro talem causam agenti? ego uero haec officia mercanda uita puto.

> . . . I see now clearly that Caesar never intended to do anything else from the beginning, other than kill Pompey. As for myself, I think of what both the mother and goddess said to him in Homer:
> "*For straightaway after Hector is your own death at hand.*"
> He replied to his mother:
> "*Straightaway then let me die, since I could not save my friend*
> *from death.*"
> Not only a "*friend*" but even a benefactor; and add to the fact that he is a great man championing a great cause. I really do think it is worth sacrificing life for such a duty.

In a moment of crisis, Cicero contemplates his own responsibility and duty to Pompey via the interchange between Thetis and Achilles in *Iliad* 18. The death of Pompey now seems to Cicero as inevitable as the death of Achilles, which is, as the quoted lines make clear (*Il.* 18.98–99), the fate which Achilles ultimately chooses. Cicero's citation of the verses emphasizes the fact that Achilles has chosen death as an expression of duty towards Patroclus, his dead friend. Indeed, Cicero's repetition of the Homeric word "friend" (ἑταῖρος) serves to refine what such an obligation of friendship meant in the Roman context: Pompey was not just ἑταῖρος to Cicero, but even more – a "benefactor" (εὐεργέτης). Cicero's *De Amicitia* (22) had emphasized the innate importance of reciprocity in friendship:[137]

> talis igitur inter uiros amicitia tantas opportunitates habet quantas uix queo dicere. principio qui potest esse *uita uitalis*, ut ait Ennius [Skutsch *op. inc.* 18], quae non in amici mutua beneuolentia conquiescit?

---

[136] Cicero's *matri ipse respondit* paraphrases in Latin part of *Il.* 18.97: τὴν δὲ μέγ᾽ ὀχθήσας προσέφη πόδας ὠκὺς Ἀχιλλεύς, "Then, greatly angered, swift-footed Achilles spoke to her."
[137] Cf. *De Off.* 1.42–47 for Cicero's discussion of the complexities behind reciprocal beneficence. On Roman friendship, see Brunt 1965.

Therefore, among men like these, friendship gives opportunities so great
that I can barely describe them. First of all, how can life be what Ennius calls
"the life worth living" if it does not depend upon the mutual goodwill of
a friend?

In the letter to Atticus, Cicero extends his theorization of friendship as
dependent upon "mutual goodwill" (*mutua beneuolentia*) to its logical end
via the Iliadic model: if Pompey dies, should Cicero, tied to him via
a mutuality of friendship compounded by the enormity of his friend's
beneficence towards him, not also die? The invocation of the Homeric
parallel not only allows Cicero to universalize the problem at hand via
literary citation, but to monumentalize the moment by modeling it upon
one of the *Iliad*'s most famous points of crisis. Noteworthy, too, is the fact
that Cicero is able to align himself with a character such as Achilles.[138] In so
doing, the emotional landscape of the *Iliad* is naturalized into Cicero's
ways of thinking: the Homeric verses express the depths of Cicero's own
concerns, and Cicero's use adapts their meaning to reflect the value of
friendship according to the contemporary Roman conception.

1.4   Latin Translations of Greek Poets

In addition to quoting Greek poets in Greek, Cicero, as is well known, also
translated Greek poetry into Latin.[139] In certain cases, Cicero's Latin
translation of Greek verses survive where the original Greek does not.[140]
For the most part, Cicero translated excerpts of Greek poets in order to
include them in his own Latin treatises, where he never quoted Greek
poetry in the original language.[141] The poets translated by Cicero from
Greek into Latin are, by and large, the canonical Greek poets, by frequency: Euripides, Homer, Aeschylus, Sophocles, *et al.*[142] Cicero's Latin

---

[138] Cicero (*Q. fr.* 3.5.4) claims the motto – αἰὲν ἀριστεύειν καὶ ὑπείροχον ἔμμεναι ἄλλων, "always to
       excel and be preeminent above all" – of Achilles (*Il.* 11.784; but also Glaucus: *Il.* 6.208) as his own.
       Instead of αἰὲν ἀριστεύειν, Cicero (*Q. fr.* 3.5.4) writes πολλὸν ἀριστεύειν ("far to excel"); see
       Behrendt 2013: 337–338.
[139] On Cicero's Latin translations of Greek poets: Ewbank 1933: 36–39, Soubiran 1972: 87–95, Jocelyn
       1973a: 73–79, Goldberg 1995: 136–157, Courtney 2003: 149–152.
[140] E.g.: 28 lines of Aeschylus' fragmentary play, *Prometheus Unbound*, are quoted by Cicero in Latin
       (*TD* 2.23–25 = Nauck fr. 193/Soubiran fr. ii).
[141] Jocelyn 1973a: 74.
[142] Euripides: *Andromeda* Nauck fr. 133 (*Fin.* 2.105; Soubiran fr. iv); *Cresphontes* Nauck fr. 449 (*TD*
       1.115; Soubiran fr. vi); *Hippolytus* 612 (*Off.* 3.108; Soubiran fr. i); *Hypsipyle* Nauck fr. 757 (*TD* 3.59;
       Soubiran fr. vii); *Orestes* 1–3 (*TD* 4.63; Soubiran fr. iii); *Phoenissae* 524–525 (*Off.* 3.82; Soubiran fr.
       ii); *Phrixos* Nauck fr. 821 (*TD* 3.67; Soubiran fr. viii); unknown tragedy Nauck fr. 964 (*TD* 3.29,
       repeated 3.58; Soubiran fr. v); unknown tragedy Nauck fr. 941 (*ND* 2.65; Soubiran fr. ix); unknown

quotations of Greek poets are, however, significantly longer than the Greek language quotations, reflecting a different citational mode – a practice of citation particular to literary composition, rather than to casual use.[143]

Perhaps the most famous and well studied of Cicero's translations is the *Aratea*, a Latin translation of Aratus' *Phaenomena*, excerpts of which Cicero embedded in his own works.[144] A point of significance is that, while Cicero, naturally, acknowledged the *Aratea* to be a translation, he nonetheless considered his role as translator as a kind of authorship. In the *De Natura Deorum* (2.104), the Stoic Balbus, about to cite a substantial portion of the poem, turns to Cicero:

> atque hoc loco me intuens, utar, inquit, carminibus Arateis, quae a te admodum adulescentulo conuersa ita me delectant quia Latina sunt ut multa ex is memoria teneam.

> Here, looking at me, he said: "I will quote the poems of Aratus, which you translated when you were quite a young man. They delight me so because they are in Latin, with the result that I still hold many lines of them in my memory."

Cicero here claims that translating Greek verse into Latin made it both more pleasurable and more memorable for a Roman reader. This passage coheres with Cicero's vision of the rivalry between Greek and Latin literature in a famous passage of the *De Finibus* (1.4–5):[145]

> iis igitur est difficilius satis facere, qui se Latina scripta dicunt contemnere. in quibus hoc primum est in quo admirer, cur in grauissimis rebus non delectet eos sermo patrius, cum idem fabellas Latinas ad uerbum e Graecis expressas non

---

tragedy Nauck fr. 973 (*Div.* 2.12; Soubiran fr. x). Homer: *Iliad* 2.299–300 (*Div.* 2.63–64; Soubiran fr. i), 6.201–202 (*TD* 3.63; Soubiran fr. ii), 9.236 (*Div.* 2.82; Soubiran fr. iv); 9.363 (*Div.* 1.52; Soubiran fr. v), 9.646–647 (*TD* 3.18; Soubiran fr. vi), 19.226–229 (*TD* 3.65; Soubiran fr. vii); *Odyssey* 12.184–191 (*Fin.* 5.49; Soubiran fr. viii); *Iliad* 7.89–91 (*De Gloria* fr. 2 [Gellius 15.6.1]; Soubiran iii), *Odyssey* 18.136–137 (*De Fato* fr. 3 [Aug. *Civ. Dei* 5.8]; Soubiran fr. ix). Aeschylus: *Prometheus Bound* 377–380 (*TD* 3.76; Soubiran fr. i), *Prometheus Unbound* Nauck fr. 193 (*TD* 2.23–25; Soubiran fr ii); Cicero (*TD* 2.23) also misattributes verses which Varro (*LL* 7.10) assigned to Accius' *Philocteta* (Dangel 208–211) to Aeschylus. Sophocles: *Trachiniae* 1045–1102 (*TD* 2.20–22; Soubiran fr. i); unknown tragedy Nauck fr. 666. Cicero also rendered other Greek poets into Latin: Solon Campbell fr. 22.5–6 (*TD* 1.117, *De Sen.* 73; Soubiran i).

[143] Many of Cicero's quotations of Greek poets in the original language are only two or three words long (see p61n121). Cicero's Latin quotations of Greek poets can be very substantial indeed: Cicero's excerpt of Sophocles' *Trachiniae* (*TD* 2.20–22, Soubiran fr. i), for example, is 45 lines long.

[144] An independent manuscript tradition of the *Aratea* (see Čulík-Baird 2018: 647) demonstrates that Cicero's Latin poem existed in a standalone edition, from which Cicero selected only parts for inclusion in his prose works. However, Cicero did not systematically translate the other Greek poets whose works he renders into Latin to embed in his philosophical works.

[145] On Cicero's attitude towards translation, see Jocelyn 1969b: 4, 46; Boyle 2006: 86; McElduff 2013: 101–103; Feeney 2016: 47.

inuiti legant. quis enim tam inimicus paene nomini Romano est, qui Ennii
Medeam aut Antiopam Pacuuii spernat aut reiciat, quod se isdem Euripidis
fabulis delectari dicat, Latinas litteras oderit? Synephebos ego, inquit, potius
Caecilii aut Andriam Terentii quam utramque Menandri legam? [5] a quibus
tantum dissentio, ut, cum Sophocles uel optime scripserit Electram, tamen
male conuersam Atilii mihi legendam putem, de quo Licinius: *ferreum
scriptorem* [*FPL* fr. 5], uerum, opinor, scriptorem tamen, ut legendus sit.
rudem enim esse omnino in nostris poetis aut inertissimae segnitiae est aut
fastidii delicatissimi. mihi quidem nulli satis eruditi uidentur, quibus nostra
ignota sunt. an *utinam ne in nemore . . .* [*TrRF* II 89] nihilo minus legimus
quam hoc idem Graecum, quae autem de bene beateque uiuendo a Platone
disputata sunt, haec explicari non placebit Latine?

It is more difficult to satisfactorily reckon with those who say that they
despise things written in Latin. First of all, I cannot fathom why the
language of their forefathers used in the most intellectually rigorous circumstances does not delight these men, when these are the same people who
would not unwillingly read plays translated into Latin word for word from
Greek. For who is so hostile to the name "Roman" that he rejects and
despises Ennius' *Medea* or Pacuvius' *Antiopa*, claiming that he is delighted
by Euripides' same plays and that he hates Latin literature? "Should I really
read Caecilius Statius' *Synephebi*," he says, "or Terence's *Andria* instead of
Menander's versions of each play?" [5] I disagree so strongly with these men
but, although I do think that Sophocles' *Electra* is a sublime piece of
literature, I nonetheless still find there to be value in reading Atilius' badly
translated version of it – because of this play, [Porcius?] Licinius called
Atilius a *writer of iron*. But, in my opinion, he is nonetheless a writer, and
therefore worth reading. To be entirely unversed in our own poets suggests
either an extreme mental inactivity or else a refinement of taste that is overly
precious. No Roman, I think, can be considered an educated man if he does
not know Latin literature. If we read *Would not that in the grove . . .* no less
than we read the same passage in Greek, why should it not also be pleasing
to read Plato's explications on morality and happiness explained in Latin?

At the outset of the *De Finibus*, Cicero struggles with the imagined reader
who would reject Cicero's philosophical work on the grounds that one
would profit more by consulting such material in the original Greek.[146]
Cicero defends himself by presenting the adaptive process behind the
production of the Latin classics as an authorizing precedent for his own
intellectual labour. While Cicero here says that the canonical Latin plays are
"word for word" (*ad uerbum*, *Fin.* 1.4) translations of Greek predecessors, his
own argument in fact problematizes this position, which in turn suggests

---

[146] Cf. *Ac.* 1.4, where Cicero has Varro make this claim explicitly.

that Cicero's claim here is a ventriloquism of the imagined reader, hostile to Latin philosophy, rather than an expression of what he himself believes. Indeed, in the *Academica*, Cicero again wrestles with the reader who rejects Greek philosophy expressed in Latin, but there explicitly says that the Latin poets "did not translate the words, but rather the essence of the Greek poets": *non uerba sed uim Graecorum expresserunt poetarum* (*Ac.* 1.10).[147] As in the *De Natura Deorum*, where Cicero's *Aratea* is said to "delight *because* it is in Latin" (*delectant quia Latina sunt, ND* 2.104), in the *De Finibus*, the Latin poets, it is implied, "delight" (*delectet, Fin.* 1.4) the Romans who happily read them.[148] Noteworthy is the fact that the Latin poets are highly regarded *not* because they write in Latin *per se*, but because they use the "language of the forefathers" (*sermo patrius, Fin.* 1.4), and thereby engage in a sense of cultural continuity with a valued past.[149]

More importantly, Cicero's characterization of the Latin classics in the *De Finibus* suggests that they had already attained a far greater cultural potency than that which mere "translation" might imply:[150] to hate Ennius' *Medea* or Pacuvius' *Antiopa* is to despise the Roman identity (*Fin.* 1.4); and no Roman could consider himself educated if he were not familiar with "our literature" (*nostra, Fin.* 1.5). Indeed, this passage of the *De Finibus* is a thesis statement regarding the canonicity of Latin poetry which is, in fact, proven by Cicero's own consistent citational practices. As we have seen, Cicero engages very minimally with the Greek poets here mentioned – Euripides, Menander, and Sophocles – yet returns over and over again to Ennius, Pacuvius, Caecilius Statius, and Terence across the entirety of his corpus. Indeed, the methods used by Cicero to engage with these poets very clearly demonstrate their centrality to the Roman educational curriculum, as Cicero here suggests.

Given that this is the case, Cicero's desire to replicate the practice of Latin poets – who, by drawing upon Greek traditions thereby augmented and amplified them – demonstrates that their cultural work was an inspiration

---

[147] Cf. *Opt. Gen.* 14: *non uerbum pro uerbo . . . sed uimque seruaui*; on which, see Feeney 2016: 47. Boyle (2006: 86) notes that an examination of the fragments of Ennius' *Medea* side-by-side with Euripides' play demonstrates that Cicero's comments in the *Academica* are "much nearer the mark."

[148] Cf. *Ac.* 1.10: *quia delectat Ennius, Pacuuius, Accius, multi alii . . .*

[149] Cicero regularly makes the Latin poets into ambassadors for the Latinity of their respective eras: Plautus and Naevius (*De Or.* 3.45; *Brut.* 60; see Hanses 2020: 53–54), Terence (*Att.* 7.3.10), Lucilius (*Fam.* 9.15.2).

[150] Evidently, Cicero is here reckoning with a contemporary hostility to translation which he does not share. Generally speaking, Cicero believes that translation into Latin amplifies the original material, e.g.: *Fin.* 1.6, *Opt. Gen.* 14.

for his own intellectual labour. Just as the Romans could simultaneously hold a deep attachment to Ennius' *Medea* alongside an appreciation for the Euripidean original, so too Cicero hopes that his explication of Platonic ideas may sit side-by-side with the treatises of Plato (*Fin.* 1.5). Indeed, Cicero goes on in the *De Finibus* (1.6) to suggest that his engagement with Plato and other Greek authorities allows him to annotate and *add to* their work.[151] In sum, Cicero's vision of the Latin poets as canonical writers who augmented precursor Greek material is the construction of an intellectual model which he himself intends to follow and further extend with his own writing.

When Cicero translated Greek verse into Latin to include in his treatises, he also used the very language of the Latin poets whom he venerated. In the *Tusculans* (2.20–22), Cicero presents a translation of part of Heracles' soliloquy from Sophocles' *Trachiniae* (1046–1102; Soubiran fr. i) to exemplify the extremes of psychic and physical pain. An examination of the first two lines of Cicero's Latin translation is sufficient to demonstrate his debt to the Latin poets (*TD* 2.20):

> o multa dictu grauia, perpessu aspera,   [Cic. Soubiran fr. i, 1–2]
> quae corpore exanclata atque animo pertuli![152]

> Oh, these many things – difficult to speak of, hard to bear –
> the sufferings which I have endured in both body and mind!

Cicero here (line 2) uses the Latin *exanclata*, "things endured" i.e. "sufferings," to expand upon Sophocles' μοχθήσας ("I have toiled").[153] *Exanclare*, as Quintilian (*Inst.* 1.6.40) would later note, is a rather unusual verb, appearing almost exclusively in the works of Cicero's favoured Latin poets,[154] where it is used to describe the endurance of great toils, as in Ennius' *Andromacha*.[155] For Cicero, the Ennian Andromacha's suffering was the *locus classicus* for the expression of psychic pain, as I discuss in Chapter 4. As a result, Cicero seems

---

[151] *Fin.* 1.6: *eisque nostrum iudicium ... adiungimus*, "to these writers, I join my own opinion."
[152] Sophocles' *Trachiniae* 1046–1047: ὤ πολλὰ δὴ καὶ θερμὰ κοὐ λόγῳ κακὰ | καὶ χερσὶ καὶ νώτοισι μοχθήσας ἐγώ; "Oh, these many things, they are hot, they are evil even to speak of; | I have toiled with both my hands and my back!" Note that Cicero's translation introduces a greater emphasis upon mental suffering than is present in the original; see Soubiran 1972: 287n2. Ewbank (1933: 251) is surely wrong to suggest that Cicero here read an uncontracted form of νοῦς ("mind"; i.e. νοόισι or νόεσσι) for νώτοισι.
[153] Given that Cicero's verse also contains *pertuli* ("I have endured"), *exanclata* ("sufferings") is an expansion upon, rather than a simple rendering of, μοχθήσας ("I have toiled").
[154] Ennius *Andromacha TrRF* II 28; Pacuvius *Periboea* Schierl fr. 213; Accius *Amphitruo* Dangel 645, *Diomedes* Dangel 538; Lucilius *Satires* Warmington 1011–12. Aside from Cicero's use of *exanclare*, which he clearly derives from these poets, the verb also appears in Apuleius, e.g. *Met.* 8.1.4.
[155] Ennius' *Andromacha* (*TrRF* II 28): *quantis cum aerumnis illum exanclaui diem*, "in the face of such great troubles, I endured that day."

to have threaded his translation of Sophocles' depiction of suffering with Ennian diction in order to map one expression of pain onto another. Indeed, that Cicero closely associated the verb *exanclare* with the extremes of suffering which test philosophical forbearance is made clear by the fact that he used it even in his prose to describe such circumstances, as in the *Tusculans* (1.118) where Cicero describes the lifespan of a human as "the endurance of all suffering" (*exanclauisset omnes labores*).[156] When Cicero (*Div.* 2.64) translated Calchas' speech in the *Iliad* (2.326–328), he also inserted the notion of endurance into the poem by using the verb *exanclare*:[157]

> nam quot auis taetro mactatas dente uidetis,   [Cic. Soubiran fr. i, 26–27]
> tot nos ad Troiam belli exanclabimus annos

> For the number of birds you see destroyed by foul tooth,
> so many years of war shall we endure at Troy.

In addition, then, to the fact that Cicero explicitly cited the Latin poets, Cicero's translation style was also, in its own way, an extension of the Latin poets. That Cicero considered his Latin translations of Greek verse to intersect spiritually with the Latin classics is made clear by the fact that he regularly entangled them, such as in the *Tusculans* (3.28–30) where Cicero quotes from a now unknown Latin tragedy (*TrRF* I 58[158]) alongside translated verses which he attributes to Euripides[159] (Soubiran fr. v; Nauck fr. 964):[160]

> ex hoc et illa iure laudantur:
> *ego cum genui, tum morituros sciui et ei rei sustuli.*   [*TrRF* I 58]
> *praeterea ad Troiam cum misi ob defendendam Graeciam,*
> *scibam me in mortiferum bellum, non in epulas mittere.*

---

[156] Cf. *Ac.* 2.108: *Herculi quendam laborem exanclatum,* "the endurance of a Herculean labour."

[157] Calchas' original utterance (*Il.* 2.328) does not explicitly contain the idea of endurance: ὡς ἡμεῖς τοσσαῦτ' ἔτεα πτολεμίξομεν αὖθι, "so shall we war there for the same number of years."

[158] Cicero attributes the speeches at *TD* 3.28, 3.39, and 3.58 to Telamo; as a result several editors attributed the verses to Ennius' *Telamo* (see *TrRF* I p231). On the Latin verses at *TD* 3.28, Jocelyn (1969a: 394) commented: "it is difficult to see why it could not equally well go into Pacuvius' *Teucer.*" As a result the *TrRF* remains agnostic.

[159] The original Greek of this fragment (Nauck fr. 964) is transmitted by Plutarch in the *Consolation to Apollonius* (*Mor.* 112d). Since Cicero and Plutarch identically note that the words were "spoken by Theseus in Euripides" (*apud Euripiden a Theseo*; ὁ παρὰ τῷ Εὐριπίδῃ Θησεύς), it is very likely that they are drawing on a common source, perhaps Crantor's *On Grief;* on Cicero's engagement with Crantor and the consolatory tradition, see Graver 2002: 185–192). Cicero (*TD* 3.76) and Plutarch (*Mor.* 102c) each also quote the same passage of Aeschylus (*PV* 377–380) in the context of consolation.

[160] This first line of this pair of citations is repeated at *TD* 3.57.

[3.29] haec igitur praemeditatio futurorum malorum lenit eorum aduentum,
quae uenientia longe ante uideris. itaque apud Euripiden a Theseo dicta
laudantur; licet enim, ut saepe facimus, in Latinum illa conuertere:

nam qui haec audita a docto meminissem uiro,　　　　[Cic. Soubiran fr. v;
futuras mecum commentabar miserias:　　　　　　　　Eur. Nauck fr. 964]
aut mortem acerbam aut exili maestam fugam
aut semper aliquam molem meditabar mali,
ut, si qua inuecta diritas casu foret,
ne me inparatum cura laceraret repens.

[3.30] quod autem Theseus a docto se audisse dicit, id de se ipso loquitur
Euripides. fuerat enim auditor Anaxagorae, quem ferunt nuntiata morte filii
dixisse: sciebam me genuisse mortalem.

For this reason even these verses are justly praised:
"The moment I fathered them, I knew they would die and I raised them for this
purpose.
Besides, when I sent them to Troy to defend Greece,
I knew that I was sending them to death-bringing war, not to a banquet."
[3.29] The anticipation of the future mitigates the approach of the bad things,
whose coming is long foreseen. And so these words, spoken by Theseus in
Euripides, are also praised. Let me, as I often do, translate them into Latin:
"For when I remembered hearing these words from the learned man,
I meditated upon my future miseries:
harsh death or the sad flight of exile
or some other mass of evil I always did contemplate,
so that, if dread chance should bring calamity,
a sudden anxiety would not distress me unprepared."
[3.30] When Theseus says he heard these things "from a learned man,"
Euripides is really speaking about himself. For he was a student of
Anaxagoras who, they say, upon the death of his son, replied: "I knew
that I had fathered a mortal."

Cicero's intellectual labour in translating Greek to Latin is presented alongside
Latin verses in order to bolster the philosophical argument at hand; namely,
that living is inherently defined by death, therefore death is not itself an evil.
Cicero's alignments in the translation allow him to extend the lexicon of the
initial Latin verses through the paragraph as a whole. The Latin poet's *cum
genui, tum morituros sciui* ("the moment I fathered them, I knew they would
die") is completed via ring-composition with Cicero's rendering of Anaxagoras'
sciebam me genuisse mortalem ("I knew that I had fathered a mortal").[161] The

---

[161] Cf. *Div.* 2.30, where verses from Ennius' *Iphigenia* (*TrRF* II 82) are made to be spoken by
Democritus.

argument of the entire citational unit therefore relies upon an essential calibra-
tion between the Latin poet's verses and Cicero's understanding of a Greek
philosophical tradition via the presence of Anaxagoras' wisdom in the verses of
his student, Euripides.

While Cicero could make Greek and Latin ideas stand together, he also
often presented them in explicit competition. In the *Tusculan Disputations*
(1.117), Cicero argued that the muted emotionality of Ennius' attitude to
death was preferable to Solon's wish to be mourned:[162]

> melior Enni quam Solonis oratio. hic enim noster
> *nemo me lacrimis decoret* inquit *nec funera fletu*
> *faxit*   [Goldberg-Manuwald F2b]
> at uero ille sapiens:
> *mors mea ne careat lacrimis: linquamus amicis*   [Cic. Soubiran fr. i;
> *maerorem, ut celebrent funera cum gemitu.*   Solon Campbell fr. 22.5–6]

> Ennius says it better than Solon. For our poet says:
> "*Let none embellish me with their tears nor a funeral*
> *with their weeping make*"
> yet this other wise man says:
> "*Let my death lack not tears. Let me leave grief*
> *for my friends, so that they fill my funeral with their wailing.*"

Cicero here deliberately pulls Ennian language (*lacrimis, funera;* "tears,"
"funeral") into Solon's verses in order to contrast the difference in their
outlook.[163] In doing so, Cicero is able to highlight the superiority (in his
view) of the Roman poet's philosophical position. Similarly, Cicero thought
that Pacuvius' depiction of Odysseus' endurance of pain was philosophically
preferable to Sophocles' depiction of Odyssean suffering: *Pacuuius hoc melius
quam Sophocles* (*TD* 2.49).[164] Cicero's juxtaposition of Latin classics alongside
canonical Greek verse, facilitated via a translation style indebted to the Latin
poets, is a testament to his investment in their value. Furthermore, his
preferential treatment of the Roman poets demonstrates a nationalistic

---

[162] Cf. *De Sen.* 73, where Solon and Ennius are likewise contrasted.
[163] The original Greek is transmitted by Plutarch (*Publ.* 24.5): μηδέ μοι ἄκλαυστος θάνατος μόλοι,
ἀλλὰ φίλοισι | καλλείποιμι θανὼν ἄλγεα καὶ στοναχάς, "May death not come to me without tears,
but in death may I leave my friends with suffering and wailing." Plutarch adds the detail that
Solon's verses were a "response to Mimnermus" (πρὸς Μίμνερμον); if Cicero knew that this was the
case, he makes Ennius respond to Solon's response, extending the recursivity of poetic competition
into the Roman literary sphere.
[164] Cicero also made such judgements between Latin poets, e.g. *TD* 1.105 where, in the competing
philosophical positions regarding the extent to which Hector's dead body was still Hector, Accius
(Dangel 160) is preferred to Ennius (*TrRF* II 23).

attachment to Latin writers that reflects a belief in the superior moral content
of their verses.[165]

Given that the majority of Cicero's citations of Greek poets can be checked
against a fully extant text, Cicero's Greek quotations present the possibility of
testing his citational "accuracy." As we have already seen, in certain cases
Cicero adjusts the Greek quotations to his own context, introducing deliberate distortions that would have been perceptible and appreciable by his
immediate reader.[166] Indeed, as we shall see, oratorical training encouraged
the adjustment, or the wholesale fabrication, of verse. But there are also
deviations which do not seem to be deliberate and instead should be classed
as errors.[167] In the *De Divinatione* (2.63–64; 2.82), Cicero translates into Latin
two passages of the *Iliad* (2.299–330; 9.236) but misidentifies the speaker in
each case.[168] Aulus Gellius (15.6.3), who was surprised to find that the error was
not corrected by Tiro (15.6.2), preserves the fact that Cicero made another
mistake with Homer in the *De Gloria* (fr. 2), where Cicero attributed three
translated verses of the *Iliad* (7.89–91) to Ajax instead of Hector.

While these errors are somewhat superficial – they could be caught, as
Aulus Gellius notes (15.6.2), by anyone who had read the original material –
they do have certain important implications. Firstly, citational mistakes in
Cicero's treatises strongly imply book use.[169] Cicero seems to have cited
these verses not from the original poems but from secondary sources; in
some cases, this meant that Cicero paid greater attention to the content of
the lines than to their immediate context, and thereby made errors.[170]
Given the certainty that Cicero makes mistakes with independently extant
poetry, it stands to reason that Cicero also makes mistakes with at least
some of the Latin verses for which there is no possibility of verification.[171]
In one interesting case, Cicero seems to misattribute some verses ostensibly
composed by a Roman poet to a Greek one; in the *Tusculans* (2.23), Cicero
quotes four anapaestic verses which, he says, come from Aeschylus:

---

[165] Cf. *Fin.* 2.106 where the gluttonous indulgence in the epitaph (Soubiran fr. x) of the Syrian king, Sardanapallus, is contrasted with the celebration of achievement in Ennius' *Scipio* (Goldberg-Manuwald F1).

[166] See p63n131.

[167] On Cicero's citational errors, see Jocelyn 1973a: 77, Soubiran 1972: 63, 266, 268, Behrendt 2013: 87.

[168] Cicero says (*Div.* 2.63) that "Agamemnon speaks" (*Agamemnon loquitur*) the lines, but it is in fact Odysseus who is speaking (*Il.* 2.278) at the beginning of the passage; later (*Div.* 2.82), Cicero introduces the speaker of *Il.* 923 as the "Homeric Ajax" (*Homericus Ajax*), but it is again Odysseus.

[169] The issue of book use and memorization is discussed on pp76–79.

[170] Jocelyn 1973a: 77: "it is less likely that he should have misattributed verses he thought of himself to illustrate a point than he misattributed verses he found already quoted in a philosophical source but lacking a full or accurate description of their original context."

[171] On "mistakes" in the citation of Latin poetry, see pp78–79.

ueniat Aeschylus, non poeta solum, sed etiam Pythagoreus; sic enim acce-
pimus. quo modo fert apud eum Prometheus dolorem, quem excipit ob
furtum Lemnium:

unde ignis cluet mortalibus clam   [Dangel 208–211]
diuisus; eum doctus Prometheus
clepsisse dolo poenasque Ioui
 fato expendisse supremo.

Let Aeschylus come forward, not only a poet but even a Pythagorean; we
accept the tradition. This is how his Prometheus bears the pain he received
because of the theft on Lemnos:
"it is from here, they say, that fire among mortals
was secretly distributed; that clever Prometheus
stole it through trickery, and paid penalty to Jupiter
 through sublime fate."

However, Varro (*LL* 7.11), quoting part of the same passage within a much
larger citation,[172] attributes the verses not to Aeschylus, but to Accius:

nam apud Accium in Philocteta Lemnio: . . .
nemus expirante uapore uides,   [Dangel 207–209]
unde ignis cluet mortalibus clam
diuisus.
quare haec quod "tesca" dixit, non errauit . . .

For in Accius' *Philocteta on Lemnos*:
"You are looking at the precinct exhaling smoke,
it is from here, they say, that fire among mortals
was secretly distributed."
It is for this reason that Accius calls the places "*tesca*," and he is
not mistaken . . .

Varro's citation incidentally gives more context to the cited verses: the
speaking character tells another, likely Philocteta, that he has come to
the legendary place on Lemnos where Prometheus originally stole fire from
the gods.[173] Varro precedes his engagement with Accius' *Philocteta* by

---

[172] Omitted here for clarity. Varro (*LL* 7.10–11) cites Accius' *Philocteta* (Dangel 228, 200–209) in order
to explain the Latin word *tesca* (according to Varro's discussion either "sacred" or "wild"), which
appears in the first line of Varro's long quotation (*LL.* 7.11; Dangel 228): *quis tu es mortalis, qui in
deserta et tesca te apportes loca*, "who are you, mortal, who bring yourself to these wild and sacred
places?" Varro quotes the remaining verses because they describe the nature of the places which
Accius designates as *tesca*.

[173] In Hesiod, Prometheus steals fire directly from Zeus (*Op.* 51) by hiding it in a hollow fennel-stalk
(*Op.* 52; *Theog.* 567). In a later tradition, Prometheus stole the fire from Hephaestus' forge on
Lemnos; see Bakola 2019: 245.

remarking that he has been reading the notes of "those who have written glosses" (*qui glossas scripserunt, LL* 7.10) on the Latin word which he is currently investigating.[174] Varro thereby signals the fact that he is using secondary literature to find the quotations needed for his linguistic work. This, coupled with the fact that Cicero quotes overlapping verses, suggests that Varro and Cicero were drawing from a shared resource. While Varro pays close attention to the content of the verses in order to further his scholarly argument, Cicero, approaching the verses with less care regarding their broader meaning, makes a mistake, attributing the verses to Aeschylus (*TD* 2.23) instead of Accius. Since Cicero follows these Accian lines with his own twenty-eight line translation of Aeschylus' *Prometheus Unbound* (*TD* 2.23–25; Soubiran fr. ii), it seems that he has accidentally attributed the prior quotation to the wrong poet via a kind of ascriptive attraction.

Cicero's engagement with the Greek poets certainly reflects the fact that an educated Roman during the late Republic might encounter Greek verse in a number of different ways. As ever, we find a degree of entanglement in Cicero's intellectual project: Cicero's Latin translations of Greek verse bear a debt to Roman poetry as well as to the Greek literary tradition. We also find that Cicero's interest in Greek poetry is deeply dependent upon his ability to discover it already embedded in other Greek writings. Yet Cicero's interest in Greek poetry was demonstrably lower than his interest in Latin poetry. This fact puts his greater interest in Latin in even higher relief.

1.5   Memory versus the Book

Cicero's sustained and complex engagement with poetry raises the question of the extent to which material texts, i.e. books, were involved.[175] On the one hand, it seems quite clear that Cicero deployed many of his quotations from memory. That Cicero calls up Latin verses in circumstances where we would not expect him to have a copy of the text at hand essentially confirm this, such as letters sent from the road.[176] Indeed, the fact that Cicero repeated many of the same quotations also suggests that he

---

[174] Cf. *LL* 7.107.

[175] As Goldberg (2005: 38) notes: "The complexity of the exercise for writer and reader alike demands a trained response and a literary consciousness that presupposes close knowledge of the books available for reference." On the book in ancient Rome, see Frampton 2019.

[176] Cicero quotes Latin verse in his letters as governor of Cilicia: a verse of an unknown comedy at camp in Mopsuhestia (*Fam.* 3.8.8); a snippet of Ennius at Loadicea (*Att.* 6.2.8); a Naevian verse at Tarsus (*Fam.* 15.6.1).

had committed them to memory, particularly in cases where he quoted identical verses several years apart.

But, of course, the fact of memorization does not rule out book use. Indeed, memorization of poetry, to some extent, presupposes both reading and writing. The ancient educational systems of Greece and Rome saw students engaging with the poets as part of their elementary training: they learned to read by scrutinizing lines of poetry, to write by copying out verse or taking it down from dictation.[177] Poetry was particularly valued as an educational resource which allowed the student to absorb both form and content, facilitating aesthetic as well as moral instruction.[178] Numerous extant materials testify to these pedagogical practices in antiquity: lines of Homer repeated over and over on potsherds, wax tablets with Menandrian *sententiae*, papyri annotated by students with excerpts of several poetic genres.[179] Seneca the younger criticized this kind of "notebook knowledge" (*commentario sapere, Ep.* 33.7) in fully grown adults who, following this literary immersion, could only quote the words and deeds of others, not write or enact their own.[180] Yet, the fullness of the Ciceronian corpus with verse quotation reflects a mature expression of such literary absorption in elite Roman education, revealing how deeply ingrained poetry was in the minds of Romans who continued to carry it with them.

Cicero himself explicitly refers to the Latin poets in the context of books and reading: Livius Andronicus' plays were, according to Cicero, not worth "reading" twice (*legantur, Brut.* 71); Cicero asks why Romans should "read" (*legantur, Fin.* 1.4; *Ac.* 1.10) Latin poets, but not Latin philosophers; and Cicero, in a Platonic mood, noted that the poets, who were "not only read but even committed to memory" (*non legantur modo sed etiam ediscantur, TD* 2.27; cf. *Rep.* 605d–e), could morally enervate their readers. "Old book copies" (*antiqui libri*) of Ennius were also thought to preserve archaic Latin orthography (*Or.* 160). Indeed, Cicero's citational practices themselves, as I note

---

[177] Bonner 1977: 172, Cribiore 1996: 46, Bloomer 2011: 116, Dickey 2016: 4.

[178] Cf. Quint. *Inst.* 1.36.2. Cribiore (1996: 44) confirms that the majority of extant writing exercises from antiquity use maxims from poetry.

[179] Limestone *ostrakon* inscribed in ink with the opening line of the *Iliad* repeated four times, Metropolitan Museum 14.1.140 (Egypt, sixth to seventh century CE); wax tablet with iambic *sententiae* from Menander written out as an exemplar by the teacher and copied (with errors) by the student, British Library Add MS 34186 (Egypt, second century BCE); see Bonner 1977: 173; papyrus roll containing excerpts from Euripides, Aeschylus, Posidippus, fragments of unknown comedy, and epigrams on Alexandria, written by a young scribe, Apollonios son of Glaukos, who claimed to be representing "the lessons of Aristhon the philosopher," P. Louvre inv. E. 7172 (Egypt, second century BCE); see Cribiore 1996: 230 (no. 244).

[180] Cf. *Rhet.* 4.4.8, where the memorization of Ennian *sententiae* is treated as only the bare minimum, not the apex, of literacy.

throughout the present work, either reveal book use, or, at the minimum, indicate prior study in environments which imply use of material texts. While Cicero sometimes quoted verse from memory, he *also* demonstrably drew on a number of written resources: in many cases, it is clear that Cicero did not excerpt the verse from the standalone poetic text, but used secondary materials – rhetorical, philosophical, or philological – to make his citations.

The fact that Cicero's philosophical treatises contain both the greatest number and the longest verse quotations in the corpus strongly suggests that Cicero consulted books for at least some of his verse quotations.[181] Cicero's *philosophica*, perhaps more than any other of his works, paint the picture of book use as part of compositional practice: in his letters, Cicero asks for books to be sent for his research;[182] in the works themselves, he describes his engagement with philosophical forebears via their books;[183] and his translations from Greek to Latin imply consultation of the source text as he worked.[184] Several of Cicero's quotations of Greek poets demonstrably derive from Greek philosophical texts, as I discuss in section 2.1. Furthermore, Cicero's book use is an extension of the fact that he had already been initiated into the intellectual circles which produced such works: Cicero's philosophical education (cf. Plut. *Cic.* 3–4) doubtless provided him with a number of philosophical resources, just as his training with the Roman scholar, L. Aelius Stilo (*Brut.* 205–207), provided him with philological texts, and his time in the oratorical schools provided him with rhetorical handbooks.

Errors in quotation can be evidence of a lapse in memory *or*, in fact, evidence of book use. A number of Cicero's quotations of Plautus and Terence use slightly different language than that which appears in their independent traditions. In a letter to Brutus (1.2a.3), Cicero slightly changes the word order of Plautus' *Trinummus* (319); and he seems on a few occasions to misremember lines from Terence's *Eunuchus* and

---

[181] Half (approx. 380 out of a total 735) of the poetic quotations in the Ciceronian corpus come from the philosophical works. The longest quotations appear in the *Tusculans* (2.20–22; 45 lines) and the *De Natura Deorum* (2.104–114; 44 discrete quotations of Cicero's *Aratea* spanning the equivalent of Aratus' *Phaenomena* 19–450, see Čulík-Baird 2018: 647).

[182] In 54 BCE, Cicero, preparing to write the *De Republica*, asked Atticus to be let into his house to use his books (*Att.* 4.14). Cicero asked Atticus for a copy of an essay by the Epicurean Phaedrus as he was writing *De Natura Deorum* (*Att.* 13.39.2 cf. Dyck 2003: 7). After Tullia's death, Cicero, preparing for the *Tusculans*, read everything in Atticus' villa at Astura to do with the lessening of grief, then he spent all his time writing (*Att.* 12.14.3).

[183] Mice are imagined eating Plato's *Republic* (*Div.* 2.59). In the *Tusculans* (3.44) Cicero says that Epicurus should have removed certain material from his book, or else thrown the entire book away.

[184] Jocelyn 1969b: 46.

Phormio.[185] However, such "misrememberences" may themselves be evidence of book use. A citational "mistake" in the *Orator* (157), where Cicero changed a word in Terence, may derive from an intermediary text, i.e. a study of Roman comedy, which, by glossing the word, introduced a textual variant.[186] As we have seen, the misattribution of verses (several Homeric quotations; the attribution of Accian verse to Aeschylus) arises from the fact that Cicero did not quote these lines directly but from a textual intermediary, leading him to include verses without proper attention to their original context. Such lapses demonstrate that Cicero was evidently more familiar with certain passages of literature than he was with others: Cicero seven times quoted the opening lines of Ennius' *Medea*, which he had clearly committed to memory, while he could not remember who precisely was speaking in various passages of Homer.[187] Cicero's citational method is therefore reflective of intellectual practice that often, but not always, relied upon the consultation of books.

---

[185] *Att.* 7.3.10 has *captam* ("seized") for *abreptam* ("carried off") in Terence's *Eunuchus* 115; *Or.* 157 has *cognatum* ("relative") for *sobrinum* ("maternal cousin") in Terence's *Phormio* 384; *TD* 3.30 omits a word (*exsilia*) from *Phormio* 242.
[186] See p163n39.
[187] *TrRF* II 89: *Inv.* 1.91, *Cael.* 18, *Fin.* 1.5, *TD* 1.45, *ND* 3.75, *Fat.* 34–45, *Top.* 61.

CHAPTER 2

Poetic Citation by Ciceronian Genre

2.1 Poetry and Philosophy

Since Cicero quotes poetry most frequently and extensively in his philosophical works, discussion of Cicero's philosophical engagement with poetry appears throughout this book. Nonetheless, some prefatory remarks ought to be made. To some extent the Greek philosophical tradition was defined by its relationship with poetry, a relationship which was at times antagonistic, at others complementary.[1] As Stephen Halliwell writes: "Greek philosophy had developed within, and was surrounded by, a culture which extensively valued the authority of the poetic word and the poet's 'voice' from which it emanated" and "familiarity with poetry had always been a force with which philosophy, in its various manifestations, needed to reckon."[2] In the *Republic* (607b), Plato referred to "the ancient dispute between philosophy and poetry"[3] which had arisen due to the competing claims of each to the possibility of knowledge, but even the framing of the relationship as a "dispute" demonstrates their deep interconnectivity.

That poetry was mimetic, i.e. it presented a representation of reality while not itself *being* a substantive instantiation of reality, is Plato's major criticism (*Rep.* 603b–c). Infamously, Plato (*Rep.* 606e) rejected Homer as the educator of Greece due to his presentation of "shameful" human behaviour – such as the open lamentation of grieving heroes (*Rep.* 605d–e) – influential upon and imitable by an audience. Under ideal circumstances, Plato would only tolerate poetry capable of social utility, hymns to the gods and praise of good men (*Rep.* 607a). Plato's apparent rejection of poetry caused great

---

[1] Indeed, the author of *On the Sublime* (13.3) explicitly figured Plato as Homer's ἀνταγωνιστής ("rival"); see Halliwell 2012: 156.

[2] Halliwell 2000: 94.

[3] *Rep.* 607b: παλαιὰ μέν τις διαφορὰ φιλοσοφίᾳ τε καὶ ποιητικῇ. Plato here (*Rep.* 607b) goes on to partially quote several verses of unknown poets criticizing the arrogance of philosophers who are ultimately dependent upon poetry, including one verse which figures philosophy as "a yelping bitch shrieking at her master" (ἡ λακέρυζα πρὸς δεσπόταν κύων).

consternation in the ancient critical tradition, since Plato's own debt to Homer was so patently obvious. If Plato – whom Cicero (*TD* 1.79), citing Panaetius, named the "Homer of the philosophers" (*Homerum philosophorum*)[4] – were to carry through his threat of banishing Homer, he would, as the fifth century CE commentator, Proclus, noted, have to banish himself as well.[5] Plato's complex and unresolved relationship with poetry is probably responsible for the later development of a dramatic episode in his biography which cast Plato as a young poet who rejected his former calling when he heard the wisdom of Socrates.[6] Diogenes Laertius (*Lives* 3.5) reports the story that, Plato, rejecting poetry, cast his work into the flames, reciting a modified verse of Homer's *Iliad*:

ἔπειτα μέντοι μέλλων ἀγωνιεῖσθαι τραγῳδίᾳ πρὸ τοῦ Διονυσιακοῦ θεάτρου Σωκράτους ἀκούσας κατέφλεξε τὰ ποιήματα εἰπών·
"Ἥφαιστε, πρόμολ᾽ ὧδε· Πλάτων[7] νύ τι σεῖο χατίζει." [*Il.* 18.392]

Afterwards, about to take part in the tragedy competition, he heard Socrates in front of the theatre of Dionysus, and then burned his own poetry. As he did so, he said:
"*Come here, Hephaestus. Plato needs you now.*"

Indeed, Plato quoted and alluded to poetry liberally in his writings.[8] Plato's engagement with Greek verse was a vehicle not only for discoursing upon philosophical problems, but also a means of dramatizing competitive engagement with philosophical rivals. Given that Greek poetry held a central position in elite education, display of its mastery was part of the repertoire of the sophists, who claimed to be able to give, or rather sell, young men the best intellectual training possible. In Plato's *Protagoras*, for example, the eponymous speaker tries to demonstrate his wisdom with an analysis of a poem by Simonides (*Prt.* 339a–346d = Campbell fr. 542),[9] and thereby to prove the value of a sophistic education. While Socrates claims that analyzing poetry in this way resembles a drunken party trick for the uneducated (*Prt.* 347c–d), the

---

[4] Plato was also named Ὁμηρικώτατος ("the most Homeric") by the author of *On the Sublime* (13.3).
[5] Proclus *In Rep.* 1.161.9–11 Kroll.   [6] Regali 2015: 173–174, with works there cited.
[7] The original verse (*Il.* 18.392) reads Θέτις instead of Πλάτων.
[8] While Plato discusses poetry at length in the *Ion*, the *Republic* esp. Books 2, 3, and 10, and the *Laws* Book 2, there are also hundreds of poetic citations across the Platonic corpus. Brandwood (1976: 991–1003) collects in an "Index of Quotations" Plato's engagements with Greek literature, the majority of which are poetic. For a criticism of the criteria behind this list and further bibliography on Plato's citations, see Halliwell 2000: 95n4.
[9] Both Socrates (who appears in Xenophon *Mem.* 1.2.56–59 as particularly well versed in the poets; see Halliwell 2000: 96n10) and Protagoras claim to know the Simonides poem well (*Prt.* 339b) and, as a result, it is deliberately not cited in full; on the entanglement of the poem fragment with Plato's text, see Carson 1992.

extended discussion of poetry in the dialogue dramatized the intellectual work which could be done with the poets and may have been an influence on Cicero.[10]

Cicero was, of course, familiar with some of Plato's poetic engagement, and in certain cases he followed Platonic opinion regarding poetry and its effects.[11] In the *Phaedrus* (245a), Plato casts the madness of divine inspiration needed for poetic composition in a positive light:[12] insanity, Plato writes, is in fact a *requirement* for poetry and, indeed, the poetry of divine madness has both greater significance and greater longevity than that composed by a rational mind.[13] Cicero knew this passage of the *Phaedrus*, and discussed it in the *De Divinatione* (1.80), where he connected the Platonic idea with an excerpt from Pacuvius' *Teucer*:

> fit etiam saepe specie quadam, saepe uocum grauitate et cantibus, ut
> pellantur animi uehementius, saepe etiam cura et timore, qualis est illa
> *flexanima tamquam lymphata aut Bacchi sacris*   [Schierl fr. 251]
> *commota in tumulis*[14] *Teucrum commemorans suum.*
> atque etiam illa concitatio declarat uim in animis esse diuinam. negat enim
> sine furore Democritus quemquam poetam magnum esse posse, quod idem
> dicit Plato. quem, si placet, appellet furorem, dum modo is furor ita
> laudetur ut in Phaedro laudatus est. quid? uestra oratio in causis, quid ipsa
> actio potest esse uehemens et grauis et copiosa, nisi est animus ipse com-
> motior? equidem etiam in te saepe uidi et, ut ad leuiora ueniamus, in
> Aesopo, familiari tuo, tantum ardorem uultuum atque motuum, ut eum uis
> quaedam abstraxisse a sensu mentis uideretur

> It often happens that the mind is greatly affected by some sight, often too by the
> power of voice and by song, often even by anxiety and fear, just as the
> woman who
> "*as though bent by madness or by the rites of Bacchus
> moved, calling for her Teucer among the graves.*"

---

[10] A translation of the *Protagoras* attributed to Cicero circulated in antiquity; see Jones 1959: 23, De Graff 1940: 145, Long 2006: 291.

[11] On Cicero and Plato more generally, see Poncelet 1957, Zoll 1962, Bishop 2019: 85–128.

[12] In the *Ion* 534b–c, however, Plato criticized the fact that poetry was divinely inspired, given that the poet, somewhat literally, "lost his mind" and thereby his intellectual capacity. There (*Ion* 534b), Plato also characterized the mad poet as a "sacred thing" (χρῆμα ἱερόν). If Cicero was aware that Plato characterized poets as sacred, he preferred to attribute the idea to Ennius instead: *noster ille Ennius sanctos appellat poetas*, "our Ennius calls poets 'sacred'" (*Arch.* 18); see Skutsch 1985: 131, Elliott 2013: 171.

[13] *Phaedrus* 245a: ἡ ποίησις ὑπὸ τῆς τῶν μαινομένων ἡ τοῦ σωφρονοῦντος ἠφανίσθη, "the poetry of the sane man vanishes before that of the inspired madman."

[14] Schierl (2006: 510) notes that either "hills" or "graves" is possible; without the full context, it is not clear whether *in tumulis* is part of the Bacchic simile, or the literal description of the woman's action. At any rate, the Latin *tumuli,* meaning, as it does "mounds of earth" may have been intended by Pacuvius to be deliberately polyvalent.

And even this disturbance makes clear that there is a divine power in the mind. Democritus says that there could be no great poet without divine frenzy, and Plato says the same thing. Let Plato call it "frenzy" if he wants, provided this frenzy is praised as it is in the *Phaedrus*. Could your speech in the courtroom, with its performance so ardent, powerful, and rich, be possible unless your mind was moved like this? Indeed, I have often seen in you, and, to take a lighter example, in Aesopus, your friend, such fire in expression and movement, that some power seems to have taken the reason from your mind.

Although this passage of *De Divinatione* is rooted (with a nod to Democritus) in Plato's *Phaedrus,* where it is argued that "frenzy" of a divine nature facilitates not only prophecy (244a–c) but also poetry (245a), Cicero has both naturalized and adapted the concept of inspiration in order to give it a broader significance in the Roman cultural context. The spark of the "divine" evident in the madness which propelled Hesiona to call out for her lost son in Pacuvius' *Teucer* is part of a continuum of inspiration which powers both Cicero's oratorical prowess and the emotional performance of the actor, Aesopus.[15] Since Varro (*LL* 7.87) also quotes verses from the same passage of Pacuvius' *Teucer* (Schierl fr. 251), it is likely that Cicero's citation derives from a secondary source used by both Varro and Cicero which studied Latin poetry. Cicero, then, who here begins with a Platonic premise, reframes Greek philosophical ideas within the context of contemporary Roman intellectual practices. Cicero is also less interested in the Platonic idea that poetry and its mad inspiration might pose a problem for rationalist discourse or epistemology, but instead accepts that such poetic inspiration exists and can manifest in himself as well. While Cicero occasionally echoes Plato's poetic moralizing – as in the *Tusculans* (2.27), where he criticizes the fact that Romans read and memorized poets who represent men incapable of withstanding pain (cf. Plato *Rep.* 605d–e) – Cicero is, generally speaking, much more invested in both the power and the cultural value of poetry.[16]

Given the fact that Cicero quotes some of the same Greek verses which appear in the Platonic corpus, Plato's use of certain poets seems to have created a canonizing focus upon them; i.e. Cicero became familiar with Greek poetry made famous by its inclusion in Plato's work. In the *De Divinatione* (1.52), Cicero explicitly says his translated line of the *Iliad* (9.363 = Soubiran fr. v) had previously appeared in Plato's *Crito*.[17] Cicero begins a letter to Atticus (*Att.*

---

[15] Aesopus' emotional intensity: *Sest.* 120–124, *De Or.* 3.102, *TD* 4.55; *Ad Her.* 3.34, Plutarch *Cic.* 5. On Aesopus' acting career, see: Wright 1931: 10–13, Boyle 2006: 145, Manuwald 2011: 89.

[16] On Ciceronian echoes of Plato's idea that poets are a bad influence, see De Graff 1940: 149, 152.

[17] *Div.* 1.52: *est apud Platonem Socrates ... dicens Critoni*; "in Plato, Socrates, speaking to Crito ... " The reference is to Plato's *Crito* (44b).

9.13.1) with a line of Stesichorus (Diehl fr. 11.1) which had appeared in Plato's *Phaedrus* (243a); given that this is Cicero's only citation of Stesichorus, it seems likely that Plato is the source. In general, however, Cicero used these Greek verses in different ways than Plato had initially. In the *Republic* (364c–e), Plato has Adeimantus quote passages of Greek verse precisely in order to problematize the general practice of poetic citation:

> τούτοις δὲ πᾶσιν τοῖς λόγοις μάρτυρας ποιητὰς ἐπάγονται οἱ μὲν κακίας
> πέρι, εὐπετείας διδόντες, ὡς
> "τὴν μὲν κακότητα καὶ ἰλαδὸν ἔστιν ἑλέσθαι   [Hesiod *Op.* 287–289]
> ῥηϊδίως· λείη μὲν ὁδός, μάλα δ' ἐγγύθι ναίει·
> τῆς δ' ἀρετῆς ἱδρῶτα θεοὶ προπάροιθεν ἔθηκαν"
> ... βίβλων δὲ ὅμαδον παρέχονται Μουσαίου καὶ Ὀρφέως, Σελήνης τε καὶ
> Μουσῶν ἐκγόνων, ὥς φασι, καθ' ἃς θυηπολοῦσιν, πείθοντες οὐ μόνον
> ἰδιώτας ἀλλὰ καὶ πόλεις ...

> In all these stories they call on the poets as witnesses. Some, giving indulgences for vice, quote the following:
> *"Indeed it is easy to obtain evil in abundance,*
> *smooth is the road, and it dwells very close by.*
> *But the gods have placed sweat in the path of virtue"*
> ... And they bring out a mass of books by Musaeus and Orpheus, descendants, as they say, of Selene and the Muses, and using these they make sacrifices, persuading not only individuals but cities ...

Cicero partially quoted in Greek one of the same verses of Hesiod (*Op.* 289; *Fam.* 6.18.5) which appears here; that this is not a coincidence is suggested by the fact that Cicero also quoted the Pindar (Snell fr. 213; *Att.* 13.38.2) quoted by Plato (*Rep.* 365b) shortly afterwards. While Adeimantus quotes Hesiod as part of an argument *against* the citation of poetry, Cicero's use of Hesiod (*Op.* 289) in the letter to Q. Lepta (*Fam.* 6.18.5) is a sincere endorsement of the verse as a maxim for Lepta's young son to learn.[18] In the *Republic* (365a–b), Adeimantus continues his criticism of poetic authority by quoting Pindar as an example of how young men can learn the wrong lessons from poetry:

> ταῦτα πάντα, ἔφη, ὦ φίλε Σώκρατες, τοιαῦτα καὶ τοσαῦτα λεγόμενα
> ἀρετῆς πέρι καὶ κακίας, ὡς ἄνθρωποι καὶ θεοὶ περὶ αὐτὰ ἔχουσι τιμῆς, τί
> οἰόμεθα ἀκούουσας νέων ψυχὰς ποιεῖν, ὅσοι εὐφυεῖς καὶ ἱκανοὶ ἐπὶ πάντα
> τὰ λεγόμενα ὥσπερ ἐπιπτόμενοι συλλογίσασθαι ἐξ αὐτῶν ποῖός τις ἂν
> [365b] ὢν καὶ πῇ πορευθεὶς τὸν βίον ὡς ἄριστα διέλθοι; λέγοι γὰρ ἂν ἐκ τῶν
> εἰκότων πρὸς αὐτὸν κατὰ Πίνδαρον ἐκεῖνο τὸ

---

[18] *Fam.* 6.18.5: *Lepta suauissimus ediscat Hesiodum et habeat in ore* τῆς δ' ἀρετῆς ἱδρῶτα *et cetera*, "Let sweet Lepta learn this passage of Hesiod and always have it on his lips – '*sweat on the path to virtue*' – and the rest."

"πότερον δίκᾳ τεῖχος ὕψιον   [Pindar Snell fr. 213.1–2]
ἢ σκολιαῖς ἀπάταις" ἀναβάς¹⁹
καὶ ἐμαυτὸν οὕτω περιφράξας διαβιῶ;

"How, dear Socrates," he said, "do we think the souls of young men will respond upon hearing all these and other similar talk about virtue and vice, and the honour attributed to them by men and gods? I mean those young men who are naturally clever and capable of flitting around all these sayings, as it were, and infer from them what sort of character they should have [365b], and what path they should take in order to lead the best life. For such a person might reasonably ask himself, in the words of Pindar:
'*Whether by justice*' that I ascend '*the higher tower,*
or by crooked deceit?'
and thus live out my life fenced in guarded security?"

Yet Cicero's quotation of this passage of Pindar to Atticus (*Att.* 13.38.2) does not focus upon the impact of poetry on a young mind, but instead takes at face value the moral question posed by the poet:

nunc me iuua, mi Attice, consilio,
πότερον δίκᾳ τεῖχος ὕψιον   [Pindar Snell fr. 213.1–2, 4]
id est utrum aperte hominem asperner et respuam
ἢ σκολιαῖς ἀπάταις ut enim Pindaro sic
δίχα μοι νόος ἀτρέκειαν εἰπεῖν
omnino moribus meis illud aptius, sed hoc fortasse temporibus.

Now, help me, dear Atticus, with your counsel,
"*Whether by justice the higher tower*"
i.e. whether I should openly reject the man and repudiate him
"*or by crooked deceit,*" as even to Pindar it seemed,
"*my mind is divided from saying certainly.*"
The first option altogether fits my character; the second, perhaps, the times we live in.

That Cicero intends his letter to echo the *Republic* is suggested by his invocation of Atticus (*mi Attice,* "my Atticus"), a parallel of Adeimantus' ὦ φίλε Σώκρατες, "dear Socrates" (*Rep.* 365a).²⁰ In Plato, Pindar is quoted to argue

---

¹⁹ Plato adjusts Pindar's third person singular verb ἀναβαίνει ("it climbs," Snell fr. 312.3) to the nominative participle ἀναβάς, shifting the question away from how the "race of men" (γένος ἀνδρῶν, Snell fr. 312.3) in general should conceptualize virtue, towards an individual reflection of the problem.

²⁰ In the beginning of this letter, Cicero also states that he had that morning been composing something "against the Epicureans" (*contra Epicureos, Att.* 13.38.1; referring either to *De Natura Deorum* or the *Tusculans* which Cicero was writing at the time of this letter, summer 45 BCE). Given that Cicero had been engaged in philosophical work, perhaps Plato's *Republic* had recently been in hand.

that poetry presents the possibility of immorality – in this case, the injustice of deception – which a receptive mind might internalize. Adeimantus, however, ultimately urges the moral necessity of acting without secrecy (*Rep.* 365d).[21] Cicero, in the midst of a conflict with his nephew, Quintus, considers whether to be open with his criticism, or to hide his true feelings. Since it was, in fact, Quintus who had been acting duplicitously towards his parents after their divorce for his own material gain,[22] Cicero's quotation of the Pindaric dilemma may be intended to meditate upon his nephew's youthful deceit. Ultimately, then, Cicero's engagement with Pindar is a refraction of the Platonic framework in which Cicero had initially encountered it. Yet, while Plato's use of Pindar underlines the justice of honesty, Cicero's redeployment accepts the complexity of this moral position in real life circumstances.

In addition to his engagement with Plato, Cicero also draws from the Aristotelian tradition.[23] While Plato was wary of mimetic poetry's deleterious effects, Aristotle, accepting poetry's mimetic character as "natural" (*Poet.* 1448b4–5), approached the poetic canon as a great repository of evidence. For Aristotle, poetry, a symbolic model of life produced by the human imagination, was a meaningful and self-reflexive artefact of human existence.[24] In Aristotle's view, poetry was humanity's mirror – the poetic image, observed by the human mind, evaluatively confirmed innate truths (*Poet.* 1448b15). In the *Metaphysics* (995a), Aristotle stated that for an argument to be persuasive, it must be naturalized to audience experiences via some kind of proof; poetry stood among these possible proofs due to the poet's ability to stand as a "witness" (μάρτυς).[25] As we have seen, Cicero's own conceptualization of poetry was in sympathy with the Aristotelian position: Cicero, too, found poetry to be reflective of human experience, and likewise approached the poets as "witnesses." Yet we should be careful about seeing a direct line of influence between Aristotle and Cicero. While Cicero certainly approached the Platonic corpus via the mediation of his own teachers as well as the writings of the subsequent philosophical tradition, he did also demonstrably have direct access to Platonic texts.[26] The works of Aristotle that Cicero knew,

---

[21] *Rep.* 365d: ἀλλ' ὅμως, εἰ μέλλομεν εὐδαιμονήσειν, ταύτῃ ἰτέον, ὡς τὰ ἴχνη τῶν λόγων φέρει, "Nonetheless, if we want to be happy, we follow the path where the footsteps of our words lead."

[22] *Att.* 13.38, 13.39, 13.41, 13.42; see Saller 1997: 129.

[23] On Cicero's engagement with Aristotle more generally, see Bishop 2019: 129–172.

[24] Halliwell 2012: 208–209.

[25] *Met.* 995a: οἱ δὲ μάρτυρα ἀξιοῦσιν ἐπάγεσθαι ποιητήν, "some expect a poet to be brought forward as a witness." Plato *Rep.* 364c (quoted p84) is a negative demonstration of the poetic "witness."

[26] De Graff (1940) collects Cicero's numerous Platonic citations and references. Cicero also explicitly refers to works of Plato in a book format: a book copy of Plato's *Republic* is imagined to be eaten by mice (*Div.* 2.59).

however, are now lost, and those that are known in modernity were only becoming available to Romans at the end of Cicero's lifetime; as a result, assessing direct contact between Cicero and Aristotle is more difficult.[27]

Nonetheless, we do find traces of Aristotle's influence in Cicero's poetic citations. In the *De Oratore* (3.141), Cicero explicitly stated his familiarity with Aristotelian verse citation when he repeated a tradition that Aristotle had altered a Greek verse in order to mock Isocrates:

> ... uersumque quendam Philoctetae paulo secus dixit: ille enim turpe sibi ait esse tacere, cum barbaros, hic autem, cum Isocratem pateretur dicere.

> ... Aristotle slightly changed a certain verse of the *Philocteta*: for that character says it is shameful for him to be silent when barbarians are allowed to speak. Aristotle says, when *Isocrates* is allowed to speak.

That Aristotle expressed his rivalry with Isocrates via a verse quotation is a well attested tradition: the story also appears in Cicero's contemporary, Philodemus, as well as in later sources.[28] Cicero paraphrased the quotation in Latin in the *De Oratore*, but he also knew the original Greek, which he later[29] quoted in a letter to Atticus (*Att.* 6.8.5):

> ... uideas quid nobis de triumpho cogitandum putes, ad quem amici me uocant. ego, nisi Bibulus, qui dum unus hostis in Syria fuit pedem porta non plus extulit quam domo sua, adniteretur de triumpho, aequo essem animo; nunc uero αἰσχρὸν σιωπᾶν ... [Nauck fr. 796[30]] sed explora rem totam, ut quo die congressi erimus consilium capere possimus.

> ... can you look into what you think about the consideration of a triumph, which my friends are calling me to? If it weren't for the fact that Bibulus is trying to get one, who so long as there was even one enemy in Syria did not put one step from the gates, any more than he did from his own house when he was consul, I would be at ease. But now it is "*shameful to remain silent.*" But do look into the whole thing, so that we can make a decision on the day we meet.

---

[27] Cicero (*Fin.* 3.10) writes that he visited Lucullus' villa to consult some of the Aristotelian *commentarii*. On Cicero's knowledge of Aristotle, see Gigon 1959, Huby 1989, Dix 2004, Long 2006: 290.

[28] Philodemus, II, P. Herc. 1015 + 832 col. 22+36.3–5; Diogenes Laertius 5.3 (where Aristotle criticizes Xenocrates, not Isocrates). Quintilian (*Inst.* 3.1.14) repeats Cicero's Latin paraphrase of the Greek original. Plutarch (*Mor.* 1108b) also reproduces part of the quotation in the context of philosophical rivalry but does not name Aristotle.

[29] *De Oratore* (55 BCE); *Att.* 6.8.5 (50 BCE).

[30] It is only Cicero (*De Or.* 3.141) and Quintilian (*Inst.* 3.1.14, following Cicero) who attribute the verse to "Philocteta"; the fragment has been assigned by modern editors to Euripides' *Philoctetes*.

Cicero, aware that Aristotle quoted Greek tragedy to mock his rival, redeploys the same verse against a rival of his own, M. Calpurnius Bibulus (cos. 59 BCE). Cicero only quotes part of the verse in his letter (αἰσχρὸν σιωπᾶν, "it is shameful to remain silent," *Att.* 6.8.5), but, in doing so, activates the memory of what has been omitted (*cum barbaros pateretur dicere*, "when barbarians are allowed to speak," *De Or.* 3.141), effectively allowing him to call Bibulus a "barbarian." Lurking behind Cicero's rivalry, as governor of Cilicia, with Bibulus, governor of Syria, over the grant of a triumph is the classic rivalry of Aristotle and Isocrates.

Cicero repeats other verses originally discussed by Aristotle, which had thereby entered the canon of philosophical exemplars. In the *Tusculans* (5.101), Cicero partially quotes the epitaph of Sardanapallus,[31] translated into Latin:[32]

> quo modo igitur iucunda uita potest esse, a qua absit prudentia, absit
> moderatio? ex quo Sardanapalli, opulentissimi Syriae regis, error agnoscitur,
> qui incidi iussit in busto:
> *haec habeo, quae edi quaeque exsaturata libido*　　　　　　[Soubiran fr. x]
> *hausit; at illa iacent multa et praeclara relicta.*
> quid aliud, inquit Aristoteles, in bouis, non in regis sepulcro inscriberes?

> How can a life without good sense or moderation be sweet? On this point,
> we recognize the mistake of Sardanapallus, the most luxuriant king of Syria,
> who ordered these lines carved on his tomb:
> *"These things I possess: what I have eaten, and what my sated desire*
> *has swallowed up; but these many and excellent things are left behind."*
> What else, Aristotle asks, would you inscribe on the tomb of a cow, not that of
> a king?

The legendary Sardanapallus, a fictive amalgamation of several historical Assyrian kings,[33] was in the Greco-Roman imagination an infamous orientalist projection of excess characterized by luxuriance and "effeminacy."[34] The original Greek of the epitaph quoted by Cicero in Latin (*TD* 5.101) is transmitted by Greek sources, some of whom were working in the same moralizing philosophical tradition.[35] Dio Chrysostom (4.135), for example, noted that those

---

[31] The name appears in Greek with a variety of spellings: Σαρδα(νά)παλ(λ)ος, see Frahm 2003: 39.
[32] Cicero also paraphrases the content of the epitaph in the *De Finibus* (2.106), where he again notes Aristotle's engagement with the verses.
[33] Frahm 2003: 39.
[34] Frahm 2003: 39–40, Rollinger 2017: 576–578, Bosak-Schroeder 2020: 61–63.
[35] The full version of the Greek epitaph appears in the *Greek Anthology* (16.27, cf. 7.326 in its shorter form). The epitaph is also quoted in Greek by Polybius (8.12.4), Diodorus Siculus (2.23.3), Strabo (14.5.9), Dio Chrysostom (4.135), Plutarch (*Mor.* 330f, 546b), and Athenaeus (8.335f–336b).

who let their love of pleasure conquer their love of honour would "frequently quote" (πολλάκις προφέρεται) the epitaph of Sardanapallus:

ὁ μὲν γὰρ καταφρονεῖ τῆς δόξης καὶ λῆρον ἡγεῖται καὶ τὸ τοῦ
Σαρδαναπάλλου προφέρεται πολλάκις ἐλεγεῖον,
"τόσσ᾽ ἔχω ὅσσ᾽ ἔφαγον καὶ ἐφύβρισα καὶ μετ᾽ ἔρωτος
τέρπν᾽ ἔπαθον· τὰ δὲ λοιπὰ καὶ ὄλβια πάντα λέλειπται"

For the one who hates fame and thinks it superficial, often cites the epitaph of Sardanapallus:
"*These things I possess: what I have eaten and vaunted over and, with love, the pleasures I experienced; but all these remaining, blessed things are left behind.*"

Plutarch (*Mor.* 546b) reports that the verses, with their philosophically abhorrent celebration of physical pleasures, were rewritten by Crates the Cynic in order to celebrate intellectual pursuits instead:

καὶ ὁ Κράτης . . . ἀντέγραψε τό:
ταῦτ᾽ ἔχω ὅσσ᾽ ἔμαθον καὶ ἐφρόντισα καὶ μετὰ Μουσῶν
σέμν᾽ ἐδάην.
καλὸς γὰρ ὁ τοιοῦτος ἔπαινος καὶ ὠφέλιμος καὶ διδάσκων τὰ χρήσιμα καὶ
τὰ συμφέροντα θαυμάζειν καὶ ἀγαπᾶν ἀντὶ τῶν κενῶν καὶ περιττῶν.

Crates . . . rewrote the verses:
"*These things I possess: what I have through study and thought and, with the Muses, the serious things I have learned.*"[36]
This kind of praise is good and helpful, teaching wonder and reverence of the useful and profitable rather than of the empty and superfluous.

Due, in all likelihood, to Aristotle's canonical engagement, the epitaph of Sardanapallus became well known to Greco-Roman audiences.[37] By choosing to frame his use of the Sardanapallus epitaph as a deliberate citation of Aristotle's criticism, Cicero demonstrates that this quotation is essentially an invocation of philosophy, not poetry.[38] References to Sardanapallus do indeed occur in the extant works of Aristotle (*Eud. Eth.* 1216a; *Nic. Eth.* 1295b), but the verses themselves do not. It has been

---

[36] The full version of Crates' verses appears in the *Greek Anthology* (7.326), following the epitaph of Sardanapallus (7.325, cf. 16.27) which it parodies.

[37] Significantly, there is also evidence of later Stoic interest in the Sardanapallus epitaph: Athenaeus (8.336a) attributes the citation to the Stoic Chrysippus; see Rollinger 2017: 578. Cicero, heavily influenced by Stoic citational practices, could have quoted the epitaph from Chrysippus instead of Aristotle.

[38] Cf. *TD* 5.25 where Cicero quotes in Latin a verse from the Greek playwright, Chaeremon: *uitam regit fortuna, non sapientia*, "it is fortune that orders life, not wisdom" (Soubiran fr. v = Nauck fr. 2); Cicero does so to note the fact that Theophrastus was criticized for approving this "maxim" (*sententia*) in the *Callisthenes*, a treatise on grief.

suggested that the Sardanapallus epitaph was quoted in Aristotle's *Protrepticus*, known today only in fragments, a work which influenced Cicero's own *Hortensius*.[39]

Cicero was clearly influenced to a certain extent by the Platonic and Aristotelian traditions, yet, it is the Stoic attitude towards poetic citation which has perhaps the greatest presence in Cicero's works. While it is clear that almost all branches of Greco-Roman philosophy engaged to some degree with poetry, the Stoics were particularly known for their philosophical use of poetic texts.[40] Indeed, the Stoic Chrysippus quoted from the tragedies of Euripides so much that one of his books is jokingly referred to as "Chrysippus'*Medea*."[41] Cicero reflects the Stoic citational practice in his own works in a number of ways. He knew, for example, that Chrysippus was fond of Euripides, and in the *Tusculans* (*TD* 3.59) echoed Carneades' criticism of Chrysippus' love of a particular Euripidean passage by translating it and inserting it into his own work.[42] Cicero also noted that Stoics were generally in the habit of quoting poetry.[43] Cicero deliberately reflected this practice in his philosophical treatises, where it is the Stoic characters among the *dramatis personae* who quote poetry extensively: Balbus in *De Natura Deorum* Book 2; Quintus in *De Divinatione* Book 1.[44] Each of these figures represent the Stoic view that literature, though "fictive," nonetheless contains within it essential truths about reality.[45] Quintus (*Div.* 1.12) claims, for example, that his Stoic beliefs can be justified by the fact that certain correlations of

---

[39] Cicero *TD* 5.101 and *Fin.* 2.106 are collected as a fragment of Aristotle's *Protrepticus* (fr. 16 Ross); see Johnson and Hutchinson 2017: 79–80.

[40] Čulík-Baird 2018: 648–651.   [41] Diog. Laert. 7.180.

[42] *TD* 3.59 quotes Euripides' *Hypsipyle* (Nauck fr. 757 = Soubiran fr. vii) in Latin.

[43] Cicero (*TD* 2.26) criticizes the Stoic Dionysius for quoting poetry badly. Augustine (*Civ. Dei* 5.8 = *De Fato* fr. 3) preserves Cicero's Latin translation of verses from the *Odyssey* (18.136–137 = Soubiran fr. ix), along with Cicero's comment that the "Stoics were in the habit of quoting them" (*Stoicos . . . uersus solere usurpare*) as evidence of the operation of fate.

[44] An exception is the figure of Cato in *De Finibus* Book 3; there are, strikingly, no poetic quotations in this book. Perhaps Cicero felt that it was not suitable to represent the austere Cato engaging in this practice. On Cicero and Cato's examination of books in *De Finibus* 3, see Frampton 2016.

[45] After quoting Ilia's dream from Ennius' *Annales* (Skutsch 34–50; *Div.* 1.40–41), Quintus adds that "even though the dream is fiction written by a poet, it is not different from how dreams actually are" (*etiamsi ficta sunt a poeta, non absunt tamen a consuetudine somniorum*). Cicero's Academic response in *De Divinatione* Book 2 is grounded in the belief that poetry is "made up" (*commenticius*, *Div.* 2.27, 2.80, 2.113), and therefore has no place in philosophical argumentation.

cause and effect have been observed by humans over a long period, observations which can be found embedded in literature:

> obseruata sunt haec tempore immenso et euentis animaduersa et notata. nihil est autem quod non longinquitas temporum excipiente memoria prodendisque monumentis[46] efficere atque assequi possit.

> These signs have been observed over a vast period of time, and they have been recognized and documented according to their outcomes. There is nothing which the stretch of time cannot accomplish and attain when human memory has excerpted it and it has been preserved by writing.

Literary sources present evidence of historically repeating patterns: if a certain phenomenon occurs consistently, then there must, the Stoics argue, be a rational law governing its behavior: human experience of nature's rationality is present like a residue in the literary products made by man.[47] Even though the poet may not intend to convey Stoic ideas, the study of verse by a Stoic philosopher reveals Stoic theory at its core. Zeno, for example, etymologizes Hesiod's "Chaos" as "primal water" from the homophony between the Greek word "chaos" (χάος) and the verb "to pour" (ἀπὸ τοῦ χέεσθαι, *SVF* 1.103–104).[48] Such an etymology demonstrates that, even though Hesiod, obviously, could not know the specific theories of physics that, according to Stoics at least, structure the cosmos, his raw perception of their effects is nonetheless rendered by his poetic activity, and could be parsed out using the tools of Stoic analysis.

The Stoic method of poetic study, which, in particular, applied etymology to individual words found in the poetic record, was alive at Rome during the late Republic due to the influence of the Roman philologist and Stoic, L. Aelius Stilo, teacher of both Cicero and Varro, as I discuss in section 3.1. In addition to the fact that Cicero dramatized Stoic attitudes towards poetry in his philosophical works, both in the crafting of character and in the details of poetic analysis, there are a number of other indications that Stoic influence filtered through Cicero's works in less immediately visible ways. In March 49 BCE, Cicero wrote to Atticus (*Att.* 9.2a.2) and quoted a Greek verse to communicate his dread in the face of civil war:

> sin cum potuero non uenero tum erit inimicus, quod ego non eo uereor ne mihi noceat, quid enim faciet?

---

[46] That Homer and Ennius are included in the category of *monumenta* (*Div.* 1.87–88), demonstrates that Quintus means for this term to include evidence from poetry as well as other cultural records.

[47] Čulík-Baird 2018: 649.

[48] Long 1992: 62. That knowledge of such Stoic engagement with poetry had filtered into Roman intellectual practices can be demonstrated by the fact that Varro (*LL* 5.19) gives Zeno's Stoic etymology of χάος, pairing it with quotations from Ennian tragedy (*TrRF* II 34; 83; 149).

τίς δ᾽ ἐστὶ δοῦλος τοῦ θανεῖν ἄφροντις ὤν;　　　　[Nauck fr. 958]
sed quia ingrati animi crimen horreo.

But if I don't go when I can, then he [= Pompey] will become hostile. I'm
not afraid that he will harm me – what can he do?
"Is he a slave who does not fear death?"
I'm afraid because I dread the charge of an ungrateful spirit.

Plutarch (*Mor.* 34b), who attributed the verse to Euripides, used it as an
exemplification of Chrysippus' citational theory, namely that the "statements of the poets can be given a wider application," i.e., that poetry can
be used metaphorically.[49] Cicero, having encountered the Euripidean
verse in the context of his Stoic training, redeployed the line during
a moment of real life drama. In his commentary to the fragments of
Ciceronian verse, Jean Soubiran (1972: 63) remarked that it is a "remark-
able coincidence" that we have the corresponding Greek for so many of
Cicero's Latin verse translations.[50] On the contrary, that these verses are
quoted by later Greek writers is not a coincidence at all but rather
evidence of a continuing Greek philosophical tradition into which
Cicero dipped his toe when he translated parts of it into Latin.
Plutarch, who regularly provides the Greek of verses translated by
Cicero into Latin, frequently gives an indication of the philosophical
context in which Cicero must have initially encountered them.
Furthermore, Plutarch attests to the fact that several of the citations
made by Cicero which appear without explicit philosophical reference
may be traced back to the Stoic citational practice.[51]

　　While Cicero was evidently drawing upon a number of Greek philosophical traditions, it is striking that Latin poetry has such a prominent role
in his own philosophical works. As Cicero makes clear (*Fin.* 1.4) there were
Romans who did not think Latin capable of expressing philosophical ideas,

---

[49] Plutarch *Mor.* 34b: τὴν δ᾽ ἐπὶ πλέον τῶν λεγομένων χρῆσιν ὑπέδειξεν ὀρθῶς ὁ Χρύσιππος, ὅτι δεῖ
μετάγειν καὶ διαβιβάζειν ἐπὶ τὰ ὁμοειδῆ τὸ χρήσιμον, "Chrysippus has correctly demonstrated that
the poet's statements can be given a wider application, saying that what is useful should be taken
over and made to apply to similar concepts." Plutarch (*ib.*) then cites Hesiod (*Op.* 348; cf. *Att.*
13.12.3, *Op. 350*) and Euripides (Nauck fr. 958).

[50] Soubiran (1972: 63) does take this phenomenon as evidence of a citational "*koine*," but does not
consider the philosophical aspect.

[51] A Greek proverb (*CPG* I p314) quoted by Cicero (*Att.* 1.19.10) was, according to Plutarch (*Life of
Aratus* 1027), also used by Chrysippus. A second Greek proverb (*CPG* II p759) which Cicero quoted
and described as "falsely ascribed to Hesiod" is also quoted by Plutarch (*Mor.* 1034e), who noted
Stoic interest in it. In the *Tusculans* (3.76), Cicero translates Aeschylus *PV* 377–380; Plutarch quotes
the original Greek in the *Consolation to Apollonius* (2). Since both Cicero and Plutarch use the
citation as part of consolation, a common philosophical source is very likely.

and yet Cicero, drawing upon the Latin poets as parallels to his own intellectual labour, committed to the possibility of Latin's expressive capability by using poetry composed in this language to exemplify philosophical precepts. While some of Cicero's poetic quotations do demonstrably derive from the Greek philosophical tradition, Cicero translated them into Latin in a manner which echoed his poetic precursors, thereby aligning Greek poetic material with the aesthetic and cultural standards of Rome.

2.2 Poetry and Oratory

The study of poetry was a key component in the education of the Roman orator.[52] In the *De Oratore* (1.154), Cicero describes a training game in which the orator memorizes a speech of Gaius Gracchus or a poem of Ennius, and tries to give an oration on the same topic without reusing any of the same words.[53] The training game anecdote demonstrates an alignment between the classics of oratory and verse, and suggests that, when it came to developing style and persuasiveness through imitation, the genre of the emulated text was not limited to oratory or even to prose.[54] Cicero (*De Or.* 1.158) goes on to say that poets, historians, and all good writers must be read closely and thoroughly analyzed:

> legendi etiam poetae, cognoscendae historiae, omnium bonarum artium doctores atque scriptores eligendi et peruolutandi et exercitationis causa laudandi, interpretandi, corrigendi, uituperandi . . .

> We ought to read even the poets, familiarize ourselves with the histories, select the experts in and writers of all good arts; we must read them often and, in training ourselves, we must praise, interpret, correct, and strongly critique them . . .

In other words, Cicero imagines a vigorous dissection of the best literary objects in whatever form they come, breaking them down under intense scrutiny in order to build up an oratorical style from composite parts. The

---

[52] See North 1952 on the role of poetry in Greek oratorical education.

[53] Cf. *Rhet. ad Her.* (4.2.4) which recommends taking *exempla* from either Ennius or Gracchus. Gracchus and Ennius as a pairing persisted in the oratorical curriculum beyond the Republican period: Fronto suggests to Marcus Aurelius, who had been reading the speeches of Gaius Gracchus alongside other "old orators" (*ueteres oratores*, *Ep.* 3.17.3), that reading Ennius' tragedies would help him write "more elevated" (*sublimiter*) verse.

[54] Subconscious internalization of exemplars, considered a benefit by Quintilian (*Inst.* 2.7.3), can have negative results. It is difficult, Cicero says (*De Or.* 1.154), to express the same concept better than the imitated orator or poet: you either use identical words (and learn nothing), or inferior ones.

author of the *Rhetorica ad Herennium* (4.3.10) similarly urges a critical approach to reading oratory and poetry: anyone can read orations and poems and enjoy them, but true understanding comes with the critical ability to see how oratorical and poetic effects are produced.[55]

Quintilian (*Inst.* 2.7.1) writes that young students of oratory should not learn their own compositions by heart for performance but should instead spend their time memorizing parts of famous orations, histories, or passages from other kinds of "books" (*uoluminum, Inst.* 2.7.3), which includes the "reading of poets" (*lectio poetarum, Inst.* 10.1.27), because doing so is better practice for the memory. Having memorized such exemplars, these students will be able to correct their own compositions because "they will always have good models to imitate within themselves" (*semperque habebunt intra se quod imitentur, Inst.* 2.7.3). Such internalization means that they will "unconsciously" (*non sentientes, Inst.* 2.7.3) reproduce the style of the passages which they have studied.[56] Literary quotations also grant an "added authority" (*plus auctoritatis, Inst.* 2.7.4) to their own orations.[57] Quintilian therefore encouraged such a deep dependence upon literary exemplars that literary citations, so thoroughly ingrained, could occur deliberately or even without the knowledge of the speaker.

Roman rhetorical theorists identify the exercises required for the degree of literary absorption which Quintilian recommended. The *Rhetorica ad Herennium* (4.7) describes the practice of copying out Ennian *sententiae* and messenger speeches from Pacuvius:

> . . . si Ennii de tragoediis uelis sententias eligere aut de Pacuuianis nuntios, sed quia plane rudis id facere nemo poterit, cum feceris te litteratissimum putes, ineptus sis, propterea quod id facile faciat quiuis mediocriter litteratus.

> . . . if you want to excerpt the *sententiae* from the tragedies of Ennius or the messenger speeches from Pacuvius and think yourself a literary elite when you do so, since a completely inexperienced person could not do this, then you're a fool, because anyone even moderately learned could do it.

---

[55] Cf. *Or.* 173.

[56] Similarly, Cicero (*De Or.* 3.39) says that eloquence is polished by "knowledge of literature" (*scientia litterarum*), which includes "the reading of orators and poets" (*legendis oratoribus et poetis*); he adds that students of "older writers" (*illi ueteres*) will not be able to avoid speaking good Latin, even if they try.

[57] The *Rhet. ad Her.* (4.2.17) applies an epistemological argument to citation: testimony is introduced to prove a point, but such testimony must itself be trustworthy (i.e. it must not itself require further proof). The best testimonies are those "taken from the most approved orators or poets" (*a probatissimis oratoribus aut poetis sumpta*).

From the perspective of this author, the memorization of selections from the tragedies of Ennius or Pacuvius is not index of great learning but rather the bare minimum for an educated person. Behind this statement is the implication that there would be students at Rome who found the memorization of poetry quite laboursome.[58] The author also sheds some light on how Roman tragedy might be studied. "Ennian *sententiae*" suggests the memorization of gnomic statements (i.e. wise utterances, proverbial sayings) detached from dramatic context for universal applicability. On the other hand, the study of "messenger speeches" (*nuntios*) from Pacuvius' tragedies indicates knowledge of how different kinds of speech functioned on the Roman stage. The role of the messenger in Greco-Roman drama, who conveyed offstage action that had not been witnessed by the audience, might, for example, be a useful template for the *narratio* of a forensic speech, where the orator was tasked with vividly, briefly, and plausibly (e.g. *Rhet.* 1.14) describing the events of the case to his own audience, who had also not experienced them.

Roman rhetorical treatises do in fact draw heavily from the Roman stage to exemplify the various partitions of oratory. The *Rhetorica ad Herennium* and Cicero's youthful *De Inventione* each illustrate the divisions of oratory with citations from Latin comedy and tragedy. In fact, these two works sometimes quote identical verses to illustrate the same oratorical concept, demonstrating that they arise out of a shared didactic tradition.[59] The *Rhetorica* and Cicero each use the opening lines of Ennius' *Medea* (*TrRF* II 89) as an example of a "remote cause," a type of flawed argumentation which locates the cause of present action too far in the past.[60] The *Rhetorica* (2.34) presents a longer verse quotation as well as a fuller explanation of the rhetorical fault:

> item uitiosa expositio est quae nimium longe repetitur ... hic id quod extremum dictum est satis fuit exponere, ne Ennium et ceteros poetas imitemur, quibus hoc modo loqui concessum est:
> *utinam ne in nemore Pelio securibus*   [*TrRF* II 89]
> *caesa accidisset abiegna ad terram trabes,*
> *neue inde nauis inchoandi exordium*
> *coepisset, quae nunc nominatur nomine*
> *Argo, quia Argiui in ea delecti uiri*
> *uecti petebant pellem inauratam arietis*

---

[58] And painful. Both Horace (*Epistle* 2.1.70–71) and Cicero (*Pis.* 73) testify to the fact that corporal punishment had a role in the study of Latin poetry in the ancient Roman classroom.

[59] Including specific citational pairings: *Inv.* 1.83 = *Rhet.* 2.42; *Inv.* 1.90 = *Rhet.* 2.40; *Inv.* 1.91 = *Rhet.* 2.34; *Inv.* 1.91 = *Rhet.* 2.39; see North 1952: 29 n88.

[60] This passage of Ennius' *Medea* (*TrRF* II 89), the opening lines of the tragedy (cf. Eur. *Medea* 1–10), are quoted a number of times by Roman authors, see *TrRF* II pp188–191. *Rhet.* 2.34 is the fullest citation of the passage; as a result, it is this text which appears as the definitive fragment in editions of Ennius.

Colchis imperio regis Peliae per dolum:
nam numquam era errans mea domo efferret pedem
Medea, animo aegro, amore saeuo saucia.
nam hic satis erat dicere, si id modo quod satis esset curarent poetae:
utinam ne era errans mea domo efferret pedem
Medea, animo aegro, amore saeuo saucia.

Again, an exposition which seeks its cause too far back is faulty ... Here
what is said last was enough for an exposition, lest we imitate Ennius and the
other poets, who are allowed to speak in the following way:
"Would that in the Pelian grove with axes
cut the firwood had not fallen to the ground as timber,
nor from there a beginning of inventing the ship
commenced, which is now named with the name
Argo because Argives, choice men, in it
were carried, seeking the ram's golden fleece
at Colchis, commanded by King Pelias, tricked:
for never would my mistress, wandering, set her foot outside the house,
Medea, sick at heart, wounded with a savage love."
If the poets cared about saying only what is enough, they would say only this:
"Would that not my mistress, wandering, set her foot outside the house,
Medea, sick at heart, wounded with savage love."

Ennius began his argument too far off in the past for oratorical toler-
ance: he started with the invention of seafaring and the voyage of the
Argo, when he could simply have begun with Medea herself, and the
love for Jason that led her to leave her home. The *Rhetorica* suggests that
it would have been better for Ennius to omit seven lines of verse. Such
a correction is not only an excision but also a foreshortening: the author
combines the first part of the opening line (*utinam ne*) with the remainder of the penultimate line cited (*era errans* ... etc.) to combine into
a new first line for Ennius' *Medea*.[61] The discussion of the *Medea* in this
oratorical context demonstrates a point stressed again and again by
Cicero: poetry and oratory have much in common,[62] but poets can go

---

[61] Cicero himself truncates verse quotations like this: e.g. *De Or.* 2.327 where Terence *Andria* 117 and
     128–129 are combined. This example clearly derives from the oratorical schools, given that it is
     immediately preceded (*De Or.* 2.326) by *Andria* 51, which also appears at *Inv.* 1.27 and 1.33.
[62] Poets have a *proxima cognatio* ("kindred connection") with orators, and orators have different styles
     in the same way that tragedians differ from one another in style (*De Or.* 3.27). Orators and poets use
     the same metaphorical "hair curlers and rouge" (*cincinnis ac fuco*) in eloquence and performance (*De
     Or.* 3.100). Despite the fact that some think that Latin is a deficient language compared to Greek,
     Cicero insists that there are good Latin orators and poets (*Fin.* 1.10). Following Theophrastus,
     Cicero believed that orators could learn prose rhythm from the poets (*De Or.* 3.184–185); indeed,

beyond the limits set for orators.[63] However, the citation of Ennius' *Medea* as a negative *exemplum*, i.e. as an example of what orators should *not* do, is still an instance of citation for didactic purposes. Assessment of Ennius' poetry, even a negative one, is guidance for the orator in training.

In the *De Inventione* (1.91), Cicero cites the same passage of Ennius' *Medea* (*TrRF* II 89) as example of the remote cause, but does so very briefly:[64]

> remotum est quod ultra quam satis est petitur . . . huiusmodi est illa quoque conquestio:
> *utinam ne in nemore Pelio securibus*   [*TrRF* II 89, 1–2]
> *caesae accedissent abiegnae[65] ad terram trabes.*
> longius enim repetita est quam res postulabat.

> A remote cause is one which is sought from farther away than is necessary . . .
> of this kind is also the following complaint:
> "*Would that in the Pelian grove with axes*
> *cut the firwood had not fallen to the ground as timber.*"
> For it was sought from farther off than the matter demands.

Cicero's brevity suggests that he is quoting an example which is well known; he does not feel the need to provide citational scaffolding for his reader to understand the point being made. Such brevity and lack of explanation may indicate that Cicero is here citing another rhetorical handbook where the quotation appeared, possibly even the *Rhetorica* itself. Quintilian (5.10.84) would later quote Ennius' *Medea* as an example of a remote cause because he had read it in earlier rhetorical treatises.[66]

Cicero (*De Or.* 3.183) quotes Ennius' *Andromacha* (*TrRF* II 23) to exemplify the cretic rhythm which orators also used.

[63] The orator should not follow the poets in everything: poets have greater "freedom of diction" (*libertas uerborum*) and greater "license with poetic figures" (*licentia figurarum,* Quint. *Inst.* 10.1.28). Poetry is more tightly constrained by metre than oratory (*De Or.* 3.184, Quint. *Inst.* 10.1.29). Neologisms are more tolerable in poetry than oratory (*Or.* 163–164).

[64] Cicero also cites the first two lines of Ennius' *Medea* (*TrRF* II 89) in the *Topica* (61) as an example of a different kind of cause: *sine quo non,* "without which something does not happen." This is a different rhetorical interpretation from that made by *Rhet.* 2.34 and *Inv.* 1.91, which both take the felling of the fir tree to make the Argo as irrelevant to the present narrative of the *Medea*. *Top.* 61 instead insists on the importance of this action, since without the invention of the ship, none of the subsequent events could have happened. The deployment of the same verses of Ennius to exemplify incompatible oratorical precepts demonstrates the malleability of the material: fertile ground for pedagogy.

[65] For the differences in the Latin text of the fragment, see *TrRF* II pp192–196.

[66] In this passage, Quintilian draws on examples he finds in Cicero (*Inst.* 5.10.85 quotes *Topica* 12), so he may have quoted Ennius' *Medea* from *Inv.* 1.91.

While Cicero's rhetorical analysis of the *Medea* passage is light, there are also cases where Cicero's *De Inventione* expands upon the *Rhetorica ad Herennium*. The *Rhetorica* (1.13) describes the different categories of *narratio*, i.e. the laying out of the facts of a case by the orator, as *fabula*, *historia,* and *argumentum*:

> id quod in negotiorum expositione positum est tres habet partes: fabulam, historiam, argumentum. fabula est quae neque ueras neque ueri similes continet res, ut eae sunt quae tragoediis traditae sunt. historia est gesta res, sed ab aetatis nostrae memoria remota. argumentum est ficta res quae tamen fieri potuit, uelut argumenta comoediarum.

> There are three types of narrative possible for laying out the facts of a case: *fabula* ("a tale"), *historia* ("history"), *argumentum* ("a proposition"). *Fabula* is the term applied to a narrative in which the events are not true and have no verisimilitude, like the tales which are passed down in tragedy. *Historia* is an account of actual occurrences remote from the recollection of our own age. *Argumentum* is a fictitious narrative which nevertheless could have occurred, just as in the propositions of comedy.

Cicero discusses identical narrative categories in the *De Inventione* (1.27) in identical language; however, instead of attributing each narrative type to a poetic genre (tragedy; comedy) in general terms, he gives explicit poetic citations from those genres:

> fabula est in qua nec uerae nec ueri similes res continentur, cuiusmodi est: *angues ingentes alites, iuncti iugo* . . .	[Pacuvius' *Medus* Schierl fr. 171] historia est gesta res, ab aetatis nostrae memoria remota; quod genus: *Appius indixit Karthaginiensibus bellum.*	[Ennius' *Annales* Skutsch 216] argumentum est ficta res, quae tamen fieri potuit. huiusmodi apud Terentium: *nam is postquam excessit ex ephebis* . . .	[Terence's *Andria* 51]

> *Fabula* is the term applied to a narrative in which the events are not true and have no verisimilitude, for example:
> "*Huge winged dragons yoked to a car . . .*"
> *Historia* is an account of actual occurrences remote from the recollection of our own age, as:
> "*War on men of Carthage Appius decreed.*"
> *Argumentum* is a fictitious narrative which nevertheless could have occurred. An example from Terence:
> "*For after he had left the school of youth . . .*"

The similarity of the two passages can only suggest a shared source, which in itself reveals an intellectual tradition of comment upon poetry in a rhetorical context. These two passages also reveal that theorization of the relationship between reality (events which actually do or do not occur) and narrative (the crafting of a story which orders events and grants them meaning) in Roman oratorical training drew from poetry. A definition of oratorical *narratio* incidentally reveals a Roman attitude to different poetic genres: tragedy contains events which are not actually possible (winged dragons); history (interestingly defined with Ennius' *Annales*, not a prose account) tells the story of ancient events; and comedy tells a story which is not true, but is very close to the truth. At the core of this is an understanding that no verbal utterance can contain the entire truth of the reality to which it refers; poetry and oratory each relate to the truth in different degrees. Poetry may often be closer to "fiction" than "fact," but the narrative perspective presented by Cicero and the *Rhetorica* reveals that despite its fictive nature, poetry can still reflect aspects of reality; like the *argumentum* of comedy, it can be like the truth, even if it is not strictly true.[67]

Roman poetry told stories, presented a variety of characters, and provoked a range of emotions. The Roman rhetorical theorists understood that poetry[68] could therefore be beneficial in the training of orators, whose purpose was to persuade through convincing narrative, construction of character, and emotional manipulation. Quintilian (*Inst.* 1.8.7) writes that comedy was capable of eloquence because it includes "every character and every emotion" (*omnes et personae et adfectus*);[69] as a result it was "useful for boys" to study (*usum in pueris*). For Quintilian (*Inst.* 1.8.11–12), Cicero himself was the prime example of how impactful Latin poetry could be on a Roman orator:

> nam praecipue quidem apud Ciceronem, frequenter tamen apud Asinium etiam et ceteros qui sunt proximi, uidemus Enni Acci Pacuui Lucili Terenti Caecili et aliorum inseri uersus, summa non eruditionis modo gratia sed etiam iucunditatis, cum poeticis uoluptatibus aures a forensi asperitate respirant. quibus accedit non mediocris utilitas, cum sententiis eorum uelut quibusdam testimoniis quae proposuere confirment.

> For especially in Cicero, but also frequently in Gaius Asinius Pollio and even in the other orators who were his contemporaries, we see that the verses of Ennius, Accius, Pacuvius, Lucilius, Terence, Caecilius Statius, and others

---

[67] Quintilian (*Inst.* 12.42) explicitly notes that while the poetry is "invented" (*ficta*), it is nonetheless trusted for its moral instruction.

[68] While drama (tragedy, comedy; even mime, e.g. *De Or.* 2.255) is generally the focus of the rhetorical treatises, epic could also be cited as an exemplar, e.g. *De Inv.* 1.91.

[69] Cf. Quint. *Inst.* 10.1.27: *namque ab his in rebus spiritus et in uerbis sublimitas et in adfectibus motus omnis et in personis decor petitur*, "from the poets we can get inspiration, sublime language, every kind of emotion, and the elegance of well-crafted characters."

are grafted into their speeches, not only evidence of the exemplary beauty of their erudition, but even of their pleasure, since the ears are refreshed from the weariness of the courtroom by the sweetness of poetry.[70] Poetic citation is very useful, since its sentiments strengthen what we orators propose, as though it were witness testimony.

Cicero, as his youthful *De Inventione* shows, had learned to study and quote poetry in the oratorical classroom, and his mature use of the technique became an exemplar for the generations of orators which followed. As Quintilian notes, Cicero was not the only orator who cited poetry: the verses of Republican poets were "grafted" (*inseri*) by Gaius Asinius Pollio, among others, into his speeches.

In addition, then, to the study of poetry as part of oratorical training, the explicit citation of poetry was also one of the rhetorical strategies available to the orator. The quotation of poetry is identified as a rhetorical technique in oratorical treatises, particularly in connection with wit or humour. Cicero writes (*De Or.* 2.255) that the most effective way to generate humour is to say something unexpected: "when we expect one thing, and another is said" (*cum aliud exspectamus, aliud dicitur*).[71] The *Rhetorica ad Herennium* (1.10) included the citation of verse alongside the use of humour to make a fatigued audience pay attention. Quintilian (*Inst.* 6.3.96) exemplified the strategy of unexpected humour by citing Cicero's citation of Ennius:[72]

> dissimulauit Cicero cum Sex. Annalis testis reum laesisset et instaret identidem accusator: dic, M. Tulli, si quid potes de Sexto Annali; uersus enim dicere coepit de libro Enni Annali sexto:
> *quis potis ingentis causas[73] euoluere belli?*   [Skutsch 164]

> Cicero subverted expectation when Sextus Annalis the witness had damaged his client and the prosecutor continuously harassed him: "Cicero, say what you can about Sextus Annalis." Cicero responded with a verse from Ennius' *Annales* Book 6:
> "*Who is able to unroll the causes of this great war?*"

---

[70] In the *Pro Archia* (12–13), Cicero also says that one of the functions of poetry is to relax and delight the wearied mind. Quintilian (*Inst.* 10.1.27) endorses Cicero's position in the *Pro Archia*.

[71] Cicero (*De Or.* 255) exemplifies the subversion of expectation for comic effect with a citation of a mime by Novius.

[72] On this passage, see North 1952: 8; 23. Discussing how an orator may use "poetic fables" (*ex poeticis fabulis*), Quintilian (*Inst.* 5.11.8) quotes a passage of Cicero's *Pro Milone* (8), which has been interpreted as an allusion to Ennius' *Eumenides* (see Jocelyn 1969a: 284).

[73] Quintilian (6.39.6) gives *causas*. Later sources (Macrob. 6.1.18, Serv. *Aen.* 9.526, Diom. 1.385) give *oras*; see Skutsch 1985: 329.

Cicero, asked to say what he "can" (*potes*) about the man "Sextus Annalis,"
chooses to interpret this as a reference to the "Sixth Annal," i.e. Ennius'
Annales Book 6. Cicero also quotes an Ennian verse which undermines the
idea that anyone "can" (*potis*) speak about such a matter.

Verse quotation for humorous effect is also described in Caesar Strabo's
excursus on wit in Cicero's *De Oratore* (2.257), where he quotes from the
comic poet, Caecilius Statius:[74]

> saepe etiam uersus facete interponitur, uel ut est, uel paululum immutatus ut
> Stati a Scauro stomachante: ex quo sunt nonnulli, qui tuam legem de ciuitate
> natam, Crasse, dicant:
> *st, tacete, quid hoc clamoris? quibus nec mater, nec pater,* [Ribbeck 245–246]
> *tanta confidentia? auferte istam enim superbiam.*

> Often even a verse is wittily introduced either as it is or changed a little, like
> the verse of Caecilius Statius quoted by a fuming Scaurus. There are some
> who would say that your own law on citizenship, Crassus, came out of this:
> *"Sh, shut up! What's this shouting? From men without mother, without father*
> *such boldness? Away with your arrogance."*

Caesar Strabo here gives an example of humorous verse citation from a recent
political situation,[75] wherein M. Aemilius Scaurus (cos. 115 BCE), angry at the
illegal adoption of Roman citizenship by Italians, quoted two verses of
Caecilius Statius.[76] These verses tell Scaurus' opponents to "shut up" (*st,
tacete!*) and accuse them of having "no mother, no father" (*nec mater, nec
pater*), i.e. of being illegitimate. The apparent "wit" of the quotation does not
come (at least solely) from the fact that the verses were cited from a Roman
comedy, but from the aptness of the verses to describe the tension between the
hostile Scaurus and the imagined Italian "bastards," perceived to be usurping
Roman civil rights.

We learn here (*De Or.* 2.257) that a line of verse can be "set within"
(*interponitur*) a speech either "as it is" (*ut est*), or "a little bit changed"
(*paululum immutatus*), or with "some other part of verse" (*aliqua pars uersus*).
The original Latin verse does not need to be quoted verbatim: in fact, part of
the humour comes from deliberate alterations (or subversions) of the original
line. Caesar Strabo (*De Or.* 2.257) gives a second example of witty verse
citation, drawing from one of the key characters of the *De Oratore* itself,

---

[74] On Caesar Strabo's discussion of wit in the *De Oratore*, see Fantham 2004: 186–208.
[75] I.e. recent to the dramatic date of the *De Oratore* (91 BCE).
[76] A reference to Crassus' citizenship law (*tuam legem de ciuitate*, *De Or.* 2.257), i.e. the *Lex Licinia
Mucia* passed by Crassus and Scaevola Pontifex in 95 BCE to investigate individuals illegally posing
as Roman citizens, see Čulík-Baird 2020: 391.

M. Antonius, who quoted a verse of a now unknown Latin comedy in the courtroom:

> nam in Caelio sane etiam ad causam utile fuit tuum illud, Antoni, cum ille
> a se pecuniam profectam diceret testis et haberet filium delicatiorem,
> abeunte iam illo, *sentin senem esse tactum triginta minis?*   [Ribbeck 45]

> For the following verse was useful for your case against Caelius, Antonius.
> He spoke as a witness in a bribery case, and, since he had a libertine son,
> when he was leaving the stand, you said: *"Don't you think this old man has
> been tricked out of thirty minae?"*

As the witness was leaving the witness stand, Antonius used a comic verse to imply, since this man apparently had a libertine son (*filius delicatior*),[77] that he, like so many *senex* figures from Roman comedy, had been fleeced by this profligate son of his, thereby characterizing him as a hapless fool and an unreliable witness. Although the phrase "*sentin senem esse tactum triginta minis*" is an iambic senarius, it may not in fact come from a Roman comedy. Antonius' witty implication that Caelius has been fleeced looks like a response to a scene from Plautus' *Epidicus* (703–705):

PERIPHANES: *dedin tibi minas triginta ob filiam?*
EPIDICUS: *fateor datas*
    et eo argento illam me emisse amicam fili fidicinam
    pro tua filia: istam ob rem te tetigi triginta minis
PERIPHANES: "Didn't I give you thirty *minae* for my daughter?"
EPIDICUS: "I admit that you did,
    and with that money I bought your son's girlfriend, the lyre girl,
    instead of your daughter: I tricked you out of thirty *minae.*"

A comparison between the Plautine exchange and Antonius' witty verse suggests that Antonius is taking elements of comic diction (*sentin, dedin*; *tactum, tetigi*; *triginta minis*) and rearranging them into something new, an Antonian verse which resembles an audience reaction to the situation between Periphanes and Epidicus. Antonius casts himself as the meta-theatrical figure in a Roman comedy who turns to his audience (the crowd at the trial), and winkingly says, "Look, folks, how silly this old fool is."

An important implication, then, of Antonius' "verse citation" in Cicero's *De Oratore* is that what at first glance appears to be a fragment of Roman comedy may in fact be something more complicated. Antonius' "*sentin senem esse tactum triginta minis*" appears in Ribbeck's edition of Roman comic fragments

---

[77] For *delicatus* as "libertine" see Cicero *In Cat.* 2.23.

as an authentic verse of an unknown *fabula palliata*.[78] But it may instead be an example of the creativity of orators who were trained to take elements of classic poetry and to rearrange them (even metrically) for comic effect. Quintilian writes that verses could be quoted with "words partially altered" (*uerbis ex parte mutatis*, *Inst. Or.* 6.3.97), and refers to another kind of verse "quotation" – the "invention of verses that resemble famous ones" (*ficti notis uersibus similes*), a technique known as "parody."

That the outright invention of verses was an oratorical strategy which existed alongside the technique of authentic citation is troubling for those of us who would wish to see as genuine the lines of poetry which appear in the works of Latin prose authors. However, the entanglement of prose and verse which this "parodic" rhetorical technique produces is also further evidence of the influence and importance of Latin poetry in the practice of Roman oratory. The ability to create verses which are humorous because they resemble famous originals is another index of how deeply Roman poetry had permeated into the common consciousness of the Romans by the late Republic. Poetry was in the DNA of oratory: orators studied it to develop and refine their craft, they deployed apt quotations in their speeches to powerful effect, and they knew the verses well enough to invent their own.

2.3 Poetry in the Speeches

Cicero's speeches contain the fewest poetic citations of all the prose genres which he composed.[79] Despite the fact that orators were evidently well versed, explicit citation of poetry would only be tolerated to a limited extent in public speaking. Indeed, verse citations and allusions to poetry are often accompanied with a performative apology.[80] Nonetheless, poetry plays an important role in a number of Ciceronian orations, and the speeches, as "receptions" of early Roman poetry, testify to the ways in which the themes of tragedy, comedy, epic, and mime could be made to align with Roman values and ways of thinking. In addition to the substantial verse quotations and allusions in the *Pro Roscio Amerino* (80 BCE), *Pro Murena* (63 BCE), *Pro Sestio* (56 BCE), and the *Pro Caelio* (56 BCE), discussed in the following sections, a further dozen Ciceronian speeches contain incidental poetic quotations and allusions.[81]

---

[78] Ribbeck *inc. pall.* 45.   [79] See Albrecht 2003: 40; and Appendix I to this work.
[80] Apologies for poetic quotation and allusion: *Rosc. Am.* 47, *Sest.* 119, *Pis.* 71, *Ph.* 2.65, *Ph.* 13.49; *Arch.* 18. See Zillinger 1911: 70–71, North 1952: 28, Hutchinson 1998: 15.
[81] In the *Verrines* (70 BCE), Cicero seems to refer to Naevius' conflict with the Metelli (*Verr.* 1.29; *TrRF* I T7, cf. Zillinger 1911: 94n3, Goldberg 1995: 34,); quotes Ennius' *Achilles* (*Verr.* 2.1.46; *TrRF* II 1); a tragic

Since Cicero's speeches, like his letters, refer to recent events, it is from the orations that we often learn about recent theatrical productions.[82] A series of poetic quotations appears in the *Pro Sestio* (118–126) because Cicero there describes dramatic performances which took place in Rome while he was in exile. In the *In Pisonem* (65), Cicero speaks in great anticipation of the inaugural *ludi* for Pompey's theatre. There are several references to Accius' *Tereus* in the *Philippics* (1.36, 2.31, 10.8) because this play was performed at the *Ludi Apollinares* of 44 BCE.[83] Indeed, since the Roman theatre was itself an inherently political site, Cicero's references to theatrical performances in the speeches are in and of themselves also political. In the *Philippics* (1.36, 2.31, 10.8), Cicero interpreted the popular reception of Accius' *Tereus* as a sign of support towards Brutus, and in the *Pro Sestio* (102–126), as we shall see in section 2.3.3, Cicero argued that when *popularis* politicians manipulated public meetings, it was the theatre at which the truest will of the people could be perceived.

Cicero's orations are full of references to the Roman stage, even if they do not have as many verbatim quotations. In the *Pro Caecina* (71–68 BCE), Cicero took advantage of a resonance between life and comedy when he described the banker, Sextus Clodius Phormio as "no less black, no less brazen" (*nec minus*

---

verse which was once attributed to Ennius' *Thyestes* (*Verr.* 2.1.81; *TrRF* II p227 = Jocelyn 295, cf. Zillinger 1911: 120); and alludes to a verse of Accius (*Verr.* 2.5.94; Dangel 700, cf. Zillinger 1911: 139) which he would later quote in the *Orator* (156). In the *Post reditum in senatu* (57 BCE), Cicero alludes (*Red. in Sen.* 33) to a verse of Accius (Dangel 42) which he would later quote in the *In Pisonem* (72). In the *De Haruspicum responsis* (56 BCE), Cicero quoted a now unknown verse (*Har. resp.* 39; *TrRF* I 17). The *De Provinciis consulariis* (56 BCE) contains a reference to Ennius' *Annales* (Skutsch 1985: 106). The *Pro Balbo* (56 BCE) quotes an unknown Ennian tragedy (*Balb.* 36; *TrRF* II 145) and Ennius' *Annales* (*Balb.* 51; Skutsch 234–235). The *Pro Plancio* (54 BCE) may contain a reference to Ennius' *Annales* (*Planc.* 20; Zillinger 1911: 107), as well as a reference to Lucilius' *Satires* (*Planc.* 33–34; Marx 1181); there is certainly a citation of Accius' *Atreus* (*Planc.* 59; Dangel 45; 62). The *Pro Scauro* (54 BCE) contains a quotation of an unknown tragedy (*Scaur.* 3; *TrRF* 35). The *Pro Rabirio Postumo* (54 BCE) contains four verse quotations in close succession (*Planc.* 28–29; *TrRF* I 31, 32, 33, 34); the last of these (*TrRF* I 34) later appears in a letter (*Att.* 7.26.1; 49 BCE). The *Pro Milone* (52 BCE) contains a poetic allusion (as Quint. *Inst.* 5.11.8 notes) which has been interpreted as a reference to Ennius' *Eumenides* (*Mil.* 8; Jocelyn 1969a: 284). The *Pro Marcello* (46 BCE) contains part of a verse (*Marc.* 14; *TrRF* I p215, cf. Zillinger 1911: 134n4) which Cicero cites in a letter to Aulus Caecina written in the same year (*Fam.* 6.6.6; Oct. 46 BCE). The *De Rege Deiotaro* (45 BCE) contains a citation of an unknown tragedy (*Deiot.* 25; *TrRF* I 45). In addition to discussion of the recent staging of Accius' *Tereus* and general references to comic stock characters, the *Philippics* (44–43 BCE) contain a citation of Accius' *Atreus* (*Phil.* 1.34; Dangel 47); a citation of Cicero's *De Consulatu Suo* (*Phil.* 2.20; Soubiran fr. vi); references to mime (*Phil.* 2.65, cf. Manuwald 2011: 181; *Phil.* 11.13, cf. Zillinger 1911: 157); a quotation of Naevius (*Phil.* 2.65; *TrRF* I 46); an allusion to a verse of Lucilius' *Satires* (*Phil.* 13.15; Warmington 176–181) previously quoted in the *Tusculans* (4.48); and there are several quotations of unknown tragedies (*Phil.* 2.104, *TrRF* I 80; *Phil.* 13.49, *TrRF* I 87 and *TrRF* I 83).

82   Manuwald 2011: 112–114.

83   Brutus as *praetor urbanus* in 44 BCE was not in Rome for the *ludi* he was responsible for organizing; he instead heard positive reports about the reception of Accius' *Tereus* from Cicero (*Att.* 16.2.3, 16.5.1). Brutus had intended to put on Accius' *Brutus* (which celebrated the heroism of his regicide ancestor), not the *Tereus* (*Att.* 16.5.1); see Manuwald 2011: 47–48, 113; Wright 1931: 7.

niger nec minus confidens, Caec. 27) than the Terentian parasite, Phormio.[84] In
the *Pro Roscio Comoedo* (77–66 BCE), Cicero, defending the Roman actor,
Quintus Roscius, claims (*Rosc. Com.* 20) that in Roscius' portrayal of Ballio the
pimp from Plautus' *Pseudolus*, he was really playing the role of his prosecutor,
C. Fannius Chaerea.[85] Similarly, in the *Philippics* (2.15), Cicero characterized
Antony's behaviour as libertine by implying that he entertained men like
Phormio, Gnatho, and Ballio: i.e. the parasites from Terence's *Phormio* and
Eunuchus, and the pimp from Plautus' *Pseudolus*.[86] Aside from these theatrical references, Cicero also (somewhat rarely) discussed individual poets: in
the *Pro Archia* (62 BCE), Cicero makes several references to Ennius as
a model exemplar of the poet who gained citizenship via his poetic service
to Rome (*Arch.* 22; 27), but this speech seems not to contain any explicit
poetic citations.[87]

There is also evidence that Cicero quoted poetry in the speeches which
no longer survive intact.[88] While Cicero suppressed the text of his defense
of Vatinius (54 BCE), he described his speech in a letter to Lentulus
Spinther (*Fam.* 1.9.19; Dec. 54 BCE):[89]

> sed tamen defendendi Vatini fuit etiam ille stimulus de quo in iudicio, cum
> illum defenderem, dixi me facere quiddam quod in Eunucho parasitus
> suaderet militi:
> *ubi nominabit Phaedriam, tu Pamphilam*   [Terence, *Eunuchus* 440–445]
> *continuo. si quando illa dicet "Phaedriam*
> *intro mittamus comissatum." "Pamphilam*
> *cantatum prouocemus." si laudabit haec*
> *illius formam, tu huius contra. denique*
> *par pro pari referto, quod eam mordeat.*

---

[84] In Terence's *Phormio* (123), Phormio is called *homo confidens*, "brazen man"; see Polt 2021: 61.

[85] *Rosc. Com.* 20: *nam Ballionem illum improbissimum et periurissimum lenonem cum agit, agit Chaeream*,
"For whenever Roscius plays Ballio, that most wicked and fraudulent pimp, he really plays Chaerea." In
Plautus' *Pseudolus*, Ballio is called *periurissumus* (351) and *fraudulentus* (266); Cicero draws on Plautus by
using *periurissimus* (*Rosc. Com.* 20), and throughout this passage he repeats the verb *fraudo* ("to cheat"),
i.e. *C. Fannium Chaeream Roscius fraudauit!*, "So it was Roscius who cheated C. Gannius Chaerea, was
it?" See Zillinger 1911: 96n3, Duncan 2006: 178–182, Hanses 2020: 49.

[86] *Phil.* 2.15: *dat nataliciam in hortis. cui? neminem nominabo: putate tum Phormioni alicui, tum Gnathoni,
tum etiam Ballioni*, "Antony is hosting a birthday party on his grounds. For whom? I won't name names,
but it's some Phormio one day, then Gnatho the next, then even Ballio." In *Phil.* 11.13, Antony is
associated with a writer of mimes (Nucula), and a man (Lento) who acted in a tragedy.

[87] When Cicero says that Ennius called poets *sancti* (*Arch.* 18; cf. 31), he may be alluding to something
Ennius actually wrote: the two word *sancti poetae* appear among Skutsch's *opera incerti fragmenta* (1985:
131; xvi). Timpanaro (1949: 198–200) suggests that *Arch.* 27 contains a quotation of Ennius' *Ambracia*.
On Cicero's characterization of Ennius in the *Pro Archia*, see Elliott 2013: 171–172; Čulík-Baird 2020.

[88] Cf. the "Sextus Annalis" joke preserved by Quintilian (*Inst.* 6.3.96); see p100.

[89] On the suppression of this text, see Crawford 1994: 301–306.

> ... quoniamque illi haberent suum Publium, darent mihi ipsi alium Publium
> in quo possem illorum animos mediocriter lacessitus leuiter repungere.

> But nonetheless, I had an incentive to defend Vatinius, which I explicitly
> stated in the trial while I was defending him: I said that I was doing what the
> parasite advises the soldier to do in the *Eunuchus*:
> "*Whenever she names Phaedria, you name Pamphila*
> *in response. If she should want Phaedria to come*
> *to dinner, you should say: 'Why not bring Pamphila*
> *to sing?' If she praises his good looks, you praise*
> *the girl's. In short: pay back what hurts.*"
> ... since they had *their* Publius, I looked for my own Publius, to sting them
> back a little in return for the mild provocation.

Jane Crawford (1994: 304–306) argued that this passage was probably not
a *bona fide* fragment of the suppressed *Pro Vatinio* precisely on the grounds
that it contained the citation of Terence's *Eunuchus*. But such an argument
does not adequately take into consideration the fact that poetic citation was
such a regular feature of Cicero's speeches or the fact that several
Ciceronian fragments are preserved precisely because they contain
poetry.[90] Regardless, the Terentian scene is core to Cicero's conception
of his political situation in 54 BCE: leading statesmen were fauning over
Publius Clodius Pulcher, so Cicero made sure to have his own Publius (i.e.
Vatinius), to provoke their jealousy. Two other fragmentary speeches are
thought to contain poetic material: Cicero's description of Clodius wear-
ing the clothes of women in the *In P. Clodium et Curionem* (Crawford
fr. 21) may include a quotation of comedy;[91] and Cicero's *Pro Q. Gallio*
(Crawford fr. 2) contained a description of a performance at recent *ludi*,
possibly a mime:[92]

> his autem ludis, loquor enim, quae sum ipse nuper expertus, unus quidem
> poeta dominatur, homo perlitteratus, cuius sunt illa conuiuia poetarum ac
> philosophorum, cum facit Euripiden et Menandrum inter se, et alio loco
> Socraten atque Epicurum disserentes, quorum aetates non annis, sed saeculis
> scimus fuisse disiunctas. atque his quantos plausus et clamores mouet! multos
> enim condiscipulos habet in theatro, qui simul litteras non didicerunt.

[90] Two fragments of the *De Republica* quote Ennian epigrams (*Rep.* fr. 1; Goldberg-Manuwald F1; *Rep.*
fr. 2; Goldberg-Manuwald F3); a fragment of *Hortensius* contains a quotation of Ennius' *Alcmeo*
(*Hort.* fr. 102; *TrRF* II 12); a fragment of *De Gloria* contains Cicero's Latin translation of *Iliad* 7.89–
91 (*Glor.* fr. 2; Soubiran fr. iii); a fragment of *De Fato* contains Cicero's Latin translation of *Odyssey*
18.136–137 (*Fat.* fr. 2; Soubiran fr. ix).
[91] Geffcken 1973: 75–79, cf. Zillinger 1911: 160; on the oratorical fragment, see Crawford 1994: 254–255.
[92] On the theory that *Pro Q. Gallio* fr. 2 refers to a performance of mime, see Crawford 1994: 154–155
with bibliography there cited, cf. Zillinger 1911: 158, Bonaria 1965: 87.

But at these games (for I speak about things which I myself recently experienced), one poet indeed dominates, a very learned man, the author of banquets of poets and philosophers, making Euripides and Menander speak to each other, and in another scene, Socrates and Epicurus, who in reality were separated not only by years, but centuries. And yet, what applause and shouts he gets with these scenes! The poet has many colleagues in the theatre, who also have not learned their letters.

When Hermogenes of Tarsus, a Greek rhetorician of the Antonine era, discussed the citation of poetry in oratory, he recommended the "inter-weaving" or "gluing" (κόλλησις) of verses into the body of the speech.[93] A consequence of this technique of subtle interweaving is that there are likely more poetic quotations in Ciceronian oratory than we are currently capable of discerning. Indeed, there are several examples in the speeches of verse citations which would be imperceptible without external indications that they are in fact there. It is due to the comment of Asconius on *Verr.* 1.29 that we have the infamous verse attributed to Naevius.[94] In the *In Pisonem* (82) Cicero quotes from Accius' *Atreus* (Dangel 42), giving no indication that he is making a verse citation.[95] Instead, we must rely on Asconius, who comments on this passage: "It is almost too well known to be worth indicating that this is a verse of the poet, L. Accius, and is said by Thyestes to Atreus."[96] Without Asconius, we would not know that Cicero was quoting Accius' *Atreus* in the *In Pisonem*; nor would we be able to perceive the allusion to this verse in *Post Reditum in Senatu* (33).[97] A short quotation of Ennius' *Achilles* (*TrRF* II 1) which appears in the *Verrines* (2.1.46) can only be identified with the help of the scholia;[98] and a passage of Ennius' *Annales* (Skutsch 247–253) partially embedded in the *Pro Murena* (30) is so thoroughly integrated into the prose that it would be impossible to find unless the passage had been partially quoted by Cicero in two of his letters (*Fam.* 7.13.2; *Att.* 15.7), and a fuller citation preserved by Aulus Gellius (20.10.4).

---

[93] *On Types of Style* 338 (Wooten 2011); cf. North 1952: 23.   [94] *TrRF* I T 7, cf. Goldberg 1995: 34.
[95] *Pis.* 82: *quamquam, quod ad me attinet,* "*numquam istam imminuam curam infitiando tibi*" [Dangel 42]; "Although, as far as I am concerned, '*I shall never lessen your anxiety by denying it.*"
[96] Asconius on *Pis.* 82: *prope notius est quam ut indicandum sit hunc uersum esse L. Acci poetae et dici a Thyeste Atreo.*
[97] *Red. in Sen.* 33: *quod numquam infitiando suspicionem hominum curamque minuerunt,* "because they never by any denial lessened men's suspicion or anxiety." This allusion was omitted by Ribbeck, see Zillinger 1911: 134.
[98] Zetzel 2007: 2.

While Cicero's speeches may not contain the most poetic quotations of the genres which he writes, it is clear that poetry was a core component of his speech-making. If more verse survived from the Republican period (and more of Cicero's speeches), we would probably see even more echoes of early Roman poetry in his oratory. Quintilian's remark upon the "unconscious" (*non sentientes, Inst.* 2.7.3) use of verse demonstrates that the orator's words were steeped in the language of the poets to the extent that he might call up a poetic phrase without even realizing it himself.[99] But it is also clearly the case that the verses which can be easily detected in Cicero's speeches were deliberately and carefully deployed.

2.3.1   Pro Roscio Amerino *(80 BCE)*

In 80 BCE, Cicero argued his first case in a criminal court (*Rosc.* 59), defending Sextus Roscius of Ameria against the charge of parricide. As one of Cicero's earliest extant speeches, the *Pro Roscio Amerino* presents an opportunity to examine how Cicero used poetic allusion as part of oratorical composition at the beginning of his career.[100] There seems to be only one explicit poetic quotation in this oration: Cicero uses a verse of Ennius (*TrRF* II 144; *Rosc.* 90) to refer to the Sullan proscriptions. Nonetheless, theatrical allusion plays a vital role in the structure of this speech. Cicero alludes to a Latin comedy by Caecilius Statius in the *Pro Roscio* (46–47):[101]

> si tibi fortuna non dedit, ut patre certo nascerere, ex quo intellegere posses, qui animus patrius in liberos esset, at natura certe dedit, ut humanitatis non parum haberes; eo accessit studium doctrinae, ut ne a litteris quidem alienus esses. ecquid tandem tibi uidetur, ut ad fabulas ueniamus, senex ille Caecilianus minoris facere Eutychum, filium rusticum, quam illum alterum, Chaerestratum? nam, ut opinor, hoc nomine est. alterum in urbe secum honoris causa habere, alterum rus supplici causa relegasse? [47] quid ad istas ineptias abis? inquies.

> If fortune has deprived you of knowing for sure who your father is, from whom you could have learned about a father's spirit towards his sons, nonetheless

99 Several of Cicero's partial verse citations in the speeches seem to be almost unconscious reuse of famous passages, e.g.: *Pro Marcello* (14) containing part of a verse (*TrRF* I p215) which Cicero cites in a letter to Aulus Caecina written in the same year (*Fam.* 6.6.6; Oct. 46 BCE); *Post Reditum in Senatu* (33) alludes to a verse of Accius (Dangel 42) which he would later quote in the *In Pisonem* (72).
100 On the *Pro Roscio* in the context of other early speeches, see Vasaly 2002: 76–82; for Cicero's assessment of the *Pro Roscio* later in life see *Or.* 108, *Brut.* 312. Cicero had delivered the *Pro Quinctio* the previous year (81 BCE; Gellius 15.28.3), on which see Lintott 2008: 43–59.
101 Goldberg 2005: 90–91, Hanses 2020: 126–127, Polt 2021: 47–48.

nature certainly endowed you with the knowledge of what it is to be human. In addition to this, there is your learned study: literature is not foreign to you. Okay, then: does it seem to you, to take an example from a play, that the Caecilian old man likes Eutychus, the rustic son, less than the other one, Chaerestratus? I think that's his name. That he kept one in the city with him to honour him, that he relegated the other to the countryside to punish him? [47] You will ask, "Why are you wandering off into such absurdities?"

Cicero deliberately presents the citation as imprecise. He does not linger on the name of the poet, but instead refers obliquely to the "Caecilian old man" *Caecilianus senex* (*Rosc.* 46).[102] He does not name this character either, but instead refers to him as a stock figure of Roman comedy (the *senex*). While the *senex* remains unnamed, the two comic figures most pertinent to Cicero's argument are: Eutychus, the "rustic son" (*filius rusticus*), and Chaerestratus, the "other one" (*alter*).[103] Cicero marks the dramatic allusion with an apologetic aside (*Rosc.* 47): *quid ad istas ineptias abis? inquies*, "you will ask, 'Why are you wandering off into such absurdities?'" Such an apology will regularly occur when Cicero uses poetry in oratory, which evidently tolerated overt citation less than other genres.[104] Cicero's effort to make the allusion deliberately vague is also communicated by his statement that he "thinks" (*ut opinor*, *Rosc.* 46) he is right about the name of one of the characters.[105]

Despite the performance of imprecision, the comic allusion is key to Cicero's defense.[106] The deceased Sextus Roscius had two sons: one, now dead, had lived with his father in Rome; the other, now on trial, had been banished to the country (*Rosc.* 42). Erucius, the prosecutor, made the claim that the elder Roscius hated his son (*Rosc.* 40), that this hatred led to the son's relegation (*Rosc.* 43), and that both of these things gave the son a motive for murder (*Rosc.* 41). The prosecution had therefore characterized the events as a family drama, the kind familiar to a Roman audience from the comic stage. Father–son conflict was a major theme of Roman

---

[102] Cicero regularly uses an adjectival version of a poet's name: *Caecilianus* (*Cael.* 37, *Fin.* 1.13, *TD* 3.56); *Terentianus* (*Caec.* 27, *Fin.* 1.3, *TD* 3.65, *De Am.* 89, *Off.* 1.30); *Plautinus* (*ad Brut.* 1.2.3.(2a.1)); *Liuianus* (*Leg.* 2.39, *Brut.* 71); *Naeuianus* (*Fam.* 5.12.7, *Leg.* 2.39, *Brut.* 60, *TD* 4.67); *Ennianus* (*Div.* 2.111); *Pacuuianus* (*De Or.* 2.156, *Rep.* 3.14, *Div.* 1.131, 2.133); *Accianus* (*Fam.* 9.16.5, *TD* 3.62); *Homericus* (*Leg.* 1.2, *TD* 3.62, 4.52, *Div.* 1.52, 1.65, 2.82).

[103] It is because Cicero names Eutychus and Chaerestratus that the play here alluded to has been identified as Caecilius Statius' *Hypobolimaeus* ("The Suppositious Son"), a *fabula palliata* based on Menander's comedy of the same name. On Cicero "often quot[ing] lines from Roman adaptations of Menander in court," see Fantham 1984: 301. Varro (*RR* 2.11.11) refers to the "young man in Caecilius' *Hypobolimaeus*" (*apud Caecilium in Hypobolimaeo . . . adulescens*).

[104] See p103n80.   [105] Goldberg 2005: 91.

[106] On comic technique in Cicero's early speeches, including discussion of Caecilius Statius in *Pro Roscio Amerino*, see Harries 2007: 129–147, esp. 134–136. On the Caecilius allusion as one part in Cicero's construction of Roscius' rustic *persona*, see Vasaly 1985.

comedy, as was the comic difference between the city and the country.[107]
Ann Vasaly (1985: 10) has suggested that the prosecution cast the younger
Roscius as a Demea-type from Terence's *Adelphoe*: the "hard-bitten old
farmer" versus "his easy-going and urbane brother." Cicero's allusion to
Caecilius' play therefore seems intended as a rival picture of comic rusti-
city, designed to combat Erucius' invocation of the Roman stage.

In the *Pro Roscio* (47), Cicero extended the theatrical allusion into
a meditation upon how Roman comedy reflected Roman life and morals:

> quasi uero mihi difficile sit quamuis multos nominatim proferre, ne longius
> abeam, uel tribulis uel uicinos meos qui suos liberos, quos plurimi faciunt,
> agricolas adsiduos esse cupiunt. uerum homines notos sumere odiosum est,
> cum et illud incertum sit uelintne ei sese nominari, et nemo uobis magis
> notus futurus sit quam est hic Eutychus, et certe ad rem nihil intersit utrum
> hunc ego comicum adulescentem an aliquem ex agro Veienti nominem.
> etenim haec conficta arbitror esse a poetis ut effictos nostros mores in alienis
> personis expressamque imaginem uitae cotidianae uideremus.

> As if it would be difficult for me to present as many as you please by name –
> not to wander too far – whether my fellow tribesmen or neighbours, who
> want their own sons to be hard-working farmers! But it is bad etiquette to
> name specific individuals, when it isn't certain that they would want to be
> named, and no one would be more known to you than this Eutychus, and
> certainly it makes no difference whether I name the comic *adulescens* or
> some young man from the countryside of Veii. Indeed, I think that these
> things were made up by poets so that we could see our own values portrayed
> in other characters, and a representative image of everyday life.

Defending his use of comic types in anticipation of the objection that comedy
is "fiction" (*conficta*),[108] Cicero claims that there is essentially no difference
between the Caecilian *adulescens*, Eutychus, and some young man from Veii,
an Etruscan town 12 miles north of Rome.[109] Although comedy is not reality, it
does mirror aspects of reality:[110] it shows "Roman values" (*nostros mores*) in
"other characters" (*alienis personis*); it gives a "representative image of everyday
life" (*expressam imaginem uitae cotidianae*). Cicero here puts into practice the
theory of the *De Inventione* (1.27), where he had cited comedy (Ter. *Andr.* 51) to

---

[107] Geffcken 1973: 23.
[108] Cicero will respond to Quintus' citation of Latin poetry in the *De Div.* with the objection that his
poetic examples are "made up" (*Div.* 2.22, 27 80, 113, 136). See Krostenko 2000: 367.
[109] Cicero (*Rosc.* 47) says he does not want to name real Romans, and instead gives stock figures from
Roman comedy; in the *Philippics* (2.15), Cicero will not name the real Romans whom Antony
entertained on his estates, and instead names parasites and pimps from Roman comedy.
[110] Hanses 2020: 127.

exemplify *argumentum*; i.e. a narrative which, while "made up" (*ficta*, *Inv.* 1.27), nonetheless could be true. Comedy is thereby figured as a realm in the Roman imagination that intersected with real life without actually being reality. Implicit here is the assumption that, by endowing fictional characters with Roman cultural values, Roman audiences were able to see aspects of themselves onstage. To some extent, then, a citation of Roman comedy had more power than a real life example, since it distilled essential truths about Roman cultural values. At any rate, the allusion suggests a certain permeability between the world of comedy and everyday life.[111]

While comedy is an important structuring feature for the characterization of Roscius in this oration, tragedy also makes an appearance. Part of Cicero's defense relies on an insistence that the crime of killing a father (*parricidium*[112]) was such a serious taboo (*Rosc.* 68) that it would never have been committed by a dutiful son like Roscius, and included an emphasis not solely on the magnitude of the crime itself but on the horror of the punishment. Cicero vividly describes the punishment for the man convicted of killing his father: to be sown up in a sack and thrown into a river (*Rosc.* 70–72).[113] Tragedy informs Cicero's depiction of the severity of the taboo of kin-killing (*Rosc.* 66–67):

> uidetisne quos nobis poetae tradiderunt patris ulciscendi causa supplicium de matre sumpsisse, cum praesertim deorum immortalium iussis atque oraculis id fecisse dicantur, tamen ut eos agitent Furiae neque consistere umquam patiantur, quod ne pii quidem sine scelere esse potuerunt? sic se res habet, iudices: magnam uim, magnam necessitatem, magnam possidet religionem paternus maternusque sanguis; ex quo si qua macula concepta est, non modo elui non potest uerum usque eo permanat ad animum ut summus furor atque amentia consequatur. [67] nolite enim putare, quem ad modum in fabulis saepenumero uidetis, eos qui aliquid impie scelerateque commiserint agitari et perterreri Furiarum *taedis ardentibus*. sua quemque fraus et suus terror maxime uexat, suum quemque scelus agitat amentiaque adficit, suae malae cogitationes conscientiaeque animi terrent; hae sunt impiis adsiduae domesticaeque Furiae quae dies noctesque parentium poenas a consceleratissimis filiis repetant.

> Do you see those men whom the poets have said exacted punishment from their mothers in order to avenge their fathers? Although they are said to have done this at the commands and oracles of the immortal gods, nonetheless

---

[111] Cf. *De Sen.* 65, where Cicero has Cato the Elder refer to Terence's *Adelphoe* as an example of what happens "in real life and on the stage" (*cum in uita tum in scaena*).

[112] Roscius was tried *de parricidio* in the Sullan murder court, the *quaestio de sicariis et ueneficiis* (Dyck 2010: 2). On *parricidium* and its "murky early history," see Riggsby 1999: 50–52.

[113] The *poena cullei*, "penalty of the sack" involved the sowing up of the guilty man in a sack with a dog, a rooster, a snake, and an ape, and thrown into water (Just. *Inst.* 4.18.6, cf. Riggsby 1999: 52).

you see how the Furies chase them vexatiously, and they are never allowed to rest, because they were not able to be pious without committing a crime. Judges, this is how the matter really is: the blood of the father and the mother possesses a great power, a great force of compulsion, a great force of prohibition. It is impossible to clean away the moral stain of this blood. It seeps into the soul. Extreme fury and madness follow. [67] Do not think, because you so often see these things in plays, that the man who commits impious and wicked crimes is really vexed and tormented by the "*burning torches*" of the Furies. It is the crime and his own fear which so greatly torments him; his own wicked deed which chases him, his madness which hounds him; his evil thoughts and his conscience terrify him. These are the constant companions of the impious, the internal Furies who night and day exact punishment for the parents from their heinous sons.

Cicero alludes to the theatrical staging ("you see in plays," *in fabulis . . . uidetis, Rosc.* 67) of the punishment of kin-killing by the Furies. Without naming the figures overtly, Cicero alludes to tragic matricides such as the figures of Alcmeo (killer of Eriphyla), who appeared in a number of Latin tragedies,[114] and Orestes (killer of Clytemnestra).[115] Since Orestes regularly appears in rhetorical treatises to demonstrate different tactics for proving or disproving guilt,[116] Cicero appears, at first, to be drawing on an oratorical tradition rather than a literary or theatrical one. Yet, Cicero's interpretation of supernatural forces, the Furies, as a poetic reflection of real human psychological processes shows an interest in how Roman drama, despite its fantastical elements, nonetheless captured certain "rationalist" truths.

Cicero's invocation of the Furies as a poetic rendering of the sensations of guilt in the *Pro Roscio* is likely a deliberately imprecise allusion. That is, while the Furies who tortured Alcmeo or Orestes may be in Cicero's mind here, it is not clear that he is making a citation of a specific play, rather than

---

[114] Alcmeo appeared in the Latin tragedies named for him, Ennius' *Alcmeo* and Accius' *Alcmeo*, and he was also a character in Accius' *Epigoni* and *Eriphyla*. The surviving fragments of Ennius' *Alcmeo*, almost all of which come from Cicero (see *TrRF* II pp49–60), focus on his torment by Furies following the killing of his mother. The extant fragments of Accius' *Alcmeo* do not give a strong enough sense of the play's action, but a reference to a father-in-law and an act of *impietas* in one fragment (Dangel 612–613) has led some scholars to connect it with Alcmeo's double marriage after the matricide (Dangel 2002: 366). Accius' *Epigoni* and *Eriphyla* seem to have staged Alcmeo's killing of his mother, Eriphyla, who had been bribed with Harmonia's necklace and dress to betray Amphiaraus, see Dangel 2002: 365, 368.

[115] Orestes appeared in Ennius' *Eumenides* (e.g. *TrRF* II 53; Jocelyn 1969a: 284), Pacuvius' *Chryses* (Schierl 2006: 198–201), *Dulorestes* (Schierl 2006: 244–247), and *Hermiona* (Schierl 2006: 291–294, 296–298. 300–308), and in Accius' *Aegisthus* (Dangel 2002: 323), *Agamemnonidae* ("Children of Agamemnon"; Dangel 2002: 325), and *Clytaemestra* (Dangel 2002: 320–322); Orestes is also named in a fragment of Accius' *Erigona* (Dangel 321–322). Orestes also appeared, or likely appeared, in Livius Andronicus' *Aegisthus*, *Hermiona*; Naevius' *Iphigenia*; and Atilius' *Electra* (Jocelyn 1969a: 284).

[116] *Rhet.* 1.17, 1.25–26; *De Inv.* 1.18–19, 1.31. Jocelyn (1969a: 284n5) discusses the prior role of these references in the Greek rhetorical tradition.

making a general reference to the theatre.[117] Nonetheless, Cicero's use of Alcmeo elsewhere in the corpus sheds light on this allusion to the tortured Alcmeo-type. When Cicero refers to Alcmeo in his philosophy, he uses the figure as an example of extreme psychological disorder against which philosophical precepts can be tested; and he quotes Ennius' *Alcmeo* to do so.[118] In the *Academica* (2.88–89), Cicero cites verses of Ennius' *Alcmeo* (*TrRF* II 13) in which the matricide describes the Furies' advance upon him:

> dormientium et uinulentorum et furiosorum uisa imbecilliora esse dicebas
> quam uigilantium siccorum sanorum. quo modo? quia, cum experrectus esset
> Ennius, non diceret se uidisse Homerum sed uisum esse, Alcmeo autem
> *sed mihi neutiquam cor consentit ...*   [*TrRF* II 13, 1]
> [2.89] quid? ipse Alcmeo tuus, qui negat cor sibi cum oculis consentire,[119]
> nonne ibidem incitato furore
> *unde haec flamma oritur?*   [*TrRF* II 13, 2]
> et illa deinceps
> *incedunt, incedunt;*[120] *adsunt, me expetunt.*   [*TrRF* II 13, 3]
> quid cum uirginis fidem implorat
> *fer mi auxilium, pestem abige a me,*   [*TrRF* II 13, 4–7]
> *flammiferam hanc uim quae me excruciat!*
> *caeruleo incinctae angui incedunt,*
> *circumstant cum ardentibus taedis.*
> num dubitas quin sibi haec uidere uideatur? itemque cetera:[121]
> *intendit crinitus Apollo*   [*TrRF* II 13, 8–10]
> *arcum auratum luna innixus,*
> *Diana facem iacit a laeua.*

You were saying that the visions of sleeping, drunk, and mad people are weaker than those seen by those who are awake, sober, sane. In what way? Because when Ennius had woken up he did not say that he had seen Homer but that he had dreamt of him,[122] but Alcmeo says,
"*in no way does my heart agree ...* "
[2.89] What? Doesn't Alcmeo himself, who denies "that his heart agrees with his eyes," in the same passage, agitated by fury say:
"*From where does this fire arise?*"

---

[117] Zillinger 1911: 109 considered *Rosc.* 67 to refer to Ennius' *Alcmeo*. Jocelyn (1969a: 186n9), however, thought that this passage more likely referred to Ennius' *Eumenides*.
[118] Cicero cites Ennius' *Alcmeo* (*TrRF* II 12c) at *TD* 4.19 as an example of the impact of *pauor* ("fear") on the mind; at *Fin.* 4.62, Alcmeo (*TrRF* II 12d) appears as the example of the wretched in contrast to the good life; at *Fin.* 5.31, Ennius' *Alcmeo* (*TrRF* II 12e) is cited as evidence of the dread of death. The emotionality of Ennius' *Alcmeo* was so distinct that it is also cited by Cicero in the *De Oratore* (3.218; *TrRF* 12b) as an example to be studied by the orator intending to simulate fear with his own speech.
[119] Prose paraphrase of *TrRF* II 13, 1.   [120] On the text here, see p25n98.
[121] A variation on *nosti quae sequuntur*; see p23.
[122] A paraphrase of Ennius' *Annales* (Skutsch 3); cf. *Ac.* 2.51.

And next the words:
"*They are coming, they are coming; they are here, they're looking for me.*"
What then, when he begs the loyalty of the young woman:
"*Bring me help, drive this contagion from me,*
this flame-bearing force which torments me!
Girt with green snakes they approach,
They stand around me with their burning torches."
Do you doubt that he seems to see these things? And the rest:
"*Long-haired Apollo stretches*
his golden bow, leaning on the moon,
Diana throws a torch from the left."

In the *Academica*, Cicero emphasizes how the verses speak to epistemological concerns, testing Alcmeo's perception of the sense data which constitute true or false impressions. But in the *Pro Roscio*, the invocation of an Alcmeo-type refers to moral issues, realigning madness as the physiological (and psychological) feeling of guilt. The vividness of the *Alcmeo* citation in the *Academica* demonstrates the torture of the Furies' chase: it is a "contagion" (*pestis*), a "flame-bearing force" (*flammiferam uim*) which "tortures" (*excruciat*). The *Academica* and the *Pro Roscio* have in common the rationalist notion that Furies are not real. While Furies could appear on stage (as in Ennius' *Eumenides*, and Seneca's *Thyestes*[123]), Cicero's insistence that Alcmeo *thinks* he sees Furies (*Ac.* 2.89), when in fact he does not, suggests that Furies manifested in that play as madness-induced hallucination.[124] In the *Pro Roscio* (67), Cicero makes a similar maneuver, stating that despite the fact that the judges "so often *see*" (or, via the stagecraft of the theatre, *think* they see) "these things in plays" (*in fabulis saepenumero uidetis*), they "should not think" (*nolite enim putare*) that the Furies are real; a guilty man is not tortured by monstrous forces but by the conscious knowledge of his own actions.

Cicero adopts the language of the stage in order to make this argument in the *Pro Roscio*. Cicero's description of the tragic avengers uses the phrase "*taedis ardentibus*" ("with burning torches," *Rosc.* 67), which also appears ("*ardentibus taedis*") in the fragment of Ennius' *Alcmeo* cited in the *Academica*.[125] In light of the fact that the orators studied poetry to the point where they might instinctually draw on its style or diction, we can interpret the use of the phrase in Cicero's *Pro Roscio* as an allusion to the Furies' appearances in the theatre, if not as an explicit citation of Ennius' *Alcmeo*. In later speeches, Cicero would

---

[123] On the Furies in Ennius, see Jocelyn 1969a: 284. An unnamed fury speaks in Seneca's *Thyestes* (23–67, 83–86, 101–121); on possible presences of Furies in other Senecan tragedies, see Boyle 2017: 98–99.
[124] Jocelyn 1969a: 187, 198.
[125] The phrase also appears in *Leg.* 1.40, which echoes the rationalist reading of the Furies as human guilt in *Rosc.* 66–67.

continue to thread his discussion of guilt and punishment with references to the tragic Furies. In the *In Pisonem* (46–47), Cicero described the madness of L. Calpurnius Piso:[126]

> nolite enim ita putare, patres conscripti, ut in scena uidetis, homines consceleratos impulsu deorum terreri furialibus *taedis ardentibus*: sua quem-que fraus, suum facinus, suum scelus, sua audacia de sanitate ac mente deturbat; hae sunt impiorum furiae, hae flammae, hae faces. [47] ego te non uaecordem, non furiosum, non mente captum, non tragico illo Oreste aut Athamante dementiorem putem . . .

> Do not think, conscript fathers, that, as you see on stage, the most heinous men are tortured at the instigation of the gods with the furious "*burning torches*." It is his own crime, his evil deed, his wickedness, his own boldness which disturbs his mind from his sanity; these are the Furies chasing impious men, these are flames, these are the brands. Must I not think that you are insane, infuriated, mentally corrupt, more out of your mind than that tragic Orestes or Athamas . . .

Just as in the *Pro Roscio Amerino* (67), Cicero warns the judges not to believe in what they have seen on the stage.[127] The invocation of the Furies in the *Pro Roscio* argues that parricide was too solemn and serious a crime to have been committed, and thereby stresses Roscius' innocence. In the *In Pisonem*, by contrast, the Furies are summoned to emphasize Cicero's claim that Piso had indeed fallen into "infuriated madness" (*furorem et insaniam*, *Pis.* 46), like Orestes or Athamas.[128] A fragment of the *In Pisonem*[129] describes both blind madness and the "burning brands of the Furies" (*ardentes furiarum faces*) driving Piso on. Indeed, Cicero calls Piso himself a Fury (*o furia*, *Pis.* 8).[130] Since "infuriation" was, according to Cicero, the psychological by-product of a guilty conscience, Piso's madness is actually evidence of his guilt. In the *Tusculan Disputations* (3.11), Cicero discusses the distinction between *insania* ("unsoundness of mind") and *furor*, the madness of "infuriation" which is

---

[126] On *Pis.* 46–47, see Kubiak 1989, Hanses 2020: 158–159. In addition to the explicit quotations of poetry in this speech (*Pis.* 43: Ennius' *Thyestes TrRF* II 132; *Pis.* 61: Plautus' *Trinummus* 419; *Pis.* 72–74: Cicero's *De Consulatu Suo* Soubiran fr. vi; *Pis.* 82: Accius' *Atreus* Dangel 42), and the apparent allusion to Ennius' *Alcmeo* at *Pis.* 46–47, Hughes (1998) noticed Cicero's use of language in *Pis.* Nisbet fr. 9 reminiscent of Roman comedy.

[127] Indeed, Cicero's phrasing is almost identical: *nolite enim putare, quem ad modum in fabulis saepenumero uidetis . . .* (*Rosc.* 67); *nolite enim ita putare, patres conscripti, ut in scena uidetis . . .* (*Pis.* 46); cf. *Har. Resp.* 62, where Cicero warns his audience not to believe that the gods "walk on earth" (*uersetur in terris*) and "talk" (*colloquatur*) among humans in the way they do on stage.

[128] Two Latin tragedies are known with the title *Athamas*; one by Ennius, another by Accius (Jocelyn 1969a: 267).

[129] *In Pisonem* fr. 4 Nisbet = Quint. *Inst.* 9.3.47.

[130] Cf. Clodius as Fury: *Vat.* 33, *De Dom.* 102, *de Har. Resp.* 39.

brought on by the kinds of intense anger, fear, and pain, suffered by Athamas, Alcmeo, Ajax, and Orestes.[131]

While the *Pro Roscio* contains very few explicit citations of verse, Cicero's use of theatrical motifs nonetheless plays a powerful role. Cicero's understanding of father–son relationships is informed by comic example. With the claimed interchangeability of a son from Veii and a comic *adulescens*, comedy is figured as a mirror of Roman reality. Cicero's understanding of guilt and innocence is also influenced by the figures of tragedy. The tragic matricide, Alcmeo, lurks in the background as a foil to the innocent Roscius; Alcmeo's madness is not only an index of guilt (absent in Roscius), but evidence of the severity of the crime of killing one's own family.

2.3.2   Pro Murena *(63 BCE)*

In the *Pro Murena*, Cicero, then consul, defended L. Murena, one of the consuls-elect for 62 BCE, against the charge of *ambitus* (electoral bribery).[132] Catiline's forces in Etruria had just been defeated (*Mur.* 79; 84), but fear of bloodshed remained. Cicero took advantage of this fear in his defense of Murena, whom he characterized as an experienced soldier (*Mur.* 31–34; 89), a man to rely on if violence came to Rome.[133] Murena was brought to trial by the famous jurist, Servius Sulpicius (cos. 51 BCE).[134] Sulpicius, one of the failed consular candidates for 62 BCE, hoped to gain the consulship for himself via a successful prosecution. As a result, Cicero's defense of Murena rests upon an insistence upon the superiority of military might over a legal mind.

Cicero devotes part of the speech to a parody of the jurists and the complexities of their profession (*Mur.* 19–30). At the culmination of his criticism (*Mur.* 30), Cicero quotes a passage of Ennius' *Annales* which emphasizes the magnitude of war-making while diminishing the importance of jurisprudence:

> omnia ista nobis studia de manibus excutiuntur, simul atque aliqui motus nouus bellicum canere coepit. etenim, ut ait ingeniosus poeta et auctor ualde bonus, proeliis promulgatis[135]

---

[131] *TD* 3.11: *quem nos furorem, μελαγχολίαν illi uocant. quasi uero atra bili solum mens ac non saepe uel iracundia grauiore uel timore uel dolore moueatur, quo genere Athamantem, Alcmeonem, Aiacem, Orestem furere dicimus,* "What we call *furor*, the Greeks call 'melancholy.' As if the mind was only affected by black bile and not often an intense anger, fear, or pain, in the sense in which we say that Athamas, Alcmeo, Ajax, and Orestes were 'infuriated.'" On Cicero's construction of a philosophy of mental derangement in the *In Pisonem*, see Gildenhard 2007: 155–167.

[132] On *ambitus*, see Lintott 1990, Yakobson 1992, Riggsby 1999: 21–49.   [133] Stem 2006: 212.

[134] On Sulpicius' role in Roman legal history, see Stein 1978: 175–184, Bauman 1985: 4–65, Frier 1985.

[135] Skutsch (1985: 433) suggests that the words *proeliis promulgatis* may also belong to Ennius.

pellitur e medio   [Skutsch 248]
non solum ista uestra uerbosa simulatio prudentiae sed etiam ipsa illa
domina rerum,
                              sapientia; ui geritur res   [Skutsch 248–249]
spernitur orator
non solum odiosus in dicendo ac loquax uerum etiam
                              bonus; horridus miles amatur   [Skutsch 249]
uestrum uero studium totum iacet.
non ex iure manum consertum, sed magis ferro   [Skutsch 252]
inquit
rem repetunt.   [Skutsch 253]
quod si ita est, cedat, opinor, Sulpici, forum castris, otium militiae, stilus
gladio, umbra soli; sit denique in ciuitate ea prima res propter quam ipsa est
ciuitas omnium princeps.

All of these efforts are knocked from our hands as soon as any new motion
begins the song of war. Indeed, as the poet of genius, a truly good witness,
says: when war is declared
"thrust from the centre"
not only is your wordy imitation of judgement but even the mistress of all
things, the real
"wisdom; the matter is carried out by force,
the orator is ignored"
– not only the annoying and long-winded speakers but even
"the good orator; the dread soldier is loved."
Truly, your entire effort is cast aside.
"They do not make claims by law but rather with steel"
he says
"they settle the matter."
If this is so, Sulpicius, let the forum yield to the camp, leisure to war, the pen
to the sword, shade to the sun! Give primacy in the state to the force by
which the state has primacy over all!

As is his usual practice in the orations, Cicero does not name Ennius
explicitly but instead calls him an *ingeniosus poeta* ("poet of genius") and
auctor bonus ("good witness"). Cicero here distributes the content of the
Ennian passage throughout his own prose. Since a fuller version of the
passage was quoted by Aulus Gellius (20.10.4 = Skutsch 248–253), we are
able, for the most part, to distinguish Ennius' words from Cicero's, unlike
in other cases.[136] Cicero adopts the high drama of Ennius' depiction of the
impact of war on "civilized" society – in times of war the sword takes the

---

[136] Cicero also partially quotes this passage in two letters (*Fam.* 7.13.2, Skutsch 252–253; *Att.* 15.7, Skutsch 252).

place of law, the "orator" is replaced with the soldier.[137] Indeed, Ennius'
Annales stands here as a symbol for war itself; the classic poem which
documented Rome's military conquest is the best possible evidence of the
primacy of military knowledge over all others.[138] However, Cicero's invocation of Ennius is also a partial subversion: according to Varro (*LL* 7.41),
Ennius used the word "*orator*" to mean "legate" or "envoy," rather than
orator in its capacity as persuasive and ethical authority, in the way that
Cicero uses in the *Pro Murena* (and, of course, more generally).[139] As a result,
Cicero inserts a retrojective interpretation: placing not wartime diplomacy,
but civic oratory in contrast with the putative valour of the soldier.[140]

Ennius' words gave the sound of war to Cicero's argument in the *Pro
Murena*, but they contained an extra sting. This Ennian passage seems to
have been a favourite of the jurists because it contained the legal phrase *ex
iure manum consertum*, "to make a claim according to the law."[141] Earlier
in the *Pro Murena* (26), Cicero had made fun of this legal language,
putting on a one-man play[142] as a parody of the over-elaborate procedure
in a land dispute: *quid tum? inde ibi ego te ex iure manum consertum uoco*,
"What next? 'I therefore summon you from the court to make a claim at
the property.'" Cicero's use of this Ennian passage in subsequent letters
further attests the fact that the jurists had a particular interest in its
language. Cicero quotes two verses from the Ennius passage in a letter
to the jurist Trebatius Testa, while he was acting as legal counsel to
Caesar in Gaul (Skutsch 252–253; *Fam.* 7.13.2); and in a letter to Atticus
(*Att.* 15.7.1[143]), Cicero quoted the verse (Skutsch 252) while discussing

[137] In the *Pro Murena* (30), all aspects of peaceful statecraft are to "yield" (*cedat*) to military might. In *De
Consulatu Suo* (Soubiran fr. vi), Cicero explicitly reversed this position: *cedant arma togae, concedat laurea
laudi*, "Let arms yield to the toga, the laurels to praise." On the infamy of this line, see Bishop 2018.
[138] Elsewhere, Cicero enlists Ennius' *Annales* for its martial flavour. In defense of another soldier,
L. Cornelius Balbus, Cicero quotes (*Balb.* 51) part of a speech of Hannibal (Skutsch 234–235) as an
argument that soldiers should be citizens of the state they fight for (see Elliott 2013: 166–167). In a letter
to Varro (*Fam.* 9.7.2; May 46 BCE), Cicero uses a verse of the *Annales* (Skutsch 309) which described the
trembling of African soil under the weight of an advancing army in reference to news of Caesar's victory
in Africa. An Ennian verse (*TrRF* II 144) quoted in the *Pro Roscio Amerino* (90) which the Gronovian
scholia identify as tragic is also used by Cicero as a reference to the Sullan proscriptions.
[139] On the change in meaning of "*orator*" = "envoy" to "*orator*" = "orator," see p224.
[140] I owe my thanks to Sander Goldberg for suggesting this interpretation to me.
[141] Skutsch 1985: 435.
[142] At *Mur.* 26, in the midst of a pretend dispute over a Sabine farm, Cicero says that he, in the role of
the *iuris consultus*, "crosses to the other side of the court like a Latin piper" (*transit idem iuris
consultus tibinicis Latini modo*). Since the *tibia* ("pipe") was played as part of the performance of
Roman comedy and tragedy, the metaphor here is theatrical; see Moore 2012: 28.
[143] That Cicero is quoting Ennius' *Annales* (Skutsch 252) at *Att.* 15.7.1, and not the legal phrase, is
indicated by *sed quae sequuntur*, " . . . but what follows."

Servius Sulpicius, the very jurist whom Cicero parodied in the *Pro Murena*.[144]

In addition to deploying a favourite verse against them, Cicero uses Ennius to redefine the concept of *sapientia* to which the jurists laid claim. Throughout the speech, Cicero contrasts the self-proclaimed "wisdom" (*sapientia*) of the jurists (*Mur.* 7; 26) with superior models: L. Lucullus,[145] Q. Catulus, and Gaius Laelius (*Mur.* 20; 36; 66). Cicero used Ennius' *Annales* to make a distinction between the jurists' understanding of wisdom, their "wordy simulation of judgement" (*uerbosa simulatio prudentiae, Mur.* 30), and true wisdom. Since Cicero insists that the jurists were overfixated in their definitions of language in the *Pro Murena* (27), his redefinition of terms was a way of using their own methods against them.[146]

In addition to Cicero's use of Ennius' *Annales* to emphasize the seriousness of war-making (and therefore the need for a soldier-consul in 63 BCE), and his humorous appropriation of an Ennian passage beloved by jurists, Cicero quotes poetry twice more in the *Pro Murena*. Cicero cites a verse from a now unknown tragedy (*Mur.* 60; *TrRF* I 13) in which an "older teacher" (*senior magister, Mur.* 60) mentors a young man.[147] Cicero (using *praeteritio*), says that he will not school Cato the Younger as this dramatic exemplar does, but will rather offer some wisdom as an experienced consul. Finally, at the end of the speech (*Mur.* 88), Cicero emphasizes the *pathos* of Murena's plight, if he is found guilty:

hunc uestris sententiis adflixeritis,[148] quo se miser uertet? domumne? ut eam imaginem clarissimi uiri, parentis sui, quam paucis ante diebus laureatam in sua gratulatione conspexit, eandem deformatam ignominia lugentemque uideat? an ad matrem quae misera modo consulem osculata filium suum nunc cruciatur et sollicita est ne eundem paulo post spoliatum omni dignitate conspiciat?

If you strike him down with a guilty verdict, where should the wretched man turn? Home? To see the bust of that famous man, his father, which he saw

---

[144] When a *grammaticus* who claimed expertise in poetry rejected the phrase *ex iure manum consertum* as legal language rather than poetic, Aulus Gellius (20.10.4) quoted this passage of Ennius' *Annales* in protest. The *grammaticus* responded that Ennius had not learned the phrase from literature but "from someone learned in law" (*set ex iuris aliquo perito*, 20.10.5). See Howley 2018: 234.

[145] Indeed, L. Lucullus (*Mur.* 20) *manum conseruit*, "joined hands" in the Ennian sense, i.e. made war.

[146] In the *Pro Balbo* (36), Cicero gives us a taste of how jurists focused on details of language to interpret legal meaning, when he himself uses a verse of Ennius (*TrRF* II 145; quoted again at *De Off.* 1.51–52) to reject his opponent's interpretation of the treaty between Gades and Rome.

[147] Some scholars have suggested that the interchange took place between Phoenix and Achilles, see *TrRF* I p193. Zillinger (1911: 132) considered *Mur.* 60 a citation of Accius' *Myrmidones*. Quintilian (*Inst.* 8.6.30) quotes Cicero *Mur.* 60 as an example of *antonomasia*.

[148] On the tragic resonance of *adflictus*, see p179.

laureled in celebration of his own deeds only a few days before, so that he can see it disfigured and mourning his disgrace? Or to his wretched mother who just recently kissed a consul when she kissed her son and is now tortured, worried that she will see this same son robbed so shortly afterwards of all his worth?

This passage clearly echoes verses quoted by Cicero in the *De Oratore* (3.217), where he had discussed their ability to make an audience feel pity:

> aliud miseratio ac maeror, flexibile, plenum, interruptum, flebili uoce:
> *quo nunc me uortam? quod iter incipiam ingredi?*   [Jocelyn 217–218/
> *domum paternamne? anne ad Peliae filias?*   *TrRF* I 25[149]]

> Another tone is used for pity and sorrow: a wavering, resounding, sobbing, tearful voice:
> *"Where now should I turn? What path can I start to tread?*
> *Towards my father's house? Or to the daughters of Pelias?"*

In *Pro Murena* 88 Cicero uses the rhetorical technique, outlined in the *De Oratore* (2.257), of "changing a verse a little bit" (*paululum immutatus*): the poet's *uortam* ("where should I turn") is altered to *uertet* ("where should he turn"); and the second verse is truncated (*domum paternamne* to *domune*). Although Cicero foreshortens the verse, he also expands upon its contents: Cicero imagines Murena, if condemned guilty, transformed into the tragic exile, turning away from the bust of his celebrated father and the embrace of his mother. In the *De Oratore* (3.214), Cicero notes that these tragic verses were also adapted to great rhetorical effect by Gaius Gracchus:[150]

> quid fuit in Graccho, quem tu melius, Catule, meministi, quod me puero tanto opere ferretur? "quo me miser conferam? quo uertam? in Capitoliumne? at fratris sanguine madet. an domum? matremne ut miseram lamentantem uideam et abiectam?"

> What about Gracchus – you remember him better, Catulus – whose words were so famous when I was young? "Where should I, a wretch, take myself? Where should I turn? To the Capitol. But it is wet with my brother's blood. Home? To my mother, so that I can see her, wretched and lamenting, downcast?"

---

[149] These verses were traditionally attributed to Ennius' *Medea* on the basis of the similarity to Euripides' *Medea* 502–504 (Jocelyn 1969a: 356), but have recently been downgraded to *incerta* by the editors of the *TrRF* (I p203). In a letter to Atticus (*Att.* 10.12.1), Cicero seems to echo this scene: *quo me nunc uertam? undique custodior. sed satis lacrimis*, "Where now should I turn? I am hemmed in on all sides. But enough of tears"; see Čulík-Baird 2021: 111–112.

[150] On Cicero's theorization of performance and emotion in *De Or.* 3.214, see Moore 2012: 91–92.

Gracchus' engagement with tragedy was indeed so famous that both the verses and the technique became enshrined in oratorical practice. Cicero himself uses the phrase *quo me uertam* ("where should I turn?") so frequently in his orations so as to suggest that its use was an intentional echo of Gracchus rather than the poet whom Gracchus was himself drawing upon.[151] Once more, Cicero's use of poetry in oratory can be demonstrated to originate from the fact that Roman rhetorical training frequently engaged with poetic exemplars.

2.3.3 Pro Sestio *(56 BCE)*

In early March 56 BCE, Cicero defended Publius Sestius (tr. pl. 57 BCE) against the charge of *uis* (public violence).[152] As tribune in the previous year, Sestius had acted in support of Cicero's recall from exile (*Sest.* 3–5), and so when Sestius was prosecuted for the use of public violence, Cicero came to the former tribune's defense. While Cicero's *Pro Sestio* is perhaps most famous for its depiction of the struggle between the *populares* and *optimates* (especially in its "excursus," *Sest.* 96–135), which had resulted in Cicero's exile at the hands of P. Clodius Pulcher,[153] the speech also contains more citations of Latin verse than any of the other orations.[154]

In the *Pro Sestio* (101), Cicero enumerates positive exemplars of resolute *optimates*, Romans who each resisted popularists: M. Aemilius Scaurus (cos. 115 BCE), Q. Metellus Numidicus (cos. 109 BCE), and Q. Catulus (cos. 78 BCE).[155] Cicero urges his audience to imitate the qualities of these men, using verses of Accius' *Atreus* to convey the difficulty of their kind of personal resolve (*Sest.* 102–103):

> haec imitamini, per deos immortalis, qui dignitatem, qui laudem, qui gloriam quaeritis! haec ampla sunt, haec diuina, haec immortalia; haec fama celebrantur, monumentis annalium mandantur, posteritati propagantur. est labor, non nego; pericula magna, fateor
> *multae insidiae sunt bonis*   [Dangel 45]
> uerissime dictum est; sed te
> *id quod multi inuideant multique expetant, inscitia est*   [Dangel 62]
> inquit,

[151] *Verr.* 2.3.155, 2.5.2; *Cluent.* 4; *Scaur.* 19; *Lig.* 1; cf. *Att.* 10.12.1, 13.13.1–2.
[152] On the background to the *Pro Sestio*, see Riggsby 1999: 89–97, Kaster 2006: 14–22.
[153] Kaster 2006: 31–37. On the "excursus" as "political manifesto," see Kaster 2006: 31 n70 with bibliography there cited.
[154] In addition to the citations here discussed (*Sest.* 102, 118, 120–126), verse citations also appear at *Sest.* 45 (*TrRF* I 16) and *Sest.* 48 (*TrRF* I 161).
[155] On Cicero's use of historical *exempla* in the *Pro Sestio*, see van der Blom 2010: 99–100, 130–132, 164–165, 215–216.

postulare, nisi laborem summa cum cura ecferas   [Dangel 63]
nollem idem alio loco dixisset, quod exciperent improbi ciues:
oderint, dum metuant   [Dangel 47]
[103] praeclara enim illa praecepta dederat iuuentuti.

Imitate these things, by the immortal gods, you who seek dignity, who seek
praise, who seek glory! These things are magnificent, they are divine, they
are immortal; they are celebrated in oral traditions, they are committed to
the monuments of the annals, they are preserved for posterity. It is work,
I do not deny it. The dangers are great, I confess it.
"Many traps are set for good men"
Most truly said. But for you,
"it is foolish to desire what many men envy, and many themselves seek,"
as he says,
"unless you summon the strength follow through with the greatest devotion."
I would wish that the same man had, in a different place, not said the words
which the worst men repeat:
"Let them hate, as long as they fear."
For in those other words he had given excellent advice to the young.

Though Cicero names neither poet nor the dramatic character, he signals his
citations with the tags *uerissime dictum est* ("most truly said") and *inquit* ("he
says").[156] *"Multae insidiae sunt bonis"* ("many traps are set for good men") is
a gnomic, proverbial phrase which calls to mind the dangers faced by those
who try to lead moral and upstanding lives, the kind of maxim that could easily
become detached from its original context. Since this Accian citation appears
in the *Pro Sestio*'s excursus on the conflict between *optimates* and *populares*
(*Sest.* 96–135), Cicero's use of the verse adds a political layer to the term *boni*; for
Accius, this may simply have meant men who did not commit evil deeds, but
for Cicero the *boni* were Rome's "best": the conservatives, the *optimates*.[157]

The same verses of Accius' *Atreus* which Cicero cites in the *Pro Sestio*
(102) would also appear in the *Pro Plancio* a few years later.[158] Cicero's use
of the *Atreus* in the *Pro Plancio* reveals more about the value of Accius'
verses as *praecepta* as well as their dramatic context. Responding to the
question of whether his own son (now the son of a consular) was more

---

[156] Cicero uses *inquit* of both poets (e.g. *inquit Accius, Off.* 3.84) and characters (e.g. *inquit Hector,
Fam.* 15.6.1). A comparison with *Pro Plancio* (59) suggests that the subject of *inquit* at *Sest.* 102 is
Atreus.

[157] Accius' plays, however, may themselves have explicitly meditated on the political upheaval of their
own era; see Boyle 2006: 126–127.

[158] Cicero defended Cn. Plancius against the charge of *ambitus* in 54 BCE. On this speech, see Craig
1990, Alexander 2002: 128–144, Lintott 2008: 119–223.

worthy of office than Cicero himself (the son of an *eques*) had been, Cicero draws upon Accius' depiction of fatherly wisdom (*Planc.* 59):

> quin etiam, ne forte ille sibi me potius peperisse iam honores quam iter demonstrasse adipiscendorum putet, haec illi soleo praecipere (quamquam ad praecepta aetas non est grauis) quae rex ille a Ioue ortus suis praecipit filiis: *uigilandum est semper: multae insidiae sunt bonis*;   [Dangel 45]
> *id quod multi inuideant . . .*   [Dangel 62]
> nostis cetera.[159] nonne, quae scripsit grauis ille et ingeniosus poeta, scripsit non ut illos regios pueros, qui iam nusquam erant, sed ut nos et nostros liberos ad laborem et laudem excitaret.

> No, indeed, so that he would not by chance think that I have already acquired honours for him rather than shown him the way to get them, I regularly teach him (even though he is not quite old enough for these lessons) what the king sprung from Jupiter[160] teaches his own sons:
> "*Always be alert: many traps are set for good men*";
> "*what many men envy . . .*"
> You know the rest. Isn't it the case that what our serious poet of genius wrote, he wrote to encourage us and our children to pursue hard work and praise, not those royal children who no longer exist?

In the *Pro Roscio*, Cicero had asserted that despite comedy's status as "fiction" (*conficta, Rosc.* 47), scenes from the theatre could nonetheless reflect Roman values. In the *Pro Plancio*, Cicero argues that Accius, unnamed but signified by *ingeniosus poeta*,[161] had "written" (*scripsit*) the scene in which a father (Atreus or Thyestes[162]) gives lessons to his sons as an exemplar for Romans and their children. Indeed, Cicero himself takes on the role of the father figure in the tragedy: just as the character "teaches his own sons" (*suis praecipit filiis*), Cicero "regularly teaches" his own (*illi soleo praecipere*). Even though this is a play in which a father, Atreus, murders his brother's children and feeds them to him, as Cicero elsewhere (*TD* 4.77) states explicitly, elements of this tragedy about cannibalism can still apparently be taken as an ethical model.

---

[159] See p23, on "*nosti quae sequuntur*" and similar phrases.

[160] Cf. *TD* 3.26 where Cicero calls Thyestes (brother of Atreus) *Iouis pronepos* ("great-grandson of Jupiter").

[161] Cf. Ennius as *ingeniosus poeta* (*Mur.* 30).

[162] On the identity of the speaker (or speakers?) of the lines from Accius' *Atreus* quoted at *Sest.* 102–103 and *Planc.* 59, see Dangel 2002: 282. At *Off.* 1.97 Cicero seems to imply that *oderint dum metuant* was spoken by Atreus; at *Sest.* 102 Cicero also seems to imply that whoever said *oderint dum metuant* also said the other verses there quoted (*idem alio loco . . .*, "the same man in a different place . . . "), but of course Cicero may be referring to Accius rather than to the tragic character. At *Planc.* 59 there is a deliberate slippage between the tragic character (*ille praecipit*) and Accius (*ille scripsit*) as producers of fatherly *praecepta*.

However, Cicero's comments in the *Pro Sestio* reveal an anxiety regarding the suitability of Accius' *Atreus* as positive exemplar: in this tragedy, the poet is simultaneously the author of good morals *and* dangerous ones. The precept "*oderint, dum metuant*" ("let them hate, as long as they fear"),[163] Cicero says, has been adopted by the "worst citizens" (*improbi ciues, Sest.* 102). This additional comment in the *Pro Sestio* allows Cicero to reassure his audience that he understands that Accius' *Atreus* is not an unambiguous moral text. In the *De Officiis* (1.97), Cicero would say that *oderint dum metuant* is an appropriate statement for a figure such as Atreus, but not for "just men" (*iusti*) such as Aeacus or Minos, the mythological judges of the underworld.[164] In the *Pro Sestio*, Atreus' maxim arises in the context of a discussion of the pursuit of honour, praise, and glory (*Sest.* 102); in the *Philippics* (1.33–34), Cicero would reprise his reading of Accius' *Atreus* as inverse *gloria*:

> quod si ita putas, totam ignoras uiam gloriae. carum esse ciuem, bene de re publica mereri, laudari, coli, diligi gloriosum est; metui uero et in odio esse inuidiosum, detestabile, imbecillum, caducum. [1.34] quod uidemus etiam in fabula illi ipsi qui
> *oderint, dum metuant*   [Dangel 47]
> dixerit perniciosum fuisse. utinam, M. Antoni, auum tuum meminisses!

> But if you think like this, then you have no idea about the path to glory. It is glorious to be a citizen who is dear to the people, to deserve well of the Republic, to be praised, to be revered, to be loved. To be feared and hated is odious, execrable, weak, vulnerable. [1.34] Even in the play we see that it was destructive to the very character who said:
> "*Let them hate, so long as they fear.*"
> Would that you, Mark Antony, remembered your own grandfather!

In addition to Cicero's adoption of the paternal persona from Accius' *Atreus*, the *Pro Sestio* also contains an extended oratorical restaging of theatrical events which took place during Cicero's exile. The theatre is a space where the Roman people showed their attitude to politicians: during the *Ludi Apollinares* of 59 BCE, Pompey was taunted by the tragic actor, Diphilus, who punningly applied a verse to him: "you are called 'Great,' and so we suffer" (*nostra miseria tu es magnus, Att.* 2.19.3; *TrRF* I 15).[165] Cicero received applause in the theatre in 54 BCE (*Att.* 4.15.6, *Q. fr.* 2.14.2), and Hortensius

---

[163] Infamously credited as a maxim of the emperors Tiberius (Suet. *Tib.* 59) and Caligula (Suet. *Gaius* 30); and the topic of philosophical discussion by Seneca (*Ira* 1.20.4; *Clem.* 1.12.4, 2.2.2).

[164] At *Off.* 1.97, Cicero adds the detail that when Atreus speaks this famous line, it arouses applause from the audience.

[165] On this passage, see Wright 1913: 5–9, Jocelyn 1969a: 238, Boyle 2006: 152–153.

was hissed at in Curio's temporary theatre in 51 BCE (*Fam.* 8.2.1).[166] In 44 BCE, Cicero described audience reactions to a performance of mime by Publilius Syrus as "good signs of popular accord" (*bona signa consentientis multitudinis, Att.* 14.2.1); one of these signs was applause for L. Cassius.[167]

In the *Pro Sestio* (115), Cicero analyzed the theatre as a mechanism by which the will of the people could be truly expressed, or maliciously falsified:[168]

> ueniamus ad ludos; facit enim, iudices, uester iste in me animorum oculorumque coniectus ut mihi iam licere putem remissiore uti genere dicendi. comitiorum et contionum significationes sunt interdum uerae, sunt non numquam uitiatae atque corruptae; theatrales gladiatoriique consessus dicuntur omnino solere leuitate non nullorum emptos plausus exilis et raros excitare; ac tamen facile est, cum id fit, quem ad modum et a quibus fiat, et quid integra multitudo faciat uidere. quid ego nunc dicam quibus uiris aut cui generi ciuium maxime plaudatur? neminem uestrum fallit. sit hoc sane leue, quod non ita est, quoniam optimo cuique impertitur; sed, si est leue, homini graui leue est, ei uero qui pendet rebus leuissimis, qui rumore et, ut ipsi loquuntur, fauore populi tenetur et ducitur, plausum immortalitatem, sibilum mortem uideri necesse est.

> Let us come to the games. For the focus of your minds and eyes upon me make me think that I can use a looser kind of speech. Applause at the assemblies and at public meetings are sometimes expressions of truth; they are sometimes falsified and corrupt. The theatrical and gladiatorial shows are said to habitually excite thin and scattered applause, bought by the fickleness of a few men.[169] But when that happens, it is easy to see how and by whom it is started, and what the real audience is doing. Why should I now tell you which men or what kind of citizen is the most greatly applauded? Everyone knows. Consider applause superficial, then; it isn't, since it is bestowed on the best. But, if it is superficial, it is only so to the most authoritative man, but to the one who relies on these most superficial things, who is gripped by rumour, and as they themselves say, the favour of the people, and is led along by them, this man must consider applause to be immortality itself, and hissing death.

---

[166] Other reports of Cicero's reception at public spectacles include: *Att.* 1.16.11 (July 61 BCE), where applause arises without the whistling of the *pastoricia fistula* ("shepherd's pipe"); see Wright 1931: 5, Kaster 2006: 346. In 44 BCE, Cicero would complain (*Att.* 16.2.3) that the audience of Accius' *Tereus* would "use their hands clapping rather than defending the state" (*manus suas non in defendenda re publica sed in plaudendo consumere*). Vanderbroeck 1987, Appendix B collects testimonia for popular support in theatrical settings.

[167] Cf. *Att.* 14.3.2. On the ability of mime to reflect popular sentiment, see Panayotakis 2010: 15.

[168] On Cicero's exaggeration of the importance of demonstrations of popular feeling, see Cameron 1976: 159.

[169] Appian (*BC* 3.24) notes that "certain men were hired" (ἐμμίσθων γάρ τινων) to shout for the recall of Brutus and Cassius at Brutus' games in 44 BCE, affecting the emotions of the other spectators.

Cicero here anticipates objections to the idea that popular responses to public men at theatrical performances could be used as evidence of a statesman's value, since he will shortly cite events which took place at the theatre during his exile as an index of the people's longing for him in his absence.[170] In the *Pro Sestio* (115), Cicero calls to mind the "authoritative man" (*homo grauis*) who finds applause at the theatre "superficial" (*leuis*). In the *In Pisonem* (65), Cicero would further develop the idea of the good statesman who does not need to value public opinion by criticizing Piso as incapable of reaching such an ideal:

> fac huius odi tanti ac tam universi periculum, si audes. instant post hominum memoriam apparatissimi magnificentissimique ludi, quales non modo numquam fuerunt, sed ne quo modo fieri quidem posthac possint possum ullo pacto suspicari. da te populo, committe ludis. sibilum metuis? ubi sunt uestrae scholae? ne acclametur times? ne id quidem est curare philosophi. manus tibi ne adferantur? dolor enim est malum, ut tu disputas; existimatio, dedecus, infamia, turpitudo: uerba atque ineptiae. sed de hoc non dubito; non audebit accedere ad ludos.

> Test this universal and bitter hatred against you, if you dare. The most magnificent and spectacular games in human memory are soon upon us, games whose kind has never existed before, and which I can't even imagine will occur like this ever again in the future. Give yourself to the people, trust yourself to the games. Do you fear the hissing? Where are your lessons? Are you afraid that they will heckle you? That is surely not an anxiety for a philosopher like you. Are you afraid of violence against you? Yes, pain is an evil, according to your system. But judgement, disgrace, dishonour, shame: those are just words, right? But about this I have no doubt: he will not dare come anywhere near those games.

Cicero claims that Piso, aware of his own bad reputation (*Pis.* 64), will avoid even the upcoming inaugural games of Pompey's theatre – greatly anticipated to be the most lavish games in recorded history – because of how the public will receive him. Testing the limits of Piso's Epicureanism, Cicero reveals the risks facing a disreputable politician when he enters the theatre: hissing, insults, and even violence. To Cicero,

---

[170] In the *De Republica* (4.11 = Aug. *Civ. Dei* 2.9), Cicero has Scipio say that, unlike in Greek comedy, where politicians (e.g. Cleon, Cleophon, Hyperbolus; even Pericles) can be named and ridiculed on stage, it was not the practice of the Roman comic playwrights (specifically Plautus, Naevius, and Caecilius Statius) to engage in libel. Yet even if this was the case (see Goldberg 1995: 36 on Naevius and the Metelli), Cicero's repeated insistence that both actors and audience at theatrical events at Rome were ready to interpret verse as reflection of the character of politicians demonstrates that there were other, more allusive ways to criticize great men in public, if not explicitly by name.

such responses to Piso in the theatre constitute genuine reflections of Piso's bad character.[171] Piso is not the *homo grauis* with nothing to fear who can dismiss popular opinion; instead, the audience at the theatre confirms the truth of Piso's shameful actions (as Cicero has construed them). In the *Pro Sestio*, Cicero mocks the lengths to which shameful politicians will go to hide themselves from such public ridicule. Appius Claudius, brother of P. Clodius and praetor in 57 BCE, manufactured dissent against Cicero at *contiones*, but would avoid the true criticism of the Roman people by sneaking into the gladiatorial games through a trapdoor, appearing suddenly like the ghost of Deipylus in Pacuvius' *Iliona* (*Sest.* 126):

> . . . contionem interrogare solebat, uelletne me redire, et, cum erat recla-
> matum semiuiuis mercennariorum uocibus, populum Romanum negare
> dicebat, is, cum cotidie gladiatores spectaret, numquam est conspectus cum
> ueniret. emergebat subito, cum sub tabulas subrepserat, ut
> *mater, te appello*   [Schierl T 55/fr. 146]
> dicturus uideretur; itaque illa uia latebrosior, qua spectatum ille ueniebat,
> Appia iam uocabatur; qui tamen quoquo tempore conspectus erat, non
> modo gladiatores sed equi ipsi gladiatorum repentinis sibilis extimescebant.

> . . . he used to ask the *contio* whether they wanted me to return, and, when the half-dead voices of his hired goons had responded "no," he said that this was the will of the Roman people. Yet this is the man who, although he went to see the gladiatorial games every day, he was never actually seen going there. He appeared suddenly, since he had crept through under the floor-boards, like the character who will say,
> "*Mother, I call upon you!*"[172]
> And so that secret path, by which he went to the games, was called the Via Appia.[173] Nonetheless when he was actually seen there, not only the gladi-ators but even their horses were scared witless by the sudden hissing!

In the *Pro Sestio*, Cicero also claims that P. Clodius, a man so familiar with the theatrical milieu that he was "not only a spectator, but an actor and

---

[171] Cf. *Deiot.* 33–34, where lack of applause for Caesar at the theatre is taken as index of low popular opinion.

[172] Cicero also refers to the appearance of the ghost of Deipylus "from the earth" (*exoritur e terra*) in the *Tusculans* (1.106). In the *Academica* (2.88), Cicero quotes *mater, te appello* again, where he says that Deipylus' appearance was part of Iliona's dream (cf. Hor. *Serm.* 2.3.60–62; Schierl 2006: 324–327). On this passage and Pacuvian spectacle, see Boyle 2006: 94–95.

[173] A pun on the Via Appia built by Appius' ancestor, Appius Claudius (censor 312 BCE), which ran from Rome to Brundisium. Cicero refers to it again in the *Pro Caelio* (34) when he takes on the role of the ancient statesman to chastize Clodia.

a buffoon" (*non solum spectator, sed actor et acroama, Sest.* 116),[174] nonetheless avoided the theatrical games during his tribunate (58 BCE), knowing what kind of response would greet him.[175] On a later occasion, in 57 BCE (*Sest.* 118), Clodius did brave the games, and the entire dramatic company playing Afranius' *Simulans* ("The Pretender") turned against him:[176]

> nam cum ageretur togata Simulans, ut opinor, caterua tota clarissima concentione in ore impuri hominis imminens contionata est:
> *huic, Tite, tua post principia atque exitus uitiosae uitae!*   [Ribbeck 304–305]
> sedebat exanimatus, et is, qui antea cantorum conuicio contiones celebrare suas solebat, cantorum ipsorum uocibus eiciebatur. et quoniam facta mentio est ludorum, ne illud quidem praetermittam, in magna uarietate sententiarum numquam ullum fuisse locum, in quo aliquid a poeta dictum cadere in tempus nostrum uideretur, quod aut populum uniuersum fugeret aut non exprimeret ipse actor.

> For when the *fabula togata*,[177] Afranius' *"The Pretender"* (I think it was), was being played, the entire troupe, singing together in the clearest harmony, made a *contio* against that filthy man as they loomed over him:
> *"This, Titus, is the sequel for you, the end of your wicked life!"*
> He was sitting there lifeless, and he, whose habit it previously was to crowd his own *contiones* with a chorus of abuse, was himself thrown out by the voices of this chorus! Since I mention the games, I will not neglect to say also this: there was never a passage among the great number of sayings from the theatre, where something said by a poet seems so pertinent to our own time, which either escaped the notice of the whole people, or the actor himself failed to pointedly express.

Verses originally written by the poet, L. Afranius, are made to apply to contemporary politics (*in tempus nostrum, Sest.* 118). Clodius, as the *popularis* who manipulated crowds with claques to alter political outcomes, is here given an ironic treatment: a genuine expression of will from the company of actors on the Roman stage. Cicero's language emphasizes the ironic inversion: Clodius as tribune had held corrupt *contiones* against Cicero (*Sest.* 106), but a throng of actors in their own way "held a *contio*"

---

174 Wright 1931: 8, 94.
175 Cicero (*Sest.* 116) asks M. Scaurus, presiding praetor and curule aedile in 58 BCE, if he remembers Clodius attending any of his games. Scaurus used three hundred and sixty columns as part of his temporary theatre (Pliny *NH* 34.36; 36.5–6; 36.113–15); see Manuwald 2011: 61.
176 On *Sest.* 118, see Moore 2012: 72–73, Hanses 2020: 123–125.
177 The *fabula togata* was a genre of comedy which, in contrast to the *fabula palliata* (i.e. the comedies of Plautus and Terence), staged plays in Roman dress and in a Roman setting, see Manuwald 2011: 156–169. Cicero quotes only the *togatae* of L. Afranius and Titinius, see Appendix II. On L. Afranius, see Wright 1931: 39.

against him (*contionata est, Sest.* 118) which expressed the true will of the people. Clodius' manipulations of popular will are thereby vitiated via dramatic response. The humiliation of Clodius in the theatre is an extension of several of comedy's essential functions: the ridicule of the powerful; the assertion of true social order via its apparent inversion; strengthening the feeling of social cohesion.[178]

Just as the true will of the people expressed itself against Clodius (and his brother), so too did the theatre allow the popular support of Cicero to manifest itself. Cicero emphasizes the argument, seeded earlier in the *Pro Sestio* (115), that applause from the public is not a superficial index of value since it is "bestowed on the best" (*optimo impertitur, Sest.* 115). The image of the *homo grauis*, the authoritative conservative who does not live or die with the fluctuations of public opinion, has given way to Cicero's more urgent argument: that the true will of the people, obscured by Clodius and his cronies at political meetings, was nonetheless perceptible in the theatre. Cicero (*Sest.* 120–121) describes how the tragic actor, Clodius Aesopus, emphasized lines of Accius' *Eurysaces* in order to make them apply to Cicero:[179]

> . . . recenti nuntio de illo senatus consulto quod factum est in templo uirtutis ad ludos scaenamque perlato, consessu maximo summus artifex et mehercule semper partium in re publica tam quam in scaena optimarum, flens et recenti laetitia et mixto dolore ac desiderio mei, egit apud populum Romanum multo grauioribus uerbis meam causam quam egomet de me agere potuissem? summi enim poetae ingenium non solum arte sua, sed etiam dolore exprimebat. qua enim
>
> *qui rem publicam certo animo adiuuerit,*   [Dangel 360–361]
> *statuerit, steterit cum Achiuis*
>
> uobiscum me stetisse dicebat, uestros ordines demonstrabat! reuocabatur ab uniuersis
>
>   *re dubia*   [Dangel 362–363]
> *haut dubitarit uitam offerre nec capiti pepercerit.*
> haec quantis ab illo clamoribus agebantur! [121] cum iam omisso gestu uerbis poetae et studio actoris et exspectationi nostrae plauderetur
> *summum amicum summo in bello*   [Dangel 364]

---

[178] On the "conspiracy of laughter," see Bergson (1912: 6–7): "However spontaneous it seems, laughter always implies a kind of secret freemasonry, or even complicity, with other laughers, real or imaginary. How often has it been said that the fuller the theatre, the more uncontrolled the laughter of the audience! On the other hand, how often has the remark been made that many comic effects are incapable of translation from one language to another, because they refer to the customs and ideas of a particular social group." On the operation of comic conspiracy in Cicero's *Pro Caelio*, see Geffcken 1973: 4.

[179] Aesopus is named as the actor at *Sest.* 123. On Aesopus the tragic actor, see Wright 1931: 10–13; Manuwald 2011: 89. On *Sest.* 120–123, see Moore 2012: 66–68, 77.

nam illud ipse actor adiungebat amico animo et fortasse homines propter
aliquod desiderium adprobabant:
summo ingenio praeditum.   [Dangel 364]

... when the news of the senate's decree passed in the Temple of Virtue
was brought to the games and the stage, before a great crowd, that
supreme artist who, by god, always played the best role in the state and
on the stage, weeping with this fresh happiness, a happiness mixed with
pain and longing for me – did this man not plead my case before the
Roman people with more authoritative words than I could have on my
own behalf? He gave force to the genius of that supreme poet not only
through his own art but with true pain. For when he said:
"The man who aided the state with unwavering conviction,
he set it straight, he stood with the Achaeans,"
he was saying that *I* had stood with *you*, he was pointing at all of the orders
here assembled! A reprise was demanded from all sides;
                                        "during uncertain times
he did not hesitate to offer his life, nor did he spare himself,"
when he performed these words the crowd shouted in such agreement! [121]
They applauded the words of the poet, the emotion of the actor, the hope of
my return, not the artifice of the stage;
"the greatest friend, in the greatest war,"
that is the phrase which the actor himself added, friendly towards me, and
perhaps the people agreed out of some longing for me:
"endowed with the greatest genius."

News of the senatorial decree which reversed Cicero's exile in 57 BCE (*Sest.* 116–
117) is brought to the theatre, where Accius' *Eurysaces* was being played.[180]
Aesopus emphasized certain tragic verses, applying them to Cicero: when
Aesopus said *"he stood with the Achaeans"* (*steterit cum Achiuis,* Dangel 361),
he meant not simply the tragic exile, but the exiled Cicero: "he was saying that
I had stood with *you*" (*uobiscum me stetisse dicebat, Sest.* 120).[181] Such metathea-
trical collapse between reality and the stage also made the audience part of the
tragedy: Roman spectators are made to take on the role of the "Achaeans." This
maneuvre allows Cicero to further his characterization of the theatre as

---

[180] Accius is named as the poet at *Sest.* 123. That the tragedy was Accius' *Eurysaces* is provided by the
Scholia Bobiensia (p136.30 St.), see Jocelyn 1969a: 239, Dangel 2002: 331. Because Cicero says that
the verses quoted in *Sest.* 120–121 come from "the same play" (*in eadem fabula*) as verses which are
known to be from Ennius' *Andromacha* (*Sest.* 121–122) and Accius' *Brutus* (*Sest.* 123), there has been
a great deal of scholarly debate as to how these fragments are to be assigned; see Jocelyn 1969a: 238–
241. It seems likely that Cicero is deliberately presenting a medley of tragic verses.

[181] The verses from Accius' *Eurysaces* may have referred either to Telamo or to Teucer, each exiled by
their own fathers; for a history of the reconstructions of the tragedy in *Sest.* 120–121, see Jocelyn
1969a: 238–241.

a microcosm of the Roman state: Aesopus' gesture to his audience was not just an invitation to a mass of spectators, but to the Roman *ordines* (*Sest.* 120), i.e. the senate, the *equites*, and the people.[182] Cicero repeated this emphasis upon the Roman audience as a civic entity when he quoted another verse from Accius' *Eurysaces* (*Sest.* 122):

> sed tamen illud scripsit disertissimus poeta pro me, egit fortissimus actor, non solum optimus, de me, cum omnis ordines demonstraret, senatum, equites Romanos, uniuersum populum Romanum accusaret:
> *exsulare sinitis, sistis pelli, pulsum patimini!* [Dangel 366]
> quae tum significatio fuerit omnium, quae declaratio uoluntatis ab uniuerso populo Romano in causa hominis non popularis, equidem audiebam, existimare facilius possunt, qui adfuerunt.

> But nonetheless the most learned poet wrote this for me, the bravest and best actor played it and made it refer to me when he pointed out all the orders – the senate, the Roman *equites*, the entire Roman people – and accused them:
> *"You allow him to be an exile, you let him be driven out, you acquiesce in his expulsion!"*
> What the whole audience then felt, what a clear demonstration of will from the entire Roman people for the cause of a man who is not *popularis*, as I later heard, can be more easily judged by those who were there.

The theatre speaks the true will of the Roman people in support of Cicero, not the *popularis* Clodius who had made claims on public opinion while deliberately distorting it. On stage, Aesopus the actor played a tragic character, but Cicero also makes Aesopus "play" Cicero himself in his absence: *egit ... grauioribus uerbis meam causam quam egomet de me agere potuissem?* "did this man not plead my case ... with more authoritative words than I could have on my own behalf?" (*Sest.* 120).[183] Since orators were surrogates for their clients, Aesopus' "pleading" of Cicero's case fulfilled the role of the orator's rhetorical surrogacy.[184] Though there is a social distance between them, actors and orators regularly appear together in Cicero's rhetorical treatises as performers with a shared repertoire: they train their bodies as well as their voices for performance; they are capable of presenting emotions as though they were

---

[182] Following the *Lex Roscia* (67 BCE), which reserved the first fourteen rows to the *equites*, the term "*ordines*" also referred to the theatre seating itself: *illud tamen audaciae tuae quod sedisti in quattuor-decim ordinibus, cum esset lege Roscia decoctoribus certus locus constitutus, quamuis quis fortunae uitio, non suo decoxisset,* "But it was your own arrogance that made you sit in the fourteen rows, when bankrupts had their place allotted to them under the *Lex Roscia,* even those whose plight was not their own fault, but just bad luck" (*Ph.* 2.44); see Manuwald 2011: 107.

[183] On *agere* as both "to act in a play" and "to plead a case," see Fantham 2002: 362–376.

[184] On oratorical surrogacy, see May 1988: 10. The terms *actor* and *orator* converge in the prologue to Terence's *Heautontimoroumenos* (11–15); on this passage, see Fantham 2002: 362.

genuine, and in so doing affect the emotions of their audiences.[185] If the theatre was a mirror image of the Roman state, the persuasive power which belonged to Cicero himself would be represented by the actor, Aesopus.[186] While Cicero wrote his own "scripts," Aesopus' was provided by the poet, Accius: thus, Accius is figured as writing "on behalf" of Cicero (*scripsit disertissimus poeta pro me, Sest.* 122).[187]

Yet, according to Cicero, Aesopus deviated from his script. Cicero says that Aesopus himself added a new verse (*Sest.* 121) which referred to Cicero as the "the greatest friend, in the greatest war" (*summum amicum summo in bello, Sest.* 121/Dangel 364). Cicero also says that Aesopus added excerpts from Ennius' *Andromacha* (*Sest.* 121/ *TrRF* II 23), in which the titular character bewailed the death of "father" Priam, and the burning of Priam's palace; these verses, Cicero says, were interpreted as referring to himself, the "father of the people" (*pater patriae, Sest.* 121), and the destruction of his house on the Palatine by Clodius. Aesopus also quoted a verse from Accius' *Brutus* (Dangel 674), in which Cicero was "mentioned by name" (*nominatim appellatus sum, Sest.* 123); it was, of course, the legendary Roman king, Servius Tullius, whom Accius named, but the mention of a "Tullius" who saved the state was applied to Marcus "Tullius" Cicero.[188] Aesopus' creative response to the contemporary events revealed, in Cicero's view, the truth of the reality; not only did the Roman stage respond to Roman politics, but the theatre itself was viewed as a microcosm of Rome.

---

[185] Indeed, Plutarch (*Cic.* 5.4) thought that Cicero was trained by Aesopus (and Roscius) as a young man. The orator ought to emulate the *gestus* ("gesture") and *uenustas* ("poise") of the actor, Roscius (*De Or.* 1.251); but not pursue the dramatic technique so far that they warm up their voice lying down (*De Or.* 1.251).

[186] In the *De Oratore* (3.217–219), Cicero presents nine citations of Roman drama to exemplify different emotions which an orator can convey: anger (*iracundia*), pity and sorrow (*miseratio*; *maeror*); fear (*metus*), force (*uis*); desire (*uoluptas*), distress (*molestia*). Among these are the verses of Ennius' *Andromacha* (3.217; *TrRF* II 23) which appear at *Sest.* 122. In the *De Oratore* (3.120), Cicero gives an assessment of the physicality of Aesopus' (if *ille alter* refers to him) performance of Ennius' *Andromacha*. Aesopus and Accius are cited by Cicero (*TD* 4.55) as examples of how actors and poets are capable of manufacturing emotions that they do not actually feel, just as Cicero himself does (for the complete opposite, cf. *De Or.* 2.193). Cicero made an equivalence between himself and Aesopus in the *De Div.* (1.80), where Cicero and Aesopus are cited together as performers whose passionate *actio* seemed like temporary madness (cf. *De Or.* 2.194). According to Plutarch (*Cic.* 5.5), Aesopus was so transported in the principal role of Accius' *Atreus* that he accidentally killed a slave who was running across the stage when he struck him with a sceptre.

[187] Cf. *De Or.* 2.194: *neque actor ... alienae personae sed auctor meae,* "I am not an actor of another character, but author of my own." On which, Fantham (2002: 363) writes: "For Cicero the stage actor merely imitated reality, whereas the orator engaged with it: the actor was only the performer of a role created by another (the poet) outside himself, but the orator was both originator of his own role and responsible for it."

[188] Cf. *Brut.* 62, where Cicero says that it would be ridiculous for him to make a claim to the Tullius who was consul in 500 BCE.

2.3.4   Pro Caelio *(56 BCE)*

In 56 BCE, Cicero defended his protégé, M. Caelius Rufus, who had been indicted under the *Lex Plautia de ui* for a number of crimes, including an attempt to poison his lover, Clodia (*Cael.* 30, 56–69).[189] Cicero's speech in Caelius' defense took place on the second day of the trial, April 4, 56 BCE, which was also the first day of the annual *Ludi Megalenses*.[190] The *lex de ui* allowed a trial to take place during these *ludi*, while regular criminal proceedings seem to have been suspended (*Cael.* 1–2; cf. *Fam.* 8.8.1).[191] Cicero therefore begins by establishing what Katherine Geffcken (1973: 2) called a "theatrical and holiday atmosphere" in order to compete with the *ludi* for Magna Mater which were simultaneously taking place on the Palatine. Cicero's effort to be as entertaining (maybe even more so) than the games reminds us that tightrope walkers and boxers drew audiences away from performances of Terence's *Hecyra*; the attention space at Roman games was inherently competitive.[192] Cicero, like Terence, projects the image of an audience that longed to be entertained elsewhere.

The *Pro Caelio* is today famous for its theatricality.[193] Indeed, the speech has been treated as exceptional for the way in which it draws upon comedy, but, as the current survey should make clear, it is not entirely unique in this regard. Certainly Cicero himself applies greater emphasis to the explicit theatricality of this speech: the *exordium* identifies the court as rival spectacle to the *ludi* on the Palatine, Cicero uses humour extensively in order to undermine the severity of Caelius' alleged crimes, and Cicero himself plays different characters over the course of the oration. However, overemphasizing the *Pro Caelio* as citationally unique has the effect of

---

[189] Austin 1960: 152–154, Wiseman 1985: 54–91, Riggsby 1999: 97.

[190] These games celebrated the cult of the Great Mother (Magna Mater or Cybele), who had been imported to Rome in 204 BCE. Once her temple on the Palatine hill at Rome was dedicated in 191 BCE or shortly before (see: Manuwald 2011: 44), theatrical productions became a part of her annual games. Plautus' *Pseudolus* was performed before the Temple of Magna Mater in 191 BCE, and four of Terence's comedies were performed during the *Ludi Megalenses* in the 160s BCE (see: Gruen 1992: 186n16). Unfortunately, Cicero does not tell us which plays were being performed during the games in 56 BCE. On the date of the trial, see Dyck 2013: 4.

[191] Austin 1960: 153, Geffcken 1973: 10, Riggsby 1999: 100. Goldberg (2005: 92 n12) notes that in 52 BCE, Milo was also prosecuted *de ui* during the *Megalenses*.

[192] Terence *Hecyra,* Prologue I, 4–5; Prologue II, 33–36. On these passages, see Goldberg 2013: 15–16.

[193] Geffcken (1973) demonstrated that motifs of Roman comedy were structurally vital to Cicero's argumentation in this speech. The importance of comic tropes to the *Pro Caelio* was further studied by Saltzman (1982), Leigh (2004), Goldberg (2005: 92–96); Hanses (2020: 130–155) correctly emphasizes that the *Pro Caelio* has multiple theatrical influences: i.e., tragedy and mime as well as comedy. Ribbeck (1855: 311) detected influence of mime on *Cael.* 65; on this passage see Hollis 1998, Hanses 2020: 151–152.

distancing it from the other orations with which it shares the techniques of quotation or allusion, as well as from the fact that the performative strategies of oratory and drama often intersect, and that each genre deliberately comments on the other. The stage, as we have seen, could reflect Roman life: citation of comedy is not a citation of another world entirely, but instead constitutes an invocation of a refracted vision of reality.

Infamously, Clodia, older sister of P. Clodius Pulcher, is made to take on several dramatic roles in the *Pro Caelio*. In an addition to Cicero's repeated insistence (*Cael.* 1, 37, 48, 49, 50, 57) that Clodia played the prostitute (*meretrix*) to Caelius' *adulescens*,[194] Cicero also refers to Clodia as an Ennian Medea (*Cael.* 18):[195]

> reprehendistis, a patre quod semigrarit. quod quidem iam in hac aetate minime reprehendendum est. qui cum et ex publica causa iam esset mihi quidem molestam, sibi tamen gloriosam uictoriam consecutus et per aetatem magistratus petere posset, non modo permittente patre, sed etiam suadente ab eo semigrauit et, cum domus patris a foro longe abesset, quo facilius et nostras domus obire et ipse a suis coli posset, conduxit in Palatio non magno domum. quo loco possum dicere id, quod uir clarissimus, M. Crassus, cum de aduentu regis Ptolemaei quereretur, paulo ante dixit:
> *utinam ne in nemore Pelio*   [*TrRF* II 89, 1]
> ac longius quidem mihi contexere hoc carmen liceret:
> *nam numquam era errans*   [*TrRF* II 89, 8]
> hanc molestiam nobis exhiberet
> *Medea animo aegra, amore saeuo saucia.*   [*TrRF* II 89, 9]
> sic enim, iudices, reperietis, quod, cum ad id loci uenero, ostendam, hanc Palatinam Medeam hanc adulescenti causam siue malorum omnium siue potius sermonum fuisse.

> You criticized him for leaving his father's house, which, at his age, is not something to criticize at all. He had just won a public case which, while annoying to me, was a glorious victory for him, and, because of his age, he was able to seek elected office. His father not only gave him permission but even persuaded him to leave and, since his father's house was far from the forum, he rented a house on the Palatine with a modest rent, so that he could more easily visit us and himself keep in touch with his clients. Here I can say what that illustrious man, M. Crassus, recently said, when he was lamenting the arrival of the King Ptolemy:

194 Leigh 2004: 303–311.
195 On *Cael.* 18, see: Austin 1960: 68–60, Geffcken 1973: 16–17, Narducci 1981, Alexander 2002: 226–229, Goldberg 2005: 93–96, Leigh 2004: 306, 308–309, Skinner 2011: 105–106, Dyck 2013: 85–86, Hanses 2020: 132–135.

"Would that not in Pelian grove ... "
I could weave this song even further.
"For never the wandering mistress,"
would be annoying us,
"Medea, sick at heart, wounded with savage love."
Thus, judges, you will discover what I will show when I come to that part of
the speech, that this Palatine Medea was the cause of all the evils which befell
this young man, or rather, of all the gossip.

M. Licinius Crassus, one of the members of Caelius' defense team, had
already quoted from Ennius' *Medea* during the trial: *paulo ante dixit*, "he
recently said" (*Cael.* 18). As we have seen, this very passage, the opening of
Ennius' *Medea*, was firmly situated in the oratorical curriculum (*Rhet.* 2.34,
Inv. 1.91); indeed, Cicero presents the verses precisely in the truncated form
recommended by the *Rhetorica*.[196] As a result, Crassus' (and Cicero's) use of
these verses does not represent a simple citation of the theatre, but a citation
of oratorical tradition as well as the Roman stage. Crassus had evidently
applied the nurse's opening monologue not to Clodia but to Ptolemy
Auletes, whose arrival at Rome had sparked the violence which precipitated
this very trial. Crassus wishes (*utinam ne*) that Ptolemy/Medea had never left
Alexandria/Colchis. In Crassus' usage, the aspect of the tragic parallel which
is most active is Medea as itinerant foreigner; not Medea the bitter lover, nor
Medea the evil woman.[197] It is Cicero who emphasizes the latter aspects
when he applies the verses to Clodia. Crassus' citation had displaced the
blame for violence away from Caelius and onto Ptolemy; Cicero's citation
likewise displaced blame, casting it upon Clodia as "Palatine Medea."[198]

In the *Pro Caelio*, Cicero puts into practice the technique advised by the
oratorical schools regarding how poetic verses could be manipulated for effect.
In the nurse's opening monologue of Ennius' *Medea*, the verse which Cicero
quotes only partially at *Cael.* 18 – *nam numquam era errans*, "for never the

---

[196] Goldberg 2005: 93. Geffcken (1973: 15) is not right to call the use of Ennius' *Medea* here
"unexpected": to anyone with oratorical training, the passage would be extremely familiar.

[197] Different aspects of tragic characters are operative in different contexts. Cicero exhorts (positively)
Trebatius to be like a Medea in a foreign land (*Fam.* 7.6); but in a different context, Medea is cited
as an example of rationality capable of great evil (*ND* 3.75).

[198] There were evidently several rival formulations of the Medea–Jason narrative in Caelius' trial: according
to Fortunatianus (*Rhet.* 3.7), the prosecutor, Atratinus, called Caelius *pulchellum Iasonem*, "pretty little
Jason" (possibly emphasizing Caelius' role as *pulcher*, i.e. Clodia's brother, Clodius Pulcher, with whom
she was supposed to have an incestuous relationship); Quintilian (*Inst.* 1.5.61) notes that Caelius called
someone *Pelia cincinnatus*, "a Pelias with curled locks," an allusion to Jason's uncle, who had sent him
on the mission for the Golden Fleece in order to be rid of him. Caelius also named Clodia *quadrantaria
Clytaemestra* (Quint. *Inst.* 8.6.53); an allusion to her adultery (and murder?) of Q. Metellus Celer (in the
role of Agamemnon), and an accusation that she charged her lovers a *quadrans* (cf. Plut. *Cic.* 29.5). See
Geffcken 1973: 15n1, Wiseman 1985: 76, Dyck 2013: 85.

wandering mistress" – was completed by *mea domo efferret pedem,* "my [mistress] would set foot outside the house." Cicero, omits this original line ending, and inserts his own substitution: *hanc molestiam nobis exhiberet,* "would [not] be annoying us."[199] Although Cicero alters the line, the spectre of the original verse remains in the audience's mind.[200] By beginning the famous line, Cicero invited his audience to mentally fill in its original conclusion, but, by breaking the verse and adding in his own comment, Cicero subverted audience expectation, thereby making the joke.[201] The verse which appears in the mind together with the subverted ending actually spoken by Cicero combine simultaneously into a singular idea: Clodia annoys us when she leaves her house. Cicero's deployment of Ennius' *Medea* in the *Pro Caelio* is fundamentally a display of several recognizable techniques from the oratorical tradition – i.e. a virtuoso oratorical performance – but the success of the citation nonetheless relies on his audience's deep familiarity with the original text. The effect of the poetic invocation is not simply to clothe Clodia as a malevolent Medea, but to play with his audience's expectations, surprising and entertaining them in a manner reminiscent of the comic stage.[202]

In the *Pro Caelio,* we see a fuller, more confident expression of the same techniques which Cicero had used early in his career. In the *Pro Roscio Amerino* Cicero had not explicitly quoted comic verses, but the speech was nonetheless deeply grounded in comedy's presentation of father–son relationships. In the *Pro Caelio,* Cicero returns to comedy's paradigms of fathers and sons, but this time he himself, as an authoritative and senior Roman, takes on a more active role among the *dramatis personae.*[203] The essential argument of the *Pro Caelio* is expressed in Cicero's citation of the comic playwrights, Caecilius Statius and Terence, for their different presentations of paternal attitudes to wayward sons (*Cael.* 37–38):[204]

> redeo nunc ad te, Caeli, uicissim ac mihi auctoritatem patriam seueritatemque suscipio. sed dubito, quem patrem potissimum sumam, Caecilianumne aliquem uehementem atque durum:

---

[199] Such an omission allows Cicero to avoid calling Clodia "my" (*mea*) mistress.

[200] Goldberg 2005: 93: "Here he expects the line not just to be completed by his jurors but to be recognized."

[201] Cicero (*De Or.* 2.255) notes that humour arises when we expect one thing and another is said.

[202] Geffcken 1973: 14.   [203] Goldberg 2005: 92–94.

[204] The fragments in *Cael.* 37–38 are notoriously difficult to disentangle from the Ciceronian prose frame. On this issue, see: Austin 1960: 98–99, Monda 1998, Goldberg 2005: 94 n18, Dyck 2013: 120–123. I here present the text and italicization of Dyck (2013), but the numeration of Ribbeck (1855) who wished to include more of the Ciceronian text among the fragments of Caecilius Statius. Other greatly entangled passages such as this one include: *Sest.* 121, *De. Or.* 1.199, *Div.* 1.132, *TD* 1.69; cf. Jocelyn 1969a: 358.

nunc enim *demum mi animus ardet, nunc meum cor cumulatur ira*
aut illum: [Ribbeck 230]
o infelix, o sceleste   [Ribbeck 231]
ferrei sunt isti patres:
egone quid dicam? egone quid uelim? quae tu omnia   [Ribbeck 232–233]
tuis foedis factis facis ut nequiquam uelim,
uix ferendi. diceret talis pater: cur te in istam uicinitatem meretriciam
contulisti?
cur illecebris cognitis non refugisti?
cur alienam ullam mulierem nosti? dide ac dissice;   [Ribbeck 237–238]
per me tibi licet. si egebis, tibi dolebit, non mihi.
mihi sat est qui aetatis quod relicuom est oblectem meae.   [Ribbeck 241–242]

[38] huic tristi ac directo seni responderet Caelius se nulla cupiditate
inductum de uia decessisse. quid signi? nulli sumptus, nulla iactura, nulla
uersura. at fuit fama. quotus quisque istam effugere potest in tam maledica
ciuitate? uicinum eius mulieris miraris male audisse, cuius frater germanus
sermones iniquorum effugere non potuit? leni uero et clementi patre, cuius
modi ille est:
fores ecfregit, restituentur; discidit   [Terence, *Adelphoe* 120–121]
uestem, resarcietur,
Caeli causa est expeditissima.

I now turn to you, Caelius, and myself take up the authority and severity of
a father. However, I'm not sure what kind of father I should be, either
a harsh and forceful father from Caecilius Statius, for
"*Only now is my mind aflame, now my heart is overfilled with anger!*"
Or this one:
"*Oh unlucky, wicked man,*"
These are iron fathers!
"*What should I say? What should I wish? Everything
you do, with your foul deeds, you make wishing hopeless.*"
Impossible to bear! Such a father would say: why have you brought yourself
into this red light district? Why did you not avoid such obvious bait?
"*Why did you become intimate with a strange woman? Waste your money,
then.*"
I allow it. If you bankrupt yourself, it's your problem, not mine.
"*I have enough to entertain me for what remains of my life.*"
[38] To this grim and rigid old man Caelius might respond that it was not
passion which led him astray from the right path. What evidence could he
give? There was no overindulgence, no spending beyond his means, no
squandering. But there was a rumour. How few there are who can avoid

rumour in this slanderous city! Are you really amazed that a neighbour of
this woman got a bad reputation, when her own brother could not avoid
scandalous talk? Perhaps I should be a gentle and forgiving father, one of this
kind:

"*He broke the doors, they will be repaired;*
he tore these clothes, they will be mended,"
I rest my case.

While Terence is not explicitly named here, we nonetheless know that the
final citation (*Cael.* 38) comes from Terence's *Adelphoe* (120–121) since this
play still survives.[205] Cicero names the severe fathers as "Caecilian," and
Quintilian (likely following Cicero) also attributed the verses to Caecilius
Statius.[206] While Cicero is very fond of Terence, he only quotes from the
Adelphoe twice: here in the *Pro Caelio* (38) and in the *De Inventione* (1.27).[207]
This suggests that, as with the citation of Ennius' *Medea*, Cicero in the *Pro
Caelio* is explicitly drawing on dramatic examples which were studied in the
rhetorical schoolroom. Cicero may be using the verses which were so often
repeated in the training of young orators in order to purposefully take on
a didactic role: his opponent, L. Sempronius Atratinus, was a seventeen year
old novice (*Cael.* 7–8).[208] Cicero could therefore "school" Atratinus with
a deployment of verses which any jury, having received the same training as
Cicero, would immediately identify as rhetorical standards.

In the *Pro Caelio*, Cicero feigns hesitation over which kind of comic
persona to adopt, choosing between the "iron fathers" (*ferrei patres*) of
Caecilius Statius or the permissive parent (Micio) of Terence's *Adelphoe*. As
with the *Pro Roscio Amerino*, the relationship between fathers and son as
presented by Roman comedy is treated by Cicero as paradigmatic. That
Cicero would present himself in the role of Micio from the *Adelphoe* is also,
to some extent, intended as a joke: Demea accuses Micio's permissiveness
of "ruining" his biological son (*Ad.* 61), and it is the stricter patriarch,

---

[205] *Adelphoe* 120–121 are spoken by the lenient father, Micio, in reponse to Demea's question (*Ad.* 112):
non est flagitium facere haec adulescentulum? "Isn't it a scandal for a young man to behave like this?"

[206] Quintilian (*Inst.* 11.1.39): *aliter enim P. Clodius, aliter Appius Caecus, aliter Caecilianus ille, aliter
Terentianus pater fingitur,* "Publius Clodius and Appius Caecus are fashioned differently [*Cael.* 33–
34, 36], as are the father in Caecilius and the father in Terence [*Cael.* 37–38]." It is notable that
Quintilian treats *personae* acted by Cicero (Clodius and Appius) in the same way as comic *personae*
cited by Cicero.

[207] Terence's *Adelphoe* (60–64) is quoted at *Inv.* 1.27 to describe a kind of *narratio* "concerned with
characters (*personae*), in which the dialogue of the characters (*personarum sermones*) and their thoughts
(*animi*) can be seen as well as the events themselves." *Ad.* 60–64 is spoken by Demea, complaining that
Micio is corrupting his biological son by allowing him to indulge himself with sex and wine.

[208] Wiseman 1985: 75.

Demea, who ultimately triumphs at the end of the play (*Ad.* 985–997), winning the submission of Aeschinus to his paternal guidance.[209] Cicero's adoption of Micio's role is a comic subversion of what we might expect from him; when Cicero wrote to his own son in the *De Officiis*, he advocated dignified restraint (e.g. *Off.* 1.15), and he was wary of his son's libertine excesses (*Att.* 12.7.1). Cicero's adoption of the role of a father who forgives his wayward son is contrary to how Cicero himself would naturally behave, but it *is* an endorsement of the status quo as defined by Roman comedy, where, as Matthew Leigh (2004: 302) writes, "the damage done through youthful exuberance is accommodated without any lasting harm to the family or to society at large."

If Cicero can play Micio in this real life drama, then Caelius can be acquitted for his actions; indeed, the *adulescens*, according to the rules of comedy, *must* triumph in the end.[210] If we take Terence's *Adelphoe* as structural template for Cicero's *Pro Caelio*, we see that Cicero is attempting to mobilize elite Roman protectiveness towards their sons at the expense of all else. Micio is not concerned that his adopted son, Aeschinus, is out in the world doing harm (*Ad.* 32–34), but that he has come into harm's way (*Ad.* 35–39). At the outset of the play, Micio is not worried that Aeschinus is behaving badly (bad behaviour is permissible), but that Aeschinus is not open to Micio about his behaviour (*Ad.* 52–54). Micio claims not to fear the misdeeds themselves, but rather a loss in father–son trust which would ultimately breed greater duplicitousness in the son towards the rest of society (*Ad.* 55–56). When Demea complains to Micio that Aeschinus has broken down doors (cf. *Cael.* 38), assaulted an entire household, and abducted a woman (*Ad.* 88–91) – acts condemned inside the play itself (*Ad.* 92–93) – Micio responds that he and Demea would have done the same as boys, if they had had the opportunity (*Ad.* 106–107). Cicero's brief invocation of Terence's *Adelphoe* endorses its worldview: bad deeds may well be worth condemnation, but, like loving fathers who care for their sons, the guilty may nonetheless be forgiven and their wrongs set right, provided that they are young, elite, freeborn men of Rome.[211]

In the world of Roman comedy, women are often playthings and objects, relegated to the background, oftentimes functioning as scenery, visual gag, or

---

[209] Indeed, Micio himself admits (*Ad.* 141–147) that what he says to Demea (the very words quoted by Cicero at *Cael.* 38), he only says because he does not want to encourage his brother's anger; despite his defense of Aeschinus to Demea, Micio is actually concerned by the boy's behaviour (*Ad.* 147–154).

[210] Leigh 2004: 303.

[211] Micio, knowing all that Aeschinus has done, nonetheless supports him: *te amo, quo magis quae agis curae sunt mihi,* "I love you. That's why I care even more about what you do" (*Ad.* 680).

plot device. In reality Clodia is a powerful member of an ancient Roman family, but recast as the *meretrix* of comedy, her actions are automatically invalidated and diminished as inconsequential. In Terence's *Adelphoe*, the wayward son, Aeschinus, not only forcibly steals an enslaved sex worker from her pimp, but, rapes and impregnates the freeborn girl next door.[212] The prostitute taken by Aeschinus appears on stage and is moved around for comic effect (*Ad.* 156–175), but does not speak; Pamphila, whose cries are heard from offstage as she goes into labour (*Ad.* 486–487), is heard but not seen. In the *Pro Caelio* (36), Cicero, in the persona of P. Clodius Pulcher, quotes a verse from a now unknown comedy, in order to minimize Clodia's complaint:

> remouebo illum senem durum ac paene agrestem; ex his igitur tuis sumam aliquem ac potissimum minimum fratrem, qui est in isto genere urbanissimus; qui te amat plurimum, qui propter nescio quam, credo, timiditatem et nocturnos quosdam inanis metus tecum semper pusio cum maiore sorore cubitauit. eum putato tecum loqui: quid tumultuaris, soror? quid insanis?
> *quid clamorem exorsa uerbis paruam rem magnam facis?*   [Ribbeck 72]

> I will take away that old, harsh and almost rustic man, and instead take up one of your relatives, your youngest brother, who is the greatest sophisticate among them. This man loves you so much; because, I think, of a fright of some kind and some vague, nocturnal fears, the young lad always slept with his elder sister. Imagine him speaking with you: why are you so agitated, sister? Why are you raving?
> "*Why do you shout so, why do you make a small thing big with your words?*"

The redeployment of comic types not *only* allows Cicero to condemn Clodia for her sexuality, her libertine ways; but it allowed him to circumscribe the rules of comedy which excluded female agency from the narrative, refocusing on homosocial discourse. Terence's *Adelphoe*, after all, is not truly about the fate of the women whom Aeschinus abducts or rapes, but about how the men in the play relate to each other. Cicero's *Pro Caelio*, likewise, is more about how elder and younger generations of Roman men interact, with the tacit assumption that youthful indiscretions will ultimately be forgiven.

While poetic quotations are not nearly as present in Cicero's speeches as they are in other genres, such citations nonetheless demonstrate the centrality of Latin poetry to the Roman oratorical education during the Ciceronian era.

---

[212] It is not the rape itself which is condemned, but Aeschinus' failure to marry Pamphila as promised (*Ad.* 471–474). Indeed, Hegio, who advocates for Pamphila and her mother, Sostrata, thinks that the rape is perfectly natural, provided that the wedding goes ahead (*Ad.* 470–471). On the subject experiences of enslaved individuals at Rome, see Padilla Peralta 2017, Richlin 2017.

Cicero's rhetorical treatises and the *Rhetorica ad Herennium* testify to the fact that poetry was used to exemplify a variety of oratorical strategies, and these works also demonstrate that the orator was trained to quote, or invent, Latin verse as part of his persuasive toolkit. Furthermore, it is also clear that the social values of Roman poetry were echoed and endorsed by Roman oratory: Cicero's use of comic tropes, for example, demonstrates a sincere belief in comedy's ability to reflect Roman values and societal roles.

2.4 Poetry in the Letters

While Cicero's epistolary corpus is one of the most important sources of historical information for the period, the letters also present vignettes of everyday life, including casual instances of verse quotation. Cicero's regular use of Latin (and Greek) poetry in the letters demonstrates Cicero's deep acquaintance with the verses cited. The presence of poetry in Cicero's letters also suggests that at least some of his correspondents were receptive to his citational habit. Because Cicero's letters reflect active dialogue and communication between himself and other Romans, they preserve evidence of other Romans quoting Latin verse. In a letter to Cicero (*Fam.* 8.2.1), Caelius quotes a verse from Pacuvius (Schierl fr. 263) to describe the spectators at the theatre hissing at Hortensius.[213] Cicero says that Atticus regularly quoted a line of Lucilius' *Satires* (609–610).[214] L. Papirius Paetus, Cicero's regular correspondent, is also frequently reported quoting Latin poetry.[215] Cicero's letters show the more casual side to poetic engagement, demonstrating the role of poetry in conveying wit among the Roman elite.

2.4.1 *A Funny Thing Happened . . .*

In a letter to Atticus from 60 BCE (*Att.* 2.1.5), Cicero recounts an exchange with P. Clodius Pulcher which happened on the way to the Forum:

> itaque iam familiariter cum ipso etiam cauillor ac iocor. quin etiam cum candidatum deduceremus, quaerit ex me num consuessem Siculis locum

---

[213] See Jocelyn 1973a: 61n4.

[214] *Att.* 6.3.7: *solit in ore esse*, "it is often on your lips." Cicero himself had partially quoted this verse (Lucilius' *Satires*, Warmington 609–610) to Atticus about a decade earlier (*Att.* 2.8.1). Cicero uses *in ore* ("on your lips") to describe intimacy with a verse: e.g. in a letter to Q. Lepta (*Fam.* 6.18.5), Cicero encourages Lepta's son to keep a verse of Hesiod *in ore*.

[215] *Fam.* 9.16.6–7: ref. to Accius' *Oenomaus*, ref. to Atellan farce; *Fam.* 9.21.1: ref. to Trabea (Ribbeck fr. iii); *Fam.* 9.22.1: Turpilius' *Demiurgus* (Ribbeck 43–44), unknown tragedies (*TrRF* I 84; 85; 86); *Fam.* 9.26.2: unknown tragedy (*TrRF* I 59).

gladiatoribus dare. negaui. at ego, inquit, nouus patronus instituam. sed soror, quae tantum habeat consularis loci, unum mihi solum pedem dat. noli, inquam, de uno pede sororis queri; licet etiam alterum tollas. non consulare, inquies, dictum. fateor; sed ego illam odi male consularem:

ea est enim seditiosa, ea cum uiro bellum gerit,

neque solum cum Metello sed etiam cum Fabio, quod eos nihili esse moleste fert.

And so, now I even make fun and joke with him as though we were friends. Indeed, when we were escorting a candidate to the Forum, he asked me whether I had been in the habit of giving a place to the Sicilians at the gladiatorial games. I said no. "But *I* will, now that I'm their new patron," he replied. "But my sister, with so much consular space, gives me only a square foot." "Don't fight over your sister's foot," I said. "You can always lift the other!" Not a very consular remark, you'll say. I admit it. But I hate the woman, herself an unworthy consular:

"she's rebellious, she wages war with man,"

not only with Metellus but even with Fabius, because he's annoyed that *they* are behaving badly.

Cicero's ironic claim that he here behaved "like a friend" (*familiariter*) towards Clodius is followed with an account of a brief battle of wits. Clodius plans to give the Sicilians a place at the gladiatorial games, if he can convince his sister, Clodia, to lend him some of the space at the games afforded to her husband, Metellus Celer, who was consul this year (60 BCE).[216] Cicero turns Clodius' reference to the foot (of space) in the consular seating into a pun on Clodia's actual foot, i.e. into a sexual reference.[217] Breaking off from his narrative of the encounter to speak to Atticus directly, Cicero illustrates the reason for his hatred of Clodia with an iambic senarius which scholars take to be a quotation of a lost play: *ea est seditiosa, ea cum uiro bellum gerit*, "she's rebellious, she wages war with man."

Since Cicero gives no indication of author or title of the play, we do not know what genre the citation comes from. Early editors of Cicero assumed that the fragment came from a comedy, and in response Ribbeck (1873, xix) printed this line in his second edition of Latin comic

---

[216] For Metellus Celer's life and career, see Skinner 2011: 79–89; for his consular year, esp. 84–87.

[217] Richlin (1992: 85) suggests "you can always get her to spread her legs" as a colloquial equivalent of *pedem tollas*. In the *Pro Caelio* (32), Cicero famously makes a deliberate "Freudian slip" (i.e. the rhetorical strategy of *correctio*; cf. *Rhet. Her.* 4.36): *mihi inimicitiae cum istius mulieris uiro – fratre uolui dicere; semper hic erro*, "my personal enmity with this woman's husband – I meant brother! I always make this mistake . . . "

fragments.[218] But the verse also bears a resemblance to a fragment of Ennius' *Andromacha* transmitted by Varro in the *De Lingua Latina* (7.82):

> apud Ennium:
> *Andromachae nomen qui indidit, recte {ei} indidit*   [Ennius' *Andromacha,*
> item: *TrRF* II 25]
> *quapropter Parim pastores nunc Alexandrum uocant*   [Ennius' *Alexander,*
>   *TrRF* II 16]
> imitari dum uoluit Euripidem et ponere ἔτυμον, est lapsus: nam Euripides quod Graeca posuit, ἔτυμα sunt aperta. ille ait ideo nomen additum Andromach<a>e, quod ἀνδρὶ μάχεται. hoc Ennii quis potest intellegere in uersu{m} significare?

> In Ennius:
> "*He who gave the name 'Andromacha,' named her correctly*"
> likewise:
> "*For this reason the shepherds now called Paris 'Alexander.'*"
> While Ennius wanted to imitate Euripides and make an etymology, he slipped. Since Euripides was writing in Greek, the etymology is self-evident. Euripides says that the name was given to "Andromacha" because she "fights with man." Who can understand that this is what is meant in Ennius' verse?

Varro quotes two verses which contain etymological puns: Andromacha was so named because she "fights with man" (ἀνήρ + μάχη); Alexander was so named because he "defends man" (ἀλέξω + ἀνήρ). Varro notes that while this etymology works in Greek, the pun is not so clear in Latin: Ennius, who wanted to imitate Euripides, "has slipped" (*est lapsus*).[219] In the verse quoted to Atticus (*Att.* 2.1.5), Cicero says that Clodia "fights with man" (*cum uiro bellum*), which is the Latin version of "ἀνδρὶ μάχεται," i.e. "Andromache." Varro's criticism that Ennius' version of "fights-with-man" is not a clear etymology in Latin because the *Latin* words do not resemble her *Greek* name raises the possibility, as Zillinger (1911: 88) suggested, that Cicero's *cum uiro bellum* is a reference to Ennius' *Andromacha*.[220] If the verse cited by Cicero in the letter to Atticus does come from Ennius, then Clodia was several times insulted by being compared

---

[218] Ribbeck (1873: 116) notes that Orelli was the first to suggest that the verse could come from comedy and that Bücheler thought that the verse could come from a comedy of Caecilius Statius or Afranius, as part of a "description of an imperious wife" (*in imperiosae descriptione coniugis*).

[219] Varro's ascription of the etymology to Euripides does not correspond to any extant passage. Varro *LL* 7.82 is taken as a testimonium for Euripides' fragmentary *Alexandros*; see Karamanou 2017: 70; T 9.

[220] *Att.* 2.1.5 is not given as a source for *TrRF* II 25, but it is there listed as a "parallel passage"; see *TrRF* II p86. Although it certainly does not decide the case conclusively, there may be significance to the

to women from the Roman tragic stage: Clodia was called "Medea of the Palatine" (*Cael.* 18), "two-penny Clytemnestra" (*quadrantariam Clytaemestram*, Quint. *Inst.* 8.6.53), and a "man-fighting" Andromacha.[221]

2.4.2   *Postcards from Home*

In April 54 BCE, C. Trebatius Testa, notable Roman jurist and younger friend of Cicero, travelled to Gaul to join Julius Caesar as legal advisor. Cicero wrote a series of letters to Testa while he was in Gaul (*Fam.* 7.6–18; May 54 to June 53), full of witticisms, from juridical jokes to quotations of Latin verse.[222] Cicero's letters imply that Testa felt his post in Gaul to be severe and remote, and, although Cicero wanted Testa to use his time under Caesar to his advantage, Cicero was nonetheless anxious for him to return. Since Testa was isolated, Cicero sent letters deliberately intended as snapshots of the Rome he missed, telegraphing Roman culture via poetic citation.[223]

The earliest extant letter from Cicero to Testa in Gaul (*Fam.* 7.6; May 54 BCE) contains a quotation of Ennius' *Medea* (*TrRF* II 90):[224]

> tu modo ineptias istas et desideria urbis et urbanitatis depone et, quo consilio profectus es, id adsiduitate et uirtute consequere. hoc tibi tam ignoscemus nos amici quam ignouerunt Medeae
> *quae Corinthum arcem altam habebant matronae opu-*   [*TrRF* II 90, 1]
> *lentae, optimates,*

---

fact that another fragment of Ennius' *Andromacha* (*TrRF* II 27) also contains the word *seditio*, "rebellion"; Cicero's fragment called Clodia *seditiosa*, "rebellious."

[221] If it is indeed Andromacha whom Cicero has in mind here, he may not necessarily be thinking of the substance of her character, but rather using the significance of her name as a referent. At *TD* 4.25, Cicero refers to the *title* of a play, rather than the substance of the play: *ut odium mulierum, quale in* Μισογύνῳ *Atilii est*, "like the hatred of women, such as in the case of Atilius' *Woman-hater*."

[222] In one letter to Testa (*Fam.* 7.13.2), Cicero quotes Ennius' *Annales* (Skutsch 252–253) to make a legalistic joke. This passage was quoted by Cicero in the *Pro Murena* (30) to undermine the knowledge of the jurist, Servius Sulpicius.

[223] Literary pursuit as a remedy for a feeling of physical remoteness is a regular feature of Roman elite behaviour. We have only to think of Ovid's *Tristia* and *Epistulae ex Ponto*, which sought to bridge the gap between Tomis and Rome; see Rosenmeyer 1997: 30–32, 44. In Gaul, Testa was in the company of men who used literary composition, in a variety of ways, to remedy remoteness. Caesar supposedly composed his *commentarii* on the Gallic war there, sending dispatches to Rome to safeguard a sense of his continued presence, while Quintus Cicero composed four tragedies in sixteen days (*Q.fr.* 3.5.7; late 54 BCE); see Goldberg 1996: 271, Boyle 2006: 145.

[224] In this letter, Cicero's citations of Ennius are intermingled with his own prose to the extent that it has been difficult to decide where Cicero ends and Ennius begins. Cicero's diction makes it clear that he is quoting Ennius (e.g. *uitio uertere*, "to blame" is an idiom of older Latin, cf. Plaut. *Capt.* 259, *Miles* 1350, 700), but the word order shows that he has rearranged the content into his own prose rather than preserving the syntax of the original. On this issue, see Jocelyn 1969a: 358–359.

quibus illa manibus gypsatissimis persuasit ne sibi
uitio illae uerterent quod abesset a patria. nam
multi suam rem bene gessere et publicam patria procul;   [*TrRF* II 90, 2–3]
multi, qui domi aetatem agerent, propterea sunt improbati.
quo in numero tu certe fuisses nisi te extrusissemus. [7.6.2] sed plura
scribemus alias. tu, qui ceteris cauere didicisti, in Britannia ne ab essedariis
decipiaris caueto et (quoniam Medeam coepi agere) illud semper memento:
qui ipse sibi sapiens prodesse non quit, nequiquam sapit.   [*TrRF* II 90, 4]
cura ut ualeas.

Put aside your silliness, your longing for the city and life in Rome, and,
follow through on what you set out to achieve with persistence and virtue.
Your friends will forgive you this, like those who forgave Medea,
"*the rich and noble matrons who held the high citadel of Corinth,*"
whom, with her hands covered in lime, Medea persuaded not to blame her
because she left her homeland. For,
"*many have managed private and public affairs well, away from the homeland;
many who spent their lives at home are wicked because of it.*"
Among whom you certainly would have been unless I had thrust you out.
[7.6.2] But I will write more at another time. You who have learned to write
caveats for others, you yourself be wary not to be tricked by the charioteers in
Britain and (since I have begun to play the *Medea*), always remember this:
"*he who, though wise, cannot help himself, is wise in vain.*"
Take care of yourself.

In his absence, Testa longs not only for the *urbs*, Rome itself, but for *urbanitas*.
In response, Cicero uses the very quality of *urbanitas* as a means to exhort Testa
towards dedication to the task at hand. In this letter, Cicero puts on a show for
Testa, who loves shows (*Fam.* 7.10.2).[225] Cicero and the rest of Testa's friends
become the women of Corinth, i.e. the chorus of Ennius' *Medea*. Testa, then, is
made to take the role of Medea. The Ennian Medea, according to Cicero, had
emphasized the importance of serving not only one's own interests (*suam rem*)
but even the state (*publicam*) by going abroad (*patria procul*).[226] The metathea-
trical aspect of this letter-as-play is emphasized by the phrase *manibus gypsatissimis*, "with hands covered in lime," which might be interpreted as a reference
to the male actor playing Medea on the Roman stage.[227] Since he has "begun to

[225] Cicero (*Fam.* 7.10.2) refers to the fact that when Testa was in Rome, he could not be torn away from
the *andabata,* the "blindfold gladiator."
[226] Jocelyn (1969a: 362–363) notes that Ennius' verses would resonate with the experience of Roman
magistrates.
[227] Jocelyn (1969a: 359–361) prefers the interpretation that *gypsum* ("lime") refers to the practice of
whitening skin with cosmetics practised by ancient women, rather than the idea that Cicero is
referring to the stage. But if Ennius, as Jocelyn thinks, was making a "contrast of the Corinthian
matronae opulentae optumates and the barbarian Medea *manibus gypsatissimis*" (p360), would this

play the *Medea*" (or "play Medea" herself), Cicero ends the letter by exhorting
Testa with a gnomic verse from the tragedy: *qui ipse sibi sapiens prodesse non
quit, nequiquam sapit*, "he who, though wise, cannot help himself, is wise in
vain."[228] The micro-staging of Ennius' *Medea* as a missive of Roman *urbanitas*
is intended to reassure Testa, anxious at the prospect of a cultural backwater,
with a familiar cultural touchstone. But it also contains a certain sternness
appropriate from an older mentor exhorting a potentially wayward youth.[229]

While Testa was in Gaul, Cicero went to the theatre in Rome.[230] Several of
Cicero's other letters to Testa contain literary or dramatic references which
telegraph the spectacle of Roman entertainments to Gaul. One letter (*Fam.*
7.16.1; Nov. 54 BCE) begins with a citation from *Equus Troianus* ("Trojan
Horse"):

> in Equo Troiano scis esse in extremo *sero sapiunt*.   [*TrRF* I *adesp.* 29[231]]

> You know that the *Trojan Horse* ends with "*they become wise late.*"

Since a play with this name had been performed at the opening of
Pompey's theatre the year before (cf. *Fam.* 7.1.2[232]), Cicero may be referring not solely to the play as text, but to Testa's memory of having attended
the event – a memorable theatrical spectacle. Cicero (*Fam.* 7.11.2;
January 53 BCE?) also warns Testa that if he stays away from Rome too
long, the mime actors will do imitations of him as a "Britannic jurist."[233] In
another letter (*Fam.* 7.10.4), Cicero again takes on a dramatic role, this
time a comic one: Chremes in Terence's *Heautontimoroumenos*:

> una mehercule nostra uel seuera uel iocosa congressio pluris erit quam non
> modo hostes sed etiam fratres nostri Haedui. qua re omnibus de rebus fac ut
> quam primum sciam.
> *aut consolando aut consilio aut re iuuero.*   [Ter. *Heaut.* 86]

---

distinction not be made clear in the staging (i.e. costuming) of the play? That is, if Cicero is
referring to the *gypsum* used to mark Medea as "other," is this not a reference to the stage either way?

[228] Quoted again at *Off.* 3.62 = *TrRF* II 90. The phrase there appears in a slightly different form: *ex quo
Ennius: nequiquam sapere sapientem, qui ipse sibi prodesse non quiret*, "On which, Ennius: 'in vain is the
wise man wise, who is not able to help himself.'" In a letter to Caesar (*Fam.* 13.15.2), Cicero quotes a verse
of Euripides (a fragment which cannot be attributed, Nauck 905) which has been taken to be its Greek
precursor: *confero me ad uera praecepta* Εὐριπίδου: μισῶ σοφιστήν, ὅστις οὐχ αὐτῷ σοφός, "I move on
to the true teachings of Euripides, 'I hate the wise man who is not wise for himself.'"

[229] In another letter Cicero jokingly writes that he will "report back" to Testa's law teachers (*Fam.* 7.8.2).

[230] Cicero writes (*Att.* 4.15.6) that he saw a revival performance of Ennius' *Andromacha* in July 54 BCE.

[231] The *TrRF* I, p206 connects this with a "proverb" in Festus (343 M.): *sero sapiunt Phryges*, "The
Trojans become wise late." There is a second verse quotation in this letter (*Fam.* 7.16.1 = *TrRF* I 30);
it may or may not belong to the *Equus Troianus*.

[232] Hanses 2020: 60–61.

[233] On this passage as a testimonium for D. Laberius, see Panayotakis 2010: 15; on the problem of
identifying "Valerius" also mentioned in *Fam.* 7.11.2, see Panayotakis 2010: 41n73.

God, one meeting between us whether serious or joking will be worth more than not only the enemy but even our Gallic "brothers," the Aedui! For which reason, make it so that I know everything as soon as possible. *"I'll help you either by consolation or advice or money."*

Since Cicero names neither play nor playwright, he must expect Testa to recognize the verse; whether Testa actually did recognize it, we do not know.[234] Cicero quotes one full line of Terence's *Heautontimoroumenos* (86), but other parts of Cicero's prose refer to verses which precede (*Heaut.* 84) and follow (*Heaut.* 87). Cicero has in his mind, then, this interchange between Chremes and Menedemus (*Heaut.* 82–87):

CHR: *si quid laborist nollem. sed quid istuc malist?*
    quaeso, quid de te tantum meruisti? MEN: *eheu!*
CHR: *ne lacruma atque istuc, quidquid est, fac me ut sciam:*
    ne retice, ne uerere, crede inquam mihi:
    aut consolando aut consilio aut re iuuero.   86
MEN: *scire hoc uis?* CHR: *hac quidem causa qua dixi tibi.*

CHR: "If there's some problem, I'm sorry. But what's wrong with you?
    Tell me, how do you deserve such punishment at your own hands?"
MEN: "Alas!"
CHR: "Stop crying! Tell me about it, whatever it is. Make it so that I know:
    Don't feel ashamed; trust me, I tell you.
    I'll help you, whether with consolation or advice or money."
MEN: "You want to know?" CHR: "Yes, for the reason I've given you."

By taking on the role of Chremes, Cicero makes Testa into his Menedemus.[235] And although Testa is hundreds of miles away, Terence's comedy provides a script for their private, epistolary dialogue. Since Menedemus is the titular "Self-tormentor" of Terence's play, Cicero can use this scene as a reflection of Testa's own anguish while also undercutting it: Testa might be in pain, but it is (in Cicero's view) one of his own making. Despite Cicero's view that Testa's psychological pain is self-inflicted, he is nonetheless a sympathetic dialogue partner: he wants to listen, and help in any way he can, as the full verse quoted states (*Heaut.* 86).

---

[234] Perhaps Testa was like the young interlocutor in *TD* 2.26 who does not recognize Cicero's verse citation.

[235] In 46 BCE, Cicero's citation of Terence's *Heaut.* (75) makes himself Menedemus; Atticus is made to take the role of Chremes (*Att.* 12.6.3(6a.1)): "*Chreme, tantumne ab re tua est oti tibi,*" ut etiam *Oratorem legas?* "'*Chreme, do you have so much free time,*' that you are even reading my *Orator?*" The answer to Menedemus' question is one of Terence's most famous lines (*Heaut.* 77): *homo sum: humani nil a me alienum puto*, "I am a man: I consider nothing of mankind foreign to me." Cicero's citation of *Heaut.* 75 sets this up to be Atticus' response.

That the letter itself is a symbol of the help Cicero wants to give, or indeed, the substance of help itself, is suggested by how Cicero uses *Heaut.* 86 when he himself is in pain. In a letter to Atticus (*Att.* 9.6.4–5; 11 March 49 BCE), Cicero returns to Terence while in deep distress:

> non angor sed ardeo dolore,
>
> οὐδέ μοι ἦτορ,   [*Iliad* 10.93–94]
>
> ἔμπεδον, ἀλλ' ἀλαλύκτημαι
>
> non sum, inquam, mihi crede, mentis compos . . . [9.6.5] tuas nunc epistulas a primo lego. hae me paulum recreant. primae monent et rogant ne me proiciam, proximae gaudere te ostendunt me remansisse. eas cum lego, minus mihi turpis uideor, sed tam diu dum lego. deinde emergit rursum dolor et αἰσχροῦ φαντασία. quam ob rem obsecro te, mi Tite, eripe hunc mihi dolorem aut minue saltem,
>
> *aut consolatione aut consilio*   [Ter. *Heaut.* 86]
>
> aut quacumque re potes. quid tu autem possis, aut quid homo quisquam? uix iam deus.

> I am not just constricted by pain but aflame with it,
>
>   "*nor is my heart firm,*
> *but I am tossed about.*"
>
> I am not, I say – and believe me – of sound mind . . . [9.6.5] I read your letters over from the beginning now. They remake me a little. The first ones advise and ask that I not rush into danger; the most recent ones show that you are happy that I stayed. When I read them, I feel less ashamed, but only while I read them. Then the pain surfaces again and the sense of shame. For which reason I beg you, my Titus, snatch this pain away from me and at the least lessen it,
>
> "*whether with consolation or advice*"
>
> or whatever you can. But what could you even do, what can any man do? A god could not even help.

Cicero's pain stems from his shame at the thought of not following Pompey, who was about to leave Italy in the face of Caesar's advance.[236] Cicero here exemplifies the intensity of his pain with Greek verse quotation, part of Agamemnon's anxious and insomniac speech to Nestor in *Iliad* 10.[237] It is Atticus' letters which lessen Cicero's pain and shame, but only while he is reading them. Cicero begs Atticus to take away his pain "whether with consolation or advice" (*aut consolatione aut consilio*), which is Terence's *Heaut.* 86 slightly changed ("*consolatione*" for

---

[236] Pompey crossed to Dyrrachium on 17 March 49 BCE.
[237] This letter (*Att.* 9.6.6) contains another (partial) Greek quotation of the *Iliad* (10.224). Cicero later quotes *Il.* 10.224 in a letter to Varro (*Fam.* 9.7.1).

"*consolando*").[238] While the paraphrase suggests that Cicero is quoting from memory, that fact in itself does not mean that Cicero has forgotten its dramatic context. This time, the quotation of Terence identifies Cicero as the "Self-tormentor." Cicero himself quotes Chremes' lines, but he takes on the position of a Menedemus trying to elicit help from Atticus in his anticipated role of Chremes.

2.4.3   Threading Connections

Since Cicero quoted some of the same Latin verses in the letters and the philosophical works, the appearance of poetry in the epistolary corpus presents a useful citational record against which to compare philosophical quotations. The appearance of the same verses in different contexts demonstrates that Cicero had memorized and internalized particular Latin verses and was capable of deploying them in different circumstances. Such citational iteration also shows Cicero's pliable approach to the application of verse: in certain cases, poetry is made to reflect his own situation, and he sees something of himself in its language or drama; in others, Cicero distances himself from the verse, presenting an analysis of its contents which removes the personal dimension. Cicero's return to these verses deepens their significance, while also creating connections between works written at different times, and for different purposes. Citationality as a building block of thought reveals the inner workings of Cicero's intellectual processes.

In a letter to L. Papirius Paetus (*Fam.* 9.26.2; late 46 BCE), Cicero wrote about a recent dinner party where the infamous mime actress, Volumnia Cytheris, was present, and imagined his friend responding with a quotation of a now unknown tragedy:

> infra Eutrapelum Cytheris accubuit. in eo igitur, inquis, conuiuio Cicero ille?
> *quem aspectabant, cuius ob os Grai ora obuertebant sua?*   [*TrRF* I 59]
> non mehercule suspicatus sum illam adfore.

> Cytheris lay next to Eutrapelus. I know what you'll say. The famous Cicero at such a dinner?
> "*Whom men gazed upon, towards whose face the Greeks turned their own?*"
> Well, I never suspected that *she* would be there!

Cicero here, somewhat melodramatically, aligns his own embarrassment with the shame felt by Telamo in his ostensible fall from grace.

---

[238] Zillinger 1911: 153. Shackleton Bailey (1961, Vol. 4: 365) has no comment on *consolatione aut consilio*.

The same verse which Cicero imagines Paetus quoting appears again a few months later in Cicero's *Tusculans* (3.39), composed during late summer 45 BCE:

> huiusne uitae propositio et cogitatio aut Thyestem leuare poterit aut
> Aeëtam, de quo paulo ante dixi, aut Telamonem pulsum patria exulantem
> atque egentem? in quo haec admiratio fiebat:
> *hicine est ille Telamon,*[239] *modo quem gloria ad caelum extulit,*   [*TrRF* I 59]
> *quem aspectabant, cuius ob os Grai ora obuertebant sua?*

> Could the idea or the consideration of such a life assuage Thyestes or Aeëta
> (about whom I spoke a little while ago), or Telamo expelled from his
> fatherland, exiled and needy? Towards whom there was such astonishment:
> *"Can this be the famous Telamon, whom glory recently raised to the sky?*
> *Whom men gazed upon, towards whose face the Greeks turned their own?"*

Comparison of the two citations reveals that when Cicero remarked "*Cicero ille*" in the letter to Paetus, this too was a tragic allusion, a playful reworking of the words "*ille Telamon*[240]" which appear in the fuller quotation in the *Tusculans*. In the *Tusculans*, Cicero quotes the two verses from a (now unknown) Latin tragedy as part of a discussion of pleasure and pain: the so-called "blessed life" of Epicureanism is all well and good (*TD* 3.38), but how can Epicurean theory help this tragic figure, who had suffered expulsion from his country, exile, need? While each individual citation communicated the notion of pain and disgrace, Cicero's relationship to the quotation changes in each iteration. In the letter (*Fam.* 9.26.2), Cicero places himself in the role of Telamo (for comic effect), while in the *Tusculans* (3.39), Cicero takes the exile's words as an exemplar of extreme psychic pain with which to disprove Epicurean theory.

In the prior example, Cicero had quoted the verse to Paetus prior to embedding it in a philosophical work. But patterns of Ciceronian citation also demonstrate simultaneity: we already know, for example, that Cicero was working on the *De Finibus* and the *Tusculans* in the summer of 45 BCE,[241] but Cicero's verse citations also show this interconnectivity.[242] Some of the verses quoted in Cicero's letters also appear in the philosoph-

---

[239] Editors print *Telamon* here (see *TrRF* I p231). Cicero speaking in his own voice (i.e. not making a verse quotation) always uses the Latin spelling, Telamo: *De Or.* 2.193, *TD* 3.58, *ND* 3.79.
[240] See n239.   [241] Marinone 1997: 214–215.
[242] *Fin.* 1.5 = *TD* 1.45 (Ennius' *Medea TrRF* II 89); *Fin.* 2.13 = *TD* 4.35 (Trabea Ribbeck 6); *Fin.* 2.94 = *TD* 2.19 (Accius' *Philocteta* Dangel 235–236); *Fin.* 5.31 = *TD* 4.18–19 (Ennius' *Alcmeo TrRF* II 12); *Fin.* 5.92 = *TD* 3.31 (ref. to Lucilius' *Satires* Marx 1300).

ical works which he was writing at the same time. While Cicero was composing the *Academica*, he sent a letter to Atticus (*Att.* 13.21.3; July 45 BCE) discussing how best to translate the Greek word ἐπέχειν ("to hold back"), in reference to the philosophical concept of withholding assent:

> nunc, ad rem ut redeam, inhibere illud tuum, quod ualde mihi adriserat, uehementer displicet. est enim uerbum totum nauticum. quamquam id quidem sciebam, sed arbitrabar sustineri remos cum inhibere essent remiges iussi. id non esse eius modi didici heri cum ad uillam nostram nauis appelleretur. non enim sustinent, sed alio modo remigant. id ab ἐποχῇ remotissimum est. qua re facies ut ita sit in libro quem ad modum fuit. dices hoc idem Varroni, si forte mutauit. nec est melius quicquam quam ut Lucilius:
> *sustineas currum, ut bonus saepe agitator, equosque*   [Warmington 1249]
> semperque Carneades προβολὴν pugilis et retentionem aurigae similem facit ἐποχῇ. inhibitio autem remigum motum habet et uehementiorem quidem remigationis nauem conuertentis ad puppim.

> Now, to return to the matter at hand. I strongly dislike your word "*inhibere*" ("to restrain"), which had really pleased me before. It is a word sailors use. I knew that already, but I thought that when oarsmen were given the order *inhibere* they held off from rowing. That this is not the case I learned yesterday when a ship put in near my villa. For they do not hold off, but row in a different way. That is very far off from "holding back." For this reason, make it so that the word in the book is what it was before. Say the same to Varro, in case he has already changed his copy. For nothing is better than what Lucilius says:
> "*Hold back your chariot and horses as a good driver often does.*"
> And Carneades always compares "holding back" to the boxer's guard and the charioteer holding in the reins. But *inhibitio* ("restraint") in the context of rowing means motion and rather powerful motion at that, turning the ship astern.

This letter reveals that Atticus and Cicero had been discussing the best Latin word for the concept of philosophical "restraint," which, in Stoic and Academic epistemological discourse, involved withholding assent to a proposition. Atticus had suggested *inhibere* ("to restrain") for ἐποχή, but Cicero, observing some rowers at Astura, realized that they used this word not for "checking" their motion, but rather reversing it. As a result, Cicero returned to his initial idea and translated ἐποχή with *sustinere*, which he had taken from a verse of Lucilius' *Satires* (Warmington 1249).[243] In the letter, Cicero asks Atticus to reverse the correction to his copy of the *Academica*, and to have Varro do the

---

[243] On Cicero's use of *inhibere* to translate ἐποχή, see Cappello 2019: 26–27.

same.[244] In our text of the *Academica*, the verb *sustinere* appears several times with the meaning of ἐπέχειν (*Ac.* 1.45; 2.48, 2.53, 2.104).[245] Since, as Cicero tells us in the *Academica* (2.102), the Academic philosopher Clitomachus had dedicated a book to the satirist, Lucilius' original verse may have been part of a metaphor for philosophical "withholding," rather than a literal description of a chariot race.[246] Significantly, in the *Academica* (2.94), Cicero also paraphrases the same verse of Lucilius *Satires* (Warmington 1249) to convey refusal:[247]

> nihil me laedit, inquit, ego enim *ut agitator* callidus priusquam ad finem ueniam *equos sustinebo*. eoquo magis si locus is quo ferentur equi praeceps erit: sic me, inquit, ante *sustineo*, nec diutius captiose interroganti respondeo.

> "It doesn't hurt me at all," he said. "For just *as* the clever *driver I will hold back my horses* before I come to the finish line. All the more so if the place where the horses are being led is treacherous. Just like him," he said, "*I hold back* beforehand, and I no longer respond to a deceptive interrogator."

The letter to Atticus, then, not only quotes the same verse which appeared in the contemporary philosophical work, but also reveals the reasons for its inclusion. Cicero's letter enriches our understanding of his composition of philosophy, but also demonstrates the influence which poetic formulations of language had on his rendering of philosophical concepts. While Cicero had entertained an alternative to his initial translation, he returned to the poet Lucilius as the best possible formulation (*Att.* 13.21.3): *nec est melius quicquam quam ut Lucilius*, "nothing is better than how Lucilius put it."

One further example demonstrates that Cicero's use of verse in both the letters and the philosophical works could be strikingly consistent, even over the course of a decade. In 55 BCE (*Fam.* 5.12.7), Cicero tried to entice the historian L. Lucceius into writing an account of Cicero's consulship, expressing the significance of Lucceius' authorization with a paraphrase of a verse from Naevius' *Hector Proficiscens* (*TrRF* I 14):

> placet enim Hector ille mihi Naeuianus, qui non tantum *laudari* se laetatur, sed addit etiam *a laudato uiro*.

---

[244] Gurd 2012: 73. On the famous example of a correction made by Cicero which is *not* in the transmitted text, see Gurd 2012: 55–56 on *Att.* 6.2.3 and *Rep.* 2.7.

[245] Seneca (*Ep.* 108.21) also has *iudicium sustinere*, "to hold back judgement." Augustine (*Contr. Ac.* 2.12) picks up the equine metaphor in Lucilius, translating ἐποχή as *refrenatio assensionis* "a reining in of assent."

[246] On Lucilius and Carneades, see Goh 2018.   [247] Zillinger 1911: 166.

The Naevian Hector pleases me because not only is he overjoyed "*to be praised*," but even adds "*by a praised man.*"

Five years later, Cicero (*Fam.* 15.6.1; 50 BCE) used the same verse to convey his respect to Cato:

> *laetus sum laudari me*, inquit Hector, opinor, apud Naeuium *abs te, pater, a laudato uiro.* ea est enim profecto iucunda laus, quae ab iis proficiscitur[248] qui ipsi in laude uixerunt.

> "*I am overjoyed to be praised*," Hector, I think, says in Naevius, "*by you father, yourself a praised man.*" For certainly praise is sweet when it arises from those who themselves have lived in praise.

Finally, in the summer of 45 BCE, Cicero quoted the full verse in the *Tusculans* (4.67):

> illud iam supra diximus, contractionem animi recte fieri numquam posse, elationem posse; aliter enim Naeuianus ille gaudet Hector:
> *laetus sum laudari me abs te, pater, a laudato uiro* [*TrRF* I 14]

> As I said earlier, it is never right for a shrinking of the spirits to happen, but an exaltation of spirits is perfectly acceptable. Naevius' Hector experiences the latter when he rejoices:
> "*I am overjoyed to be praised by you, father, yourself a praised man.*"

In this case, the final, philosophical use of the verse sheds further light on the significance of the prior iterations. Cicero, writing to men he admires, indicates this esteem with a verse spoken – presumably by Hector to his "father" (*pater*), i.e. Priam – to convey the mutual respect between them, a tensile kind of social dynamic which Cicero hopes will be replicated in his dealings with Lucceius and Cato. In the *Tusculans* (4.67), Cicero treats this verse as part of his philosophical analysis of emotion: while hedonistic pleasures are to be avoided, there is a virtuous kind of pleasure, one which comes from being "praised by a praised man" (*laudari . . . a laudato uiro*).[249] Cicero's focus upon the necessity for elites to act in mutually respectful cooperation is conveyed in his letters via the same verse citation which is ultimately selected as an exemplum of ethical behaviour in the context of philosophical analysis. Once more we see Cicero

---

[248] Cicero's *proficiscitur* ("arises") is a pun on the title of the play: *Hector Proficiscens,* "Hector's Departure."
[249] Cicero (*TD* 4.67) contrasts this virtuous kind of pleasure with the excesses of sexual pleasure by pairing the positive exemplum of Naevius' *Hector Proficiscens* (*TrRF* I 47) with a negative exemplum from a comedy by Trabea (Ribbeck 1–5). For the relationship between *laetari* and *elatio*, see p171n53.

approaching the same verse from multiple angles, and the repetitions deepen our understanding of the significance of the verse.

Cicero's use of Latin verse in his letters demonstrates the extent to which Latin poetry was naturalized into everyday life, and also reveals threads of interconnection between his epistolary corpus and other intellectual works. Furthermore, Cicero's use of poetic citation in the letters conforms to the rhetorical strategy of deploying verse as part of the conveyance of wit, and, to some extent, Cicero's informal, off-the-cuff citation in the letters most closely resembles the use of verse in the oratorical corpus. However, given that many verses used in Cicero's letters also appear in his philosophical works, Cicero's correspondence allows us to see that Cicero could approach the same verse in a variety of different ways.

CHAPTER 3

Roman Comedy and Scholarship

At the time of their original performance, Plautus' plays were not made available to the public in book form, but copies – scripts or transcripts – were kept in the private archives.[1] The first book copies of Plautine comedy probably appeared in the mid second century BCE, a time when the plays of the now dead playwright were being restaged.[2] By the end of the second century BCE, a lively scholarly activity had developed around Plautine comedy in particular.[3] Grammatical writers made collections of the plays in book rolls (*uolumina*).[4] Republican scholars became preoccupied with trying to discover which of the comedies then circulating under Plautus' name were genuine: several Roman scholars, all active during Cicero's youth, compiled "lists" (*indices*) of authentic Plautine comedies.[5] Among their number were L. Aelius Stilo, about whom we shall hear more shortly. And it was on the foundations built by these Roman scholars that Varro worked when he turned his

---

[1] Reynolds 1983: 302, Deufert 2002: 23. A "script" is the plan of what will occur; "transcript" the documentation of what did occur; see Marshall 2006: 274.

[2] Reynolds 1983: 303, Deufert 2002: 23. The prologue to Plautus' *Casina* (13–15) describes the fact that this play is being restaged. Terence, whose plays were staged in the 160s, describes careful use of scripts in his defense against plagiarism at the beginning of his *Eunuchus* (19–33). One of the earliest Roman writers that we know of to quote from Plautus was the satirist, Lucilius, which may make him one of the first users of a book copy of Plautus; see Deufert 2002: 45.

[3] According to Aulus Gellius (3.3.13), so many plays were attributed to Plautus because he partially rewrote scripts of older Latin comedies and had them staged as his own.

[4] Ferri 2014: 774.

[5] The authors of Plautine *indices* named by Aulus Gellius (3.3.1) are the following: L. Aelius Stilo (see section 3.1); Volcacius Sedigitus, who also composed a canon of comic playwrights in *senarii* (Gell. 15.24; see Courtney 2003: 93); Servius Clodius, a scholar and Stilo's son-in-law, said to have stolen one of Stilo's books (Suetonius, *Gramm.* 3); Q. Aurelius Opillus (often written as *Opilius* in mss.; see Kaster 1995: 110, Zetzel 2018: 17, 27–28, 98); L. Accius, poet and scholar who held a prominent position in the *collegium poetarum* c. 120 BCE (see Boyle 2006: 111), and was the dedicatee of Varro's work on the Latin alphabet (*De Antiquitate Litterarum*); and a certain Manilius, possibly a senator (see Rawson 1985: 4, 273). According to Cicero, Servius Clodius, Stilo's son-in-law, could identify a single isolated verse as Plautine (*Fam.* 9.16.4, see Zetzel 2018: 23). Servius Clodius' library was given to Cicero in 60 BCE as a gift by his friend L. Papirius Paetus, a close relative to Clodius (*Att.* 1.20.7, see Dix 2013: 217). On the Republican scholarship as a stage in the reception of Roman comedy, see Hanses 2020: 46–47.

attention to the authentication of Plautine comedy.[6] By the Ciceronian period, then, Roman comedy, with Plautus in a place of prominence, had become a fertile ground for linguistic inquiry. Cicero's use of comic verse to explore grammatical and philosophical questions can fruitfully be contextualized within this contemporary scholarly interest in the comic poets.

3.1 The Roman Scholar

Both Cicero and Varro studied with the Roman scholar, L. Aelius Stilo ("the Pen") as young men.[7] In different ways, Stilo's influence on each of them was indelible, a testament to the potentially long-lasting effects of early mentorship in the Roman intellectual world. Cicero's praise of Stilo in the *Brutus* (205) extends from his excellence as a prominent member of the social elite to his knowledge of both Greek and Latin literature, presenting him as an expert in the works and lives of ancient writers:

> fuit is omnino uir egregius et eques Romanus cum primis honestus idemque eruditissimus et Graecis litteris et Latinis, antiquitatisque nostrae et in inuentis rebus et in actis scriptorumque ueterum litterate peritus. quam scientiam Varro noster acceptam ab illo auctamque per sese, uir ingenio praestans omnique doctrina, pluribus et inlustrioribus litteris explicauit.

> Stilo was altogether an outstanding individual: a Roman knight, honoured among the best men, and also most learned in both Greek and Latin literature, a lettered expert in Roman antiquity in regard to both the creations and deeds of ancient writers. Our own Varro inherited this knowledge from Stilo, and augmented it in his own right. Himself a man of unsurpassed expertise in every subject, he has furthered Stilo's research with his many impressive writings.

For Cicero, Stilo's prestige derived from his devotion to scholarly pursuits in Roman culture and the Latin language. The extant notices of Stilo's intellectual corpus essentially confirm Cicero's picture: he studied Plautus, and wrote commentaries on foundational Roman texts such as the Hymn

---

[6] Varro set aside twenty-one plays of Plautus as the comedies which he considered genuine without a doubt. It is these same twenty-one comedies that have been preserved through the middle ages, except for the last in the alphabetical series, the *Vidularia* (see Reynolds 1983: 305–306). On Varro's twenty-one plays being identical with our twenty-one, see Reynolds 1983: 303, Rawson 1985: 273, Deufert 2002: 45. The existence of lists of authentic plays did not stop the non-canonical comedies circulating as texts: during the Antonine period there were around 130 comedies under Plautus' name (Gellius 3.3.11); see Hanses 2020: 11. Varro himself in the *De Lingua Latina* includes quotations from Plautine plays which he had excluded from his canon: twenty-one of sixty-one quotations; see Piras 2015: 65.

[7] On Stilo, see Kaster 1995: 68–70, Zetzel 2018: 17n7, 29.

of the Salii and the Twelve Tables.[8] Stilo, then, was interested in studying and elucidating the artefacts of Rome's textual past. If we look beyond the immediate testimony of Stilo's late Republican students to his impact among imperial writers, we see that Stilo's legacy was as an authority on the Latin language.[9] For Cicero (*Brut.* 205), it was Varro who "inherited and augmented" (*acceptam auctamque*) Stilo's scholarly knowledge and voice. In the *Academica* (1.8), Cicero has Varro say that he has tried to teach the Romans things that could not be learned from anyone else since the death of Stilo:

> quae autem nemo adhuc docuerat nec erat unde studiosi scire possent ea quantum potui (nihil enim magnopere meorum miror) feci ut essent nota nostris. a Graecis enim peti non poterant ac post L. Aelii nostri occasum ne a Latinis quidem.

> But the things which no one up till now had taught, and there was nowhere that students could even learn them, I have worked hard as I could (I do not have any great admiration of my own work) to make known to the Romans. These things cannot be learned from the Greeks, and, after the death of Lucius Aelius Stilo, not even from those who speak Latin.

Varro's *De Lingua Latina*, a tour de force which used hundreds of quotations of Latin poetry to make its definitions and etymologies, clearly depended upon Varro's initiation into the field of Roman scholarship facilitated by Stilo and his colleagues.[10] Indeed, Varro engaged Stilo explicitly, often offering correctives to his teacher's theories, and linguistic debate between Varro and Stilo took place using old Roman poetry as its battle ground. An extant grammatical fragment, for example, describes a debate between Stilo and Varro over an ancient text of now uncertain genre, the *Carmen Nelei* ("Song of Neleus").[11] Stilo and Varro argue over

---

[8] Stilo's writings: study of Plautus (Gellius 3.3); speeches for elites (*Brut.* 169, 205–207; see Della Corte 1970: 32), a book which was stolen by his son-in-law, the scholar Servius Clodius (Suet. *Gramm.* 3); the *Commentarium De Proloquiis* (Gellius 16.8.2); a commentary on the *Carmen Saliare* (*LL* 7.2); possible commentary on the Twelve Tables (*De Leg.* 2.59, *Topica* 10, *De Off.* 1.37).

[9] Aulus Gellius (5.12.3) relates an anecdote regarding a learned friend who accidentally used the form *pluria* (for *plura*) because he had read older Latin literature so frequently. When he is corrected by a dilettante, Gellius' friend responds (5.12.6) that the term was used in such a form by Stilo alongside other authorities such as Cato the Elder, P. Nigidius Figulus, and Varro, as well as other unnamed orators and poets.

[10] On Varro and Stilo: Lehmann 1997: 96–106, Dangel 2001: 103, Piras 2015: 66, Spencer 2019: 21. On Varro's scholarship, see Zetzel 2018: 31–58.

[11] There are five extant fragments of the *Carmen Nelei* (*FPL* fr. inc. 7a) transmitted by Festus and Charisius. Charisius (106 B (84)) writes that the poem is "just as ancient" (*aequo prisco*) as Livius Andronicus' *Odyssey*.

whether a word for "daughter" should be written *puer* or *puera* (*GRF* 47/
250[12]):[13]

> puer et in feminino sexu antiqui dicebant, ut Graeci ὁ παῖς καὶ ἡ παῖς, ut in
> Odyssia uetere, quod est antiquissimum carmen:
> *mea puer, quid uerbi ex tuo ore audio?*   [Livius' *Odyssia, FPL* 3]
> et in Nelei carmine, aeque prisco:
> *saucia puer [filia[14]] sumam*
> ubi tamen Varro cum a puera putat dictum, sed Aelius Stilo magister eius et
> Asinius [Pollio] contra.

> The ancients also used *puer* ("boy") in the feminine grammatical gender,
> like the Greeks use ὁ παῖς ("the male child") and ἡ παῖς ("the female child"),
> as in the old *Odyssey*, which is a very ancient poem:
> *"My daughter, what word do I hear from your mouth?"*
> And in the *Song of Neleus*, which is just as ancient:
> *"wounded child, daughter, I will take … (?)"*
> Varro thinks that it should be written *puera* (with an "*a*"), but Aelius Stilo,
> his teacher, and Asinius Pollio think otherwise.

Influential, too, upon Varro and Cicero alike, was Stilo's application of
Stoic theory in his study of language. Cicero tells us that Stilo "aspired to
be a Stoic" (*Aelius Stoicus esse uoluit, Brut.* 206), and there is evidence of
a consistent preoccupation with etymology, a favoured tool of Stoicism, in
the fragmentary remains of Stilo's corpus. According to Augustine (*De
Dialectica* 6), who drew upon a lost work of Varro, the Stoics used three
etymological categories: "phonetic imitation" (*similitudo*), "transferred
resemblance" (*uicinitas*), and "opposition" (*contrarium*).[15] One of Stilo's
etymologies containing both the *uicinitas* and the *contrarium* types is
quoted by Varro in the *De Lingua Latina* (5.17–18) as he discusses
Pacuvius' *Chryses* and Lucilius' *Satires*:

> sic caelum et pars eius, summum ubi stellae, et id quod
> Pacuuius cum demonstrat dicit:
> *hoc uide circum supraque quod complexu continet terram*   [Schierl fr. 79, 1]
> cui subiungit:
> *id quod nostri caelum memorant*   [Schierl fr. 79, 2]
> a qua bipertita diuisione Lucilius suorum unius et
> uiginti librorum initium fecit hoc:
> *aetheris et terrae genitabile quaerere tempus*   [Warmington 1]

---

[12] Charisius 106 B (84): Stilo *GRF* 47 = Varro *GRF* 250.
[13] On correct grammatical gender as an important part of *Latinitas* according to the Roman philolo-
      gists, see Zetzel 2018: 83.
[14] *Filia* appears to be a gloss on *puer*; see Steuart 1921: 36.   [15] Long 2005: 37.

[5.18] caelum dictum scribit Aelius [*GRF* 7], quod est caelatum, aut contrario nomine, celatum quod apertum est.

So "sky" is both a part, high up where the stars are, and what Pacuvius points to when he says:
"*Look at this around and above, which holds the earth in its embrace*"
to which he adds:
"*that which we call sky . . .* "
From such a bipartite division, Lucilius made the beginning of his own twenty-one books:
"*Seeking the time generative of the earth and sky.*"
[5.18] Aelius writes that the word "*caelum*" derives from the fact that it is "*caelatum*," i.e. "raised above the surface"; or from the opposite, "*celatum*" i.e. "hidden" because it is open.

Varro says that Stilo explained the meaning of the Latin word *caelum* ("sky") from the fact that it is "raised above the surface" (*caelatum*); or, alternatively, since the sky is "exposed" (*apertum*), that it received its name from the opposite idea, *celatum* ("hidden").[16] Given that Varro's citation of Stilo's Stoic explication of *caelum* appears in close proximity to quotations of Pacuvius and Lucilius, it is tempting to think that Varro excerpted these verses from Stilo. Indeed, that Cicero quotes part of the same passage of Pacuvius' *Chryses* (Schierl fr. 79, 2) in the Stoic book of *De Natura Deorum* (2.91) makes this virtually certain. Several of Stilo's Stoic etymologies are reproduced by his students. Varro (*LL* 5.21) reports that Stilo (*GRF* 39) had etymologized *terra* ("earth") from *teritur* ("trodden"), an example of the *similitudo* type.[17] Cicero embeds an etymology of the Ursa Major constellation (*Septentriones*) into his Latin translation of Aratus' *Phaenomena* which derives from Stilo's etymology of the Latin word -*triones* from *terra* (*GRF* 42).[18] In the *De Divinatione* (1.93), Cicero puts into the mouth of the Stoic character, Quintus, the etymology of *monstrum* ("portent") from *moneo* ("to warn") which also derives from Stilo (*GRF* 17).

Cicero and Varro demonstrably learned to apply the Stoic tool of etymology to Latin poetry from Stilo. They were also influenced by

---

[16] Another example of etymology from opposition appears with Stilo's (*GRF* 15) derivation of *miles* ("soldier") from *mollitia* ("softness").
[17] Although he does not signal that the etymology derives from Stilo, Varro's (*LL* 5.72) etymology of *nuptiae* ("marriage") from *nuptus* ("veiling") can be found among Stilo's fragments (*GRF* 23).
[18] Čulík-Baird 2018: 658.

his method of quoting Latin poetry as evidence for a variety of linguistic and cultural phenomena.[19] The extant fragments of Stilo's work, meagre as they are, contain many quotations of poetry: a citation of the *Iliad* is used to etymologize the Roman concept of unploughed soil; a verse from Plautus' non-canonical *Faeneratrix* is cited to explain a proverbial use of language; and part of Ennius' *Sota* is quoted to discuss the dialect of the Praenestini.[20] As far as we can tell, Stilo seems to have used Roman comedy in particular as a baseline of linguistic clarity through which he could bring order to other sanctified Roman texts: for example, a Naevian comedy is quoted to explain the Latin *sonticus* ("critical," "dangerous") used in the Twelve Tables to describe a serious illness (*GRF* 36).[21]

Among the insights that we gain from examining the interaction between Stilo and Varro is the importance of book technology and annotation for the ancient study of Roman literature. Scholars have recognized that Varro's general citational practices imply consultation of books, although not necessarily direct examination of the poets whom he excerpts (i.e. a book copy of Ennius' *Annales*), but the writings of other Roman intellectuals such as Stilo.[22] The appearance, for example, of alphabetical lists in the *De Lingua Latina* has been taken as evidence of Varro's use of secondary sources.[23] Varro also consistently uses the verb *scribere* ("to write") when he refers to scholarly opinions, implying consultation of their books, and inconsistencies in citation method likely imply book use as well.[24] We learn from Varro, too, that Roman scholars

---

[19] Stilo's study of early Roman texts such as the Twelve Tables was certainly influential upon Cicero, who repeats several of Stilo's explanations of Roman legal terminology: *Top.* 10, *Leg.* 2.21, 2.59; see Zetzel 2018: 26.

[20] Stilo quotes the *Iliad* 18.547 (νειοῖο βαθείης τέλσον, "the end of deep soil") to give a precedent for the Latin idiom *noualis ager,* "unploughed soil" (*GRF* 21); Varro, by contrast, derives *noualis* from *nouare,* "to renew" (*LL* 5.39). Stilo quoted Plautus' non-canonical *Faeneratrix* (*GRF* 44) to explain its proverbial phrase, *uapula Papiria* ("Get whipped, Papiria"); and from Ennius' *Sota* in reference to the dialect of the Praenestini (*GRF* 40).

[21] A *fabula togata* by L. Afranius was cited by Stilo, possibly as part of his commentary on the Hymn of the Salii (*GRF* 38).

[22] Stilo himself is explicitly cited three times in the extant portions of Varro's *De Lingua Latina* (5.25, 5.66, 7.2).

[23] At *LL* 7.107, Varro works through examples from plays of Naevius in mostly alphabetical order: *Aesiona, Clastidium, Dolus, Demetrius, Lampadio, Nagido, Romulus, Stigmatias, Technicus, Tarentilla, Tunicularia*; on such alphabetical lists, see Dangel 2001: 99, who also notes Varro's use of a military lexicon (*LL* 7.55–58), a list of Greek calques (*LL* 7.86–89), and a compendium of animal noises (*LL* 7.103–104). On alphabetization as a general phenomenon in grammatical works, see Zetzel 2018 *passim*.

[24] Dangel 2001: 100, Piras 2015: 66 n30.

wrote notes on individual words or phrases as marginal glosses.[25] Varro (*LL* 7.107) found one of his etymologies in a glossed line of Naevius' *Demetrius*:

> in Demetrio persibus a perite: itaque sub hoc glossema callide subscribunt.

> In the *Demetrius*, the term "*persibus*" comes from "*perite*" ("very knowing"): and so they write under this the gloss, "*callide*" ("shrewdly").

If Varro used intermediary texts to find his poetic citations, then the same must be true for Cicero, who, as we know, by 60 BCE owned books that had belonged to Stilo's son-in-law, the Plautine scholar Servius Clodius (*Att.* 1.20.7).[26] Replication of material from Stilo and his colleagues is significant not simply because it demonstrates the intellectual environment in which comedy and other Latin poetry was used, but the fact that late Republican writers such as Varro and Cicero found the examples they needed not always from a book copy of the poem or play, but from a book containing scholarly discussion of Latin poetry. Cicero's interest in verse was therefore facilitated by a whole network of scholarly interest in poetry and its ability to exemplify both Latin language and Roman culture. However, while Cicero had been trained in Roman scholarship by Stilo, he did not follow this path in his own intellectual career: it was Varro (*Brut.* 205), in Cicero's view, who was the spiritual heir of this scholarly tradition. Instead, Cicero took what he needed from the Roman scholarship, and, at times, worked outside of it.

3.2 Looking outside the Canon

That Plautus' plays did not circulate as book copies until the time when Stilo and his colleagues began to work on them meant that there were certain mysteries surrounding Plautus that were simply not the case for other comic playwrights. Plautus' comedies possibly existed for half a century without a published or critical form, but the interval between performance and publication for Terence was much shorter.[27] The question of authenticity which exercised the late

---

[25] These marginal or interlineal additions, intended to elucidate the text, probably also introduced textual variants; see Lindsay 1904: 4. On marginal notes in Roman scholarship, see Zetzel 2018 *passim*.
[26] Dix 2013: 217.
[27] This much is suggested by the fact that in the transmission of Terence there are far fewer interpolations and textual doublets; see Victor 2013: 343, 2014: 699.

Republican philologists about Plautus also seems not to have existed for Terence.[28]

There is very little evidence of scholarly interest in Terence in the Republican period.[29] No citations of Terence can be found among the fragments of Stilo, and we know even less about the scholarship on other Roman comic writers, such as Caecilius Statius. If these poets were the objects of philological activity, a possibility given Cicero and Varro's interest in them, their texts did not raise the same problems of authenticity as the Plautine corpus.[30] Republican intellectuals did, however, exert effort to put their comic poets into qualitative hierarchies. Volcacius Sedigitus, one of the writers of a Plautine *index* (Gellius 3.3.3), composed a poem in *senarii* which ranked the Roman comic poets (Gellius 15.24).[31] Terence appears sixth in this list, possibly reflecting a lack of scholarly interest in his works at this time.[32]

For Varro, Plautus was one of the privileged sources for his linguistic research: the only poet Varro quotes more than Plautus in what remains of *De Lingua Latina* is Ennius (Plautus 61, Ennius 78).[33] Cicero, however, was barely interested in Plautus: he only quotes Plautus five times in the extant corpus, four of which come from the same play, the *Trinummus*.[34] Cicero was much more interested in Terence, whom he quotes almost forty times, from all of his plays except the *Hecyra*.[35] He also quotes from several other comic poets, such as Caecilius Statius, Trabea, Atilius, Sextus Turpilius, and the composer

---

[28] A book copy of Terence's comedies designed to be read (rather than for use in the theatre) seems to have arisen at some point between Terence's time and the end of the first century BCE, and it is this reading text from which our copies ultimately derive, rather than a stage text; see Victor 2013: 343, Monda 2015: 111. An ancient editor gave all but one of Terence's comedies brief introductions, known as *didascaliae*; see Reynolds 1983: 412, Goldberg 2005: 69–75, Hanses 2020: 45.

[29] Scholarly work on Terence seems to get underway in earnest only after the Republican period, as far as we can tell; see Zetzel 2018: 253–257. In his commentary on Terence's *Phormio*, Donatus presents textual readings from Nigidius Figulus on lines 182, 190, 233 (*GRF* 35–37); see Victor 2014: 351. Verrius Flaccus, who became tutor to Augustus' grandsons c. 10 BCE, seems to have studied Terence's language: *GRF* 20 on *Adelphoe* 962; see Victor 2014: 352. From Donatus, we learn that M. Valerius Probus wrote a commentary upon Terence in the Flavian period: *ad Andria* 720, *ad Phormio* 49; see Victor 2014: 699. In the Imperial period, Terence received several commentaries: a complete set of commentaries by Aemilius Asper (first to second century CE), on *Eunuchus* and *Adelphoe* by Helenius Acro (third century CE), on *Phormio* by Arruntius Celsus (fourth century CE), and at least an introduction by Evanthius (fourth century CE); see Reynolds: 1983: 412 n7.

[30] Piras 2015: 67.   [31] Courtney 2003: 93–94.

[32] On Terence and Volcacius Sedigitus, see Hanses 2020: 15, 45. However, Terence would become one of the most studied dramatic poets: at the end of the fourth century CE, Arusianus Messius composed an alphabetical phraseology of Latin idiomatic phrases which took its examples exclusively from the canonical *quadriga* of Terence, Cicero, Sallust, and Virgil; see Hanses 2020: 14.

[33] Piras 1998: 106, Dangel 2001: 97.

[34] *Aulularia* 178 (*Div.* 1.65); *Trinummus* 23–26 (*De Inv.* 1.95), 319 (*Ep. ad Brut.* 1.2.5(2a.1)), 419 (*Pis.* 61), 705 (*De Or.* 2.39).

[35] Spahlinger 2005: 234–239, Monda 2015: 155 n57.

of *fabula togata*, L. Afranius.[36] Varro, by contrast, barely engages these poets in what remains of the *De Lingua Latina*.[37] If Varro's apparent disinterest in these poets is not simply the result of the fact that *De Lingua Latina* does not fully survive to demonstrate such interest, then Cicero, in his citation of the Roman comic poets, seems to be working outside of the canonical texts upon which Roman scholarship had focused Varro's attention. Nonetheless, Cicero used the tools and resources of Roman scholarship to mine the poets and parse out the significance of their verses.

3.3   A Grammar Lesson

While, as we have seen, Cicero did also draw upon the dramatic qualities of Roman comedy, many of the comic citations in the Ciceronian corpus are used to discuss an aspect of language, reflecting comedy's central position within Roman scholarship.[38] That comedy could be used to define "good" and "bad" Latin was a large part of its attraction for Cicero. Cicero, whose philosophical treatises sought to demonstrate the power of Latin to a Roman audience (*Fin.* 1.4), insisted upon the high status of the language. As a result, Cicero's attitude towards the investigation of Latin was driven by a simultaneously moral and political impulse: good Latinity, in Cicero's view, reflected a good Roman.

Roman comedy could be used to establish and defend acceptable Latin usage. In the *Orator* (157), Cicero quotes from Terence's *Phormio* (384, 390) to justify colloquial Latin verb forms:

> nosse, iudicasse uetant, nouisse iubent et iudicauisse? quasi uero nesciamus in hoc genere et plenum uerbum recte dici et imminutum usitate. itaque utrumque Terentius:
> *eho tu, cognatum*[39] *tuom non noras?*   [*Phormio* 384]
> post idem
> *Stilponem, inquam, noueras.*   [*Phormio* 390]

> They forbid us from using *nosse*, "to know" and *iudicasse*, "to have judged." As if we do not know in this case that the full word is correct usage, and the contraction colloquial. Terence uses either:
> *"Hey, you, don't you know your own cousin?"*
> A little bit later:

---

[36] See Appendix II.   [37] Piras 1998: 106.   [38] Hanses 2020: 55.

[39] Cicero has changed Terence's *sobrinum* ("maternal cousin") to *cognatum* ("relative"). This example of citational "mistake" may be the result of a textual variant introduced by a gloss. Since the quotation from the *Phormio* in the *Orator* takes places in the midst of a long series of poetic quotations used to exemplify elements of Latin usage (between *Orator* 149–184 there are around 30 discrete quotations), it may come from an intermediary work by one of the Roman philologists.

"I am saying you knew Stilpo."

The authority of Roman comedy allowed Cicero to resist the overcorrection of organic Latin.[40] In a letter (*Att.* 7.3.10), Cicero defends a use of Latin which Atticus considered a mistake with a citation of Roman comedy:[41]

> uenio ad Piraeëa, in quo magis reprehendendus sum quod homo Romanus Piraeëa scripserim, non Piraeum (sic enim omnes nostri locuti sunt), quam quod addiderim in. non enim hoc ut oppido praeposui sed ut loco. et tamen Dionysius noster et qui est nobiscum Nici as Cous non rebatur oppidum esse Piraeëa.

> I come, then, to the term "Piraeus." In this matter, I am more to be blamed, as a Roman man, for writing *"Piraeëa"* instead of *"Piraeum"* (for this is what we Romans all say), than for adding the preposition. I added the preposition as though it were a place, not a town. After all, our friend Dionysius and Nicias of Cos, who is staying with us, think Piraeus is not a town.

Atticus had objected to Cicero's use of the phrase *in Piraeëa* in a previous letter (*Att.* 6.9.1) because he used a preposition with a name of a town.[42] Cicero says that, if anything, "as a Roman man" (*quod homo Romanus*) his mistake was using the Greek form *Piraeëa* rather than the Latin *Piraeum*, a note which points towards the importance of performative Latinity to the cultural elite. Cicero goes on to defend his choice by arguing that the Piraeus, Athens' harbour, was not big enough to merit the use of the accusative without a preposition. The grammatical issue therefore centred upon whether Piraeus was a "town" (*oppidum*) or a "place" (*locus*).[43] To answer this question, Cicero first consults Dionysius, Atticus' learned freedman, and the grammarian Nicias of Cos[44] – both men who appear in Cicero's letters engaging in

---

[40] During the first century BCE, there was ongoing debate over the nature of language which fell into two opposing sides: the analogists and the anomalists. Analogy, developed by Alexandrian scholars, sought to impose regularity of language, whereas anomaly, championed by the Stoics, understood language to follow usage. In 54 BCE, Caesar composed a treatise *De Analogia*, which he dedicated to Cicero (Suetonius, *Iul.* 56, see Bonner 1977: 27). Both Cicero (*Brut.* 258) and Varro (*LL* 9.12) use *consuetudo* ("accustomed use") as the Latin term for the opposite of analogy. Cicero favoured *consuetudo*, and he was followed by Quintilian in this opinion (*Inst.* 1.6.3, see Bonner 1977: 206). On *consuetudo*, see Zetzel 2018 *passim*.

[41] Bonner 1977: 202–203, Monda 2015: 109.

[42] In Latin, direction towards the names of towns and small islands was usually expressed in the accusative case without a preposition.

[43] Varro gives etymologies for each of these words: *oppidum* (*LL* 5.141) from *ops* ("strength") and *opus esse* ("need"); *locus* (*LL* 5.14) from the verb *locare* ("to place"), illustrated with quotations from Plautus (*Aulularia* 191–192) and Ennius (*TrRF* II 167); see Spencer 2019: 235.

[44] Dionysius Pomponius was a freedman of Atticus (*Att.* 7.18.3) who accompanied Cicero to Cilicia in 51 BCE, where Dionysius taught Cicero's son and nephew (*Att.* 6.1.12); see Treggiari 1969: 119–121, Rawson

3.3 A Grammar Lesson

literary and philological activity.[45] Having consulted these two, Cicero (*Att.* 7.3.10–11) goes further and presents verses from Caecilius Statius and Terence's *Eunuchus* which authorize his use of a preposition:

> nostrum quidem si est peccatum, in eo est, quod non ut de oppido locutus sum, sed ut de loco, secutusque sum non dico Caecilium
> *mane ut ex portu in Piraeum* [Ribbeck 258]
> malus enim auctor Latinitatis est, sed Terentium, cuius fabellae propter elegantiam sermonis putabantur a C. Laelio scribi:
> *heri aliquot adulescentuli coiimus in Piraeum* [*Eunuchus* 539]
> et idem
> *mercator hoc addebat: captam e Sunio* [*Eunuchus* 114, 115[46]]
> quod si δῆμους oppida uolumus esse, tam est oppidum Sunium quam Piraeus. [7.3.11] sed quoniam grammaticus es, si hoc mihi ζήτημα persolueris, magna me molestia liberaris.

> If I made a mistake it is in the fact that I spoke of the Piraeus not as a town, but as a place, and I have precedents for this; not Caecilius Statius, although he says
> "*in the morning from the port to the Piraeus*"
> for he is a bad example of Latinity, but Terence, the speeches of whose plays were so fine that they were thought to have been written by Gaius Laelius:
> "*yesterday several of us lads went to the Piraeus,*"
> and:
> "*the merchant added this: she was taken from Sunium.*"
> If we are going to say that demes are towns, then Sunium is as much a town as Piraeus. [7.3.11] But since you are playing the scholar, perhaps you will solve this dispute for me, and free me from this great annoyance.

Caecilius Statius wrote *in Piraeum*, but Caecilius' suspect Latinity, in Cicero's judgement, makes him a "bad authority" (*malus auctor Latinitatis*), therefore Cicero also cites Terence's *Eunuchus*.[47] For Cicero, Terence's plays contained such high quality Latin that they "could have been written by Laelius himself" (*putabantur a C. Laelio scribi, Att.* 7.3.10). Such a statement is reminiscent of the

---

1985: 70–71. The man known to Cicero as *Nicias Cous* is generally taken to be the same person Suetonius calls *Curtius Nicias;* see Syme 1961: 25, Rawson 1985: 71. Suetonius (*Gramm.* 14) notes that Nicias was friends with C. Memmius, Lucretius' patron, and wrote a commentary on Lucilius' *Satires.*

[45] In 56 BCE, Dionysius organized Cicero's library (*Att.* 4.4a.1; 4.8.2). Cicero (*Fam.* 9.10, cf. Suet. *Gramm.* 14) describes Nicias' use of Alexandrian notation: *Aristarchus hos obelizei: ego tanquam criticus antiquus iudicaturus sum, utrum sint* τοῦ ποιητοῦ *an* παρεμβεβλημένοι, "Like an Aristarchus, he marked it with an obelus – I will have to play the role of the ancient critic, to find out whether the words are the poet's or a forgery."

[46] Cicero combines the beginning and end of two consecutive lines from Terence's *Eunuchus* 114–115. This technique of truncation is recommended by *Rhet.* 2.34.

[47] Varro also quoted *Eunuchus* 539 as part of a discussion of metre (*GRF* 39).

well-known passage of *De Oratore* (3.45) in which Crassus praises his mother-in
-law, Laelia, Laelius' daughter, for her Latinity, which apparently resembled the
"unspoiled antiquity" (*incorruptam antiquitatem*) of Plautus and Naevius.[48] In
the *Brutus* (258), the age of Laelius and Scipio Aemilianus is likewise figured as
the time of optimal Latinity; there, too, Cicero censures Caecilius, alongside
Pacuvius, as "bad speakers of Latin" (*male locutos*). While Cicero makes clear
that it is the genre of Roman comedy that best reflects elite speech, not all poets
were evidently capable of reaching that level.

3.4 "Beyond the Second Step"

Cicero's discussion of Latin on the level of language via poetic citation
demonstrates the fact that correct usage was deeply embedded in the
performance of elite identity at Rome. That access to knowledge of the
Latin language was hierarchically stratified is also argued by Varro in the *De
Lingua Latina* (5.7–9):

> nunc singulorum uerborum origines expediam, quorum quattuor expla-
> nandi gradus. infimus quo populus etiam uenit: quis enim non uidet unde
> "argentifodinae" et "uiocurus"? secundus quo grammatica escendit antiqua,
> quae ostendit, quemadmodum quodque poeta finxerit uerbum, quod con-
> finxerit, quod declinarit; hic Pacui:
>
> *rudentum sibilus*   [Pacuvius' *Teucer*, Schierl fr. 241]
> hic:
> *incuruiceruicum pecus,*   [Pacuvius' *Teucer*, Schierl fr. 238]
> hic:
> *clamide clupeat bracchium.*   [Pacuvius' *Hermiona*, Schierl fr. 134]
> [5.8] tertius gradus, quo philosophia ascendens peruenit atque ea quae in
> consuetudine communi essent aperire coepit, ut a quo dictum esset
> "oppidum," "uicus," "uia." quartus, ubi est adytum et initia regis: quo si non
> perueniam <ad> scientiam, at opinionem aucupabor, quod etiam in salute
> nostra nonnunquam facit cum aegrotamus medicus. [5.9] quodsi summum
> gradum non attigero, tamen secundum praeteribo, quod non solum ad
> Aristophanis lucernam, sed etiam ad Cleanthis lucubraui. uolui praeterire
> eos, qui poetarum modo uerba ut sint ficta expediunt.

> Now I will extricate the origins of individual words. There are four steps of
> explanation. The first step is the one to which even regular people arrive: for
> who cannot see where the words "silver mines" and "road manager" come

[48] Naevius and Plautus are each described as reflecting old and elite speech; where records of the past
are not available, deductions can be made from these two poets: *De Or.* 3.45, *Brut.* 60. Varro
followed the judgement of Stilo when he said that – if the Muses could speak Latin, they would have
spoken like Plautus (*GRF* 50); see Hanses 2020: 46.

from? To the second step has ascended ancient philological study, which shows how the poet has fashioned each word, what he has fabricated, what he has derived. For example, Pacuvius'
"the whistling of ropes"
and
"curve-necked flock"
and
"shields the arm in cloak."
[5.8] The third step is the one to which philosophy, climbing, arrived, and there began to open up the words which are in common use, explaining, for example, the origin of "town," "street," "road." The fourth step is where lies the inner sanctum and the sacred rites of the priest: if I do not reach this stage of knowledge, I will still hunt around for an explanation, which the doctor sometimes does when we are ill, even in the matter of our own health. [5.9] But if I have not reached that highest level, I will nonetheless go beyond the second step, working by nocturnal light not only with Aristophanes but also Cleanthes. I aspire to go beyond those who explain only how the words of poets are made up.

While many Romans, Varro says, were able to etymologize words which self-evidently indicated their own origins, the finer degrees of investigation required initiation into deeper modes of inquiry. Varro distinguishes between the superficial knowledge of "everyday people" (*populus*), who remain on the "lowest step" (*infimus gradus*) of linguistic understanding, and the ascending degrees of linguistic specialization which culminate in unattainable, mystical knowledge. At the second stage, *grammatica,* the study of poetry, could explain the unusual words invented by poets like Pacuvius. Beyond that lay philosophy, at which stage the origin of more complex words (such as *oppidum*, cf. *Att.* 7.3.10) and their true meaning could be revealed. Varro (*LL* 5.9) therefore characterizes his study of the Latin language as a fundamentally philosophical endeavour, one inspired by the Stoic Cleanthes. While linguistic understanding is rooted in detailed examination of poetry, it is ultimately philosophy, Varro says, that uses those building blocks to construct deeper understanding.

Cicero was in sympathy with Varro's depiction of philosophy as the highest attainable stratum of linguistic knowledge. In his philosophical works, Cicero applied the techniques of poetic citation and analysis established by Roman scholarship as part of his philosophical argumentation. In the *De Finibus* (2.12), Cicero takes issue with the claim that non-Epicureans do not understand what Epicureans mean by the term *uoluptas* ("pleasure"), approaching the problem from a linguistic perspective:

> itaque hoc frequenter dici solet a uobis, non intellegere nos quam dicat Epicurus uoluptatem. quod quidem mihi si quando dictum est (est autem dictum non parum saepe), etsi satis clemens sum in disputando, tamen interdum soleo subirasci. egone non intellego, quid sit ἡδονή Graece, Latine "uoluptas"? utram tandem linguam nescio? deinde qui fit, ut ego nesciam, sciant omnes quicumque Epicurei esse uoluerunt? quod uestri quidem uel optime disputant, nihil opus esse eum qui futurus sit philosophus scire litteras.

> And you are in the frequent habit of saying that we do not understand what Epicurus means by pleasure. Whenever I hear this, and I have heard it many times, even though I'm a pretty easy-going discussant, still I tend to get a bit angry every now and then. What do I not understand: the Greek word for pleasure, or the Latin one? Which language do I not know? How can it be that I do not know something that all who aspire to be Epicureans know? Let me rather bring in the fact that Epicureans argue that there is no need for the aspiring philosopher to know his letters.

To the Epicurean claim that non-adherents do not have a sufficient understanding of Epicurus' definition of pleasure, Cicero responds that the Epicureans themselves have an insufficient grasp of language. While it is, Cicero continues, sometimes difficult to find exact equivalents for Greek words in Latin, there is no Greek-Latin pairing more apt than ἡδονή-*uoluptas*. In order to demonstrate that this is the case, Cicero (*Fin.* 2.13) quotes verses from Roman comic playwrights, Trabea and Caecilius Statius:[49]

> nullum inueniri uerbum potest quod magis idem declaret Latine quod
> Graece, quam declarat uoluptas. huic uerbo omnes qui ubique sunt qui
> Latine sciunt duas res subiciunt, laetitiam in animo, commotionem suauem
> iucunditatis in corpore. nam et ille apud Trabeam
> *uoluptatem animi nimiam*   [Trabea, Ribbeck 6]
> laetitiam dicit, eandem quam ille Caecilianus quia
> *omnibus laetitiis laetum*   [Caecilius, Ribbeck 252]
> esse se narrat. sed hoc interest, quod uoluptas dicitur etiam in animo (uitiosa
> res, ut Stoici putant, qui eam sic definiunt: sublationem animi sine ratione
> opinantis se magno bono frui), non dicitur laetitia nec gaudium in corpore.

---

[49] The comic poet, Trabea, took 8th position in Volcacius Sedigitus' canon of Roman comic playwrights (see Gellius 15.24; see Courtney 2003: 93). The only two known fragments of Trabea come from Cicero: Ribbeck 1–5 (*TD* 4.67), Ribbeck 6 (*Fin.* 2.13, *TD* 4.35, *Fam.* 2.9.2).

There is no word to be found which more closely reflects Greek ἡδονή than the Latin "*uoluptas.*" To this word everyone everywhere who knows Latin attributes two meanings: mental joy, and the sweet feeling of pleasantness in the body. For the character in Trabea says:
"*excessive mental pleasure*"
is called "joy." This same feeling is what the character in Caecilius Statius means when he says that he is
"*joyful with every joy.*"
But there is a difference, since "*uoluptas*" is used even for mental pleasure (a moral fault, as the Stoics think, who define it as an irrational elevation of a mind that considers itself to be enjoying a great good), whereas neither "*laetitia*" ("joy") or *gaudium* ("gladness") are used of bodily pleasure.

Cicero begins at the bottom step of linguistic inquiry: just as Varro considered "even regular people" (*etiam populus, LL* 5.7) capable of knowing the true meaning of certain Latin words, Cicero here emphasizes the fact that "everyone, everywhere who knows Latin" (*omnes qui ubique sunt qui Latine sciunt, Fin.* 2.13) understands that *uoluptas* can mean either mental or bodily pleasure.[50] Cicero then, arriving at the "second step" (*secundus gradus, LL* 5.7) of the Varronian framework, draws upon the poets to define his terms. Given that it was Roman comedy which was central to the Roman scholarly tradition, Cicero again turns to comic playwrights for authorizing examples of Latin usage: Trabea's verse is used to exemplify *uoluptas* ("pleasure"); while Caecilius Statius defines the related feeling of *laetitia* ("joy").

Cicero is not content to ascend only the first two Varronian steps of linguistic comprehension, but reaches the third by applying a philosophical reading to his poetic selections. Following the claim that *uoluptas* corresponds appropriately to the Epicurean definition of ἡδονή, Cicero (*Fin.* 2.14–15) then substantiates the Epicurean thesis that true "pleasure" is essentially neutral, i.e. an absence of extreme pleasure or pain (cf. Epic. *Men.* 131–132), with citations from Caecilius Statius, Terence, and an unknown poet:

in eo autem uoluptas omnium Latine loquentium more ponitur, cum percipitur ea quae sensum aliquem moueat iucunditas. hanc quoque iucunditatem, si uis, transfer in animum (iuuare enim in utroque dicitur ex eoque iucundum), modo intellegas inter illum qui dicat
tanta laetitia auctus sum ut nihil constet   [Unknown comedy, Ribbeck 37]

---

[50] In his letter to Atticus (*Att.* 7.3.10), Cicero writes that "everyone who speaks Latin" (*sic enim omnes nostri locuti sunt*) uses *Piraeum* rather than *Piraea.*

et eum qui
nunc demum mihi animus ardet . . .   [Caecilius, Ribbeck 230]
quorum alter laetitia gestiat, alter dolore crucietur, esse illum medium:
quamquam haec inter nos nuper notitia admodum est   [Ter. *Heaut.* 53]
qui nec laetetur nec angatur; itemque inter eum qui potiatur corporis
expetitis uoluptatibus et eum qui crucietur summis doloribus esse eum qui
utroque careat. [2.15] satisne igitur uideor uim uerborum tenere, an sum
etiam nunc uel Graece loqui uel Latine docendus?

But according to the custom of all those who speak Latin, "*uoluptas*" is
understood to mean the perception of a pleasantness that moves the senses.
Transfer this pleasantness, if you like, to the mind (the verb "*iuuare*," "delight,"
is used for both mind and body, and the adjective "*iucundus*," "delightful"
derives from it), as long as you understand the difference between he who says:
"*I am so swollen with joy that nothing makes sense*"
and the one who says:
"*Only now is my mind aflame . . .*"
The first character is in a state of delighted "joy" ("*laetitia*"), while
the second is tortured in pain. A third figure treads a middle path:
"*Although our friendship is only quite recent.*"
This character is neither overjoyed nor pained. And so, between the man
who obtains the most exquisite bodily pleasures and the man who is tortured
with most severe pains, there is a man who lacks either extreme. [2.15] Are
you satisfied with my understanding of these words, or must I still, even
now, be taught to speak Greek or Latin?

Three characters from Roman comedy are brought onto Cicero's philosophical stage to exemplify three states of being: the first speaker, from an
unknown play, expresses extreme "joy" (*laetitia*); the second, a character
from Caecilius Statius, extreme pain; the third exemplar, from Terence, feels
"neither joy nor pain" (*nec laetetur nec angatur*), and therefore typifies the
"neutral" (*medium*) state of Epicurean "pleasure." Just as Cicero (*Att.* 7.3.11)
had closed his linguistic analysis of the Piraeus as *oppidum* by teasing Atticus
for playing the role of the *grammaticus*, Cicero here ends his definition of
uoluptas with rhetorical indignation to underline the role of language in
philosophical discourse: "are you satisfied . . . or must I still, even now, be
taught to speak Greek or Latin?" (*satisne igitur uideor . . . an sum etiam nunc
uel Graece loqui uel Latine docendus?*). Cicero's framing of the issue as
a fundamentally linguistic problem allows him to engage the techniques of
Roman scholarship, centering Roman comedy as the established baseline of
the Latin language.
    That Cicero is drawing from a scholarly tradition for his linguistic
investigations is further suggested by the similarities between his analysis

of *uoluptas* in the *De Finibus* and a passage of Varro's *De Lingua Latina*. Varro (*LL* 6.50) quotes from the comic poet, Iuventius, to justify his etymology of the verb *laetari*, "to be joyful":[51]

> laetari ab eo quod latius gaudium propter magni boni opinionem diffusum. itaque Iuuentius ait:
>
> > gaudia   [Ribbeck 2–4]
> > *sua si omnes homines conferant unum in locum.*
> > *tamen mea exsuperet laetitia.*
> > sic cum se habent, laeta.

> *"laetari"* ("to be joyful") comes from the fact that gladness (*"gaudium"*) is spread "more widely" (*"latius"*), because it is widely considered a great good. And so, Iuventius says:
> *"If all men collected their own happiness together into a single spot,*
> *nonetheless my joy would surpass theirs."*
> When things are like this, they are "joyful."

Varro defines the Latin verb *laetari* ("to be joyful") as "gladness" (*gaudium*) which is spread "more widely" (*latius*); a Stoic etymology of the *similitudo* type (*laet-; lat-*). Varro's comment that joy is "considered a great good" (*magni boni opinionem*) connects with Cicero's (*Fin.* 2.13) statement on the Stoic attitude to mental pleasure:

> uitiosa res, ut Stoici putant, qui eam sic definiunt: sublationem animi sine ratione opinantis se magno bono frui.

> a moral fault,[52] as the Stoics think, who define it as an irrational elevation of a mind that considers itself to be enjoying a great good.

Both Varro and Cicero refer to the fact that joy is "considered a great good" (*magni boni opinionem*; *opinantis se magno bono frui*), and Cicero's description of mental pleasure as an "elevation" (*sub-latio*) echoes Varro's definition of *laetari* from *latius*.[53] The true meaning of *laetitia* ("joy") as a form of movement, put forward by both Varro and Cicero, is an endorsement of the Stoic view of emotion.[54] Among the fragments of the Greek Stoics, we find

---

[51] Iuventius is cited by Varro by name twice more in the *De Lingua Latina* (7.65, 7.104). Unless a verse of Iuventius appears among the anonymous quotations, Cicero never cites him.

[52] Cf. *TD* 4.34–35, where *uitiositas* ("faultfulness") resulting in agitated movements of the soul is exemplified with the two citations of comedy which had also appeared the Cicero's definition of *uoluptas*: Trabea Ribbeck 6 = *Fin.* 2.13, *TD* 4.35; unknown comedy Ribbeck 37 = *Fin.* 2.14, *TD* 4.35.

[53] In the *De Finibus* (3.35), the Stoic figure, Cato, defines ἡδονή as "joy" (*laetitia*) which is like "the pleasurable elevation of an exulting mind" (*gestientis animi elationem uoluptaria*); cf. *Fin.* 2.13, where Cicero describes the character from Caecilius Statius as "exulting in joy" (*laetitia gestiat*).

[54] Stoic theory of emotion as movement: *TD* 4.11, *Fin.* 2.13; Epictetus fr. 9 = Long-Sedley 65Y.

a definition of "pleasure" (ἡδονή) as "an irrational uplifting" (ἄλογος ἔπαρσις).[55] Cicero (*Fin.* 2.13) reflects the Stoic belief that mental pleasure is "irrational" (*sine ratione*) and that mental pleasure is a form of "elevation" (*sublatio*); but the Latin terms used by Cicero to convey these ideas are deeply rooted in a specifically Roman form of linguistic investigation. The etymological explanation of *laetari* from *lat-* confirms a Stoic thesis but it is dependent upon the structure of the Latin language, not Greek. Since Cicero and Varro had both quoted from Roman comedy to reveal the true meaning of *laetari*, their philosophical definitions were facilitated by the study of Latin poetry on the detailed level of language.

Situated within the context of Roman scholarship, which viewed Roman comedy as the privileged site of Latin textual analysis, we are able to see that Cicero's engagement with the comic poets is deeply influenced by the techniques developed and in current use by those who studied the Latin language. Roman comedy was most reflective of good Latinity, and allowed Cicero to define grammatical usage, as well as to explore even more complex questions regarding the meaning of individual Latin words. Techniques and poetic sources used by Varro appear in Cicero's corpus too, suggesting the engagement by each in a shared scholarly tradition, one deeply influenced by the work of their teacher, L. Aelius Stilo. Just as the study of poetry in the rhetorical classroom influenced Cicero's deployment of verse in his speeches, so too did Cicero's study with the Roman scholar influence his use of Latin verse in his philosophical works.

---

[55] *SVF* 3.391 = Long-Sedley 65B.

CHAPTER 4

Singing in Cicero

In the Republican period, music in its theory and practice was part of the intellectual interests of the elite, but also part of the regular experience of an average Roman. Aside from spellsongs – guarded against by the Roman legal code – song, both lyric and melodic, played a part in weddings, triumphs, religious celebrations, funerals, and lamentations. One of the most important musical settings in Republican culture was the Roman theatre, which was highly musical: 48 percent of Plautus' output was performed in the longer iambo-trochaic metres (septenarii and octonarii) which were recited, in a manner often compared to the recitative of modern opera, to musical accompaniment provided by the "pipes" (*tibiae*).[1] Another 14 percent of Plautus consisted of full, melodious songs, known as *cantica*, written in metres such as bacchiacs, cretics, and anapaests. The remaining 38 percent of Plautus was performed in the spoken metre, the iambic senarius, which was considered by both Aristotle and Cicero most closely to reflect the pattern of everyday speech.[2]

Extant Roman theatrical texts show that the *tibia* was playing more than it was silent. Terence may have far fewer set songs (there are only three in his corpus,[3] amounting to 25 lines), but like Plautus, the longer, recited metres make up the bulk of the play (almost 48 percent). Although some modern scholars doubt our ability to detect the musicality of Republican tragedy from fragmentary sources (e.g. Landels 1999: 182), we can none-theless see metrical patterns in their remains which strongly suggest a musical quality.[4] The Roman stage was also much more musical than

---

[1] These percentages for Plautus and Terence come from Maltby 2012: 25. Boyle (2006: 61 n21) gives a slightly different set of percentages for Plautus: 56 percent recited, 11 percent *cantica*.

[2] Aristotle *Poetics* 1449a24–6, *Rhetoric* 1404a32; cf. *Or.* 184.

[3] *Andria* 481–6, 625–38; *Adelphoe* 610–17.

[4] We appear to have evidence of song in Roman tragedy from its beginning, such as the cretic dimeters from *Equus Troianus*, which Fraenkel compared with cretic *cantica* in Plautus: *da mihi hasce opes | quas peto quas precor | porrige opitula* (*TrRF* I, 14) "Give me the resources | which I seek, which I pray for | hold them out! help me!" cf. *Curc.* 148, *Men.* 116, *Rud.* 208, *Cas.* 194; Fraenkel 2007: 378.

its Greek predecessor. When Roman writers adapted Greek plays, they made song where there had been none previously.[5] Additionally, the musical accompaniment to Roman plays seems to have had a tremendous amount of variety. From the production notices (*didascaliae*) which have been transmitted with Terence's plays, we know that he used several different kinds of pipe – *tibiae pares*, "of equal length"; *tibiae impares*, which probably played at an interval of an octave from one another; *tibiae Sarranae*, which may have come from a Semitic musical tradition.[6] Given that what differentiated the *tibiae* was their length and therefore their pitch, the fact that different types of pipe were used for different plays suggests different melodic ranges for each play.[7]

Music was also a part of the elite Roman education.[8] Although we read anecdotes concerning the apparent moral turpitude brought on by musical training which discourage the idea that the Roman elite valued musical amateurism, we nonetheless get a sense that music was in fact taught to children, both boys and girls, as part of their liberal education.[9] In the *De Oratore* (3.86–87), Cicero's Crassus mentions the professional Valerius who used to sing everyday, but also Numerius Furius, a well-respected Roman equestrian and *paterfamilias*, who, having learnt to sing when he had to as a boy, now sang whenever he could. While Quintilian (*Inst.* 1.12.14) says that the student of oratory should not become consumed with the granular technicalities of ancillary arts, he adds that the student does

---

70 percent of Ennius' surviving tragic verses are thought to have been sung or recited to the *tibia*; see Boyle 2006: 61.

[5] Such as Caecilius Statius' adaptation of Menander's *Plokion*, preserved by Aulus Gellius (2.23.9–10), who compares the two passages; the presence of song in plays of Plautus that are based upon Menander (*Bacchides, Cistellaria, Stichus*), who did not write songs; or Ennius' adaptation (*TrRF* II 97) of the iambic trimeters from Euripides' *Medea* 1069–73 into song: *saluete optima corpora | cette manus uestras measque accipite*, "Goodbye, my sweet creatures | give me your hands, and take mine"; see Fraenkel 2007: 228.

[6] Landels 1999: 189, Moore 2012: 57.

[7] When the pipes were unequal, they played different notes: Varro tells us that one of the two pipes played the melody (*incentiua*), while the other played the accompaniment (*succentiua*, *RR* 1.2.15–17). On the *tibiae* ("pipes") and *tibicines* ("pipe-players"), see Moore 2012: 26–63; on the *tibiae* and comic delivery, see Marshall 2006: 234–244.

[8] Wille 1967: 406, Bonner 1977: 44.

[9] Seneca the Elder (*Contr.* 1 *pr.* 8) mentions the practice of singing and training the voice as part of a luxuriant and effeminate lifestyle, the current vogue among young men. Cicero (*Cat.* 2.23) characterizes the young men at Catiline's banquets in a similar way. Nepos' *Life of Epaminondas* (1.2) begins with a plea that the reader not judge the habits of other cultures by their own standard, noting that the Romans thought that great men should stay away from music. According to Plutarch (*Pom.* 55), Pompey's wife, Cornelia, was well educated in literature, geometry, and in playing the lyre. Sallust (*BC* 25) describes Brutus' mother, Sempronia, as shameful because she was too good at playing the lyre and dancing for an elite woman.

not need to train his voice like a singer or "take down songs in musical notation" (*musicis notis cantica excipiat*).[10] Musical training was a possibility, even if the orator was not encouraged to linger.

Roman intellectuals were also well acquainted with the theory of music, with its connections to mathematics and ethics in the Greek philosophical tradition.[11] In the *De Legibus* (2.38), Cicero says that he agrees with Plato (cf. *Rep.* 424c–d) that nothing is more influential upon an impressionable young mind than "the varied notes of songs" (*uarios canendi sonos*), capable of arousing the dull and soothing the excited.[12] Cicero also says (*Leg.* 2.39) that he is aware of the theory that innovations in music create losses of ethical virility and vice versa, an opinion that is rooted in the association with certain musical scales and even specific notes with masculinity or femininity (discussed further on pp184–185). Cicero (*Leg.* 2.39) also noticed a difference between how Roman audiences used to react to the "sweet severity" (*seueritas iucunda*) of the music of Livius Andronicus and Naevius, and the physical reactions which modern audiences have to Roman music:[13]

> ... solebat quondam conpleri seueritate iucunda Liuianis et Naeuianis modis, nunc ut eadem exultet ceruices oculosque pariter cum modorum flexionibus torqueant.

> ... where once the theatre was full of the sweet severity of the music of Livius Andronicus and Naevius, now the same place is full of energy, with necks and eyes alike twisting to the sound of the music.

Cicero, who discussed prose rhythm in the context of oratorical style, demonstrates an awareness of the role of melody in shaping the impact and meaning of poetry. In the *Orator* (183–184) Cicero quotes from a *Thyestes*[14] to show that, without musical accompaniment, certain kinds of verse would essentially be prose:[15]

---

[10] Cf. *De Or.* 1.251.

[11] The Epicurean Philodemus opposed the idea that melody or song could instill in its listener any ethical value (*De Mus.* 4; Anderson 1966: 154, Comotti 1991: 43–44). Varro's *De Musica*, now lost, was highly influential upon later writers and engaged with a number of theories regarding acoustics and ethics, see: Wille 1967: 414; Comotti 1991: 52. On Cicero's (*Rep.* 6.18) discussion of the Pythagorean theory of acoustic consonances, see Comotti 1991: 27.

[12] Moore 2012: 26n4

[13] On this passage as an echo of Plato's criticism of "New Music," see Moore 2012: 140.

[14] Both Pacuvius and Ennius wrote a *Thyestes*. This excerpt is most commonly attributed to Ennius (= *TrRF* II 133).

[15] Moore 2012: 154.

sed in uersibus res est apertior, quanquam etiam a modis quibusdam cantu
remoto soluta esse uideatur oratio maxumeque id in optumo quoque eorum
poetarum qui λυρικοί a Graecis nominantur, quos cum cantu spoliaueris,
nuda paene remanet oratio. quorum similia sunt quaedam etiam apud nostros,
uelut illa in Thyeste:

quemnam te esse dicam? qui tarda in senectute   [*TrRF* II 133]
et quae sequuntur;[16] quae, nisi cum tibicen accessit, orationis sunt solutae
simillima.

In poetry the operation of rhythm is more obvious, although with certain
metres when the song is removed it looks like prose, especially in the best of
the poets called "lyric" by the Greeks. When you remove the song from
them, what remains is almost naked prose. We even have similar cases
among our own poets, such as in the *Thyestes*:
"Who should I say you are? Who in slow old age . . . "
and what follows. If there were no pipe-player accompanying these verses,
they would be very much like prose.

Greek lyric, Cicero says, was given its formal sense not simply by its metre
but also by a melody which might clarify the metre.[17] Cicero's insistence
that certain Latin verses were also sung to the *tibia* stresses the importance
of melody and verse for those citations, and, importantly, demonstrates
that Cicero himself was aware that some of the verses he quoted had
a melody. Interestingly, Cicero's point, that music is needed to understand
the metre of some poetry, is proven by the example that he gives. While
some editors categorize *TrRF* II 133 as a series of bacchiacs, a textual
emendation (*senectute* for *senecta*) was required to make the verse fit this
structure.[18] Cicero relies upon the fact that a contemporary reader of his
work will recognize the metre of the verse by using their knowledge of the
missing melody, something which we now cannot recover. A reader who
does not know the *Thyestes* can only see these words as prose without the
tibia's accompaniment.

  Knowledge of the melodies which enriched and, in certain cases,
gave measure to the poetic verses of the Roman stage seems to have
come principally from continued exposure to the performances of
these theatrical texts. Roman spectators grew to know the songs of
the stage because they had experienced them firsthand. In the

---

[16] See p23 on "*nosti quae sequuntur*" and similar phrases.
[17] Horace (*Ode* 4.2.11) writes that Pindar composed certain songs *numeris lege solutis*, "in free unregu-
   lated rhythms." Quintilian (*Inst.* 9.4.53) adds that it was the pedantic *grammatici*, not the poets
   themselves, who forced lyric into regular metres
[18] Jocelyn 1969a: 422; cf. *TrRF* II p267.

Academica (2.20, cf. 2.86), Cicero remarks that those with technical knowledge of music were able to recognize certain tragedies from their opening notes.[19] Cicero also writes that even an untrained listener was capable of evaluating music: hearing when instruments are out of tune or rhythms are off their beat.[20] While Cicero emphasizes the ability of Roman audiences to appreciate and evaluate live performances of song, the fact that Cicero himself engaged with Roman songs in a textual manner – i.e. Cicero reproduced their lyrics in the texts of his own works, presumably by consulting a text in which they appeared – raises the question of whether the book copies of the Roman plays (or other works in which Cicero found these citations) available to Cicero had any graphic representation of their musicality.

Whether a Roman play's music was written down or transmitted in a written form is not known.[21] We also do not know for certain whether the music of a play's first performance in the second century BCE was the same as what Cicero heard when he saw the revivals of these plays.[22] However, contemporary evidence suggests that tragic lyric could be annotated, and thereby differentiated, in a variety of ways. A number of papyri contain musical notation for songs from Greek tragedies: one fragment, dated to the beginning of the first century BCE, preserves part of the first choral song of Euripides' *Orestes*.[23] Musical papyri are usually thought to be esoteric texts used only by the professional musicians who had the specific literacy to decipher musical notation, and it is certainly not clear that Cicero would know how to do so. Yet a text did not necessarily have to be marked with musical notation in order to demonstrate that a certain passage was musical. P. Köln VI 252, a small papyrus fragment from the second or first century BCE, partially represents lines 134–142 of, again, Euripides' *Orestes*. The arrangement of the text on the shred of

---

[19] Manuwald 2011: 329.

[20] Cicero (*De Or.* 3.195–197) writes that the orator who wants to use prose rhythms should not worry about metrical intricacies going over the heads of his audience since humans have a natural instinct for judging rhythm and melody. In the theatre, the audience drives actors off stage if they make mistakes: *De Or.* 3.196, *Or.* 173, *Paradoxa* 26, *De Off.* 1.145.

[21] In the nineteenth century it was thought that certain markings over a verse of Terence's *Hecyra* represented ancient musical notation, but reconsideration now identifies the graphics as neumes from the tenth or eleventh centuries, see: Ziolokowski 2000, Pöhlmann 1970: 41–42, Moore 2012: 13 n27.

[22] Cicero's (*Leg.* 2.39) remark regarding the difference between the music of older Roman plays and modern ones suggests that a play's music was *not* changed. A late source (Donatus *De Com.* 8.9) says that the Roman playwrights did not compose the music to their own plays, which may have made changes to musical accompaniment relatively easy to make.

[23] Vienna Pap. G2315/Rainer inv. 8029 = Euripides' *Orestes* 338–344, see West 1992: 247, Landels 1999: 221.

papyrus suggests that the lyric passage was deliberately marked off from the previous iambic dialogue with an "indent."[24]

In addition to evidence of efforts to mark lyric in book copies of Greek tragedy, there is also evidence of contemporary intellectuals using text to reflect upon the ways in which songs were performed. Dionysius of Halicarnassus (*De Comp.* 11.19–21), who, interestingly, quotes part of the same *Orestes* passage as appears in P. Köln VI 252,[25] states that the three opening words of Electra's song (σῖγα σῖγα, λευκὸν, "Be silent, silent! Light … ") were sung "on the same note" (ἐφ᾽ ἑνὸς φθόγγου). Dionysius' engagement with the lyrics on their melodic level has led scholars to wonder whether he was looking at a musical "score."[26] We are here presented with the possibility that annotations of tragic texts helped to facilitate intellectual engagement with the performative (i.e. musical) qualities of ancient plays.[27]

4.1 Tragic *Cantica* in the *Tusculan Disputations*

In the *Tusculans* (2.27), Cicero, following Plato (*Rep.* 605d–e), blames the poets for representing the psychological breakdown of their characters:

> sed uidesne, poetae quid mali adferant? lamentantes inducunt fortissimos uiros, molliunt animos nostros, ita sunt deinde dulces, ut non legantur modo, sed etiam ediscantur. sic ad malam domesticam disciplinam uitamque umbratilem et delicatam cum accesserunt etiam poetae, neruos omnes uirtutis elidunt. recte igitur a Platone eiciuntur ex ea ciuitate quam finxit ille, cum optimos mores et optimum rei publicae statum exquireret.

> But do you see the harm that poets do? They represent the bravest men wailing, they render our spirits soft. But they are so appealing that not only is their poetry read but even learned by heart. Thus when the influence of poets is added to bad education at home and a lifestyle of dreaming and indulgence, it entirely strikes out the very marrow of virtue. Plato was right, then, to remove poets from his ideal state, when he was seeking the best customs and the best conditions for the state.

The poets, Cicero says, present negative exemplars of philosophical endurance which are destructive to the observer whose own capacity for endurance is weakened by witnessing and subsequently internalizing or mimicking the

---

[24] For the text see Gronewald 1980.
[25] P. Köln VI 252 = *Orestes* 134–142; Dionysius (*De Comp.* 11.19–211) = *Orestes* 140-142.
[26] Pöhlmann 1960: 19–24, West 1992: 248, Hall 2002: 10 n26, Prauscello 2006: 23.
[27] An ancient scholiast also happens to have recorded (schol. on *Orestes* 176) the fact that the actor playing Electra sang at a very high pitch when asking the chorus to be quiet; see Damen 1990.

symptoms of moral failure. The problem, in particular, is that the poets present "the bravest men" (*fortissimos uiros*) openly "vocalizing" (*lamentantes*) their pain. Cicero (*TD* 2.31) goes on to state that it is beneath the dignity of a *man* (again, in particular) to indulge his pain by expressing it vocally:

> nam dum tibi turpe nec dignum uiro uidebitur gemere, eiulare, lamentari, frangi, debilitari dolore, dum honestas, dum dignitas, dum decus aderit, tuque in ea intuens te continebis, cedet profecto uirtuti dolor et animi inductione languescet.

> While you consider it disgraceful and unworthy of a man to groan, shriek, wail, break down, and be enervated by pain, so long as honour, so long as nobility, so long as worth remain, and so long as you control yourself by keeping your eyes upon them, pain will surely give way to virtue and grow ineffective by your exertion of will.

Operative in Cicero's assertion that it is "not appropriate for a *man*" (*nec dignum uiro uidebitur*) to vocally express his pain is the contemporary Roman elision of notional "manhood" (*uirtus*) with the fact of being a "man" (*uir*).[28] Throughout the *Tusculans*, Cicero presents passages of poetry which exemplify a failure to be "manly" and, consequently, a failure to have "virtue." Such philosophical failure, Cicero makes clear, depends on whether the individual gives voice to their pain. Significantly, the terms Cicero uses for vocalizing pain *derive* from Latin poetry: the words used to forbid unmanly crying out in pain – *gemere* ("groan"), *eiulare* ("shriek"), etc. – are taken directly from Accius' *Philocteta* (Dangel 214–216), quoted at *TD* 2.33:

> adflictusne[29] et iacens et lamentabili uoce deplorans audieris, o uirum fortem? te uero ita adfectum ne uirum quidem quisquam dixerit . . . sed ille certe non fortis, qui iacet
>
> ia⁶   . . . *in tecto umido,*   [Dangel 214–216]
> *quod eiulatu, questu, gemitu, fremitibus*
> *resonando mutum flebiles uoces refert.*

> Will you be heard weeping with a crying voice, pained and prostrate, brave man? No one could even call you a man in such a state . . . But he is certainly not brave, he who lies
>   "*. . . in a wet cave,*
> *which returns shrieking, complaints, groaning, moaning,*
> *echoing his weeping cries, though mute itself.*"

---

[28] Cicero makes the connection clear via the etymology *ex uiro uirtus* (*TD* 2.43).
[29] Cf. *TD* 4.18 where *adflictatio* is defined as *aegritudo cum uexatione corporis* ("suffering accompanied by bodily pain").

The words which Accius uses to describe Philocteta's cries – *eiulatus* ("shriek"), *gemitus* ("groan") – are coopted by Cicero and converted into philosophical terminology (*TD* 2.31). It is therefore Philocteta's screams of pain which Cicero takes to be the classic example of failure to endure. In these verses from Accius' *Philocteta*, the cave on Lemnos where Philocteta had been abandoned is a lonely and wretched place which "echoes back" (*resonando*) his cries while itself remaining resolutely mute; Philocteta's cries are psychologically intensified via this resounding amplification.[30] The prostrate position of Philocteta is also a point of significance which allows Cicero to closely associate "lying down" (*iacens; iacet*) with a broken spirit. The mockery of Philocteta's failure to be a "brave man" (*o uirum fortem?*) returns to Cicero's original thesis: that poets are wrong to show "brave men crying" (*lamentantes fortissimos uiros*, *TD* 2.27).

In the *De Finibus* (2.94), Cicero repeated the same passage of Accius' *Philocteta* in order to assert once more that shrieks of pain are unmanly and therefore shameful:

> fortitudinis quaedam praecepta sunt ac paene leges, quae effeminari uirum
> uetant in dolore. quam ob rem turpe putandum est, non dico dolere – nam
> id quidem est interdum necesse – sed saxum illud Lemnium clamore
> Philocteteo funestare
>
> ia⁶ *quod eiulatu, questu, gemitu, fremitibus*   [Dangel 215–216]
> *resonando mutum flebiles uoces refert.*
> huic Epicurus praecentet, si potest, cui
> ia⁶ *e uiperino morsu uenae uiscerum*   [Dangel 235–236]
> *ueneno inbutae taetros cruciatus cient.*
> sic Epicurus: "Philocteta, st! breuis dolor." at iam decimum annum in
> spelunca iacet. "si longus, leuis; dat enim interualla et relaxat."

> Bravery has its own rules, laws really, which forbid a man from being
> womanly when he is in pain. As a result, we ought to think it shameful,
> I would not say to *feel* pain (sometimes that is unavoidable), but to defile
> that Lemnian rock with the Philoctetan cry:
> *"which returns shrieking, complaints, groaning, moaning,*
> *echoing his weeping cries, though mute itself."*
> Let Epicurus sing back to him, if he can, the man whom
> *"from viper's bite, veins of his entrails*

---

[30] In Sophocles' *Philoctetes*, he speaks of the cave "as a lonely sight" (ὄμμασιν μόνην θέαν, 536) that no other man but him could bear, and that he himself had only learned to love because of necessity (536–538). In the fragments of Euripides, Philoctetes refers to the cave several times as an unbearable sight to see (Nauck fr. 789; fr. 790).

tinctured with venom, rotting cruelties compel."
Epicurus says: "Hey, Philocteta! Severe pain is short." But he's already been lying in that cave for ten years. "If pain is long, it is light. It gives intervals of relief."

Cicero's insistence that the vocalization of pain is not suitable for men is here made even more explicit: a man's failure to endure results in his "becoming a woman" (*effeminari*), something which the "laws of bravery" (*fortudinis . . . leges*) "forbid" (*uetant*).[31] Additionally, Cicero is more explicit about the fact that the cry of pain is not only philosophically but also morally abhorrent: crying out in pain is "shameful" (*turpe*), and Philocteta's cry "pollutes" (*funestare*) his surroundings. In the context of the anti-Epicurean argument of *De Finibus*, Epicurus is drawn into the citation in order to demonstrate (in Cicero's view) the inherent impracticability of the Epicurean attitude towards pain. The Epicurean maxim that severe pain is short, long pain light can be disproved, Cicero argues, by the fact that Philocteta has suffered extreme pain for a decade.

While the verses of Accius' *Philocteta* quoted at *Fin.* 2.94 and *TD* 2.33 were not themselves sung, they do *describe* song.[32] Cicero imagines Epicurus "singing back" (*praecentet*) to Philocteta's shrieks as an ineffective remedy. In the *Tusculans* (2.19), Cicero quotes part of Philocteta's anapaestic song:

aspice Philoctetam, cui concedendum est gementi; ipsum enim Herculem uiderat in Oeta magnitudine dolorum eiulantem. nihil igitur hunc uirum sagittae quas ab Hercule acceperat tum consolabantur cum
ia[6]   *e uiperino morsu uenae uiscerum*   [Dangel 235–236]
       ueneno inbutae taetros cruciatus cient.
       itaque exclamat auxilium expetens, mori cupiens:
an[4]   *heu! qui salsis fluctibus mandet*   [Dangel 237–240]
       me ex sublimo uertice saxi?
       iam iam absumor: conficit animam,
       uis uulneris, ulceris aestus.
       difficile dictu uidetur eum non in malo esse, et magno quidem qui ta clamare cogatur.

Look at Philocteta. We must pardon his groans, since he had seen Hercules shrieking in great pain on Mt. Oeta. In no way did the arrows which he had received from Hercules console this man when
"from viper's bite, veins of his entrails
tinctured with venom, rotting cruelties compel."

---

[31] Cf. *TD* 2.53, where Cicero comments on the "current effeminate vogue" (*opinio est enim quaedam effeminata*) of voicing both pleasure and pain.
[32] Dangel 215–216 are iambic senarii, i.e. the spoken metre.

And so he cries out, looking for help, longing for death:
"Alas! who will to the salt waves deliver
me from the high summit of rock?
now, now I am consumed – my spirit conquered by
strength of wound, the lesion's heat."
It seems difficult to say that he is not suffering, when even he – though
great – is compelled to scream in this way.

In the prose frame to the citation, Cicero describes the cries in Accian
vocabulary: Hercules – who has set a bad example to Philocteta (cf. *TD*
2.31) – "shrieks" (*eiulans*), Philocteta himself "groans" (*gemens*).[33] The
content of this "groan" is the anapaestic song (Dangel 237–240) which
follows, in which Philocteta gives voice to the extremes of his own suffering, both spiritual and physical. Subsequently (*TD* 2.55–56), Cicero insists
that above all the "Philoctetan cry" (*clamor Philocteteus*) is to be avoided:[34]

> sed hoc idem in dolore maxime est prouidendum, ne quid abiecte, ne quid
> timide, ne quid ignaue, ne quid seruiliter muliebriterue faciamus, in primisque
> refutetur ac reiciatur Philocteteus ille clamor. ingemescere non numquam uiro
> concessum est, idque raro, eiulatus ne mulieri quidem. et hic nimirum est
> "lessus," quem duodecim tabulae in funeribus adhiberi uetuerunt. [2.56] nec
> uero umquam ne ingemescit quidem uir fortis ac sapiens, nisi forte ut se
> intendat ad firmitatem, ut in stadio cursores exclamant quam maxime
> possunt.

> But the most important provision when it comes to pain is that we do not in
> any way behave in a downcast manner, fearfully, like a coward, a slave, or
> a woman. First and foremost, we must keep in check and reject the
> Philoctetan cry. It is sometimes, although rarely, allowed that a man
> groan aloud, but not even women are permitted to shriek. And this, no
> doubt, is the form of "wailing" which the Twelve Tables have banned from
> taking place at funerals. [2.56] Nor is it ever allowed for a brave and wise
> man to groan, unless he is stretching himself towards a state of endurance,
> like the runners in the stadium who shout as much as they can.

Cicero once more uses Accian vocabulary as philosophical terminology: a man
may only rarely "groan" (*ingemescere*); and no one, not even a woman, may
"shriek" (*eiulatus*). The failure of manhood is here formulated as a socially
constructed and gendered moral concern: to behave less than is expected of

---

[33] In Sophocles' *Trachiniae*, Hercules vocalizes his extreme pain in a manner which he himself calls
"womanly" (θῆλυς, 1075). Cicero (*TD* 2.20–22) translates a passage of this play and connects it with
Accius' *Philocteta*, as discussed on p184.
[34] In *De Finibus* (2.94), the iambic senarii from Accius' *Philocteta* (Dangel 215–216) are quoted and
likewise described as conveying the *clamor Philocteteus*.

a man is to become a figure with low moral stature in the Roman social hierarchy – a slave (*seruiliter*), or a woman (*muliebriter*). Cicero goes on to gloss the Latin term *eiulatus*: it must represent, he says, what the Twelve Tables call *lessus*, i.e. the act of lamentation by women at public funerals.[35] In the *De Legibus* (2.59), Cicero quotes this passage of the Twelve Tables, which further investigates the meaning of *lessus*:

> extenuato igitur sumptu "tribus reciniis et tunicla purpurea et decem tibici-
> nibus" tollit etiam lamentationem: "mulieres genas ne radunto neue les-
> sum funeris ergo habento." hoc ueteres interpretes Sex. Aelius, L. Acilius
> non satis se intellegere dixerunt, sed suspicari uestimenti aliquod genus
> funebris, L. Aelius lessum quasi lugubrem eiulationem, ut uox ipsa significat.

> Expense is limited to "three small veils, a purple tunic, and ten pipe-
> players." Mourning is also limited: "Women shall not tear their cheeks,
> nor have a *lessus* at a funeral." The older scholars, Sextus Aelius and Lucius
> Acilius, said that they did not completely understand this word, but inferred
> that it was some kind of a mourning garment. Lucius Aelius explained *lessus*
> as a kind of "sorrowful wailing," for that is what the word itself signifies.

Cicero's acceptance of L. Aelius Stilo's explanation of *lessus* as *eiulatio* ("shriek-ing") reveals an association between this kind of vocalization and specifically female song. In the *Tusculans* (4.18), Cicero closely connected lamentation and *eiulatus*.[36] Indeed, the association of *eiulatio* (or *eiulatus*) with women's songs of lamentation is found throughout Roman literature. Commenting on Horace's description of the sound as "unmanly" (*non uirilis heiulatio, Epode* 10.17), Porphyrio notes that *eiulatio* was a word for a "weeping groan" (*gemitus flentis*). Servius interpreted the "woman's lament" (*femineo ululatu*) which filled Carthage at Dido's death in the *Aeneid* (4.667) as a form of *eiulatio*. According to a late grammatical source (Cass. *Gramm.* VII 200,16), the verb *eiulo* (or *eiulor*) literally meant "to say *heu*," and some Roman lyrics do indeed use this word when tragic characters sing in pain:[37]

---

[35] All of the known manuscripts of the *Tusculans* give *fletus* ("weeping") at *TD* 2.55, but following Muretus' claim to have seen *lessus* in old manuscripts which are not longer extant (see Dougan 1905: 225), editors have emended *fletus* to *lessus* based on Cicero's quotation of the Twelve Tables in *De Legibus* (2.59).

[36] *TD* 4.18: *lamentatio aegritudo cum eiulatu*, "lamentation is suffering accompanied by shrieking."

[37] Plautine characters also use *eiulatio* to denote highly emotional singing. In *Aulularia*, Lycomides comes across the slave, Euclio, outside his house and asks who the "wailing man" (*eiulans*, 727) could be; Euclio had just finished an anapaestic song (713–721), in which he had voiced the words *heu me miserum* ("alas, I am wretched," 721). Act II of the *Captiui* begins with a song in mixed metres (195–241) in which the overseer advises Philocrates and Tyndarus to bear their new status as slaves with patience. To their *extra metrum* cries (200), the overseer tells them that there is no need for *eiulatio* (201).

an⁴   *heu! qui salsis fluctibus mandet*   Accius' *Philocteta* (Dangel 237–240)
           me ex sublimo uertice saxi?
           iam iam absumor: conficit animam,
           uis uulneris, ulceris aestus

           Alas! who will to the salt waves deliver
           me from the high summit of rock?
           now, now I am consumed – my spirit conquered by
           strength of wound, the lesion's heat.

an⁴   *retinete, tenete! opprimit ulcus,*   Pacuvius' *Niptra* (Schierl fr. 199, 8–9)
           nudate, heu, miserum me! excrucior.

           Hold back, hold! The wound is overpowering.
           Uncover it, alas, I am wretched! I am tortured.

When Cicero translates a passage of Sophocles' *Trachiniae* in the *Tusculans* (2.21), he inserts a *heu* at the moment where Hercules feels shame at the "womanly" nature of his wailing in pain:[38]

ia⁶   *heu! uirginalem me ore ploratum edere,*   Soubiran fr. i, 25–27
           quem uidit nemo ulli ingemescentem malo!
           ecfeminata uirtus adflicta occidit.

           Alas! Think of my lips uttering girls' laments,
           a man whom none saw groaning over any evil!
           Crushed is my manhood, fallen effeminate.

The condemnation of "womanly" song in Cicero's *Tusculans* is not only a reflection of the highly gendered construction of Roman morals, but also betrays a debt to the theory of music in Greco-Roman philosophy. The association of *eiulatus* with female lament and infirm male voices suggests that this kind of "shrieking" was done at a higher pitch than was considered usual for the speech of men. In the fifth century BCE, the Greek musicologist Damon influentially classified specific notes as female or male according to

---

[38] Cicero (*TD* 2.20–22) gives a 45 line Latin translation of the *Trachiniae* 1046–1102 (= Soubiran fr. i); the following three lines quoted at *TD* 2.21 represent *Trachiniae* 1070–1075 (= Soubiran fr. i, 25–27). The Greek passage of the *Trachiniae* which Cicero translates is in iambic trimeters, and his translation reflects this as Latin iambic senarii. The passage from Sophocles' *Trachiniae* which Cicero translates is preceded in the original by lyrics performed by Heracles, his son Hyllus, and the old man (1004–1043), during which Heracles emits *extra metrum* shrieks (1004, 1015), and sings of his sensations of pain. Sophocles' Heracles says that he remained ἀστένακτος, "ungroaning," during his labours (1074), but now, due to his vocal expression of pain, has been revealed a θῆλυς, "female" (1075).

their supposed ethical effects, characterizing scales as female or male according to the proportion of their notes.[39] In the *Republic* (424c), Plato attributed to Damon the argument that the introduction of new music was a threat to the state.[40] Indeed, it is this Platonic reference to Damon that lurks behind Cicero's (*Leg.* 2.39) own statement regarding the physiological effects of modern music in the Roman theatre.

Traces of Varro's *De Musica,* a work which is itself lost but which echoes through later Latin sources, suggest that Roman theory continued to describe musical notes according to the analogy of the gendered human body.[41] Isidore of Seville (*Etym.* 3.20.11), drawing upon Varro, writes that women, children, and "people in pain" (*aegrotantes*) had voices that were "thin" (*subtiles*) and sounded "like string instruments" (*ut neruis*);[42] such "thin" voices are contrasted with the "rich voices of men" (*pingues uoces . . . uirorum, Etym.* 3.20.12). Isidore (*Etym.* 3.20.12) also remarks that these thin, string-like voices are "sharp" (*acuta*) and "high" (*alta*), suggesting an association of voice tone with pitch. The idea that women and "people in pain" (*aegrotantes*) were thought to have the same vocal quality underlies Cicero's decision to quote the specific tragic *cantica* which appear in the *Tusculan Disputations*. After all, Cicero (*TD* 2.64) used the same language to describe (and criticize) those who "could not endure their pain like men" (*aegrotare uiriliter non queunt*). As we have seen, Cicero focused heavily on the figure of the wounded Philocteta as the classic example of the failure to hold back from singing in pain. The rest of the tragic *cantica* cited in the *Tusculans* also fit the vocal category of women and *aegrotantes*: the song of wounded Ulixes in Pacuvius' *Niptra* (*TD* 2.48–50; Schierl fr. 199); a song from a now unknown tragedy (*TD* 3.25–26; *TrRF* I 55–56[43]); and the famous aria of Ennius' *Andromacha* (*TD* 3.44–46; *TrRF* II 23).

4.2 Pacuvius' *Niptra*

Quoting songs allowed Cicero to present negative exemplars of endurance, and to meditate upon the extent to which each departed from the

---

[39] Anderson 1966: 91, Csapo 2004: 231, Wallace 2015: 151. According to Plutarch (*Mor.* 645c), the Athenian playwright, Agathon, received a reputation for effeminacy because he had introduced the chromatic scale, evidently seen as "feminine," into tragic music.

[40] Comotti 1991: 31.

[41] Comotti 1991: 52. On the performative characteristics of female speech (i.e. "female Latin") in Roman comedy, see Dutsch 2008.

[42] Cf. *De Or.* 3.216 where Cicero also likens the human voice to "the strings of a lyre" (*ut nerui in fidibus*).

[43] These verses have traditionally been attributed to Ennius' *Thyestes* (Jocelyn 293–295), but have recently been downgraded to *adespota* (*TrRF* I 55–56).

philosophical ideal. In the *Tusculans* (2.48–50), Cicero quoted *cantica* from Pacuvius' *Niptra* which reflect upon the possibility of such endurance even at the very moment of failure:

> non nimis in Niptris ille sapientissimus Graeciae saucius lamentatur uel modice potius:

an⁴   *pedetemptim,* inquit, *ac sedatu nisu,*   [Schierl fr. 199, 1–3]
           ne succussu arripiat maior
           dolor . . .

> [2.49] Pacuuius hoc melius quam Sophocles; apud illum enim perquam flebiliter Ulixes lamentatur in uulnere: tamen huic leuiter gementi illi ipsi, qui ferunt saucium, personae grauitatem intuentes non dubitant dicere:

an⁴   *tu quoque, Ulixes, quamquam grauiter*   [Schierl fr. 199, 4–7]
           cernimus ictum, nimis paene animo es
           molli, qui consuetus in armis

> intellegit poeta prudens ferendi doloris consuetudinem esse non contemnendam magistram. [2.50] atque ille non inmoderate magno in dolore:

an⁴   *retinete, tenete: opprimit ulcus,*   [Schierl fr. 199, 8–9]
           nudate, heu, miserum me: excrucior.

> incipit labi; deinde ilico desinit:

an⁴   *operite, abscedite, iam iam,*⁴⁴   [Schierl fr. 199, 10–12]
           mittite; nam attrectatu et quassu
           saeuum amplificatis dolorem.

> uidesne ut obmutuerit non sedatus corporis, sed castigatus animi dolor? itaque in extremis Niptris alios quoque obiurgat idque moriens:

tr⁷   *conqueri fortunam aduersam, non lamentari decet;*   [Schierl fr. 200]
           id uiri est officium: fletus muliebri ingenio additus.

In the *Niptra*, the wisest hero of Greece when wounded does not wail extravagantly but instead with moderation:
"*March step-by-step,*" he says, "*evenly straining
lest from a jolt there seize me a great
pain . . .*"
[2.49] Pacuvius' version is better than Sophocles'. For in Sophocles the wounded Ulixes wails very pitifully: nevertheless those who carry the wounded man, having an eye to the dignity of his character, do not hesitate to say to him when he softly groans:
"*You too, Ulysses, although grievously
stricken we see, yet you show too soft a
spirit for a soldier accustomed to a life
of war.*"

---

⁴⁴ Cf. *iam iam* in Accius' *Philocteta* (Dangel 239).

The wise poet sees that the custom of bearing pain is a teacher not to be despised. [2.50] And then Ulixes in his great pain speaks not immoderately:
"Hold back, hold! The wound is overpowering.
Uncover it, alas, I am wretched! I am tortured."
He begins to slip. Then suddenly he stops.
"Cover it. Leave me, already, let go.
You make the savage pain worse
with your touching and shaking."
Do you see how it is not the pain of the body which has been quieted and reduced to silence, but the pain of the soul
which has been chastened by rebuke? And so at the end of the *Niptra* he rebukes others as well, and that in his last moments:
"It befits you to complain of adverse fortune, not bemoan;
This is man's duty: on women's nature weeping was bestowed."

The Pacuvian Ulixes struggles with an immense wound which pains him especially when he moves. Cicero, arguing that the lapse of an individual's endurance could be remedied via peer pressure, praises the criticism of those who carry the wounded Ulixes: they "protect his dignity" (*grauitatem intuentes*) by drawing attention to the fact that he does not bear his pain like the seasoned soldier he is.[45] Ulixes initially "groans" (*gemens*) in pained anapaestic song (Schierl fr. 199, 8–9; 10–12), but, checked by his comrades, returns to soldierly forbearance "at the end" (*in extremis*) of the play.[46] His renewed endurance is reflected not only in the content of his words – like Cicero, the Pacuvian Ulixes believes it is "man's duty" (*uiri est officium*) to avoid voicing pain – but in the way these words are performed: anapaestic song is replaced with the recitative of trochaic septenarii. While Ulixes is not able entirely to resist shrieking in pain, he nonetheless presents a useful philosophical lesson in that his resolve is ultimately restored. Cicero (*TD* 2.49) also prefers Pacuvius' treatment since Sophocles, apparently, allowed Odysseus to shriek in pain.[47] Cicero (*TD* 2.50) precedes the quotation of Pacuvius' *Niptra* by stating that if reason fails to rein in excessive lamentation, then it "must

---

[45] Cf. *TD* 2.31: *dum honestas, dum dignitas, dum decus aderit, tuque in ea intuens te continebis,* "so long as honour, so long as nobility, so long as worth remain, and so long as you control yourself by keeping your eyes upon them."

[46] Cicero not only describes Ulixes' anapaestic song as a "groan" (*gemens, TD* 2.49), but Ulixes himself says *heu* (*TD* 2.50; Schierl fr. 199, 9), i.e. he performs *eiulatus*.

[47] Schierl (2006: 386) notes that while Cicero compares Pacuvius to Sophocles, it is not clear that Pacuvius' *Niptra* was actually an adaptation of Sophocles.

be fettered and bound by the guardianship of friends and acquaintances"
(*uinciatur et constringatur amicorum propinquorumque custodiis*). The
Pacuvian song is therefore a self-reflexive philosophical exemplar which
dramatizes both the failure to endure *and* its remedy.

4.3   The Unknown Tragedy

While the Accian Philocteta and the Pacuvian Ulixes represent tragic
figures suffering extreme physical pain, Cicero also condemned the
lamenting song which originated in psychological distress. In the
Tusculans (3.25–26), Cicero quotes from a now unknown tragedy (*TrRF*
I 55–56[48]) to criticize once more the lack of forbearance, this time stem-
ming from mental anguish:

> id enim sit propositum, quandoquidem eam tu uideri tibi in sapientem
> cadere dixisti, quod ego nullo modo existimo; taetra enim res est, misera,
> detestabilis, omni contentione, uelis, ut ita dicam, remisque fugienda. [3.26]
> qualis enim tibi ille uidetur

tr⁷ *Tantalo prognatus, Pelope natus, qui quondam a socru*   [*TrRF* I 55]
     Oenomao rege Hippodameam raptis nanctust nuptiis?
     Iouis iste quidem pronepos. tamne ergo abiectus tamque
     fractus?

ba⁴ *nolite*, inquit, *hospites ad me adire, ilico istic!*   [*TrRF* I 56]
ba⁴ *ne contagio mea bonis umbraue obsit!*
cr⁴ *<meo> tanta uis sceleris in corpore haeret!*
     tu te, Thyesta, damnabis orbabisque luce propter *uim sceleris* alieni?

> Let that be the point of our discussion, since you said that it seems to you that
> a wise man is susceptible to distress, which I don't agree with. For the state of
> distress is foul, wretched, execrable, and to be avoided with every effort, with
> full sail and, so to speak, quick oars. [3.26] Does such a man as the
> *"descendant of Tantalus, son of Pelops, who once won*
> *Hippodamea in stolen wedlock from a royal father-in-law"*
> seem like this to you? In fact he was the great-grandson of Jupiter. And so
> how can he be so downcast and broken?
> *"Don't come near me, friends!"* He says, *"there, over there –*
> *don't let my touch or shadow infect good men.*
> *Such force of sin adheres to my body."*
> Thyestes, will you condemn yourself and orphan yourself from light
> because of another man's *"force of sin"*?

---

[48] Traditionally attributed to Ennius' *Thyestes*, these verses have recently been downgraded by the
TrRF. See p185n43.

While Cicero presents endurance as a rule that applies to all, he is here especially concerned with the idea that individuals with moral responsibilities live up to certain philosophical standards. The "wise man" (*sapiens*) must be impervious to distress, but so too, Cicero implies, ought the kings and nobility of the tragic stage. Thyestes is not only, as the poet notes, a "descendant of Tantalus" and "son of Pelops" (*Tantalo prognatus, Pelops natus*), but also, Cicero adds, "the great-grandson of Jupiter" (*Iouis pronepos*) – Thyestes' lineage is not only noble, but divine.[49] Yet Thyestes, according to Cicero, behaves like a "broken man" (*fractus*); and such "brokenness" is manifested in his song of distress. Indeed, Cicero (*TD* 2.31) closely associated "breaking down" (*frangi*) with the words for wailing song (i.e. *eiulatus, gemitus*).[50] Cicero (*TD* 3.25) also calls Thyestes "downcast" (*abiectus*); he had earlier (*TD* 2.55), in connection with the "Philoctetan cry," insisted that behaving in a "downcast manner" (*abiecte*) was to be avoided.[51] While Thyestes' song figures the guilt of eating his own children as a physical rot, his suffering stems from a psychological torment rather than an external wound. Cicero (*TD* 3.26) does not think that Thyestes is at fault but has internalized the guilt of "someone else" (*alieni*), i.e. his brother, Atreus. As a result, Thyestes' song, which desperately asks for friends and good men to stay away, is taken by Cicero as a failure to understand his moral position; if the wise man and the king alike apply the lessons of philosophy, then they will not, he says, fall into Thyestean wretchedness via false moral reasoning. Thyestes, according to Cicero, loses sight of self-respect, and so his wailing song becomes an index of his fundamental "brokenness."

4.4 Ennius' *Andromacha*

In the *Academica* (2.20; 2.29), Cicero writes that those with knowledge of music were able to recognize the *Antiopa* or the *Andromacha* from their opening notes.[52] Since *Antiopa* and *Andromacha* were the names of plays by

---

[49] Cicero (*TD* 3.26) goes on to quote lines (*TrRF* I 57) spoken by Aëeta, child of the sun, to demonstrate that he could not live philosophically according to what was demanded by his divine lineage.

[50] *TD* 2.31 quoted p179.

[51] Cf. Gaius Gracchus' tragic parody, reported by Cicero (*De Or.* 3.214): *matremne ut miseram lamentantem uideam et abiectam*, "To my mother, so that I can see her, wretched and lamenting, downcast?"

[52] *Ac.* 2.20: *qui primo inflatu tibicinis Antiopam esse aiunt aut Andromacham*, "there are those who, when the piper plays their first note, can say: 'this is the *Antiopa*' or 'this is the *Andromacha*.'"; *Ac.*

Pacuvius and Ennius respectively, it is possible to view this statement as a reference to full productions of these tragedies at the dramatic festivals.[53] During the Ciceronian period, however, tragic songs were also performed independently of their plays.[54] That a song could be detached from its script suggests that some were very famous in their own right. This seems to be the case for the aria from Ennius' *Andromacha* (*TrRF* II 23), which Cicero quotes in the *Tusculans* (3.44–46):

	ecce tibi ex altera parte ab eodem poeta	
ia^6	*ex opibus summis opis egens Hector tuae*	[*TrRF* II 23, 3^{55}]
	huic subuenire debemus; quaerit enim auxilium[56]	
cr^4	*quid petam praesidi aut exequar? quoue nunc*	[*TrRF* II 23, 4–9]
	auxilio exili aut fugae freta sim?	
	arce et urbe orba sum. quo accedam? quo applicem?	
tr^7	*cui nec arae patriae domi stant, fractae et disiectae iacent,*	
	fana flamma deflagrata, tosti alti stant parietes,	
	deformati atque abiete crispa ...	
	scitis quae sequantur.[57] et illa in primis:	
an^4	*o pater, o patria, o Priami domus,*	[*TrRF* II 23, 10–14]
	saeptum altisono cardine templum.	
	uidi ego te adstante ope barbarica	
	tectis caelatis laqueatis,	
	auro ebore instructam regifice.	

o poetam egregium! quamquam ab his cantoribus Euphorionis contemnitur. sentit omnia repentina et necopinata esse grauiora. exaggeratis igitur regiis opibus, quae uidebantur sempiternae fore, quid adiungit?

an^4	*haec omnia uidi inflammari*	[*TrRF* II 23, 15–17]
	Priamo ui uitam euitari	
	Iouis aram sanguine turpari	

praeclarum carmen! est enim et rebus et uerbis et modis lugubre.

2.89: *et simul inflauit tibicen a perito carmen agnoscitur,* "as soon as the piper plays a note, the song is recognized by someone who knows"; see Manuwald 2011: 329.

[53] Ennius' *Andromacha* was performed at the *Ludi Apollinares* of 54 BCE (*Att.* 4.15.6). But since Cicero quotes from the play in *Pro Sestio* 121 (56 BCE) and *De Oratore* 3.102, 183, 217 (55 BCE), his initial exposure must have come before that year.

[54] Jocelyn (1969a: 253–254) took the references to *Antiopa* and *Andromacha* at *Ac.* 2.20 to refer to performances of theatrical song at funerals, rather than of complete tragedies. Songs from Pacuvius' *Armorum Iudicium* and Atilius' *Electra* were performed at the funeral of Julius Caesar (Suet. *Iul.* 84; Manuwald 2011: 113). Suetonius (*Iul.* 84) notes that these songs were chosen because they were appropriate for grief.

[55] *TD* 1.105 (*TrRF* II 23, 1–2) quotes two lines (iambic senarii) taken to be the beginning of this fragment.

[56] Cf. *TD* 2.19: *itaque exclamat auxilium expetens,* "and so [Philocteta] cries out, looking for help."

[57] A variation on *nosti quae sequuntur*; see p23.

Take another example from the same poet:
"*From the heights of power, now without your protection, Hector –* "
We ought to help her, she's asking for aid.
"*What defenses should I seek or find? What help could I rely on now*
for escape or flight? I have lost my citadel and my city.
Where to kneel, where appeal,
when the altars of my homeland no longer stand,
lie broken, scattered, the shrines consumed by fire,
the high walls stand burnt, misshapen, the wood warped . . . "
you know the rest, especially this part:
"*Oh father, oh fatherland, oh house of Priam,*
the temple closed by shrill-sounding doors,
I saw you when your barbaric wealth still stood,
the carved paneled ceilings inlaid with gold and kingly ivory."
Oh excellent poet! Despite the fact that he is undervalued by those singers of
Euphorion. He feels that everything sudden and unexpected is that much
heavier to bear. After the account of heaped up, royal riches, which were
expected to last forever, what does he say?
"*Everything in sight set alight,*
Priam's life by might unlifed,
altar of Jove in blood blighted."
An excellent song! Mournful in its content, its diction, and its melody.

As with Cicero's previous citations of tragic *cantica*, Ennius' *Andromacha* is
excerpted in the *Tusculans* as part of a meditation upon pain. Cicero uses
Andromacha's extreme pain to test (and fail) Epicurean philosophy, just as he
had done with Accius' *Philocteta* (*Fin.* 2.94). In addition to the fact that Cicero
quotes anapaests and cretics (i.e. the poetic metres used in song on the Roman
stage), Cicero explicitly comments upon the song's musicality: *praeclarum
carmen! est enim et rebus et uerbis et modis lugubre,* "an excellent song –
mournful in its content, its diction, and its melody."[58] When Cicero had
previously quoted parts of the anapaestic song in the *Tusculans* (1.85), he
remarked that if Priam had died before the destruction of his kingdom, then
Andromacha's aria would never have been sung:

at certe ei melius euenisset nec tam flebiliter illa canerentur:
an⁴   *haec omnia uidi inflammari*   [*TrRF* II 23, 15–17]
       Priamo ui uitam euitari
       Iouis aram sanguine turpari

[58] Cicero also contrasts Ennius' song with the "singers of Euphorion" (*cantores Euphorionis, TD* 3.45);
see Shackleton Bailey 1983: 240, Knox 2011: 192.

But certainly everything would have turned out better for him, and these
verses would not so tearfully be sung:
"Everything in sight set alight,
Priam's life by might unlifed,
altar of Jove in blood blighted."

Cicero here describes Andromacha's aria as sung "tearfully" (*flebiliter,*
TD 1.85). Latin words for tears appear so regularly in descriptions of
tragic song that we might take this to be another index of musicality.[59]
When Cicero returned to this passage of Ennius' *Andromacha* for a third
time in the *Tusculans* (3.53), it was to compare her aria to the songs of
slaves:

> quod ita esse dies declarat, quae procedens ita mitigat, ut isdem malis
> manentibus non modo leniatur aegritudo, sed in plerisque tollatur.
> Karthaginienses multi Romae seruierunt, Macedones rege Perse capto; uidi
> etiam in Peloponneso, cum essem adulescens, quosdam Corinthios. hi
> poterant omnes eadem illa de Andromacha deplorare:
> *haec omnia uidi . . .*   [*TrRF* II 23, 15]
> sed iam decantauerant fortasse.

> That this is the case is made clear by the passing of time which softens pain
> as it goes, to the extent that it gets easier to bear the suffering of the same
> evils even though they remain; in many such cases, suffering ceases entirely.
> Many Carthaginians were slaves at Rome, many Macedonians too, when
> King Perseus was captured. I myself saw some Corinthian slaves in the
> Peloponnese when I was young. These slaves could have, all of them, cried
> out the same verses from the *Andromacha*:
> *"Everything in sight . . . "*
> But maybe they were long sung out.

Strikingly, Cicero connects the real suffering of people enslaved by Romans
with the pain expressed in Ennius' *Andromacha*.[60] Cicero, we recall, forbade
men from vocalizing their pain "like slaves or women" (*seruiliter muliebriterue,*
TD 2.55). In Ennius' play, the tragic figure of Andromacha inhabits both
categories – woman and slave – simultaneously. After the death of Hector
and the fiery destruction of the Trojan palace, which her song vividly describes,
Andromacha is left in a state of utter destitution: no family, no home; no means

---

[59] Accius describes Philocteta's song as *flebiles uoces,* "weeping voices" (Dangel 216; *Fin.* 2.94); Cicero
describes the Pacuvian Ulixes as *flebiliter lamentatur,* "weepingly wails" (*TD* 2.49); Ulixes himself
calls *fletus,* "weeping," a female trait (Schierl fr. 200, 2; *TD* 2.50).
[60] Čulík-Baird 2019: 191. On the dramatization of experiences of enslaved individuals on the Roman
comic stage, see Richlin 2017, Padilla Peralta 2017.

of escape.[61] On the Greco-Roman stage, Andromacha was always a slave: Euripides' and Seneca's *Troades* dramatized the Greeks dividing up the elite women of Troy as part of the spoil; Euripides' *Andromache* depicted her as a sex slave to Neoptolemus.[62] The tragic Andromacha's deep suffering was her inherent characteristic. In Ennius' tragedy, she gave full, emotive expression to that suffering in a song which became famous for doing so.

In the *Tusculans*, Andromacha's aria appears alongside several other tragic *cantica* which allow Cicero to vividly describe the effects of extreme pain, and to morally condemn the vocalization of pain which tragedy's songs represented. In *De Oratore* (3.102), Cicero dissects Andromacha's song in a manner which reflects a technical understanding of the actor's performance, which could be studied and emulated by orators:[63]

	quid ille alter	
cr^4	*quid petam praesidi?*	[*TrRF* II 23, 4]
	quam leniter, quam remisse, quam non actuose! instat enim:	
an^4	*o pater, o patria, o Priami domus!*	[*TrRF* II 23, 10]

in quo tanta commoueri actio non posset si esset consumpta superiore
motu et exhausta. neque id actores prius uiderunt quam ipsi poetae,
quam denique illi etiam qui fecerunt modos, a quibus utrisque sum-
mittitur aliquid, deinde augetur, extenuatur, inflatur, uariatur,
distinguitur.

To give another example:
"*What defenses should I seek?*"
how gently, how softly, how un-actively Roscius performs these lines! He urges forward again:
"*Oh father, oh fatherland, oh house of Priam!*"
Such a performance would not be possible to execute if he had already used up his energy in the previous movement. Actors did not see this before poets themselves did, or indeed before the composers who wrote the music; both poets and composers lower the notes, then raise, fill, vary, and differentiate them.

---

[61] Hector's death is referenced at the beginning of the passage (*TrRF* II 23, 3; *TD* 3.44). Another fragment of Ennius' *Andromacha* (*TrRF* II 30), which describes a "boy" (*puer*) placed "on a shield" (*in clipeo*), is usually interpreted as referring to the death of Astyanax after the sack of Troy since Cicero refers to Astyanax as a character in a revival of Ennius' *Andromacha* (*Att.* 4.15.6); see *TrRF* II p91. On Andromacha's "social death," see Čulík-Baird 2019: 188–193.

[62] On the connection between Andromache's lament and her status as sex slave in Euripides' *Andromache*, see Dué 2006: 154.

[63] On the importance of bodily movement (*gestus* and *actio*) to the performance of these verses, see Moore 2012: 69.

Cicero's analysis of Roscius performing tragic verses results in a detailed list of "stage directions." The actor treats some verses lightly in order to emphasize the more weighty lines and to save his full energy for their performance: the cretic section of Andromacha's song is "gently" (*leniter*) performed, while the anapaestic section is given full energy. Cicero credits actors, poets, *and* musicians with the capacity to articulate poetic phrases using their own talents via their body, words, and music respectively. Poets (*poetae*) are distinguished from composers of music (*illi qui fecerunt modos,* "those who made the measures"); the two groups (*utrisque*) understand how to variegate words and melody, but they are nonetheless distinct groups. That Cicero mentions the composers at all again demonstrates Cicero's awareness of the musical quality of these verses; indeed, knowledge that these verses are song are fundamental to his argument.

Later in *De Oratore* (3.217), Cicero quotes again from the *Andromacha* in order to demonstrate that different vocal techniques produce specific emotional responses in an audience:

	aliud miseratio ac maeror, flexibile, plenum, interruptum, flebili uoce:	
ia⁶	*quo nunc me uortam? quod iter incipiam ingredi?*	[Jocelyn 217–218/
	domum paternamne? anne ad Peliae filias?	*TrRF* I 25]
	et illa:	
an⁴	*o pater, o patria, o Priami domus.*	[*TrRF* II 23, 10]
	et quae sequuntur:⁶⁴	
an⁴	*haec omnia uidi inflammari,*	[*TrRF* II 23, 15–16]
	Priamo ui uitam euitari.	

> Another tone is used for pity and sorrow: a wavering, resounding, sobbing, tearful voice:
> "*Where now should I turn? What path can I start to tread?*
> *Towards my father's house? Or to the daughters of Pelias?*"
> And these verses:
> "*Oh father, oh fatherland, oh house of Priam!*"
> and what follows:
> "*Everything in sight set alight,*
> *Priam's life by might unlifed.*"

Anapaests from Ennius' *Andromacha* appear under the rubric of *miseratio* ("pity") and *maeror* ("sorrow"),⁶⁵ preceded by the famous set of verses

---

⁶⁴ A variation on *nosti quae sequuntur;* see p23.
⁶⁵ According to Suetonius (*Iul.* 84), the songs from Pacuvius' *Armorum Iudicium* and Acilius' *Electra* were chosen for Caesar's funeral precisely because they inspired *miseratio.*

frequently echoed by Cicero in his oratory.[66] In the philosophical context of the *Tusculans* (4.18), Cicero defines *maeror* ("sorrow") as a "weeping suffering" (*aegritudo flebilis*). In an oratorical context, Andromacha's song becomes a test case for emulation: if an orator can understand the performance techniques which make the verses so powerful, he too can influence audiences into feeling these emotions. Cicero (*De Or.* 3.217) analyzes the vocal qualities of Andromacha's song: the terms *flexibilis*[67] ("wavering"), *plenus* ("resonant"), *interruptus* ("sobbing"), and *flebili uoce*, ("with a tearful voice") refer to the timbre of the human voice and its tone, pitch, modulation. In the *Pro Sestio* (121), Cicero described Aesopus bringing a Roman audience to tears when he performed Andromacha's song:[68]

> iam illa quanto cum gemitu populi Romani ab eodem paulo post in eadem fabula sunt acta!
> *o pater*   [*TrRF* II 23, 10]
> me, me ille absentem ut patrem deplorandum putabat, quem Q. Catulus, quem multi alii saepe in senatu patrem patriae nominarant. quanto cum fletu de illis nostris incendiis ac ruinis, cum patrem pulsum, patriam adflictam deploraret, domum incensam euersamque, sic egit ut, demonstrata pristina fortuna, cum se conuertisset,
> *haec omnia uidi inflammari*   [*TrRF* II 23, 15]
> fletum etiam inimicis atque inuidis excitaret!

> A little later in the same play, how greatly the Roman people groaned when they heard these words spoken by the same actor.
> "*Oh father!*"
> He meant me, me, absent and to be mourned as a father, whom Quintus Catulus, whom many others often called father of the fatherland in the senate. With what great weeping did he lament our burned down ruins, a father expelled, a fatherland wounded, a house burned and toppled over. When he acted the lines that describe a former prosperity converted,
> "*Everything in sight set alight!*"
> What weeping he aroused in even my enemies and rivals!

When Aesopus the actor, who, as we have seen, is a surrogate for the orator (*Sest.* 122), played Andromacha, the intense emotionality of his performance compelled his audience to feel pity and grief, to "groan" (*gemitus*) and to "weep" (*fletus*). Tragic song, itself a representation of "groaning"

---

[66] See p120.
[67] Moore 2012: 90: "*Flexibilis*, along with *canorus, clarus,* and *suauis,* is one of the Latin words most often used in praise of the voice."
[68] On *Sest.* 120–123, see Moore 2012: 66–8, 77.

(*gemitus*), "shrieking" (*eiulatus*), and "weeping" (*fletus*), is demonstrated to cause these very emotions in an audience.

Here we come back full circle to Cicero's Platonic assertion in the *Tusculans* (2.27), that poets are wrong to represent "the bravest men weeping" (*lamentantes fortissimos uiros*) because an audience which internalizes their words will emulate these actions and fail to meet the moral standards of philosophical forbearance. That the verses chosen by Cicero to exemplify vocalization of pain were sung, and recognizably musical to his contemporary readership, is a crucial component of his argumentation. Cicero's invocation of the music of tragedy in his philosophical and rhetorical treatises represents a striking hybridity between the fixed nature of the Ciceronian text, and the live performance of the Roman stage. Quotation of tragic *cantica* enlivens Cicero's own writing with the musical and emotional colour of contemporary drama, and Cicero's engagement with the Roman stage in his treatises leaves behind a crystalized artefact of how live performance influenced intellectual work in the late Republic.

CHAPTER 5

Poetry as Artefact

uetustas pauca non deprauat, multa tollit. quem puerum uidisti formosum, hunc uides deformem in senecta. tertium seculum non uidet eum hominem quem uidit primum. quare illa quae iam maioribus nostris ademit obliuio, fugitiua secuta sedulitas Muci et Bruti retrahere nequit. non, si non potuero indagare, eo ero tardior, sed uelocior ideo, si quiuero. non mediocres enim tenebrae in silua ubi haec captanda neque eo quo peruenire uolumus semitae tritae, neque non in tramitibus quaedam obiecta quae euntem retinere possent.

There is little that time does not distort, much it obliterates completely. The boy you then saw as beautiful, you now see ugly in his agedness. The third generation does not see a person as the first generation did. It is because of this that the things which oblivion has taken from our ancestors, these fugitives, could not be hunted down by the diligence even of Publius Mucius Scaevola and Marcus Junius Brutus. If I cannot track them down, this will not make me slower, but even swifter, if I am able. The darkness in the woods where these things are to be caught is considerable, there are no trodden paths to the place we want to go, and there are obstacles in these paths which could hold back the hunter on his way.

In this passage of the *De Lingua Latina* (5.5), Varro figures the Roman researcher as a hunter in dark woods with many obstacles in his path.[1] Obstacles to knowledge stem from the old age of the material: *uetustas* ("time"), Varro notes, destroys most of the historical record, and leaves behind only a limited representation of what once was.[2] Varro's attitude towards the ongoing processes of historical loss may be compared to Gerda

---

[1] On Varro's use of the hunt as a metaphor for intellectual inquiry, see Spencer 2011: 57–80.

[2] The word *uetustas* for the Romans signified both time itself and the effects of time: a long duration that, once endured, left a human or object old. Cicero (*De Or.* 2.36) called history the "messenger of antiquity" (*nuntia uestustatis*), figuring *uetustas* as a place from which we can receive only messages which must travel a long distance. Livy (2.21.4) noted the difficulty in establishing early Roman history: the cause of the problem was "ancientness" (*uetustas*, 2.21.4); both of the "events" (*rerum*), but also the "sources" (*auctorum*).

Lerner's (1986: 15) problematizing of the belief that ancient evidence survives because of an inherent superiority:

> That which succeeded and survived was by the very fact of its survival considered superior to that which vanished and had thus "failed."

Late Republican intellectuals knew that their own past had not been satisfactorily transmitted, and they developed strategies to try to recover it. Indeed, Varro's research is figured by Cicero as a foundational moment for Roman cultural recovery and historical self-knowledge. Before Varro, Cicero (*Ac.* 1.9) says, Romans were strangers in their own home:

> nam nos in nostra urbe peregrinantis errantisque tamquam hospites tui libri quasi domum deduxerunt, ut possemus aliquando qui et ubi essemus agnoscere.

> We were wandering and straying about like foreigners in our own city. Varro's books led us, so to speak, back home again, and enabled us at last to realize who and where we were.

Without Varro's work, Cicero says, the Romans were unable fully to come to terms with, interpret, or understand the city around them; Varro's research planted Rome in its spot, and revealed its identity.[3] The need for a historical consciousness facilitated by intellectual investigation into Rome's past is understood by Cicero to be deeply rooted in questions of national identity. Elsewhere, Cicero (*Or.* 120) presented historical knowledge as a prerequisite for individual maturity, arguing that to be ignorant of events which happened before one's lifetime was "to remain a child forever" (*semper esse puerum*).[4] The two images – a stranger at home, an eternal child – graphically portray the state of historical ignorance that Cicero thought was possible.

Rome's past was therefore felt to be remote, and such remoteness was an obstacle towards its understanding.[5] Roman history was, at times, so obscure that only the names of certain significant historical figures were recorded.[6] The nature of Roman historical writing also presented a

---

[3] Goldberg 2005: 97.   [4] Wiseman 1999: ix.

[5] When Cicero first started writing his *De Republica*, our earliest surviving narrative account of Roman history, he received criticism that setting the dialogue even in 129 BCE was to put words in the mouths "of such ancient men" (*tam antiquis hominibus*, *Q.fr.* 3.5.1–2) that the work would seem "fictitious" (*ficta*); see Zetzel 1995: 3–8.

[6] *Rep.* 2.33: *sed obscura est historia Romana*, "but Roman history is obscure." Cornell (2001: 43) interprets *De Republica*'s historical vagueness as part of Cicero's characterization of Scipio as a noble Roman who does not want to lecture fellow Roman luminaries on the stories that they know

number of other obstacles. Cicero was personally averse to Roman historiography because of its style, which he found to be dry, lapidary, and
uninspiring.[7] In Cicero's view (*De Or.* 2.54), Roman historians were only
reporting history, not elaborating on the significance of the events they set
down; the task of the historian was therefore antithetical to the task of the
orator, who amplified and monumentalized certain events, presenting an
interpretation of their meaning.[8] Cicero also, importantly, found Roman
historiography to be partisan: eulogies of the famous dead, used as historical sources, introduced distortions into the historical record (*Brut.* 61–62;
cf. Livy 8.40.3–5).[9] Cicero did not explicitly cite the Roman historians very
often for these reasons.[10] We do, however, regularly find Cicero engaging
with Roman poetry as part of his efforts to understand Roman history.

5.1 Researching the Past

In May and June of 45 BCE, Cicero was engaged in historical research for a
composition he described as a "political conference" set at Olympia in the
year 146 BCE.[11] In a series of letters, Cicero describes his research practices
and preparations for writing.[12] A letter to Atticus (*Att.* 13.30.2; May 45 BCE)
gives a sense of the complexity of trying to reconstruct the past:

> mi, sicunde potes, erues, qui decem legati Mummio fuerint. Polybius non
> nominat. ego memini Albinum consularem et Sp. Mummium; uideor audisse
> ex Hortensio Tuditanum. sed in Libonis annali XIIII annis post praetor est
> factus Tuditanus quam consul Mummius. non sane quadrat. uolo aliquem
> Olympiae aut ubiuis σύλλογον more Dicaearchi, familiaris tui.

---

[7] Cicero (*De Or.* 2.52–53) says that the histories of Fabius Pictor, Cato the Elder, and L. Calpurnius
Piso (cos. 133 BCE) resemble the pontifical record, a style of writing (described at *Leg.* 1.6 as the
"driest possible"; *nihil potest esse ieiunius*) that records dates, names, places, and events without
ornament. C. Licinius Macer's histories read to Cicero like the work of a "scribal copyist" (*ex
librariolis, Leg.* 1.7).
[8] And introducing their own distortions: *concessum est rhetoribus ementiri*, "orators can distort history"
(*Brut.* 42).
[9] Contemporary aristocrats, tasked with commemorating their illustrious ancestors, might also
accidentally introduce errors: Q. Caecilius Metellus Scipio (cos. 52 BCE) erected a statue to Scipio
Nasica Serapio (cos. 138 BCE) but used a statue-type and inscription of Scipio Aemilianus as an
exemplar, thereby attributing a censorship to Serapio, though he had never attained the censorship.
Cicero calls this a "shameful ahistoricity" (ἀνιστορησίαν *turpem, Att.* 6.1.17).
[10] Rambaud (1953: 25–26) lists Cicero's engagements with Roman historians.
[11] There is no evidence that Cicero completed the project. Shackleton Bailey (1966, Vol. 5: 349)
suggests that "he soon jettisoned this idea."
[12] *Att.* 13.30, 13.31, 13.32, 13.33, 13.6, 13.4, 13.5, 13.8.

If you can, please dig out for me somewhere the names of Mummius' ten
commissioners. Polybius does not name them. I remember the consular
Albinus and Spurius Mummius. I think I have heard Hortensius mention
Tuditanus. But in Libo's *Annales,* Tuditanus became praetor fourteen years
after Mummius became consul. It doesn't square up. I want to stage a sort of
"Political Conference" at Olympia or wherever in the manner of your old
friend Dicaearchus.

Cicero has set his sights on a specific moment in time: the immediate
aftermath of the capture of Corinth in 146 BCE. Cicero tries in this series of
letters to find appropriate characters for his work. Although Cicero would
always remake the historical figures of his dialogues in his own image, these
letters show that his starting point was nonetheless historicist; Cicero is
concerned to ensure that his chosen *personae* were actually at Olympia
when he says they were. Cicero asks Atticus to try to "dig up" (*erues*[13])
historical information for him: he wants to know the names of the legates
that organized Greece in 146 BCE after L. Mummius' capture of Corinth.[14]
When Atticus (*Att.* 13.32.3) reveals the fact that the Postumius among the
commissioners sent to Greece was in fact Aulus Postumius (and therefore
the consul of 151 BCE), Cicero says that Atticus has done him a great service
by giving him exactly the "right kind of person" (*persona idonea, Att.*
13.32.3) for his dialogue, and he hopes that Atticus will find others of
similarly high calibre.[15]

This letter demonstrates the variety of historical sources at Cicero's
disposal, as well as the limitations of those sources.[16] Cicero's tools for
historical inquiry in these letters are the following: a) he can draw on his
own memory; b) consult Atticus, his historian friend; c) consult a book copy
of Polybius, a Greek historical source contemporary to the event he is
interested in; d) draw on someone *else's* memory, in this case Hortensius',
an older colleague whom he respected; e) use a book copy of a Roman
historian, the annalist L. Libo. But poetry also offered Cicero an opportunity

[13] In an oration against the Rullan land bill of 63 BCE, Cicero spoke of the tribune investigating, finding, and "digging out from the shadows" (*ex tenebris erueris, Agr.* 1.3) something ancient to help his case. In the *Tusculans* (1.29), Cicero speaks of "examining old things" (*scrutari uetera*) to "try to dig out" (*eruere coner*) further evidence.
[14] L. Mummius destroyed Corinth as consul in 146 BCE. A tablet (*ILS* 20) found at Rome on the *Mons Caelius* commemorating the event was dedicated in 142 BCE. Mummius also left dedications at Delphi, Olympia, and many other sites (*ILLRP* 327–31); Polybius 39.6.102, Paus. 5.10.5, 5.24.4, Strabo 8.6.23.
[15] In *De Amicitia* (4), Cicero writes that Gaius Laelius seemed like an *idonea persona* for a dialogue on friendship.
[16] Rawson (1972: 41) stresses the "extreme variety" of sources generally used by Cicero in his historical inquiries.

to establish historical "facts." Cicero writes (*Att.* 13.6.4) that he was certain that Spurius Mummius, brother of L. Mummius, was also present at Corinth:

> Tuditanum istum, proaum Hortensi, plane non noram et filium, qui tum non potuerat esse legatus, fuisse putaram. Mummium fuisse ad Corinthum pro certo habeo. saepe enim hic Spurius, qui nuper est <mortuus>, epistulas mihi pronuntiabat uersiculis factas[17] ad familiaris missas a Corintho. sed non dubito quin fratri fuerit legatus, non in decem.

> I had never heard of that Tuditanus, Hortensius' great-grandfather, and I had thought that it was his son who was the commissioner, who could not have then been even legate. I am certain that Spurius Mummius was at Corinth. For often Spurius, the one who recently died, recited to me his letters made from little verses, sent to his friends from Corinth. But I do not doubt that he was a legate to his brother, rather than among the ten commissioners.

Cicero had known a descendant of Spurius Mummius, perhaps his grandson, a man with the same name. This younger Spurius once read to Cicero some epistolary poems that his relative had written at Corinth and sent back to his friends at Rome (*Att.* 13.6.4).[18] Cicero took these poems as evidence of Mummius' presence there, and so Cicero considered including him as a character in his fictional dialogue set in 146 BCE.

That Mummius' letters circumscribed an elite Roman sociality was precisely what made them good historical evidence for Cicero. They placed the second century BCE Spurius Mummius at a specific location and time, and connected him to other historical figures. In addition to the consultation of sources which we may consider "historical" in the traditional sense, Cicero found evidence of the Roman past in poetic sources. Indeed, Cicero had in fact made this elder Spurius Mummius into a character in the *De Republica* (1.18, 1.34, 3.46–48, 5.11), although unfortunately he says only a little in the extant version of this text.[19] Nonetheless, we have here evidence

---

[17] Or *facetis*, "witty." See Shackleton Bailey (1966, Vol. 5: 360).

[18] Scholars consider Spurius Mummius' "letters made in little verses" (*epistulas uersiculis factas, Att.* 13.6.4) an immediate precursor to the poetry of Lucilius the satirist, see Krenkel 1970: 17, Coffey 1976: 221 n61, Raschke 1987: 304, von Albrecht 1997: 254, Gärtner 2001: 90. Raschke (1987: 305) suggested that the earliest of Lucilius' satires, written in the context of Scipio Aemilianus' campaign at Numantia in Spain (134–133 BCE; Vell. Pat. 2.9.4, see Gruen 1992: 281), were an emulation of Mummius' Corinthian letters. Gärtner (2001: 90) recognized "reminiscences" of Mummius' letters in the fragments of Lucilius which contained scenes from Scipio's Spanish campaign (Books 11, 14, and 30).

[19] See Zetzel 1995: 10. At *Rep.* 3.46–48, Mummius takes the position against a "democratic" form of government. At *Rep.* 5.11, Mummius is "filled with a kind of hatred for rhetors" (*erat enim odio quodam rhetorum inbutus*).

of Cicero composing a character from a literary artefact that he had
encountered, applying his imagination to historical evidence in order to
create his own work.

5.2 "Without Lucilius We Wouldn't Know ... "

Cicero tells us that, in certain cases, earlier Roman literature stood as a
means of recording historical events that were otherwise lost.[20] In the
Brutus (160), Cicero says that if Lucilius the satirist had not written
about L. Licinius Crassus (cos. 95 BCE) dining with a herald called
Granius, no one would ever have known that Crassus had held the
tribunate in 107 BCE:[21]

> sed ita tacitus tribunatus ut, nisi in eo magistratu cenauisset apud praeco-
> nem Granium idque nobis bis narrauisset Lucilius, tribunum plebis nesciri-
> emus fuisse.

> But his tribunate was so quiet that, unless he had dined with the herald,
> Granius, during this magistracy, and unless Lucilius had twice told the
> story, we wouldn't know that he had even held the tribunate.

In the *Orator* (132), Cicero writes that Crassus published very few of his
orations.[22] Because regular publication of speeches did not become common until Cicero's lifetime, the absence of a record could evidently create
problems for establishing even relatively recent Roman history. Cicero here
tells us that Lucilius the satirist had "twice told the story" (*bis narrauisset,
Brut.* 160) of Crassus dining with the herald, Granius, and that this scene of
satire preserved the fact that Crassus had held the tribunate in 107 BCE.[23]
Cicero's citation of Lucilius as evidence that Crassus held the tribunate

---

[20] Rambaud 1953: 65.
[21] Cicero refers to Granius' wit via Lucilian citation a number of times; see Chahoud 2010: 90. In the
Brutus (172), Granius is referred to as the man "about whom Lucilius said so much" (*de quo multa
Lucilius*; cf. Warmington 448–449). In the *Pro Plancio* (34), this Granius is said to have made
"sarcastic remarks" (*asperioribus facetiis*) about Crassus and Marcus Antonius (Marx 1181). In the *De
Oratore*, Granius' buffoonish, mime-like wit is contrasted with Crassus' austere humour (*De Or.*
2.244); a verse citation of Scipio Africanus *apud Lucilium* (Warmington 1135) is followed by a
paraphrase of Granius (*De Or.* 2.254), suspected to be a paraphrase of Lucilius (Marx 1181); two
further witticisms of Granius are cited (*De Or.* 2.281–282). Cicero also refers to Granius (alongside
Lucilius) as a positive example of Latinity in a letter to Paetus (*Fam.* 9.15.2); the verse of Lucilius that
was so often on Atticus' lips (*Att.* 6.3.7; Warmington 609–610) was spoken by Granius.
[22] Fantham 2004: 30. After Cicero's résumé of Crassus' oratorical career (*Brut.* 159–164), his interlocutor (Brutus) responds (*Brut.* 163) with a wish that Crassus had written more.
[23] Broughton (1951, Vol. 1: 551); Lucilius' *Satires* (Marx 1180).

appears in Cicero's *Brutus* as part of a résumé of Crassus' career, at least as far as Cicero could textually reconstruct it:

a) as a young man (*adulescens*), he rose to fame through his role in the indictment of C. Papirius Carbo in 119 BCE (*Brut.* 159);[24]
b) he defended the Vestal Virgin, Licinia, when he was 27 (*Brut.* 160);[25]
c) as a young man (*adulescens*) he was one of the *duouiri* who founded Narbo in 118 BCE (*Brut.* 160);[26]
d) he was tribune in 107 BCE, according to Lucilius (*Brut.* 160);
e) he gave a speech in support of the *Lex Seruilia* the year after his tribunate (106 BCE), when he was 34, the year Cicero was born (*Brut.* 161);[27]
f) he defended Q. Caepio during his consulship of 95 BCE (*Brut.* 162);
g) he was successful in the *Causa Curiana* of 94 BCE (*Brut.* 144–145);[28]
h) he gave a speech as censor in 92 BCE when he was 48 (*Brut.* 162) against Cn. Domitius Ahenobarbus (*Brut.* 164).[29]

In the *Brutus,* Cicero is careful to tell us that he had derived this résumé from Crassus' extant writing: Cicero knew that Crassus defended the Vestal, Licinia, because "he left behind certain written parts of that oration" (*orationisque eius scriptas quasdam partis reliquit, Brut.* 160); he knew about the Narbo colony because Crassus' oration on the law for its establishment still "survived" (*extat, Brut.* 160);[30] he knew that Crassus supported the *Lex Seruilia* in 106 BCE because the speech had been "published" (*edita oratio est*) and Cicero could assume that his interlocutor had "often read it" (*saepe legisse certo scio, Brut.* 161).[31] While Cicero would discuss other court cases in the *De Oratore*, his résumé for Crassus in the

---

[24] In *De Oratore* (3.74), Cicero has Crassus begin the overview of his own career with this case, cf. *De Or.* 1.40 where Antonius says: "Crassus, you crushed Carbo as a rather young man" (*C. ipsum Carbonem, quem tu adulescentulus perculisti*). Cicero included part of this speech in the *De Oratore* (2.170 = 14 *ORF*). On this trial, see Gruen 1968: 107–109, Alexander 1990: no. 30.

[25] Unsuccessfully (Val. Max. 3.7.9).

[26] Coinage from Narbo (RRC 228) establishes that the other was Cn. Domitius Ahenobarbus (cos. 96 BCE, cens. with Crassus 92 BCE). That the colony of Narbo was established in 118 BCE relies on this passage of Cicero, but the date is not, in fact, certain: see Sumner 1973: 96.

[27] On Cicero's birth as a dating mechanism in *Brut.* 140, 160–161, see Steel 2002: 208.

[28] On the notorious *Causa Curiana* (*De Or.* 1.180, 1.238, 2.242–244; 2.24, 2.140–141, 2.220–222; *Inv.* 2.122–123; *Brut.* 144–145, 194–198, 256; *Top.* 44; *Pro Caec.* 53, 67, 69), see Vaughn 1985: 208–222, Alexander 1990: no. 93, Fantham 2004: 119–120, Dugan 2012: 119–128, 2013: 211–225.

[29] Also discussed at *De Or.* 2.45, 2.227, 2.230, 2.242.   [30] Mankin 2011: 30.

[31] Cicero included part of this speech in the *De Oratore* (1.255 = 24 *ORF*). In the *De Oratore* (2.223) and the *Pro Cluentio* (140–141), Cicero describes Brutus (son of the jurist, M. Iunius Brutus) ordering two of these speeches (on Narbo; on the *Lex Seruilia*) to be read out by two *lectores* with the aim of highlighting their political inconsistencies. Fantham (2004: 27) notes that Cicero describes Crassus' speech from 106 BCE (on the *Lex Seruilia*) as his "virtual teacher." Cicero refers to this speech again at *De Off.* 2.63.

Brutus included only the events which Cicero could date with certainty based on firm textual evidence.[32] In short, Cicero's presentation of Crassus' oratorical and political career in the *Brutus* relied heavily on inferences from surviving textual evidence, among which Lucilius' *Satires* numbered, supplying data where oratorical texts were lacking.[33] Indeed, the date of 107 BCE for Crassus' tribunate, provided by Cicero's interpretation of Lucilius' *Satires*, is still the linchpin for modern reconstructions of the dates for his earlier magistracies.[34]

Cicero's *Brutus* discusses the difficulties of trying to reconstruct oratorical history from textual evidence. Despite the ability of circulated orations to leave a record of a kind, published speeches did not always convey the true oratorical power of their author (e.g. *Brut.* 91). In some cases, Cicero and his contemporaries had no evidence at all for an orator's eloquence, but had to "infer" (*suspicari*, *Brut.* 55) eloquence from historical circumstances.[35] In the context of Cicero's inferences and investigations into Rome's past, Lucilius' *Satires* become an important piece of contemporary evidence which granted Cicero a textual view of Crassus, an individual he was greatly interested in, but who died early in Cicero's life.[36]

Crassus was a character, and one of the chief speakers, in Cicero's *De Oratore* (55 BCE), a historical fiction which presented individuals from the

---

[32] Several lines of Crassus' résumé, omitted in the *Brutus* (159–164), had appeared in the *De Oratore*: a defense of L. Calpurnius Piso Caesoninus (c. 114 BCE; Mankin 2011: 30n127), *De Or.* 2.265, 2.285; oration against C. Memmius (c. 111 BCE), *De Or.* 2.240, 2.267; oration against the consul, L. Marcius Philippus (91 BCE), *De Or.* 3.2; defense of C. Sergius Orata, *De Or.* 1.178 (*Off.* 3.67); defense of Cicero's uncle, C. Visellius Aculeo, *De Or.* 2.269, 2.262; defense of Cn. Plancus, *De Or.* 2.220–226 (*Clu.* 140). Crassus was also proconsul in Gaul (Val. Max. 3.7.6) in 94 BCE. He had also been a member of the augural college (*De Or.* 1.39, 1.24, 3.1–8).

[33] Many of the historical anecdotes which appear in *De Oratore* are considered to have derived from Lucilius. Zillinger (1911: 160–168) took almost every reference to the second century BCE in *De Oratore* as a citation or an allusion to Lucilius: *De Or.* 1.72 (Marx 1241); *De Or.* 2.22 (Laelius and Scipio in the countryside); *De Or.* 2.25 (Warmington 635); *De Or.* 2.224 (Marx 1181); *De Or.* 254 (Warmington 1135); *De Or.* 2.254 (Marx 1181); *De Or.* 2.263 (otherwise unknown quarrel between Glaucia and Metellus in 102 BCE); *De Or.* 2.267 (witticism of Scipio at Numantia); *De Or.* 2.268 (witticism of Scipio against Asellus); *De Or.* 2.277 (witty banter between Q. Opimius and Egilius); *De Or.* 2.281 (Marx 1181); *De Or.* 2.284 (Lucilius? and the *ager publicus*); *De Or.* 3.86 (Warmington 182–183); *De Or.* 3.164 (*stercus curiae*, cf. Warmington 430–431); *De Or.* 3.171 (Warmington 84–85, 86). On *De Or.* 2.262 and Lucilius (Marx 173), see Chahoud 2010.

[34] Broughton (1951, Vol. 1: 546) gives 109 BCE as "the latest probable date" for Crassus' quaestorship (*De Or.* 1.45, 2.365, 3.75), based on a date of 107 BCE for the tribunate. Cicero writes that Crassus and Q. Mucius Scaevola (his fellow cos. 95 BCE), were aediles together (*Off.* 2.57, *Verr.* 2.4.133), but the exact date (between 105–100 BCE, Broughton p575) is not known.

[35] Dugan 2005: 291.

[36] Crassus died on September 19, 91 BCE (*De Or.* 3.1, 3.6). Cicero was fifteen years old.

Roman past, now dead,[37] alive and discussing oratorical precepts together at a specific moment in time, the *Ludi Romani* of 91 BCE.[38] In the preface to Book 2 (*De Or.* 2.2), Cicero describes how he and his brother, as young boys, observed Crassus:

> quos tum, ut pueri, refutare domesticis testibus patre et C. Aculeone propinquo nostro et L. Cicerone patruo solebamus, quod de Crasso pater et Aculeo, quocum erat nostra matertera, quem Crassus dilexit ex omnibus plurimum, et patruus, qui cum Antonio in Ciliciam profectus una decesserat, multa nobis de eius studio et doctrina saepe narrauit; cumque nos cum consobrinis nostris, Aculeonis filiis, et ea disceremus, quae Crasso placerent, et ab eis doctoribus, quibus ille uteretur, erudiremur, etiam illud saepe intelleximus, cum essemus eius domi, quod uel pueri sentire poteramus, illum et Graece sic loqui, nullam ut nosse aliam linguam uideretur, et doctoribus nostris ea ponere in percontando eaque ipsum omni in sermone tractare, ut nihil esse ei nouum, nihil inauditum uideretur.

> When we were boys, we used to argue against those men[39] with witnesses from our own house: our father, and Gaius Aculeo, our near relative, and our uncle, Lucius Cicero. Father and Aculeo, who was married to our aunt and whom Crassus loved above all others, told us about Crassus; and our uncle, who went to Cilicia with Antonius and was with him when he left the province, often told us many things about Antonius' commitment to learning. When we (with our cousins, Aculeo's sons) were instructed in the things which pleased Crassus, from the learned men with whom he associated, even we often understood (to the extent that boys can understand – we were at his house), that he spoke Greek as though he did not know any other language, and set out precepts before our teachers in his questioning, and handled himself in the discourse in such a way that nothing seemed new, or unheard of to him.

While many scholars have suggested that Cicero was closely mentored by Crassus,[40] Cicero here nonetheless gives the impression that there were several filters between himself and the orator whom he revered.[41] Cicero would go on (*De Or.* 2.3) to say that he asked the great orator, Marcus

---

[37] L. Licinius Crassus d. 91 BCE, M. Antonius d. 87 BCE, Q. Mucius Scaevola Augur d. 87 BCE, Q. Lutatius Catulus d. 87 BCE, C. Julius Caesar Strabo Vopiscus d. 87 BCE, C. Aurelius Cotta d. 74/73 BCE, P. Sulpicius Rufus d. 88 BCE. See Mankin 2011: 30–35.

[38] *De Or.* 1.24; see Mankin 2011: 30.

[39] I.e. those who claimed that L. Licinius Crassus and M. Antonius were not educated (cf. *De Or.* 2.1).

[40] Kennedy 1972: 103–104, May-Wisse 2001: 7, 14. Mankin 2011: 29n120 more cautiously avoids overstating their relationship.

[41] Fantham 2004: 26n1: "Since Cicero was himself not yet 16 when Crassus died, he has to authenticate his knowledge through intermediaries."

Antonius, as many questions as "the modesty of my young age would allow" (*quantum illius ineuntis aetatis meae patiebatur pudor*), but he never explicitly refers to a conversation with Crassus.[42] Instead, Cicero describes the men who knew Crassus, and helped Cicero learn about him: his own father,[43] and his uncle by marriage, Gaius Visellius Aculeo (*de Crasso pater et Aculeo ... narrauit*).[44]

If Cicero observed Crassus from afar as a young man, he nonetheless relied on the memories of trusted men to convey historical knowledge to him.[45] At the beginning of the *De Oratore*, Cicero had described the content of the dialogue as a "fuzzy recollection of an old memory" (*ueteris cuiusdam memoriae non sane satis explicata recordatio, De Or.* 1.4), a dramatization of a conversation which he remembered being told to him (*dici mihi memini, De Or.* 1.24).[46] That knowledge of Roman elders was filtered through this kind of paternalistic memory is likewise enacted in the preface to the *De Amicitia* (1), where Cicero connects himself to the figures of Laelius and Scipio via the memories of Q. Mucius Scaevola ("Augur," cos. 117 BCE), son-in-law of Gaius Laelius.[47]

5.3   *Lusit in Persona*

But evidently such memory could also be supplemented by consultation of poetry.[48] Indeed, Cicero has Crassus himself quote Lucilius' *Satires* in the *De Oratore* (3.171) in this very way:

> collocationis est componere et struere uerba sic ut neue asper eorum con-
> cursus neue hiulcus sit, sed quodam modo coagmentatus et leuis; in quo
> lepide soceri mei persona lusit is qui elegantissime id facere potuit, Lucilius:
> *quam lepide* λέξεις *compostae! ut tesserulae omnes*   [Warmington 84–85]

---

[42] Fantham (2004: 28) also notes that Cicero elsewhere (*TD* 5.55) calls Marcus Antonius "the most eloquent man that I have myself heard" (*M. Antonii, omnium eloquentissimus quos ego audierim*). Cicero may not have heard Crassus speak in court.

[43] Cicero and his dramatic characters regularly relate historical information which they say they had "heard from their fathers": *De Or.* 3.133: *audiui de patre*, on Sextus Aelius Catus (cos. 198 BCE); *ND* 2.11: *e patre audiebam*, on Tiberius Gracchus (tr. pl. 133 BCE); *ND* 2.11: *e patre audiebam*, on the solar "doubling" in 129 BCE (cf. *Rep.* 1.15); *De Off.* 3.77: *audiebam de patre nostro*, on Gaius Flavius Fimbria (cos. 104 BCE).

[44] Fantham 2004: 27. Cicero describes a land dispute case between M. Marius Gratidianus and C. Sergius Orata, in which Crassus and Antonius opposed each other (*De Or.* 1.178, *Off.* 3.67). Since Marius was Cicero's relative, Cicero's knowledge of the case may have come from his family's memory; see Fantham 2004: 30.

[45] Rawson 1991: 26.   [46] Mankin 2011: 29.

[47] Cf. *De Or.* 2.22, where Cicero has Crassus recall a memory from his father-in-law (*ex socero meo*), i.e. Q. Mucius Scaevola, recalling a memory from *his* father-in-law (*socerum suum*), Gaius Laelius.

[48] Rawson 1972: 41.

arte pauimento atque emblemate uermiculato
quae cum dixisset in Albucium illudens, ne a me quidem abstinuit:
Crassum habeo generum, ne rhetoricoterus tu sis. [Warmington 86]
quid ergo? iste Crassus, quoniam eius abuteris nomine, quid efficit? illud
quidem – scilicet, ut ille uult et ego uellem, melius aliquanto quam
Albucius: uerum in me quidem lusit ille, ut solet.

Arrangement involves putting together and building words in such a way
that there is neither a harsh assemblage of them, nor a gaping hole, but the
words are well and smoothly joined. In reference to this, Lucilius, in the
persona of my father-in-law, joked in that neat way that he could:
*"Speech so charmingly put together! Like all the little stones
in a paved mosaic, an intricate panel."*
He had jokingly spoken those words against Albucius, and didn't even
spare me:
"I have Crassus as a son-in-law, so don't get too 'rhetorical.'"
What then? Since you abuse this "Crassus" by name, Lucilius, what did he do?
The same thing as Albucius. To be sure, just as he says and I could only wish,
Crassus did it far better than Albucius. But truly he teased me, as was his way.

Cicero's Crassus here quotes three verses of Lucilius' *Satires*, in which Crassus
himself appeared as a character.[49] Lucilius the poet had spoken *in persona*[50]
(*De Or.* 3.171) of Q. Mucius Scaevola, Crassus' father-in-law.[51] Since Scaevola
was a character in Book 1 of *De Oratore*, the reference to him here is not merely
an ornamental flourish but an internal link to the dialogue's worldbuilding.[52]
In the scene of satire, Lucilius as Scaevola had joked about the overwrought
oratorical style of Titus Albucius (pr. 105 BCE), which apparently included a
humorous aside against Crassus as well.[53] Lucilius' *Satires*, then, preserved

[49] Cf. *De Rep.* 1.30 where Sextus Aelius Catus (cos. 198 BCE), who appeared in Ennius' *Annales* (Skutsch 329), is represented quoting Ennius' *Iphigenia* (*TrRF* II 82).
[50] Chahoud 2004: 35. Cicero quotes these verses three times (*De Or.* 3.171, *Or.* 149; *Brut.* 274 is a partial quotation); twice referring to the fact that the character speaking Lucilius' verses is Scaevola: *in soceri mei persona, De Or.* 3.171 (said from the perspective of Crassus); *exagitat in Albucio Scaeuola* (*Or.* 149). Cicero explicitly attributes the verses to Lucilius in all three cases: *Lucilius* (*De Or.* 3.171), *apud Lucilium* (*Or.* 149), *ut ait Lucilius* (*Brut.* 274). It is from Cicero alone that we learn that these lines of Lucilius were spoken by Scaevola about Albucius (*in Albucium, De Or.* 3.171; *in Albucio, Or.* 149). The later Roman writers who quote this passage (Pliny *NH* 36.185, Quintilian 9.4.113) do not refer to either Albucius or Scaevola.
[51] Their relationship is preserved in Lucilius' *Crassum habeo generum*, "I have Crassus for a son-in-law" (Warmington 86).
[52] Cicero decided to remove Scaevola from the latter parts of *De Oratore*, following, he says (*Att.* 4.16.2), the example Plato's Cephalus in the *Republic*; an old man who would not be capable of sustaining a conversation for too long (*Att.* 4.16.3).
[53] Lucilius' *Satires* (Warmington 87–93) included an exchange between Scaevola and Albucius, the infamous philhellene, at Athens; see Gruen 1992: 290–291, Chahoud 2004: 31–34, Goldberg 2005: 161–162. This passage is cited by Cicero in the *De Finibus* (1.8–9). Cicero referred to T. Albucius a

something even more important than chronological data: Lucilius depicted Cicero's oratorical heroes living and breathing, joking with one another and, via their depiction in elite play, created a series of vignettes which preserved the cultural values attractive to Cicero.[54]

For Cicero, then, Lucilius' poetry did not simply convey "history," but cultural and intellectual history. Lucilius' comparison of oratory to the mosaic style known as *opus uermiculatum* became embedded in Cicero's own language of oratorical assessment.[55] The best kind of "arrangement" (*collocatio*) in oratory, Cicero has Crassus say (*De Or.* 3.171), is achieved by a deliberate and careful "joining" (*coagmentatus*) of words which avoids "harshness" (*asper*) or "hiatus" (*hiulcus*), and this construction of speech resembles the careful laying out of mosaic. Individual words which make up a well-crafted speech are like the individual pieces of coloured marble, the *tesserulae* (as Lucilius writes), which combine to create an image. The *opus uermiculatum* mosaic style used particularly small cubes of marble (as small as 1mm squared), fitting so closely that they created a mosaic with the appearance of a painting. The mosaic of the drinking doves discovered at Hadrian's villa is thought to be a reproduction of an original made during Lucilius' lifetime by Sosus of Pergamum.[56] As such, the *opus uermiculatum* was a good metaphor for oratorical technique: precise and detailed work combined to produce an image that was more than a sum of its own parts.

Scaevola's comment that Albucius' speech was like *opus uermiculatum* was a tongue-in-cheek criticism of overwrought oratory, but the theory that an oration should be like a mosaic was, nonetheless, sound. Indeed, that is Cicero's very point in the *De Oratore* (3.171): Crassus' emphasis on the fact that words must be smoothly joined is positively exemplified by Lucilius' λέξεις *compostae ut tesserulae*, "words joined together like little pieces of stone" (Warmington 84). When Cicero assessed the oratorical style of M. Calidius (pr. 57 BCE), he remarked that "you could see every word set up like the individual stones in a mosaic (*in uermiculato*

---

number of times: *Brut.* 131, *Brut.* 102, *De Or.* 2.281, *De Prov. Cons.* 7, *Pis.* 38, *Div. in Caecil.* 19, *Off.* 2.14, *TD* 5.37.

[54] Cicero, like Lucilius, wrote *in persona*. Cicero described Book 2 of *De Oratore* as written *per personam* of Marcus Antonius (*Fam.* 7.32.2). Taking on the role of another person was a rhetorical technique which Cicero himself used in the lawcourts (e.g. *Cael.* 33–34; *Pis.* 59) and it was a fundamental compositional strategy for many of his philosophical works, where he took on the voices of Roman historical figures: Scipio (*De Republica*); Cato the Elder (*De Senectute*); Gaius Laelius (*De Amicitia*).

[55] Pliny (*NH* 36.185) also treats Lucilius as a historical source when he cites this passage as evidence of the fact that this kind of mosaic existed before the Cimbric War (113–101 BCE).

[56] Smith 1983: 117; Pliny *NH* 36.184.

emblemate), as Lucilius says" (*Brut.* 274). The application of the Lucilian phrase is at first used to praise Calidius for his technical skill in producing flowing, well-joined oratory, but Cicero ultimately finds Calidius' lacking because he failed to move the emotions of his audience (*Brut.* 276).[57] Discussing "arrangement" (*collocatio*) again in the *Orator* (149–150), Cicero quotes Lucilius' mosaic passage once more, commenting that he would not want the detailed construction of a speech to be overtly visible.[58] To use the mosaic of the drinking doves as a metaphor: Cicero wants us to focus on the doves, not the individual tiles from which they are constructed.

For Cicero, then, Lucilius' *Satires* provided a literary world in which the historical *personae* whom he admired could be seen in aristocratic play. Cicero observed the Lucilian depictions of these elite men and used aspects of the poetic characters to develop his own versions of historical Romans. The language which Lucilius placed in the mouths of these elites became the very language which Cicero used to discuss intellectual or moral issues. Lucilius presented not just versions of L. Licinius Crassus and Q. Mucius Scaevola, men whom Cicero himself had known (to differing degrees), but other esteemed historical figures who were more remote. As such, Lucilius, like Ennius, was a conduit by which Cicero could access aristocratic memory.[59]

Cicero therefore treated Latin poetry as an artefact of Roman history. Cicero regularly quoted the words of Scipio or Gaius Laelius from Lucilius as though they had been authentically preserved by the poet. In the *De Finibus* (2.24–25), Cicero used a passage of Lucilius' *Satires* to discuss Gaius Laelius' avoidance of overexcess at dinner; Cicero there praises the words of Laelius, not Lucilius.[60] In the *De Oratore* (2.253), Cicero quoted the "famous saying of Africanus, which is in Lucilius" (*ut illud Africani, quod est apud Lucilium,* Warmington 1135). That Lucilius played a role in valorizing these men is suggested by how Cicero uses some of the anecdotes

---

[57] Dugan 2005: 162–163.

[58] *Or.* 150: *nolo haec tam minuta constructio appareat,* "I do not want such detailed construction of a speech to be visible." Quintilian (9.4.113) would follow Cicero in citing Lucilius's mosaic passage to describe excessive attention to detail in composition.

[59] Cicero presents vignettes of Ennius with Scipio Nasica (*De Or.* 2.276) and "his neighbour" (*suus uicinus*) Servius Sulpicius Galba (*Ac.* 2.51).

[60] A few months later, Cicero quoted the same passage (Warmington 206–207) in a letter to Atticus (*Att.* 13.52.1; Dec. 45 BCE) after witnessing a banquet during the Saturnalia where Julius Caesar was on an emetic diet and therefore able to eat and drink to excess. For a discussion of *Fin.* 2.24–25 and *Att.* 13.52.2, see Goh 2018: 259–260. On the echoes of this passage of Lucilius in Horace *Epode* 2.57, see Goh 2016: 77–79.

he derived from the poet. Cicero wrote that according to Lucilius, M. Licinius Crassus (pr. 126 BCE) only ever laughed once in his life (*TD* 3.31, *Fin.* 5.92); both passages present the severe Lucilian Crassus alongside traditional wisdom figures: Socrates (*TD* 3.31); and Polycrates of Samos (*Fin.* 5.92).[61] For Cicero, then, Lucilius' treatment of Roman historical figures in the *Satires* not only preserved them but enshrined them.

5.4   History and Historicity

While Lucilius had written about men of his own time, some of whom Cicero would claim to know personally, Ennius, who was himself long dead and had written about events from Rome's deep past as well as his own time, was a more remote figure. As we have seen, Cicero regularly cited Ennius' *Annales* for linguistic or philosophical, rather than strictly "historical" reasons. Nonetheless, Cicero's citations of Ennius' *Annales* also show that he considered the poem to be an authoritative telling of Roman history, one which captured moments of high drama in the Roman saga, and enshrined the names of Roman heroes into common memory.[62] A letter to Atticus (*Att.* 2.19.2) demonstrates how late Republican Romans carried Ennius' *Annales* in their minds:

> scito nihil umquam fuisse tam infame, tam turpe, tam peraeque omnibus generibus, ordinibus, aetatibus offensum, quam hunc statum qui nunc est, magis mehercule quam uellem, non modo quam putarem. populares isti iam etiam modestos homines sibilare docuerunt. Bibulus in caelo[63] est, nec qua re scio, sed ita laudatur quasi
> *unus homo nobis cunctando restituit rem.*   [Skutsch 363]

> Know that no other time has ever been so disgraceful, so shameful, so uniformly destructive to all types, ranks, ages, than this one right now, more than I could have wished, let alone expected. Those *populares* have taught even the temperate to hiss.[64] Bibulus is elevated, I don't know why, but he is praised like the "*one man*" who "*by delaying restored the republic for us.*"

In this letter Cicero contrasts the state of Rome during Caesar's consulship with the Rome of the past. M. Calpurnius Bibulus, Caesar's conservative

---

[61] Cf. *TD* 1.117 where Ennius is aligned with Solon.

[62] For a discussion of Cicero's citation of Ennius' *Annales*, see Elliott 2013: 152–195.

[63] The phrase "*in caelo*" may also be a deliberate Ennianism. It appears in a verse of Ennius' *Annales* (Skutsch 110 = *TD* 1.28, *De Or.* 3.154) which describes the apotheosis of Romulus.

[64] Cf. Caelius' letter to Cicero (*Fam.* 8.2.1; 51 BCE), which describes the crowd hissing at Hortensius in Curio's theatre with a citation of Pacuvius (Schierl fr. 263).

colleague, is worshipped for his resistance to Caesar's popularist agenda as though he were one of the most famous Romans of all time, Q. Fabius Maximus Cunctator, the man whose delaying tactics preserved Roman strength during the war against Hannibal. (Such a comparison would, of course, make Caesar Hannibal.)[65]

Cicero would later quote this passage of Ennius' *Annales* (Skutsch 363–365) more fully in the *De Senectute* (10) and in the *De Officiis* (1.84); in both places, the Ennian passage is cited to praise Q. Fabius Maximus.[66] In the *De Senectute* (10), Cicero presents Cato the Elder quoting Ennius:

> hic et bella gerebat ut adulescens, cum plane grandis esset, et Hannibalem iuueniliter exsultantem patientia sua molliebat; de quo praeclare familiaris noster Ennius:
> *unus homo nobis cunctando restituit rem.*   [Skutsch 363–365]
> *noenum rumores ponebat ante salutem.*
> *ergo postque magisque uiri nunc gloria claret.*

> Fabius was waging war like a youth despite the fact that he was advanced in years, and he tamed Hannibal's puerile pride with his own patience. Our friend, Ennius, excellently says of Fabius:
> "*One man by delaying restored the republic for us.*
> *He did not put his reputation before our safety.*
> *More and more, therefore, glory now brings him renown as a man.*"

Since Cato the Elder appeared in Ennius' *Annales*, we here have another example of Cicero making a historical figure who had been enshrined in a poetic text quote the very text in which they appeared, just as Crassus had quoted Lucilius' *Satires* in the *De Oratore*.[67] Cato (*Sen.* 10) here calls Ennius his "friend" (*familiaris*);[68] Crassus too had called Lucilius *familiaris* (*De Or.* 1.72).[69] Cicero evidently interpreted the appearance of historical Romans in the works of poets as evidence of association between poet and statesman. Cicero's depiction of the relationships between poets and

---

[65] Cicero quotes Hannibal positively in the *Pro Balbo* (51), where verses of Ennius' *Annales* (Skutsch 234–235) spoken by the Carthaginian are used to support the soldier's claim to Roman citizenship. On this passage, see Elliott 2013: 166–167.

[66] On *De Off.* 1.84 see Elliott 2013: 164–165.

[67] Skutsch 1985: 1, 527, 273, 642, 782. Cicero (*Arch.* 22) says that Cato the Elder "is raised to the skies" (*in caelum . . . Cato tollitur*) by Ennius. For a sceptical reading of *Arch.* 22, see Zetzel 2007: 9.

[68] According to Nepos (*Cato* 1.4; cf. Jerome *Chron.* 1777), it was Cato who brought Ennius to Rome from Sardinia. The connection between Ennius and Cato has been questioned by Badian (1972: 155–162) and Zetzel (2007: 11), but has otherwise been generally accepted, see Goldberg 1995: 114 n6.

[69] D. Brutus Callaicus (cos. 138 BCE) is called Accius' *familiaris* (107). Laelius (*Am.* 24) calls Pacuvius *hospes* ("guest") and *amicus* ("friend").

historical Romans is, of course, idealized.[70] Yet it is nonetheless a point of
interest that, despite the historical distortions which Cicero himself introduces via his romanticizing of the Roman past, Cicero rooted his historical
understanding in poetic sources.[71]

Indeed, Cicero has Cato the Elder reflect several times on his own
relationship to the poets in the *De Senectute*. Cato says that Scipio and
Laelius, his younger interlocutors, were able to remember Ennius (*quem
quidem probe meminisse potestis*, *Sen.* 14), since he had died in 169 BCE, only
nineteen years before the dramatic date of the work.[72] Cicero (*Sen.* 14) here
gives an overabundance of chronological information for the year 169 BCE,
suggesting his desire to stress the historicity of Cato's association with
Ennius, even if Cicero had only inferred that association from Cato's
presence in Ennius' poetry.[73] Cicero also has Cato say that he had personally seen Livius Andronicus when he was an old man (*uidi senem Liuium*,
Sen. 50), even though Livius had put on a play six years before Cato's birth
(240 BCE).[74] That Livius had put on a play in 240 BCE was a recent literary
theory; Cicero, following the research of Varro and Atticus, had criticized
Accius in the *Brutus* (72–74) for placing the event in 197 BCE.[75] As a result,
Cicero's depiction of Cato in the *De Senectute* evidently also relied on
recent research into Roman literary history. Cicero makes Cato the Elder
inscribe himself into the history of Rome as it had been recently recon-
structed by late Republican intellectuals.[76] Cicero's *De Senectute* is a
historical fiction, but it relied on an understanding of poetry and the
history of poetry.

---

[70] Zetzel 2007: 10.

[71] On Lucretius' engagement with Ennian historiography, see Nethercut 2021: 101–114.

[72] The dramatic date of the *De Senectute* is 150 BCE (*Sen.* 14); Ennius was therefore thought to have
died in 169 BCE. Cicero gives the same date in the *Brutus* (78), where he associates it with a
performance of Ennius' *Thyestes*. See Zetzel 2007: 10.

[73] Cicero (*Sen.* 14) names the consuls in 169 BCE, Q. Marcius Philippus and Cn. Servilius Caepio
(including the fact that Philippus was holding it for the second time), says that Cato was 65 years old,
and that Cato had supported the *Lex Voconia* in this year.

[74] *Sen.* 50: *Centone Tuditanoque consulibus*, "during the consulship of C. Claudius Centho and M.
Sempronius Tuditanus," i.e. 240 BCE.

[75] On Roman literary history before Varro, Atticus, and Cicero, see Welsh 2011.

[76] The importance of Roman literary figures in the history of Roman culture is made clear in Cicero's
Brutus, where early Roman poets allow Cicero to characterize different periods of Roman eloquence: Naevius' poetry is presented as a possible representation of the style of the late third century
BCE (*Brut.* 60); Ennius' comment (Skutsch 207–209) on the *Fauni* who sang before him is
compared to the poets who sang before Homer (*Brut.* 71), marking a self-consciously pre-classical
and post-classical moment in literary history (see Hinds 1998: 64–65); the simultaneity of elder and
younger poets, Pacuvius and Accius, characterizes the relationship between Hortensius and Cicero
(*Brut.* 229); the Latinity of Pacuvius and Caecilius is contrasted against that of Laelius and Scipio
(*Brut.* 258).

While Cicero fabricated a historicist amalgam for the stuff of his philosophical dialogues, he also explicitly problematized historicism as a straightforward concept. Cicero revealed his attitude to history in the *Brutus* (42–44),
where he presented a self-critical view of his own romanticizing of historical
figures.[77] Atticus, in his role as historian, complained that Cicero's version of
the death of Coriolanus was oversensationalized, embellished in the manner
of orators and tragic poets (*rhetorice et tragice ornare, Brut.* 43).[78] As Atticus
says, "orators can distort history" (*concessum est rhetoribus ementiri, Brut.* 42)
to make their argument more convincing; and, indeed, Cicero wants to keep
his embellished version of Coriolanus despite Atticus' objections (*Brut.* 42).
For Cicero, historical poetry conveyed certain ethical, cultural truths even if it
did not meet the standard of the historians.

Cicero was certainly aware that Ennius had taken certain poetic licenses
which affected the "historicity" of the *Annales*. But from Cicero's perspective, Ennius shared this quality with the famous historians. In the *De
Divinatione* (2.115–116), Cicero, in the role of a sceptical Academic, accuses
Herodotus and Ennius alike of introducing historical impossibilities, or at
least implausibilities:

> sed iam ad te uenio,
> *o sancte Apollo, qui umbilicum certum terrarum obsides,*   [*TrRF* I 77]
> *unde superstitiosa primum saeua euasit uox fera.*
> tuis enim oraculis Chrysippus totum uolumen impleuit partim falsis, ut ego
> opinor, partim casu ueris, ut fit in omni oratione saepissime; partim flex-
> iloquis[79] et obscuris, ut interpres egeat interprete, et sors ipsa ad sortes
> referenda sit; partim ambiguis, et quae ad dialecticum deferendae sint. nam
> cum illa sors edita est opulentissimo regi Asiae:
> *Croesus Halyn penetrans magnam peruertet opum uim.*   [Soubiran fr. viii]
> hostium uim se peruersurum putauit, peruertit autem suam.
> [2.116] utrum igitur eorum accidisset, uerum oraclum fuisset. cur autem hoc
> credam umquam editum Croeso? aut Herodotum cur ueraciorem ducam
> Ennio? num minus ille potuit de Croeso quam de Pyrrho fingere Ennius?
> quis enim est qui credat Apollinis ex oraculo Pyrrho esse responsum?
> *aio te, Aeacida, Romanos uincere posse.*   [Skutsch 167]
> primum Latine Apollo numquam locutus est; deinde ista sors inaudita
> Graecis est; praeterea Pyrrhi temporibus iam Apollo uersus facere desierat;
> postremo, quamquam semper fuit, ut apud Ennium est,
>   *stolidum genus Aeacidarum,*   [Skutsch 197–198]

---

[77] On this passage, see Walbank 1955: 13n58, Brunt 1979: 331–332, Wiseman 1979: 31–32, Fornara 1983:
136n57, Woodman 1988: 116.
[78] The association here of Coriolanus with Themistocles (*Brut.* 42) also appears at *Att.* 9.10.3, and *De
Am.* 42. Livy (2.35) dated Coriolanus' exile to 491 BCE.
[79] Cf. "*uersutiloquas*" ("twisty-speaking") quoted at *De Or.* 3.154, *Or.* 164 (= *TrRF* I 19).

bellipotentes sunt magis quam sapientipotentes
tamen hanc amphiboliam uersus intellegere potuisset, "*uincere te Romanos*"
nihilo magis in se quam in Romanos ualere; nam illa amphibolia quae
Croesum decepit, uel Chrysippum potuisset fallere, haec uero ne Epicurum
quidem!

But now I come to you,
"*Oh sacred Apollo, you who set your eye upon the fixed navel of the earth,
whence first escaped the prophetic, wild voice.*"
Chrysippus filled up a whole volume with your oracles, some of them false,
as I think, some of them true but only by coincidence, as often happens with
regular speech; some so twisty-speaking and inscrutable, that their interpreter needs an interpreter, and the oracles must be returned to the oracle;
some of them so equivocal that they need to be brought to the dialectician.
When the oracle was given to the richest king of Asia:
"*Croesus crossing over the Halys will destroy the mighty power of an empire.*"
He thought that he would destroy his enemy's empire but instead he
destroyed his own. [2.116] But the oracle would have been true either way!
Why should I even believe that this oracle was ever given to Croesus? Why,
for that matter, should I consider Herodotus more truthful than Ennius?
Was Herodotus really less able to invent things about Croesus than Ennius
was with Pyrrhus? Who is there who believes that this was the response to
Pyrrhus from Apollo's oracle?
"*I say that you, son of Aeacus, are able to conquer the Romans.*"
First of all, Apollo never spoke Latin. Next, the Greeks have never heard of
this oracle. Additionally, by the time of Pyrrhus, Apollo had long since
stopped making verses. Lastly, although the "*race of Aeacus*" was always, as it
is in Ennius, "*slow of mind, more powerful in war than powerful in intellect*"
nonetheless, Pyrrhus could have understood the ambiguity of the verse;
namely that "*you . . . the Romans conquer*" – has no less force against himself
than it does against the Romans. The ambiguity which deceived Croesus
might well have been able to fool Chrysippus, but not even Epicurus would
be tricked by this one!

Cicero's hostility to literary sources in *De Divinatione* Book 2 is part of a
careful construction of an Academic persona brought into conflict with the
Stoic practice of using literature as evidence of its philosophical system.
Cicero as Academic in the *De Divinatione* (2.80) said: *nihil debet esse in
philosophia commenticiis fabellis loci*, "contrived stories should have no
place in philosophy."[80] As a result, all of the verse quotations in *De*

---

[80] At *Div.* 2.112 Cicero repeats the citations of Ennius (*TrRF* II 151) which Quintus had made (*Div.*
1.67; 1.114), and comments: *num igitur me cogis etiam fabulis credere? . . . auctoritatem quidem nullam
debemus nec fidem commenticiis rebus adiungere*, "Are you really forcing me to believe in these stories?
. . . we should not attach authority or faith to these contrived things." However, Cicero in his own

Divinatione Book 2 are deliberately chosen to undercut Quintus' argument, ironically and effectively turning the Stoic citational method against him.[81] Indeed, Cicero (*Div.* 2.104) quotes a passage of Ennius' *Telamo*, part of which had been cited by Quintus (*Div.* 1.132; *TrRF* II 117), to undermine Quintus' prime Stoic argument – that the gods care for mankind:[82]

> primum enim hoc sumitis: si sunt di, benefici in homines sunt. quis hoc uobis dabit? Epicurusne? qui negat quicquam deos nec alieni curare nec sui. an noster Ennius? qui magno plausu loquitur assentiente populo:
> *ego deum genus esse semper dixi et dicam caelitum,*   [*TrRF* II 117]
> *sed eos non curare opinor, quid agat humanum genus.*
> et quidem cur sic opinetur rationem subicit; sed nihil est necesse dicere quae sequuntur;[83] tantum sat est intellegi, id sumere istos pro certo, quod dubium controuersum sit.

> You start with this proposition: if there are gods, they show goodwill to mankind. Who will grant you this? Epicurus, who says that the gods do not care about themselves or anyone else? Or our Ennius, who speaks to great applause from the people in support of his position?
> *"I always said that the race of celestial gods exists, and I will always say so,*
> *but I believe that they do not care about what happens to the human race."*
> And indeed, he includes why he believes so, but I do not need to say the lines which follow. It is enough to understand that what the Stoics take as certain is actually a subject of doubt and discussion.

The criticism of the implausibility of Ennius' *Annales* in the *De Divinatione* (2.115–116) therefore arises from the perspective of an

---

voice had quoted this very play in a letter to Atticus (*Att.* 8.11.3; Feb. 49 BCE), in which he compared himself to the dramatic speaker, Cassandra, and, like her, he foretells "an *Iliad* of evils" (*malorum* Ἰλιάς).

[81] At *Div.* 2.45 Cicero dismisses his brother's citation of his own *De Consulatu Suo* (Soubiran fr. ii) at *Div.* 1.19; at *Div.* 2.82 Cicero quotes a translated verse of *Iliad* 9.236, which describes Jupiter thundering "on the right" (Cicero: *his dextris*; Homer: ἐνδέξια σήματα), in order to contradict Ennius' *Annales* (Skutsch 541): *tum tonuit laeum*, "then Jupiter thundered on the left." Likewise, Cotta in *De Natura Deorum* Book 3, in response to Balbus' Stoic citations, quotes verses which undercut the Stoic thesis: *ND* 3.10 and 3.40 repeat Ennius' *Thyestes* (*TrRF* II 134) quoted at *ND* 2.4 and 2.65; *ND* 3.40 alludes to Achilles' famous criticism of astrologers in Ennius' *Iphigenia* (*TrRF* II 82; also quoted at *Div.* 2.57) in response to Balbus' extensive citation of Cicero's *Aratea* (1.110–114); at *ND* 3.72 verses from Caecilius' *Synephebi* are said to be argued using "the Academic method" (*Academicorum more*); verses spoken by tragedy's villains are cited as examples of perverted *ratio* (*ND* 3.65–75).

[82] *Div.* 1.10: *mihi uero, inquit, satis est argumenti et esse deos et eos consulere rebus humanis*, "'It is enough,' Quintus said, 'for my argument that the gods exist and that they care about human affairs'"; cf. *ND* 2.4: *consulere eos rebus humanis*.

[83] The Academic Cotta had cited the verse here omitted (*ND* 3.79; *TrRF* II 117): *nam si curent, bene bonis sit, male malis; quod nunc abest*, "for if they cared, good men would prosper, bad men suffer; this is not the case now." On *nosti quae sequuntur* and similar phrases, see p23.

artificially constructed cynicism, and should not be taken as a program-matic statement of Cicero's stance on Ennius' perceived historicity. Indeed, what the passage comparing oracles in Herodotus and Ennius shows is that Ennius' *Annales* was considered to exist in the same category as the classic historians who wrote in prose.[84] Similarly, during the debate in the *De Legibus* (1.4) on the historicity of Cicero's epic poem, the *Marius*, Herodotus and Theopompus are cited as writers of histories which contain "numerous fabulous tales" (*innumerabiles fabulae*). Although their accounts contained material which strained belief, their status as historical narrative is not automatically invalidated by that fact.

Cicero, trained in the rhetorical tradition which armed advocates to make alternative interpretations of real events, understood that different kinds of narrative had different relationships to truthfulness, historicity, or plausibility.[85] In the *De Inventione* (1.27), Cicero had illustrated the rela-tionships of different kinds of "narrative" (*narratio*) to the truth with examples from tragedy, epic, and comedy:

> fabula est in qua nec uerae nec ueri similes res continentur, cuiusmodi est:
> *angues ingentes alites iuncti iugo ...*   [Pacuvius' *Medus* Schierl fr. 171]
> historia est gesta res, ab aetatis nostrae memoria remota, quod genus:
> *Appius indixit Karthaginiensibus bellum.*   [Ennius' *Annales* Skutsch 216]
> argumentum est ficta res, quae tamen fieri potuit, huiusmodi apud
> Terentium:
> *nam is postquam excessit ex ephebis ...*   [Terence's *Andria* 51]
>
> *Fabula* is the term applied to a narrative in which the events are not true and
> have no verisimilitude, for example:
> *"Huge winged dragons yoked to a car ..."*
> *Historia* is an account of actual occurrences remote from the recollection of
> our own age, as:
> *"War on men of Carthage Appius decreed."*
> *Argumentum* is a fictitious narrative which nevertheless could have occurred.
> An example from Terence:
> *"For after he had left the school of youth ... "*

---

[84] Elliott 2013: 192: "Paradoxically, even as Cicero highlights the fictitiousness of the incidents Ennius and Herodotus relate, he builds on and thus strengthens the basic assumption that what they say represents a truthworthy account of an historical reality."

[85] *Narratio* in the courtroom was the advocate's version of the events at stake in the case. The *narratio* was required to be "like the truth" (*uerisimilis, De Or.* 2.80) and "believable" (*credibilis, Or.* 124). It was not to be conveyed in "the style of history" (*nec historico, Or.* 124), but in everyday speech, which would likely increase the feeling of organic verisimilitude. On the relationship of rhetorical *narratio* and historiography, see Woodman 1988: 83–88.

In the youthful *De Inventione,* which drew uncynically from contemporary thought, Ennius' *Annales* is cited as the exemplar for "historical narrative" (*historia*) describing a "real event" (*gesta res*) which happened a long time ago; in this case, Appius Claudius Caudex (cos. 264 BCE) formally beginning the First Punic War.[86] Even though the *Annales* contained fabulous elements, it nonetheless appears as an authoritative account of events which "really happened."

5.5   Poetic Authority

However, Cicero was less invested in the idea of poetry as a faithful historical record than he was interested in its power to augment and elevate the historical figures whom it represented. In the *De Legibus* (1.2), Cicero had his brother, Quintus, claim an immortalizing power to one of Cicero's own historical epics, the *Marius*:[87]

> nisi forte Athenae tuae sempiternam in arce oleam tenere potuerunt, aut, quod Homericus Ulixes Deli se proceram et teneram palmam uidisse dixit, hodie monstrant eandem; multaque alia multis locis diutius commemoratione manent quam natura stare potuerant. quare
> *glandifera*   [Soubiran fr. i]
> illa quercus, ex qua olim euolauit
> *nuntia fulua Iouis miranda uisa figura*   [Soubiran fr. ii]
> nunc sit haec. sed cum eam tempestas uetustasue consumpserit, tamen erit his in locis quercus, quam Marianam quercum uocabunt.

> Unless you think your Athens has been able to eternally preserve the olive tree on the acropolis, or that the tall and slender palm tree which the Homeric Ulixes said he had seen on Delos is the same one which they show there today. Many other things in many places remain longer in the memory than they are allowed to do in reality. That is why the

---

[86] For discussion of the apparent inconsistency between *Inv.* 1.27's quotation of Ennius' *Annales* (Skutsch 216), a reference to the beginning of the First Punic War, and *Brut.* 76, where Cicero (citing Skutsch 206–207) claims that Ennius "passed over" (*reliquisset*) the First Punic War, see Skutsch 1985: 385–386. Elliott (2013: 61) notes that whatever *reliquisset* may mean, *Brut.* 76 is evidence "that Ennius was highly selective in what he treated."

[87] On *Leg.* 1.1–5, see Woodman 1988: 98–101, Feeney 1991: 258–260, Wiseman 2002: 339–340, Henderson 2004a: 166–168, Fox 2007: 141–144, Elliott 2013: 202–205. On Cicero's *Marius*, see Soubiran 1972: 42–50, Courtney 2003: 174–178, Gee 2013a: 98–101. It is a point of some significance that when Cicero quotes the augury passage from his *Marius* at *De Div.* 1.106 (= Soubiran fr. iii), it is there (*Div.* 1.107–108) paired with the Romulus and Remus augury from Ennius' *Annales* (Skutsch 72–91); see Goldberg 1995: 157. Such juxtaposition clearly demonstrates that Cicero considered the *Annales* to be a prototype for his own epic; and, of course, that he wished his own poems to be inscribed into the poetic canon: cf. *Or.* 152 where Cicero cites Ennius' *Scipio* (Goldberg-Manuwald F3) alongside his own *Aratea* (Soubiran fr. xxiii) to exemplify hiatus.

"acorn-bearing"
oak, out of which once flew
"the tawny messenger of Jupiter, a miraculous sight to see"
may be this one. But when time and old age have destroyed this oak,
nonetheless there will be an oak here, which they will call the Marian oak.

Quintus argues that foundation myths (Athena's olive tree in Athens) and
literature (Odysseus in *Odyssey* 6.162–163) alike, though "fictional" (in
different ways and to different extents), nonetheless exert a powerful
force on the landscape of cultural memory. Atticus, again playing the
role of historian, responds (*Leg.* 1.3) by asking Cicero if the eagle did
actually appear to Marius (*ita factum*), as Cicero had described it, or
whether the scene was a purely poetic invention. Cicero responds that
certain stories which are "handed down" (*est traditum, Leg.* 1.3) would not
stand up to Atticus' historical test.[88] All of the tales named by Cicero
appeared in Ennius' *Annales*: Romulus' apotheosis (*Leg.* 1.3); Numa and
the nymph, Egeria (*Leg.* 1.4); the eagle placing the cap on Tarquinius
Priscus' head (*Leg.* 1.4).[89] Although Cicero goes on (*Leg.* 1.5) to say that
the aim of history is to present "truth" (*ueritas*), while poetry is "mostly"
(*pleraque*[90]) for entertainment, the dramatic exchange between Quintus,
Atticus, and Cicero actually implies a greater significance for poetry.[91]
Cicero's *Marius* created an image of the Roman general so powerful that
it would persist long after ravages of "time" (*uetustas*) had destroyed its
historical referent. As a result, questions of historicity fade away in the face
of the persistent image of Marius.

The poetic power to grant persistence is most regularly the aspect of
Ennius which Cicero invoked. In the *Tusculans* (1.34), Cicero used Ennius'

---

[88] Atticus (*Leg.* 1.4) is asking for truth as though he were cross-examining a witness in a courtcase (*a teste*), not a poet (*a poeta*); cf. *De Or.* 2.62 where history is called the "witness" (*testis*) of truth, on which see Brunt 1979: 311–322, Dyck 2004: 68, Elliott 2013: 204.

[89] Zillinger 1911: 102 takes *Leg.* 1.4 as a reference to Ennius' *Annales*. Romulus' apotheosis was dramatized in Ennius' *Annales* (Skutsch 110 = *TD* 1.28, *De Or.* 3.154); the nymph Egeria is named in a fragment of the *Annales* (Skutsch 113); on the interpretation of a fragment (Skutsch 146) as a reference to the eagle lifting and replacing Tarquin's hat, see Skutsch 1985: 301–302.

[90] On the importance of *pleraque*, see Wiseman 2002: 340.

[91] It is not quite the case, as Elliott (2013: 192) writes, that Cicero here "is made to assume that the distinction ... between an historical object or act and its literary representation is not significant." Atticus' essential suggestion here is that there *is* a truthful version of history (whether or not that is captured by poetry); for Quintus and Cicero, however, the truth of history is a piece of trivia compared to the lasting impact of the cultural object which poetry creates. The Marian oak lives on whether or not there ever was one; the tales of early Roman history live on despite their suspect "historicity."

epitaphs as evidence of the human desire for glory as a kind of life after death:

> loquor de principibus, quid poetae? nonne post mortem nobilitari uolunt? unde ergo illud?
> *aspicite, o ciues, senis Enni imaginis formam:* [Goldberg-Manuwald F2a, 1–2]
> *hic uestrum panxit maxuma facta patrum*
> mercedem gloriae flagitat ab iis quorum patres adfecerat gloria. idemque:
> *nemo me lacrimis decoret nec funera fletu* [Goldberg-Manuwald F2a, 3–4]
> *faxit. cur? uolito uiuos per ora uirum*
> sed quid poetas? opifices post mortem nobilitari uolunt. quid enim Phidias sui similem speciem inclusit in clipeo Mineruae, cum inscribere non liceret? quid nostri philosophi? nonne in iis libris ipsis, quos scribunt de contemnenda gloria, sua nomina inscribunt?

> I speak about leading men, but what about poets? Do they not want to be known after death? What about this?
> *"Look, o citizens, on the form of the image of old Ennius:*
> *he opened up the greatest deeds of your fathers."*
> He demands the reward of glory from those whose fathers he gave glory. The same poet writes:
> *"Let none embellish me with their tears nor a funeral*
> *with their weeping make. Why? I fly, alive, on the lips of men."*
> But why just poets? Artists want to be known after death. For why did Pheidias insert his likeness on the shield of Minerva, though not allowed to inscribe his name on it? What about philosophers? Do they not write their names on the very books they write about contempt of glory?

When Cicero tried to convince the historian, L. Lucceius to write a history of his own achievements (*Fam.* 5.12.4), he emphasized that it was not solely the hope of immortality which motivated him, but the fact that Cicero would be praised with the "authority of Lucceius' testimony" (*auctoritate testimoni, Fam.* 5.12.1). That is, the *ethos* of the man rendered into textual form – whether prose history or historical epic – was augmented by the *ethos* of the author. Indeed, Cicero sought from Lucceius, using the austere words of Naevius, to be "praised by a praised man" (*laudari ... a laudato uiro, Fam.* 5.12.7; *TrRF* I 14). That a poet or a historian might render a Roman statesman immortal with his words was therefore only one part of the equation; authoritative praise by a distinguished literary personality was just as important, as this created substantive evidence of the statesman's true worth. Cicero's inability to attract the historian, Lucceius, or the poet, Archias,[92]

---

[92] In the *Pro Archia*, Cicero represented Archias as a modern day Ennius, asserting that the Syrian poet's ties to Roman statesmen and generals (*Arch.* 6), presented a parallel to Ennius' association

was a source of embarrassment because it meant that Cicero could not have his own image externally verified, reflected in a textual artefact which stood as concrete evidence of his reputation.[93] In the *De Officiis* (1.77–78), Cicero discussed the poem which he himself wrote on his consulship, treating the epic as a concrete substantiation of his legacy:

> illud autem optimum est, in quod inuadi solere ab improbis et inuidis audio:
> *cedant arma togae, concedat laurea laudi.*   [Soubiran fr. vi]
> ut enim alios omittam, nobis rem publicam gubernantibus nonne togae arma cesserunt? . . . [1.78] licet enim mihi, M. fili, apud te gloriari, ad quem et hereditas huius gloriae et factorum imitatio pertinet.

> But this is the best maxim, although I hear that it is the habit of shameful and jealous men to attack it:
> "*Let arms yield to the toga; to praise the laurel.*"
> to leave out other cases, did not arms yield to the toga when we were guiding the state? . . . [1.78] For I can have pride with you, my son, to whom both the inheritance of this pride and the imitation of the deeds belong.

While the poem itself had been criticized, as Cicero admits here,[94] the record which epic created is figured as a lasting memory, one which is to be kept alive and emulated by Cicero's son, Marcus. Cicero's *gloria* is, in theory, validated via its epic representation, and this poetic image is figured by Cicero as the "inheritance" (*hereditas*) passed from father to son. It is not a line of the Catilinarian orations which Cicero presents as an icon of his consulship, but *cedant arma togae* – a verse which elevates the events of 63 BCE from a series of mere political struggles into a greater narrative with moral potency.

Poetry therefore constituted a "historical" record to the extent that it captured evidence of the reputations of historical figures, and, indeed, augmented those reputations by providing a persistent image more powerful than texts which those men may themselves have produced. In the *Brutus*, Cicero had demonstrated the importance of reputation above all other evidence: Servius Sulpicius Galba (cos. 144 BCE) is described as

---

with the great men whom he praised in his poetry (*Arch.* 20; 27). According to Cicero, Archias began a poem on the Cimbric War as a young man, which pleased Marius (*Arch.* 19); he wrote more than one book (*libri*) on the Mithridatic War, which praised Lucullus (*Arch.* 21); and at the time of the trial, Archias had begun a poem on Cicero's consulship (*Arch.* 28), which, infamously, never materialized (*Att.* 1.16.15), see Steel 2001: 83, Dugan 2005: 47, Čulík-Baird 2020.

[93] On negative reception of Cicero's poetry, see Gee 2013a, Bishop 2018.

[94] In the *In Pisonem* (72–74), Cicero schools Piso for his criticism of *cedant arma togae*; see Dyck 1996: 209, Dugan 2005: 62.

"preeminently eloquent without controversy" (*sine controuersia Ser. Galba eloquentia praestitit, Brut.* 82), but, despite his preeminent reputation, his surviving orations are "rather meagre" (*exiliores, Brut.* 82), and not, in fact, better than those left behind by his contemporaries, Laelius, Scipio, or Cato.[95] That Galba was *thought* to be eloquent is itself evidence, perhaps even better evidence, of his eloquence than his surviving speeches. Similarly, despite the fact that the speech of Appius Claudius (censor 312 BCE) apparently still survived (*Brut.* 61),[96] Cicero turned instead to Ennius' version in the *De Senectute* (16):[97]

> ad Appi Claudi senectutem accedebat etiam ut caecus esset; tamen is cum sententia senatus inclinaret ad pacem cum Pyrrho foedusque faciendum, non dubitauit dicere illa quae uersibus persecutus est Ennius:
> *quo uobis mentes, rectae quae stare solebant*   [Skutsch 199–200]
> *antehac, dementes sese flexere †uia?*
> cetera grauissime;[98] notum enim uobis carmen est, et tamen ipsius Appi exstat oratio.

> In addition to his old age, Appius Claudius was also blind. Nonetheless, when the opinion of the senate was leaning towards making a peace treaty with Pyrrhus, he did not hesitate to speak these words which Ennius rendered[99] in verse:
> "*down what road* (?) *have your senses, which before used to stand upright, wandered off senseless.*"[100]
> And the rest, so impressively put; for you know this poem well,[101] and, anyway, Appius' speech still survives.

Ennius' version of Appius' speech to the senate following Roman defeat at the hands of Pyrrhus was evidently a more powerful example for Cicero to draw upon because it enshrined a vision of the censorious figure's persuasive

---

[95] Servius Galba also appears as an *exemplum* of supreme eloquence in *De Or.* 1.54.

[96] On the prose version of this speech which circulated among the historiographers, see Elliott 2013: 161n81 and bibliography there cited.

[97] On this passage, see Elliott 2013: 160–163.

[98] *Cetera* here acts as an equivalent for *nosti quae sequuntur;* see p23.

[99] In the context of historical inquiry, Cicero uses *sequor* and *persequor* to refer to following a trusted historical authority (*Brut.* 72: *post Romam conditam autem quartodecimo et quingentensimo, ut hic ait, quem nos sequimur,* "five hundred and fourteen years after the foundation of Rome according to the authority whom I follow"), or else the careful study of chronology (*Rep.* 1.29: *eos qui diligentissime persecuti sunt temporum annales,* "those who have made careful study of the annalistic records").

[100] On the text of Skutsch 199–200, see p33n10.

[101] A variation on *nosti quae sequuntur;* see p23.

power into common memory.[102] The real text of Appius' speech was
evidence that the event had taken place, but Ennius' rendering of the speech
was evidence of the importance of the event within the epic narrative of the
Roman saga. For Cicero, this kind of subjective historiography, which
elevated certain moments over others, held greater significance than the
"objective" historical narratives which interested Atticus. As a powerful
engine of cultural memory, Ennius' *Annales* defined the canonical moments
of Roman history. Some kinds of evidence might have proved that certain
events had happened; Ennius' *Annales* proved that certain selected events
mattered.

In the *Brutus* (57–60), Cicero finds the beginning of documented
Roman oratory not in the ancient extant orations, but in the epic poem
of Ennius' *Annales*:[103]

> quem uero exstet et de quo sit memoriae proditum eloquentem fuisse et ita
> esse habitum, primus est M. Cornelius Cethegus, cuius eloquentiae est
> auctor et idoneus quidem mea sententia Q. Ennius, praesertim cum et ipse
> eum audiuerit et scribat de mortuo; ex quo nulla suspicio est amicitiae causa
> esse mentitum. [58] est igitur sic apud illum in nono, ut opinor, annali:
> *additur orator Cornelius suauiloquenti*   [Skutsch 304–306]
> *ore Cethegus Marcus Tuditano collega*
> *Marci filius*
> et oratorem appellat et suauiloquentiam tribuit, quae nunc quidem non tam
> est in plerisque: latrant enim iam quidam oratores, non loquuntur; sed est ea
> laus eloquentiae certe maxuma:
>   *is dictust ollis popularibus olim,*   [Skutsch 306–308]
> *qui tum uiuebant homines atque aeuum agitabant,*
> *flos delibatus populi*
> [59] probe uero; ut enim hominis decus ingenium, sic ingeni ipsius lumen
> est eloquentia, qua uirum excellentem praeclare tum illi homines florem
> populi esse dixerunt:
> *suadai medulla.*   [Skutsch 308]
> ... [60] et id ipsum nisi unius esset Enni testimonio cognitum, hunc
> uetustas, ut alios fortasse multos, obliuione obruisset.

Cethegus is the first extant example of Roman eloquence, the first for whom
it is recorded that he was eloquent and that he was considered so. The
witness of Cethegus' eloquence – in my opinion a fitting one – was Quintus

[102] Appius Claudius dissuading the senate from making peace with Pyrrhus is the most frequently
mentioned event of his life; see Powell 1988: 136: *Ph.* 1.11, *Brut.* 61; Plut. *Pyrrhus* 19; *An seni* 794e;
Val. Max. 8.13.5; Sen. *Ep.* 114.13; Tac. *Dial.* 18.4; 21.7; [Livy] *Periocha* 13.6; Quint. *Inst.* 2.16.7.
Ennius' depiction of Pyrrhus was particularly influential on Lucretius, see Nethercut 2021: 95–101.
[103] On Ennius' *auctoritas*, see Goldberg 2005: 40.

Ennius, especially since he actually heard him speak while he was alive, but wrote about him when he was dead, removing the suggestion that he altered his account because of their connection. This is how Ennius describes him in, I think, Book 9 of the *Annales*:

"The orator, Cornelius Cethegus, with lips
of sweet speech, is added as a colleague to
Tuditanus, son of Marcus."

Ennius both calls Cethegus an "*orator*" and he attributes "*sweet speech*" to him, a quality which very few have even now, for the orators, such as they are, bark, they do not "speak." The praise of his eloquence is certainly great:

"He was called then by each and every one
who was then alive and living out the age,
the choice flower of the people."

[59] Well said indeed. For as inborn talent is man's glory, so is eloquence the lamp of talent. It is for Cethegus' excellence in eloquence that the men of that time rightly called such a man, the flower of the people:

"the marrow of persuasion."

. . . [60] If the knowledge of his eloquence were not known to us by the sole testimony of Ennius, time would have consigned him to oblivion as it has doubtless many others.

In the figure of Cethegus, Cicero says, the Romans could see oratory valued for the first time in their history. Ennius' *Annales* contained the first extant use of the word *orator* with the meaning which Cicero and his contemporaries understood it to have, with the fullest sense of persuasive, intellectual, and ethical capability. Varro (*LL* 7.41) notes that there was a time in the earlier period when the word *orator* had only the meaning of "envoy," using Ennius' *Annales* as evidence:

apud Ennium:
orator sine pace redit regique refert rem.   [Skutsch 202]
orator dictus ab oratione: qui enim uerba haberet publice aduersus eum quo legabatur, ab oratione orator dictus; cum res †maiore ratione, legebantur potissimum qui causam commodissime orare poterant. itaque Ennius ait:
oratores doctiloqui.   [Skutsch 593]

In Ennius:
"The orator returned without peace and conveyed the matter to the king."
"*Orator*," i.e. "speaker" is derived from "speech": the one who has words publicly before the man to whom he was sent as an envoy, it is from this kind of speech that he is named "*orator*." When the matter was more serious, the most capable men were sent as envoys because they were able to speak on the issue best. And so, Ennius says:
"Orators learned in speech."

While these envoys, Varro argues, are sent precisely because of their oratorical capabilities, they are not yet the political figures recognizable to late Republican Romans. In the *Brutus,* then, Cicero has pin-pointed the moment in history when the modern Roman consciousness comes online and the term *"orator"* takes on a new definition. In this moment of redefinition, the Roman orator appears for the first time with specific characteristics: not only is he *suauiloquens* ("sweet-speaking," Skutsch 304);[104] but, crucially, he is *praised* for his eloquence: the Roman people call Cethegus *flos delibatus* ("choice flower," Skutsch 308) and *suadai medulla* ("the marrow of persuasion," Skutsch 308). Cicero is not interested in Cethegus solely because of his talent, but because his talent is recognized. Within the narrative of Ennius' poem, the poetic characters praise Cethegus; outside of the narrative, Ennius' authorial decision to elaborate upon the moment is evidence of its historical and cultural significance.

Cicero also explicitly reflects upon the power and veracity of Ennius' account as historical testimony. Ennius' account of Cethegus' eloquence is, Cicero argues, especially trustworthy because the poet "actually heard him" (*ipse eum audiuerit, Brut.* 57), i.e. Ennius was an "eye"-witness.[105] Since Ennius wrote after the consul's death, there was also "no suspicion that he distorted the record because of their friendship" (*nulla suspicio est amicitiae causa esse mentitum, Brut.* 57). Unlike Roman prose historiography, with its tendency to bloat the praise of famous Romans due its reliance upon funerary orations (*Brut.* 61–62), Ennius could, according to Cicero, present a vision of history untainted by political preference, or, at least, untainted by the political perspective with which Cicero himself disagreed.[106] It is significant, too, that Cicero calls Ennius the "author" (*auctor*) of Cethegus' eloquence: Ennius is not only an "author," i.e. the "writer" of these verses, but also the "authorizer" of Cethegus' eloquence.[107] Just as Cicero (*De Sen.* 16) had turned to Ennius' version of Appius Claudius' speech instead of the speech itself, here Cicero sees Ennius as a faithful author of Roman eloquence in the simultaneity of his testimony and the descriptive craft of his poesis. Finally, just as Cicero relied upon Lucilius (*Brut.* 160) to

[104] *Rep.* 5.11.2 where Cicero calls Menelaus *suauiloquens.*
[105] Elliott (2013: 158): "[Cicero] suggests that the quality of Ennius' narrative and the reason to trust it lie in the author's autoptic (or rather aut-otic!) relationship to his subject matter."
[106] Ennius did, of course, praise famous Romans preferentially, and Cicero celebrated this (e.g. *Arch.* 22).
[107] On *auctoritas*, authority, and authorship, see Guastella 2017: 125–135.

preserve the record of Crassus' oratorical career, Cicero emphasizes
Ennius' role in the conservation of Roman history (*Brut.* 60):

> et id ipsum nisi unius esset Enni testimonio cognitum, hunc uetustas, ut
> alios fortasse multos, obliuione obruisset.

> If the knowledge of his eloquence were not known to us by the sole
> testimony of Ennius, time would have consigned him to oblivion as it has
> doubtless many others.

Without Ennius' account, Cicero says, *uetustas* ("time") would have destroyed the memory of Roman eloquence, consigning it to oblivion. Like
Lucilius, Ennius had the power to preserve moments of deep significance
and to testify to their significance in the act of preservation.

Cicero's engagement with Latin poetry was therefore historically
minded to the extent that it fulfilled Cicero's own desire to have contact
with a world of Rome that was slowly receding from him. Cicero's nostal-
gia for the periods represented by Ennius and Lucilius was certainly not
motivated by a sense of historical "objectivity" (to the extent such an ideal
is even attainable), since Cicero did not particularly care about objectivity.
Orators, in Cicero's own words (*Brut.* 42), were allowed to "distort history"
(*ementiri*). Indeed, it was precisely the subjectivity of the poetry preserving
snapshots of the Roman past which interested him, in line with the
Naevian maxim that it was honourable "to be praised by a praised man"
(*laudari a laudato uiro*).[108] The Roman poets augmented and authorized
events and characters of the Roman past by enshrining them in their own
work.

---

[108] *TrRF* I 14.

Envoi

In *The Sociology of Philosophies* (1998), Randall Collins describes the power of the sanctified text in intellectual discourse:[1]

> This, then is the intellectual ritual. Intellectuals gather, focus their attention for a time on one of their members, who delivers a sustained discourse. That discourse itself builds on elements from the past, affirming and continuing or negating. Old sacred objects, previously charged up, are recharged with attention, or degraded from their sacredness and expelled from the life of the community; new candidate sacred objects are offered for sanctification. By reference to texts past and texts future, the intellectual community keeps up the consciousness of its projects, transcending all particular occasions on which they were enacted. Hence the peculiar guiding sacred object – truth, wisdom, sometimes also the activity of seeking or researching – as both eternal and embodied in the flow of time.

Elements of the past, interwoven, annotated, redefined, are threaded into the Ciceronian corpus via the citation of Latin poets from prior generations. The quotation of these poets not only allowed Cicero to link his own work and life to the past, but also imbued his own text with greater significance. The poet is an authorizing figure for Cicero, but Cicero also authorizes the poet via invocation. It is from this mutual reinforcement that the citation of poetry takes its essential power: poetry is reactivated and given greater meaning due to Cicero's insistence of its potency. Cicero's commitment to the significance of poetry in Roman life and thought also manifests a single instance of a broader cultural consciousness. According to Collins' framework, the focus of the group may rest, for a time, on the performance of a single individual, but the act is, at its core, initiated by the community. Cicero's sustained engagement with Roman poems identifies them as "sacred objects" of Republican life, charging and recharging them with every return.

---

[1] Collins 1998: 28.

Poetry symbolically reflects reality, and acts as a preservative substance. As an ethical, aesthetic, historic artefact, old Latin poetry guided late Republican thought, and presented itself as an authoritative text. Within its own context, such "text," according to Hayden White, was "an entity that once had an assuring solidity and concreteness, indeed a kind of identity that allowed it to serve as a model of whatever was comprehensible in both culture and nature."[2] Latin poetry's significance in the Roman consciousness is affirmed by the degree to which it permeated Cicero's own textual corpus: wherever Cicero's own thoughts roamed, Latin verse was there as a touchstone or guide, offering a reassuring sense of continuity. Absorbed to such a degree, Latin poetry reentered the community in Cicero's own authoritative utterances, filtered through the words and ideas of a cherished past. Materiality of text and power of performance each impacted Cicero's vision of poetry: words found in books, studied by mentors, guided Cicero's own intellectual practice; yet, he also experienced those same words, given electric new life on the Roman stage, in emotive, embodied forms. Cicero's encounters with poetry were entangled with so many discrete parts of his intellectual life that he was able to see the same verses from different angles: theorization and study of Latin poetry which took place in one part of the corpus expressed itself in a fully persuasive capability in another; verse taken as an expression of deeply personal emotions in one context appears in another with a purely analytical capacity. The deep connection between poetry and the notion of "Latinity" ensured Cicero's dependence upon earlier Latin verse as the definitive lexicon of Roman expression.

Cicero's engagement with the Latin poets in many ways demonstrates the primacy of their position in the consciousness of late Republic Rome, and by embedding choice excerpts, he ensured the memory of that primacy by his own textual survival, even when the original poems themselves faded away. By enshrining the voices of the poets in his own corpus, Cicero exerted a canonizing focus upon them which influenced his own future readers. Seneca (*Ep.* 108.34) demonstrates how the Latin poets were read by subsequent Romans through a Ciceronian frame:

> esse enim apud Ciceronem in his ipsis de re publica hoc epigramma Enni
> *si fas endo plagas caelestum ascendere cuiquam est,*   [Goldberg-
> *mi soli caeli maxima porta patet.*   Manuwald F3b]

---

[2] White 1990: 186.

For there is an Ennian epigram in the same book of Cicero's *De Republica*:
"If it is right for anyone to ascend to the realms of the gods,
for me alone that great gate lies open."

By quoting Ennius from Cicero's *De Republica*, Seneca in fact preserved a passage of the Ciceronian work which does not otherwise exist. Subsequent Latin writers continued to quote Latin poetry because Cicero had done so first. Quintilian (*Inst.* 11.3.31) invoked Cicero's reading of Ennius' *Annales* in the *Brutus* (57–60) for his own definition of eloquence:

ita fiet illud quod Ennius probat cum dicit
suauiloquenti ore   [Skutsch 304–305]
Cethegum fuisse, non quod Cicero in iis reprehendit quos ait latrare, non agere.

This is how to achieve what Ennius approves when he says that Cethegus had
"lips of sweet speech"
and to avoid what Cicero criticizes in those who, he says, don't plead, but bark.

Augustine (*Civ. Dei* 2.21), like Seneca, quoted Ennius through Cicero's *De Republica*:[3]

sicut etiam ipse Tullius non Scipionis nec cuiusquam alterius sed suo sermone loquens in principio quinti libri commemorato prius Ennii poetae uersu quo dixerat
moribus antiquis res stat Romana uirisque   [Skutsch 156]
quem quidem ille uersum, inquit, uel breuitate uel ueritate tamquam ex oraculo quodam mihi esse effatus uidetur.

Similarly, Cicero himself at the beginning of the fifth book speaks in his own person, and not in the person of Scipio or anyone else, when he quotes the line of Ennius:
"the Roman state stands in its ancient ways, and in its men"
and indeed this verse, he says, resembles the utterance of an oracle due to its pith and truth.

In time, Cicero would become the principal source for the Latin poets, and modern readers saw the old Latin poets through the eyes of Cicero.[4] That Cicero's survival ensured the fragmentary survival of the Latin poets is significant given the fact that Cicero drew on poetry for its power to confer

---

[3] In doing so Augustine, like Seneca, preserved an otherwise lost passage of Cicero's *De Republica*.
[4] Petrarch (*Fam.* 3.18.4): *Ennii nomen in Officiorum libris audivi,* "I heard Ennius' name in the *De Officiis.*"

immortality. In the *Tusculan Disputations* (1.34), Cicero approvingly quoted Ennius' epitaph:

> loquor de principibus, quid poetae? nonne post mortem nobilitari uolunt? unde ergo illud?
> *aspicite, o ciues, senis Enni imaginis formam:*   [Goldberg-Manuwald F2a, 1–2]
> *hic uestrum panxit maxuma facta patrum*
> mercedem gloriae flagitat ab iis quorum patres adfecerat gloria. idemque:
> *nemo me lacrimis decoret nec funera fletu*   [Goldberg-Manuwald F2a, 3–4]
> *faxit. cur? uolito uiuos per ora uirum.*

> I speak about leading men, but what about poets? Do they not want to be known after death? What about this?
> *"Look, o citizens, on the form of the image of old Ennius:*
> *he opened up the greatest deeds of your fathers."*
> He demands the reward of glory from those whose fathers he gave glory. The same poet writes:
> *"Let none embellish me with their tears nor a funeral*
> *with their weeping make. Why? I fly, alive, on the lips of men."*

Cicero obeyed Ennius' command to celebrate the glory of a poet who had glorified Roman ancestors, and did so by enshrining him alongside other Latin poets. Due to Cicero's deep interest in the old Latin poets, they continue to fly *per ora uirum*.

Note to Appendices

The following Appendices are based upon lists of Latin and Greek verse in the Ciceronian corpus compiled by Zillinger (1911) and Shackleton Bailey (1995, 1996), updated with cross-references to newer editions. On the editions of fragments here cited, see *Note on Editions of Fragments* (pxii) as well as the list of *Abbreviations* (ppxiii–xiv). Following Zillinger, I include not only "verbatim" quotations, but document a wide variety of different kinds of "reference": e.g. *Att.* 16.11.1 contains a reference to Lucilius' *Satires*, but not an explicit quotation; *De Or.* 1.154 contains a reference to Ennius as a person, but does not cite his poetry. Several fragments included in this list have contested attributions: e.g. *TD* 1.10 contains a verse which has been assigned either to Ennius' *Annales* or to Lucilius' *Satires*. In such cases, since my aim here is to document rather than to adjudicate, I give both available options. Given that Cicero's citational practices often render the quotation near invisible to modern eyes – e.g. the quotation of Ennius' *Achilles* at *Verr.* 2.1.46 (see p107) – there are many Ciceronian passages which seem to contain poetic quotation or reference but which cannot be confirmed with absolute certainty; I mark such tentative attributions with a question mark ("?"): e.g. the possible quotation of Ennius' *Annales* at *Planc.* 20 (see Zillinger 1911: 107). Many fragments contained within the Ciceronian corpus cannot be assigned to a particular poet or a particular work. While I have here collected these as fragments of "Unknown tragedy" or "Unknown comedy," according to attributions made by previous editors, many of the verses likely do not belong to the genre to which they have been assigned (see p20).

I would, finally, like to emphasize the fact that many of the attributions here documented are still open to contestation. By curating lists of perceptible verse quotations in the Ciceronian corpus, I mean to make these citations more visible and accessible to students and scholars as well as to emphasize their fundamental ubiquity, but not, necessarily, to endorse the unshakeable authority of these attributions. As I discuss in this book, attributions of fragments are always in flux, subject to new interpretations and assignments. I offer these Appendices as a roadmap to further examination of these fragments, and welcome future additions, revisions, and reassignments.

Appendix I By Ciceronian Work

Letters

Att. 1.1.4	Homer's *Iliad*	22.159
Att. 1.12.1	Menander	*Monostichoi* 726
Att. 1.15.1	Homer's *Iliad*	22.268
Att. 1.16.1	ref. to Homer	
Att. 1.16.1	Unknown comedy	Ribbeck 63
Att. 1.16.5	Homer's *Iliad*	16.112–113
Att. 1.16.13	ref. to *Faba* (mime)	Zillinger 1911: 157
Att. 1.16.15	ref. to Caecilius Statius	
Att. 1.18.1	Unknown tragedy	*TrRF* I 14
Att. 1.19.10	Greek proverb	*CPG* I p314
Att. 1.20.3	Euripides' *Telephus*/	Nauck fr. 723/
	Greek proverb	*CPG* I p307
Att. 1.20.3	Rhinthon?	Kaibel 1899: 189
Att. 2.1.5	Ennius' *Andromacha*?	*TrRF* II p86
Att. 2.3.4	Cicero's *De Consulatu Suo*	Soubiran fr. viii
Att. 2.3.4	Homer's *Iliad*	12.243
Att. 2.5.1	Homer's *Iliad*	22.105/6.442
Att. 2.5.1	Homer's *Iliad*	22.100
Att. 2.7.4	Sophocles' *Tympanistai*	Nauck fr. 579
Att. 2.8.1	Lucilius' *Saturae*	Warmington 610
Att. 2.9.3	Homer's *Iliad*	24.369
Att. 2.11.2	Homer's *Odyssey*	9.27–28
Att. 2.13.2	Homer's *Odyssey*	10.82
Att. 2.15.3	Ennius' *Annales*/	Skutsch *dub.* 5/
	Cicero: unknown work	Soubiran 1972: 300
Att. 2.16.2	Sophocles: unknown tragedy	Nauck fr. 701
Att. 2.16.4	Homer's *Iliad*	6.181
Att. 2.19.1	Terence's *Phormio*	232–233
Att. 2.19.2	Ennius' *Annales*	Skutsch 363
Att. 2.19.3	Unknown tragedy	*TrRF* I 15a
Att. 2.25.1	Euripides' *Andromache*	448
Att. 2.25.1	Euripides' *Phoenissae*	393
Att. 4.1.8	Unknown tragedy	*TrRF* I 160a
Att. 4.2.1	Unknown tragedy	*TrRF* I 160b
Att. 4.3.3	Unknown comedy	Ribbeck 71
Att. 4.6.2	Euripides' *Telephus*/	Nauck fr. 723/
	Greek proverb	*CPG* I p307

(*cont.*)

Att. 4.7.2	Homer's *Odyssey*	22.412
Att. 4.7.3	Homer's *Odyssey*	17.488/20.384
Att. 4.8.1	Sophocles' *Tyro*	Nauck fr. 601
Att. 4.8a.2	Unknown Greek comedy	Kock fr. 189
Att. 4.11.2	Menander	*Epitrepontes* fr. 2
Att. 4.15.6	ref. to Ennius' *Andromacha*	*TrRF* II T 18
Att. 4.15.7	Homer's *Iliad*/ *Odyssey*	23.326/ 11.126
Att. 5.10.3	Aristophanes' *Wasps?*	1431
Att. 5.11.5	Greek proverb	*CPG* II p44
Att. 5.12.1	Archilochus	Diehl fr. 56.2
Att. 5.15.3	Unknown comedy	Ribbeck 66–67
Att. 6.1.8	Euripides: unknown tragedy	Nauck fr. 918.3
Att. 6.1.22	Homer's *Iliad*	6.236
Att. 6.1.23	Homer's *Iliad*	7.93
Att. 6.2.8	Ennius' *Annales?*	Skutsch 589
Att. 6.3.7	Lucilius' *Saturae*	Warmington 609–610
Att. 6.8.5	Euripides' *Philoctetes*	Nauck fr. 796
Att. 6.9.3	Callimachus' *Epigrams*	32.2
Att. 6.9.5	Unknown tragedy	*TrRF* I 36
Att. 7.1.2	Homer's *Odyssey*	7.258/9.33
Att. 7.1.4	Homer's *Iliad*	22.105/6.442
Att. 7.1.4	Homer's *Iliad*	22.100
Att. 7.1.9	Homer's *Iliad*	18.112/19.65
Att. 7.3.5	Euripides' *Troades*	455
Att. 7.3.10	Caecilius Statius: unknown comedy	Ribbeck 258
Att. 7.3.10	Terence's *Eunuchus*	539
Att. 7.3.10	Terence's *Eunuchus*	114–115
Att. 7.6.2	Homer's *Odyssey*	12.209
Att. 7.8.4	Homer's *Iliad*	18.309
Att. 7.11.1	Euripides' *Phoenissae*	506
Att. 7.11.3	Homer's *Iliad*	9.524
Att. 7.12.3	Homer's *Iliad*	22.105/6.442
Att. 7.13.4	Euripides: unknown tragedy	Nauck fr. 973
Att. 7.18.4	Greek proverb	*CPG* II p759
Att. 7.26.1	Unknown tragedy	*TrRF* I 34b
Att. 8.5.1	Callimachus	Pfeiffer fr. 732
Att. 8.8.2	Euripides: unknown tragedy	Nauck fr. 918.1-3
Att. 8.11.3	Ennius: unknown tragedy	*TrRF* II 151a
Att. 8.16.2	Homer's *Iliad*	22.105/6.442
Att. 9.2a.2	Euripides: unknown tragedy	Nauck fr. 958

(cont.)

Att. 9.5.3	Homer's *Iliad*	18.96, 98-99
Att. 9.6.4	Homer's *Iliad*	10.93-94
Att. 9.6.5	Terence's *Heaut.*	86
Att. 9.6.6	Homer's *Iliad*	10.244
Att. 9.7.3	Homer's *Odyssey*	11.634
Att. 9.7.5	Leonidas	*Ath. Pal.* 10.1.1
Att. 9.8.2	Homer's *Odyssey*	3.22
Att. 9.9.2	Unknown tragedy	*TrRF* I 56[1]
Att. 9.13.1	Stesichorus	Diehl fr. 11.1
Att. 9.15.3	Homer's *Odyssey*	20.18
Att. 9.15.4	Homer's *Odyssey*	3.26-27
Att. 9.18.3	Leonidas	*Ath. Pal.* 10.1.1
Att. 10.1.1	Homer's *Iliad*	22.304-305
Att. 10.2.1	Leonidas	*Ath. Pal.* 10.1.1-2
Att. 10.2.2	Unknown comedy	Ribbeck 28-29
Att. 10.5.2	Greek proverb	*CPG* I p207
Att. 10.12a.1	Homer's *Iliad*	18.112/19.65
Att. 10.12.1	Ennius' *Medea?*	Jocelyn 217–218/*TrRF* I 25
Att. 12.5.1	Ennius' *Annales*	Skutsch 290
Att. 12.5.1	Pindar's *Nemeans*	1.1
Att. 12.6.3(6a.1)	Terence's *Heaut.*	75
Att. 12.6.3(6a.1)	ref. to Aristophanes	
Att. 12.6.3(6a.1)	ref. to Eupolis	
Att. 12.51.3	Unknown tragedy	*TrRF* I 67a
Att. 13.11.1	Euripides' *Ion*	585
Att. 13.12.3	Hesiod's *Works and Days*	350
Att. 13.13(14).2	Homer's *Iliad*	22.105/6.442
Att. 13.21a.1	Greek proverb	*CPG* I p116
Att. 13.21.3	Lucilius' *Saturae*	Warmington 1249
Att. 13.24.1	Homer's *Iliad*	22.105/6.442
Att. 13.25.3	Homer's *Iliad*	11.654
Att. 13.34	Terence's *Andria*	185
Att. 13.38.2	Pindar	Snell fr. 213.1–2, 4
Att. 13.47.1	Unknown tragedy	*TrRF* I 68a
Att. 13.52.1	Lucilius' *Saturae*	Warmington 206–207
Att. 14.2.1	ref. to Publilius Syrus	
Att. 14.13.1	Homer's *Iliad*	9.228–230
Att. 14.13.2	Homer's *Iliad*	5.428–429
Att. 14.10.1	Aeschylus' *PV*	682
Att. 14.12.2	Unknown tragedy	*TrRF* I 83a
Att. 14.14.1	Pacuvius' *Iliona*	Schierl fr. 147
Att. 14.20.3	Atilius: unknown comedy	Ribbeck 1–2

[1] *TrRF* I 56, 3 (preserved by *TD* 3.26) contains the phrase "*tanta uis sceleris.*" This phrase appears at *Att.* 9.9.2, but this is not noted in the *TrRF*.

(*cont.*)

Att. 14.21.3	Unknown tragedy	*TrRF* I 67b
Att. 14.22.2	Unknown Greek tragedy	Nauck fr. 105
Att. 15.1.4	Unknown comedy?	Palmer 1883: 446[2]
Att. 15.7.1	Ennius' *Annales*	Skutsch 252
Att. 15.11.3	Unknown Greek tragedy	Nauck fr. 106
Att. 15.11.3	Unknown tragedy	*TrRF* I 83b
Att. 16.2.3	ref. to Accius' *Tereus*	
Att. 16.2.3	Afranius: unknown comedy	Ribbeck 411
Att. 16.3.1	ref. to Ennius' *Annales*/ Cicero's *De Senectute*	Skutsch 337
Att. 16.5.1	ref. to Accius' *Tereus*	
Att. 16.5.1	ref. to Accius' *Brutus*	
Att. 16.5.5	Homer's *Iliad*	17.280
Att. 16.6.1	Homer's *Odyssey*	3.169
Att. 16.6.2	Unknown Greek tragedy	Nauck fr. 106
Att. 16.11.1	Homer's *Iliad*	22.308
Att. 16.11.1	ref. to Lucilius' *Saturae*	Marx 1317
Att. 16.11.2	ref. to Aristophanes	
Att. 16.11.2	ref. to Archilochus	
Att. 16.11.6	Homer's *Iliad*	7.93
Att. 16.13.1–2	Homer's *Odyssey*	3.169, 172, 171
Brut. 1.2.3(2a.1)	Plautus' *Trinummus*	319
Brut. 1.10.2	Unknown tragedy	*TrRF* I 160c
Fam. 1.9.19	Terence's *Eunuchus*	440–445
Fam. 2.8.2	Lucilius' *Saturae*?	Marx 1372
Fam. 2.9.2	Unknown comedy	Ribbeck 38
Fam. 2.9.2	Unknown comedy	Ribbeck 39
Fam. 2.9.2	Unknown comedy	Ribbeck 40
Fam. 2.9.2	Caecilius: unknown comedy	Ribbeck 252
Fam. 2.9.2	Trabea: unknown comedy	Ribbeck 6
Fam. 3.7.6	Homer's *Iliad*	1.174–175
Fam. 3.8.8	Unknown comedy	Ribbeck 49
Fam. 3.11.5	ref. to Homer	
Fam. 5.10.2	Unknown comedy	Ribbeck 30
Fam. 5.12.7	ref. to Homer	
Fam. 5.12.7	Naevius' *Hector Proficiscens*	*TrRF* I 14
Fam. 6.6.6	Unknown tragedy	*TrRF* I 44
Fam. 6.18.5	Hesiod's *Works and Days*	289
Fam. 7.1.2	Unknown tragedy	*TrRF* I 27

[2] Shackleton Bailey 1967: 243: "I believe that the senarius is accidental and the words C.'s own."

(cont.)

Fam. 7.1.2	ref. to Accius' *Clytemestra*	
Fam. 7.1.2	ref. to *Equus Troianus*	
Fam. 7.3.4	Unknown comedy	Ribbeck 90–91
Fam. 7.6.1–2	Ennius' *Medea*	*TrRF* II 90a
Fam. 7.10.4	Terence's *Heaut.*	86
Fam. 7.11.2	ref. to D. Laberius	
Fam. 7.11.2	ref. to Valerius	
Fam. 7.13.2	Ennius' *Annales*	Skutsch 252–253
Fam. 7.16.1	*Equus Troianus*	*TrRF* I *adesp.* 29a
Fam. 7.16.1	Unknown tragedy	*TrRF* I 30
Fam. 7.28.2	Unknown tragedy	*TrRF* I 83d
Fam. 7.30.1	Unknown tragedy	*TrRF* I 83c
Fam. 7.31.2	Pomponius: unknown *Atellana*	Ribbeck 191
Fam. 7.33.1	Accius' *Philocteta*	Dangel 221–222
Fam. 8.2.1	Pacuvius: unknown tragedy	Schierl fr. 263
Fam. 9.7.1	Homer's *Iliad*	10.224
Fam. 9.7.1	Terence's *Andria*	112
Fam. 9.7.2	Ennius' *Annales*	Skutsch 309
Fam. 9.7.2	Unknown Greek tragedy	Nauck fr. 107
Fam. 9.15.2	ref. to Lucilius	
Fam. 9.16.4	ref. to Plautus	
Fam. 9.16.6–7	ref. to Accius' *Oenomaus*	Dangel 2002: 113
Fam. 9.16.7	ref. to Atellan farce	
Fam. 9.16.7	ref. to mime	
Fam. 9.21.1	ref. to Trabea	Ribbeck fr. iii
Fam. 9.22.1	Turpilius' *Demiurgus*	Ribbeck 43–44
Fam. 9.22.1	Unknown tragedy	*TrRF* I 84
Fam. 9.22.1	Unknown tragedy	*TrRF* I 85
Fam. 9.22.1	Unknown tragedy	*TrRF* I 86
Fam. 9.26.2	Unknown tragedy	*TrRF* I 59b
Fam. 10.13.2	ref. to Homer	
Fam. 12.14.7	Unknown Greek tragedy	Nauck fr. 411
Fam. 12.18.2	ref. D. Laberius	
Fam. 12.18.2	ref. to Publilius Syrus	
Fam. 12.25.5	Terence's *Andria*	189
Fam. 13.15.1	Homer's *Odyssey*	7.258
Fam. 13.15.1	Homer's *Odyssey*	1.302/3.200
Fam. 13.15.1	Homer's *Iliad*/ *Odyssey*	17.591/ 24.315
Fam. 13.15.2	Homer's *Iliad*	22.304–305
Fam. 13.15.2	Euripides	Nauck fr. 905
Fam. 13.15.2	Homer's *Iliad*	1.343
Fam. 13.15.2	Homer's *Iliad*	6.208/11.784
Fam. 15.6.1	Naevius' *Hector Proficiscens*	*TrRF* I 14

(*cont.*)

Q. fr. 1.2.1	Homer's *Odyssey*	9.513
Q. fr. 1.2.13	Aeschylus' *PV*	750
Q. fr. 2.(7).8.1	ref. to Cicero's *De Temp.*	Soubiran iii
Q. fr. 2.9.2	Sophocles: unknown tragedy	Nauck fr. 877
Q. fr. 2.10.3	ref. to Lucretius	
Q. fr. 2.11.3	Unknown tragedy	*TrRF* I 28
Q. fr. 2.14.5	Euripides' *Suppliants*	119
Q. fr. 2.16.3	ref. to Sophocles' *Syndeipnoi*	
Q. fr. 3.1.13	ref. to Quintus' *Erigona*	Courtney 2003: 181
Q. fr. 3.1.24	ref. to Cicero's *De Temp.*	Soubiran ii
Q. fr. 3.4.2	ref. to Lucilius' *Saturae*	
Q. fr. 3.5.4	Homer's *Iliad*	6.208/11.874
Q. fr. 3.5.7	ref. to Quintus Cicero's tragedies	
Q. fr. 3.5.7	ref. to Quintus' tragedies	Courtney 2003: 181
Q. fr. 3.5.8	Homer's *Iliad*	16.385–386, 387–388
Q. fr. 3.7.1	Homer's *Iliad*	4.182/8.150
Q. fr. 3.7.2	Homer's *Iliad*	8.355
Q. fr. 3.7.6	ref. to Quintus' *Erigona*	Courtney 2003: 181
Q. fr. 3.7.6	ref. to Cicero's epic for Caesar	Courtney 2003: 181

Speeches

Pro S. Roscio 67	ref. to Ennius' *Alcmeo?*	Zillinger 1911: 109
Pro S. Roscio 90	Ennius: unknown tragedy	*TrRF* II 144a
Pro Q. Roscio 20	ref. to Plautus' *Pseudolus*	
Verr. 1.29	ref. to Naevius?	*TrRF* I T7
Verr. 2.1.46	Ennius' *Achilles*	*TrRF* II 1a
Verr. 2.1.81	Ennius' *Thyestes?*	Jocelyn 295/*TrRF* II p227
Verr. 2.5.94	ref. to Accius: unknown tragedy	Dangel 700
Pro Caecina 27	Terence's *Phormio*	123
Pro Murena 30	Ennius' *Annales*	Skutsch 248, 248–249, 249, 252, 253
Pro Murena 60	Unknown tragedy	*TrRF* I 13a
Pro Murena 88	ref. to Gaius Gracchus/ Ennius' *Medea?*	Jocelyn 217–218/TrRF I 25
Pro Archia 18	Ennius' *Annales?*	Skutsch 1985: 131; xvi
Pro Archia 19	ref. to Homer	
Pro Archia 22	ref. to Ennius	
Pro Archia 24	ref. to Homer	
Pro Archia 27	ref. to Accius	
Pro Archia 27	ref. to Ennius	
Pro Archia 31	Ennius' *Annales?*	Skutsch 1985: 131; xvi
Red. in sen. 33	ref. to Accius' *Atreus*	Dangel 42
Har. resp. 39	Unknown tragedy	*TrRF* I 17

(cont.)

Pro Sestio 45	Unknown tragedy	*TrRF* I 16
Pro Sestio 48	Unknown tragedy	*TrRF* I 161
Pro Sestio 102	Accius' *Atreus*	Dangel 45, 62, 63, 47
Pro Sestio 118	Afranius'*Simulans*	Ribbeck 304–305
Pro Sestio 120	Accius' *Eurysaces*	Dangel 360–361, 362–363
Pro Sestio 121	Accius' *Eurysaces*	Dangel 364
Pro Sestio 121	Ennius' *Andromacha*	*TrRF* II 23a
Pro Sestio 122	Accius' *Eurysaces*	Dangel 366
Pro Sestio 123	Accius' *Brutus*	Dangel 674
Pro Sestio 126	Pacuvius' *Iliona*	Schierl fr. 146/T 55
Pro Caelio 18	Ennius' *Medea*	*TrRF* II 89c
Pro Caelio 36	Unknown comedy	Ribbeck 72
Pro Caelio 37	Caecilius: unknown comedy	Ribbeck 230, 231, 232–233, 237–238, 241–242
Pro Caelio 38	Terence's *Adelphoe*	120–121
Pro Caelio 61	Terence's *Andria*	126
Pro Caelio 65	ref. to mime	Ribbeck 1855: 311
De Prov. Cons. 20	ref. Ennius' *Annales*	Skutsch 1985: 106
Pro Balb. 36	Ennius: unknown tragedy	*TrRF* II 145a
Pro Balb. 51	Ennius' *Annales*	Skutsch 234–235
In Pisonem 43	Ennius' *Thyestes*	*TrRF* II 132a
In Pisonem 46	ref. to Ennius' *Alcmeo*?	Zillinger 1911: 109
In Pisonem 61	Plautus' *Trinummus*	419
In Pisonem 72–74	Cicero's *De Consulatu Suo*	Soubiran fr. vi
In Pisonem 82	Accius' *Atreus*	Dangel 42
Pro Plancio 20	Ennius' *Annales*?	Zillinger 1911: 107
Pro Plancio 33–34	ref. to Lucilius' *Saturae*	Marx 1181
Pro Plancio 59	Accius' *Atreus*	Dangel 45, 62
Pro Scauro 3	Unknown tragedy	*TrRF* I 35
Pro Rab. Post. 28	Unknown tragedy	*TrRF* I 31
Pro Rab. Post. 29	Unknown tragedy	*TrRF* I 32
Pro Rab. Post. 29	Unknown tragedy	*TrRF* I 33
Pro Rab. Post. 29	Unknown tragedy	*TrRF* I 34a
Pro Milone 8	ref. to Ennius' *Eumenides*?	Jocelyn 1969a: 284
Pro Marcello 14	Unknown tragedy	*TrRF* I p215
Pro Reg. Deiot. 25	Unknown tragedy	*TrRF* I 45
Phil. 1.34	Accius' *Atreus*	Dangel 47
Phil. 1.36	ref. to Accius' *Tereus*	
Phil. 2.15	ref. to Terence's *Phormio*	
Phil. 2.15	ref. to Terence's *Eunuchus*	
Phil. 2.15	ref. to Plautus' *Pseudolus*	
Phil. 2.20	Cicero's *De Consulatu Suo*	Soubiran fr. vi
Phil. 2.31	ref. to Accius' *Tereus*	
Phil. 2.65	ref. to mime	Ribbeck 1855: 311
Phil. 2.65	Naevius: unknown tragedy	*TrRF* I 46
Phil. 2.104	Unknown tragedy	*TrRF* I 80b

(cont.)

Phil. 10.8	ref. to Accius' *Tereus*	
Phil. 11.13	ref. to Nucula (mime writer)	
Phil. 13.15	ref. to Lucilius' *Saturae*	Warmington 176–181
Phil. 13.49	Unknown tragedy	*TrRF* I 87
Phil. 13.49	Unknown tragedy	*TrRF* I 83e
In Clod. et C.		
Crawford fr. 21	Unknown comedy	Zillinger 1911: 160
Pro Q. Gallio		
Crawford fr. 2	ref. to mime	
Rhetorical Writings		
De Inv. 1.27	Pacuvius' *Medus*	Schierl fr. 171
De Inv. 1.27	Ennius' *Annales*	Skutsch 216
De Inv. 1.27	Terence's *Andria*	51
De Inv. 1.27	Terence's *Adelphoe*	60–64
De Inv. 1.33	Terence's *Andria*	49–50
De Inv. 1.33	Terence's *Andria*	51
De Inv. 1.33	Terence's *Andria*	157
De Inv. 1.33	Terence's *Andria*	168
De Inv. 1.83	Unknown tragedy	*TrRF* I 9
De Inv. 1.90	Pacuvius' *Medus*	Schierl fr. 186
De Inv. 1.91	Ennius' *Medea*	*TrRF* II 89b
De Inv. 1.91	Ennius: unknown tragedy	*TrRF* II 143b
De Inv. 1.94	ref. to Pacuvius' *Antiopa*	Schierl T 46
De Inv. 1.95	Plautus' *Trinummus*	23–26
De Or. 1.72	ref. to Lucilius' *Saturae?*	Marx 1241
De Or. 1.154	ref. to Ennius	
De Or. 1.198	Ennius' *Annales*	Skutsch 329
De Or. 1.199	Ennius: unknown tragedy	*TrRF* II 146
De Or. 1.246	ref. to Pacuvius' *Teucer*	
De Or. 2.22	ref. to Lucilius' *Saturae?*	Zillinger 1911: 167
De Or. 2.25	Lucilius' *Saturae*	Warmington 635
De Or. 2.39	Plautus' *Trinummus*	705
De Or. 2.40	Caecilius: unknown comedy	Ribbeck fr. xxv
De Or. 2.155	ref. to Pacuvius' *Antiopa*	Schierl T 47
De Or. 2.155–156	Ennius: unknown tragedy	*TrRF* II 147a
De Or. 2.172	Terence's *Andria*	110–112
De Or. 2.187	Pacuvius' *Hermiona*	Schierl fr. 139
De Or. 2.193	Pacuvius' *Teucer*	Schierl fr. 243
De Or. 2.222	Ennius: unknown tragedy	*TrRF* II 148
De Or. 2.224	ref. to Lucilius' *Saturae?*	Marx 1181
De Or. 2.242	Unknown comedy	Ribbeck 1
De Or. 2.253	Lucilius' *Saturae*	Warmington 1135
De Or. 2.254	ref. to Lucilius' *Saturae?*	Marx 1181
De Or. 2.255	Novius: unknown *Atellana*	Ribbeck 115

(cont.)

De Or. 2.257	Caecilius Statius: unknown comedy	Ribbeck 245–246
De Or. 2.257	Unknown comedy	Ribbeck 45
De Or. 2.259	ref. to *Tutor* (mime)	
De Or. 2.262	Lucilius' *Saturae*?	Marx 173
De Or. 2.263	Lucilius' *Saturae*?	Zillinger 1911: 167
De Or. 2.267	Lucilius' *Saturae*?	Zillinger 1911: 162
De Or. 2.268	Lucilius' *Saturae*?	Marx 396
De Or. 2.274	Unknown mime	Ribbeck 1–2
De Or. 2.274	Unknown mime	Ribbeck 3–4
De Or. 2.274	Unknown mime	Ribbeck 5
De Or. 2.276	ref. to Ennius	
De Or. 2.277	Lucilius' *Saturae*?	Marx 421
De Or. 2.279	Novius: unknown *Atellana*	Ribbeck 113–114
De Or. 2.281	ref. to Lucilius' *Saturae*?	Marx 1181
De Or. 2.284	Lucilius' *Saturae*	Zillinger 1911: 161
De Or. 2.285	Novius: unknown *Atellana*	Ribbeck 116
De Or. 2.326	Terence's *Andria*	51
De Or. 2.327	Terence's *Andria*	117, 128–129
De Or. 3.27	ref. to Ennius	
De Or. 3.27	ref. to Pacuvius	
De Or. 3.27	ref. to Accius	
De Or. 3.43	ref. to Q. Valerius Soranus	
De Or. 3.45	ref. to Plautus	
De Or. 3.45	ref. to Naevius	
De Or. 3.57	ref. to *Iliad* 9.443[3]	
De Or. 3.86	Lucilius' *Saturae*	Warmington 182–183
De Or. 3.102	Unknown tragedy	*TrRF* I 18
De Or. 3.102	Ennius' *Andromacha*	*TrRF* II 23b
De Or. 3.137	ref. to Homer	
De Or. 3.141	ref. to Euripides *Philoctetes*	Nauck fr. 796
De Or. 3.154	Ennius' *Alcmeo*	*TrRF* II 12a
De Or. 3.154	Unknown tragedy	*TrRF* I 19a
De Or. 3.154	Ennius' *Annales*	Skutsch 110
De Or. 3.154	Unknown tragedy	*TrRF* I 52b
De Or. 3.157	Pacuvius' *Teucer*	Schierl fr. 239
De Or. 3.158	Unknown tragedy	*TrRF* I 20
De Or. 3.162	Ennius: unknown tragedy	*TrRF* II 149a
De Or. 3.162	Unknown tragedy	*TrRF* I 21a
De Or. 3.164	ref. to Lucilius' *Saturae*?	Zillinger 1911: 167

---

[3] Not in Soubiran's collection. However, Cicero's *oratorem uerborum actoremque rerum* (*De Or.* 3.57) clearly renders μύθων τε ῥητῆρ' ἔμεναι πρηκτῆρά τε ἔργων (*Il.* 9.443).

(cont.)

De Or. 3.164	Ennius' *Thyestes?*	Jocelyn 290/ *TrRF* I 22
De Or. 3.164	Ennius' *Thyestes?*	Jocelyn 293–294/ *TrRF* I 56b
De Or. 3.166	Unknown tragedy	*TrRF* I 23a
De Or. 3.166	Unknown tragedy	*TrRF* I 24a
De Or. 3.167	Ennius' *Annales*	Skutsch 309
De Or. 3.167	Pacuvius' *Chryses*	Schierl fr. 63
De Or. 3.167	Ennius' *Scipio*	Goldberg-Manuwald F1
De Or. 3.167	Ennius' *Scipio*	Goldberg-Manuwald F2
De Or. 3.168	Ennius' *Annales*	Skusch 560–561
De Or. 3.168	Ennius' *Annales*	Skutsch 525
De Or. 3.171	Lucilius' *Saturae*	Warmington 84–85, 86
De Or. 3.183	Ennius' *Andromacha*	*TrRF* II 23c
De Or. 3.197	ref. to *epulae solemnes*	
De Or. 3.197	ref. to the Hymn of the Salii	*FPL* p3
De Or. 3.214	ref. to Gaius Gracchus/ Ennius' *Medea*	Jocelyn 217–218/ *TrRF* I 25
De Or. 3.217	Accius' *Atreus*	Dangel 58–59
De Or. 3.217	Pacuvius' *Teucer*	Schierl fr. 243
De Or. 3.217	Accius' *Atreus*	Dangel 64
De Or. 3.217	Ennius' *Medea?*	Jocelyn 217–218/ *TrRF* I 25
De Or. 3.217	Ennius' *Andromacha*	*TrRF* II 23d
De Or. 3.218	Ennius' *Alcmeo*	*TrRF* II 12b
De Or. 3.219	Accius' *Atreus*	Dangel 29–32
De Or. 3.219	Unknown comedy	Ribbeck 32–34
De Or. 3.219	Pacuvius' *Iliona*	Schierl fr. 150/ *TrRF* I 26a
De Or. 3.225	ref. to Porcius Licinius	
Brut. 15	Hesiod's *Works and Days*	350
Brut. 40	ref. to Homer	
Brut. 50	ref. to Homer	
Brut. 58	Ennius' *Annales*	Skutsch 304–306
Brut. 59	Ennius' *Annales*	Skutsch 306–308
Brut. 59	Ennius' *Annales*	Skutsch 308
Brut. 60	ref. to Naevius	
Brut. 60	ref. to Plautus	
Brut. 71	ref. to Homer	
Brut. 71	Ennius' *Annales*	Skutsch 207–209
Brut. 71	ref. to Livius Andronicus' *Odyssia*	
Brut. 71	ref. to Livius Andronicus' *fabulae*	
Brut. 72	ref. to Livius Andronicus	
Brut. 72	ref. to Ennius	
Brut. 72–73	ref. to Accius	
Brut. 73	ref. to Ennius	
Brut. 73	ref. to Plautus	

(*cont.*)

Brut. 73	ref. to Naevius	
Brut. 75	ref. to *carmina conuiualia*	*FPL* p2
Brut. 76	Ennius' *Annales*	Skutsch 206–207
Brut. 76	ref. to Naevius *Bellum Punicum*	
Brut. 78	ref. to Ennius' *Thyestes*	
Brut. 79	ref. to Ennius	
Brut. 99	ref. to Lucilius' *Saturae*	Warmington 635
Brut. 107	ref. to Accius	
Brut. 132	ref. to Furius Antias	
Brut. 160	ref. to Lucilius' *Saturae*	Marx 1180
Brut. 167	ref. to C. Titius	
Brut. 167	ref. to L. Afranius	
Brut. 169	ref. to Q. Valerius Soranus	
Brut. 172	ref. to Lucilius' *Saturae*	Warmington 448–449
Brut. 177	ref. to Julius Caesar Strabo Vopiscus	
Brut. 229	ref. to Accius	
Brut. 229	ref. to Pacuvius	
Brut. 258	ref. to Caecilius Statius	
Brut. 258	ref. to Pacuvius	
Brut. 274	Lucilius' *Saturae*	Warmington 85
Or. 4.	ref. to Homer	
Or. 4	ref. to Archilochus	
Or. 4	ref. to. Sophocles	
Or. 29	ref. to Aristophanes' *Acharnians*	530–531
Or. 36	ref. to Ennius	
Or. 36	ref. to Pacuvius	
Or. 36	ref. to Accius	
Or. 93	Ennius' *Andromacha*	*TrRF* II 23e
Or. 93	Ennius' *Annales*	Skutsch 309
Or. 109	ref. to Homer	
Or. 109	ref. to Ennius	
Or. 147	Unknown comedy?	Ribbeck 30
Or. 149	Lucilius' *Saturae*	Warmington 84–85
Or. 152	Naevius: unknown tragedy	*TrRF* I 41
Or. 152	Naevius: unknown tragedy	*TrRF* I 42
Or. 152	Ennius' *Scipio*	Goldberg-Manuwald F3
Or. 152	Cicero's *Aratea*	Soubiran fr. xxiii
Or. 153	Ennius' *Alcmeo*	*TrRF* II p55
Or. 153	Unknown tragedy	*TrRF* I 37

(*cont.*)

Or. 153	Unknown tragedy	*TrRF* I 38
Or. 153	Unknown tragedy	*TrRF* I 39
Or. 155	Ennius: unknown tragedy	*TrRF* II 151b
Or. 155	Ennius: unknown tragedy	*TrRF* II 152
Or. 155	Ennius: unknown tragedy	*TrRF* II 153a
Or. 155	Pacuvius' *Chryses*	Schierl fr. 76
Or. 155	Pacuvius: unknown tragedy	Schierl fr. 264
Or. 156	Accius: unknown tragedy	Dangel 700
Or. 156	Accius: unknown tragedy	Dangel 701
Or. 157	Terence's *Phormio*	384, 390
Or. 157	Unknown tragedy	*TrRF* I 40
Or. 157	Ennius' *Annales*	Skutsch 206
Or. 157	Ennius' *Annales*	Skutsch 504
Or. 160	Ennius: unknown tragedy	*TrRF* II 151
Or. 161	Ennius' *Annales*	Skutsch 63
Or. 161	Lucilius' *Saturae*	Warmington 173
Or. 163–164	Unknown tragedy	*TrRF* I 41
Or. 164	Unknown tragedy	*TrRF* I 26b
Or. 164	Unknown tragedy	*TrRF* I 42
Or. 164	Unknown tragedy	*TrRF* I 19b
Or. 166	Unknown tragedy	*TrRF* I 43a
Or. 171	Ennius' *Annales*	Skutsch 207, 210
Or. 184	Ennius' *Thyestes*	*TrRF* II 133
De opt. gen. 2	ref. to Ennius	
De opt. gen. 2	ref. to Pacuvius	
De opt. gen. 2	ref. to Caecilius	
De opt. gen. 3	ref. to Terence	
De opt. gen. 3	ref. to Accius	
De opt. gen. 6	ref. to Homer	
De opt. gen. 6	ref. to Menander	
De opt. gen. 17	Lucilius' *Saturae*	Warmington 172–175
De opt. gen. 18	ref. Terence's *Andria*	
De opt. gen. 18	ref. to Caecilius' *Synephebi*	
De opt. gen. 18	ref. to Ennius' *Andromacha*	
De opt. gen. 18	ref. to Pacuvius' *Antiopa*	
De opt. gen. 18	ref. to Accius' *Epigoni*	
Top. 55	ref. to Homer	
Top. 55	Unknown tragedy	*TrRF* I 43b
Top. 55	Unknown tragedy	*TrRF* I 67c
Top. 61	Ennius' *Medea*	*TrRF* II 89h
Top. 61	Unknown tragedy	*TrRF* I 78

(*cont.*)

Philosophical Works

Rep. 1.1[4]	Lucilius' *Saturae*	Warmington 632–634
Rep. 1.3	Ennius' *Annales*	Skutsch 590
Rep. 1.25	Ennius' *Annales*	Skutsch 153
Rep. 1.30	Ennius' *Annales*	Skutsch 329
Rep. 1.30	Ennius' *Iphigenia*	*TrRF* II 82a
Rep. 1.30	ref. to Pacuvius' *Antiopa*	Schierl T 48
Rep. 1.30	Ennius: unknown tragedy	*TrRF* II 147b
Rep. 1.49	Ennius: unknown tragedy	*TrRF* II 150a
Rep. 1.56	ref. to Cicero's *Aratea*	Soubiran fr. i
Rep. 1.56	ref. to Homer	
Rep. 1.64	Ennius' *Annales*	Skutsch 105–109
Rep. 2.18	ref. to Homer	
Rep. 2.19	ref. to Homer	
Rep. 3.6	Ennius' *Annales*	Skutsch 456
Rep. 3.14	ref. to Pacuvius' *Medus*	Schierl T 61
Rep. 4.5[5]	ref. to Homer	
Rep. 4.11[6]	ref. to Plautus	
Rep. 4.11	ref. to Naevius	
Rep. 4.11	ref. to Caecilius Statius	
Rep. 5.1[7]	Ennius' *Annales*	Skutsch 156
Rep. 6.10	ref. to Homer	
Rep. 6.10	ref. to Ennius' *Annales*	Skutsch 1985: 151
Rep. fr. 1 Powell[8]	Ennius: epigram	Goldberg-Manuwald F1b
Rep. fr. 2 Powell[9]	Ennius: epigram	Goldberg-Manuwald F3b
De Leg. 1.2	Cicero's *Marius*	Soubiran fr. i
De Leg. 1.2	ref. to Homer	
De Leg. 1.2	Cicero's *Marius*	Soubiran fr. ii
De Leg. 1.4	ref. Ennius' *Annales*?	Zillinger 1911: 102
De Leg. 1.33	Terence's *Heaut.*	77
De Leg. 1.40	ref. to Ennius' *Alcmeo*?	Zillinger 1911: 109
De Leg. 2.7	Cicero's *Aratea*	Soubiran fr. i
De Leg. 2.37	ref. to Aristophanes	
De Leg. 2.39	ref. to Livius Andronicus	
De Leg. 2.39	ref. to Naevius	
De Leg. 2.54	ref. to Accius	
De Leg. 2.57	Ennius: epigram	Goldberg-Manuwald F1a
De Leg. 2.62	ref. to *nenia*e	
De Leg. 2.68	Ennius: unknown work	Goldberg-Manuwald F3a
Par. Stoic. 34	Unknown comedy	Ribbeck 75
Hortensius		
fr. 102 Grilli[10]	Ennius' *Alcmeo*	*TrRF* II 12f

---

[4] *Rep.* 1.1 = Pliny *NH* pf. 7. [5] *Rep.* 4.5 = Nonius 308 M. [6] *Rep.* 4.11 = Aug. *Civ. Dei* 2.9.
[7] *Rep.* 5.1 = Aug. *Civ. Dei* 2.21. [8] *Rep.* fr. 1 Powell = Sen. *Ep.* 108.33.
[9] *Rep.* fr. 2 Powell = Sen. *Ep.* 108.34. [10] *Hortensius* fr. 102 Grilli = Prisc. *Inst.* II p 250, 12–16.

(cont.)

De Gloria fr. 2[11]	Homer's *Iliad* 7.89–91	Soubiran fr. iii
De Fato fr. 3[12]	Homer's *Odyssey* 18.136–137	Soubiran fr. ix
Ac. post. 1.10	ref. to Ennius	*TrRF* II T 27
Ac. post. 1.10	ref. to Pacuvius	Schierl T 24
Ac. post. 1.10	ref. to Accius	Zillinger 1911: 132
Ac. pr. 2.20	ref. to Pacuvius' *Antiopa*	Schierl T 40
Ac. pr. 2.20	ref. to Ennius' *Andromacha*	*TrRF* II T 28
Ac. pr. 2.51	ref. to Ennius	Goldberg-Manuwald T 27
Ac. pr. 2.51	Ennius' *Annales*	Skutsch 3
Ac. pr. 2.51	Ennius' *Epicharmus*	Goldberg-Manuwald F1
Ac. pr. 2.52	Ennius' *Alcmeo*	*TrRF* II 13a
Ac. pr. 2.66	Cicero's *Aratea*	Soubiran fr. vii
Ac. pr. 2.88	ref. to Ennius' *Annales*	Skutsch 3
Ac. pr. 2.88	Ennius' *Alcmeo*	*TrRF* II 13b
Ac. pr. 2.88	Ennius' *Annales*	Skutsch 4
Ac. pr. 2.88	Pacuvius' *Iliona*	Schierl T 56/fr. 146
Ac. pr. 2.88	Pacuvius' *Iliona*	Schierl fr. 147
Ac. pr. 2.89	Unknown tragedy	*TrRF* I 21b
Ac. pr. 2.89	Ennius' *Alcmeo*	*TrRF* II 13b
Ac. pr. 2.94	Lucilius' *Saturae*	Warmington 1249
Ac. pr. 2.102	ref. to Lucilius	Warmington 1938: x
Fin. 1.3	Terence's *Heaut.*	69
Fin. 1.4	ref. to Ennius' *Medea*	*TrRF* II T 29
Fin. 1.4	ref. to Pacuvius' *Antiopa*	Schierl T 25
Fin. 1.4	ref. to Euripides	
Fin. 1.4	ref. to Caecilius' *Synephebi*	
Fin. 1.4	ref. to Terence's *Andria*	
Fin. 1.4	ref. to Menander	
Fin. 1.5	ref. to Sophocles' *Electra*	
Fin. 1.5	ref. to Atilius' *Electra*	
Fin. 1.5	Porcius Licinius	*FPL* fr. 5
Fin. 1.5	Ennius' *Medea*	*TrRF* II 89d
Fin. 1.5	ref. to Euripides' *Medea*	
Fin. 1.7	ref. to Homer	
Fin. 1.7	ref. to Ennius	
Fin. 1.7	ref. to L. Afranius	
Fin. 1.7	Lucilius' *Saturae*	Warmington 635
Fin. 1.9	Lucilius' *Saturae*	Warmington 87–93

[11] *De Gloria* fr. 2 = Gellius *NA* 15.6.1.   [12] *De Fato* fr. 3 = Aug. *Civ. Dei* 5.8.

(cont.)

Fin. 1.51	Ennius' *Annales*	Zillinger 1911: 105[13]
Fin. 2.13	Trabea: unknown comedy	Ribbeck 6
Fin. 2.13	Caecilius: unknown comedy	Ribbeck 252
Fin. 2.14	Unknown comedy	Ribbeck 37
Fin. 2.14	Caecilius: unknown comedy	Ribbeck 230
Fin. 2.14	Terence's *Heaut.*	53
Fin. 2.15	Lucilius' *Saturae*?	Zillinger 1911: 167
Fin. 2.18	Unknown tragedy	*TrRF* I 46
Fin. 2.22	Caecilius' *Hymnis*	Ribbeck 70
Fin. 2.23	Lucilius' *Saturae*	Warmington 1226–1227
Fin. 2.24	Lucilius' *Saturae*	Warmington 200–205
Fin. 2.25	Lucilius' *Saturae*	Warmington 206–207
Fin. 2.41	Ennius: unknown tragedy	*TrRF* II 155
Fin. 2.71	Unknown tragedy	*TrRF* I 47
Fin. 2.79	ref. to Pacuvius' *Chryses*	Schierl T 51
Fin. 2.94	Accius' *Philocteta*	Dangel 215–216, 235–236
Fin. 2.105	Cic. trans. Eur. *Andr.* Nauck fr. 133	Soubiran fr. iv
Fin. 2.106	ref. to epitaph of Sardanapallus	Soubiran fr. x
Fin. 2.106	Ennius' *Scipio*	Goldberg-Manuwald F1
Fin. 2.115	ref. to Homer	
Fin. 2.115	ref. to Archilochus	
Fin. 2.115	ref. to Pindar	
Fin. 2.116	ref. to Homer	
Fin. 2.116	epitaph of A. Atilius Calatinus	*FPL* pp13–14
Fin. 4.62	Ennius' *Alcmeo*	*TrRF* II 12d
Fin. 4.68	Accius: unknown tragedy	Dangel 724
Fin. 5.28	Terence's *Heaut.*	147, 148
Fin. 5.29	Terence's *Heaut.*	80
Fin. 5.31	Ennius' *Alcmeo*	*TrRF* II 12e
Fin. 5.31	Pacuvius: unknown tragedy	Schierl fr. 265
Fin. 5.32	Accius' *Philocteta*	Dangel 217–219
Fin. 5.49	Cic. trans. *Ody.* 12.184–191	Soubiran fr. viii
Fin. 5.63	Pacuvius' *Chryses*?	Schierl fr. 69/ *TrRF* I 48
Fin. 5.92	ref. to Lucilius' *Saturae*	Marx 1300

---

[13] The phrase *noctesque diesque* (*Fin.* 1.51) appears in a fragment of Ennius' *Annales* (Skutsch 336), however Skutsch does not use *Fin.* 1.51 as a source. *Noctesque diesque* appears frequently in poetry: Skutsch 336, Plautus' *Amphitruo* 168, Cic. *Aratea* Soubiran fr. iii, 2, Virg. *Aen.* 6.556, Horace *Sat.* 1.1.76, Lucan *BC* 8.292, Manilius *Astr.* 3.383, Statius *Theb.* 3.76, 7.503, 12.396, 12.485; *Silv.* 2.1.210; *Ach.* 1.637, Martial *Ep.* 12.38.1.

(*cont.*)

TD 1.3	ref. to Homer	
TD 1.3	ref. to Hesiod	
TD 1.3	ref. to Archilochus	
TD 1.3	ref. to Livius Andronicus	
TD 1.3	ref. to Ennius	
TD 1.3	ref. to Plautus	
TD 1.3	ref. to Naevius	
TD 1.3	ref. to Ennius	
TD 1.3	ref. to *carmina conuiualia*	*FPL* p2
TD 1.10	Unknown tragedy	*TrRF* I 49
TD 1.10	Ennius' *Annales*?/	Skutsch (*dubia*) 3–4
	Lucilius' *Saturae*	Marx 1375–1376
TD 1.18	Ennius' *Annales*	Skutsch 329
TD 1.27	Ennius' *Annales*	Skutsch 22
TD 1.28	Ennius' *Annales*	Skutsch 110–111
TD 1.31	Caecilius' *Synephebi*	Ribbeck 210
TD 1.34	Ennius: epigram	Goldberg-Manuwald F2a
TD 1.37	Unknown tragedy	*TrRF* I 50
TD 1.37	ref. to Homer	
TD 1.37	Unknown tragedy	*TrRF* I 51
TD 1.45	Ennius' *Medea*	*TrRF* II 89e
TD 1.45	Ennius' *Annales*	Skutsch 302
TD 1.48	Unknown tragedy	Jocelyn 1969a: 255
TD 1.65	ref. to Homer	
TD 1.68	Accius' *Philocteta*	Dangel 242–243
TD 1.69	Unknown tragedy	*TrRF* I 52a
TD 1.79	ref. to Homer	
TD 1.85	Ennius' *Andromacha*	*TrRF* II 23f
TD 1.94	Unknown comedy	Ribbeck 43–44
TD 1.98	ref. to Homer	
TD 1.98	ref. to Hesiod	
TD 1.101	Cic. trans. Simonides	Soubiran fr. ii
TD 1.105	Ennius' *Andromacha*	*TrRF* II 23g
TD 1.105	Accius' *Epinausimache*	Dangel 160
TD 1.106	Pacuvius' *Iliona*	Schierl fr. 146
TD 1.107	Ennius' *Thyestes*	*TrRF* II 132b
TD 1.115	Cic. trans. Eur. *Cresph.*	Soubiran fr. vi
	Nauck fr. 449	
TD 1.116	ref. to *Iphigenia*	
TD 1.117	Ennius: epigram	Goldberg-Manuwald F2b
TD 1.117	Cic. trans. Solon	Soubiran fr. i
	Campbell fr. 22.5–6	
TD 2.1–2	Ennius: unknown tragedy	*TrRF* II 147c
TD 2.13	Accius' *Atreus*	Dangel 43–44
TD 2.19	Accius' *Philocteta*	Dangel 235–236, 237–240

(*cont.*)

TD 2.20–22	Cic. trans. Soph. *Trach.* 1046–1102	Soubiran fr. i
TD 2.23	Accius' *Philocteta*	Dangel 208–211[14]
TD 2.23–25	Cic. trans. Aesch. Nauck fr. 193	Soubiran fr. ii
TD 2.33	Accius' *Philocteta*	Dangel 214–216
TD 2.34	Unknown tragedy	*TrRF* I 53
TD 2.36	Unknown tragedy	*TrRF* I 54
TD 2.38–39	Ennius: unknown tragedy	*TrRF* II 153b
TD 2.41	Lucilius' *Saturae*	Warmington 173
TD 2.44	Pacuvius' *Iliona*	Schierl fr. 147
TD 2.47	ref. to Pacuvius' *Hermiona*	Schierl fr. 139
TD 2.48–50	Pacuvius' *Niptra*	Schierl fr. 199
TD 2.50	Pacuvius' *Niptra*	Schierl fr. 200
TD 2.67	Unknown tragedy	*TrRF* I 162
TD 3.5	Ennius: unknown tragedy	*TrRF* II 156
TD 3.18	Cic. trans. *Iliad* 9.646–647	Soubiran fr. vi
TD 3.20	Accius' *Melanippus*	Dangel 536
TD 3.26	Unknown tragedy	*TrRF* I 55[15]
TD 3.26	Unknown tragedy	*TrRF* I 56a
TD 3.26	Unknown tragedy	*TrRF* I 57
TD 3.28	Unknown tragedy	*TrRF* I 58
TD 3.29	Cic. trans. Eur. Nauck fr. 964	Soubiran fr. v
TD 3.30	Terence's *Phormio*	241–246
TD 3.31	ref. to Lucilius' *Saturae*	Marx 1300
TD 3.39	ref. to unknown tragedy	*TrRF* I 57
TD 3.39	Unknown tragedy	*TrRF* I 59a
TD 3.44	Ennius: unknown tragedy	*TrRF* II 157
TD 3.44–46	Ennius' *Andromacha*	*TrRF* II 23h
TD 3.45	ref. to Euphorion	
TD 3.53	Ennius' *Andromacha*	*TrRF* II 23i
TD 3.56	Caecilius: unknown comedy	Ribbeck 266
TD 3.58	Unknown tragedy	*TrRF* I 58
TD 3.59	Cic. trans. Eur. Nauck fr. 964	Soubiran fr. v
TD 3.59	Cic. trans Eur. *Hyps.* Nauck fr. 757	Soubiran fr. vii

[14] Cicero attributes these verses to Aeschylus. However, part of this same passage was quoted by Varro (*LL* 7.10), who attributed it to Accius' *Philocteta* (= Dangel 208–211).

[15] Verses quoted at *TD* 3.25–26 have traditionally been assigned to Ennius' *Thyestes* (Jocelyn 291–292, 293–295), but have been recently downgraded to *adespota* (*TrRF* I 55–56).

(cont.)

TD 3.62	Accius: unknown tragedy	Dangel 696
TD 3.63	Cic. trans. *Iliad* 6.201–202	Soubiran fr. ii
TD 3.63	Ennius' *Medea*	*TrRF* II 91
TD 3.65	Terence's *Heaut.*	147-148
TD 3.65	Terence's *Heaut.*	135
TD 3.65	Cic. trans. *Iliad* 19.226–229	Soubiran fr. vii
TD 3.67	Cic. trans. Eur. *Phrixos* Nauck fr. 821	Soubiran fr. viii
TD 3.71	Cic. trans. Soph. Nauck fr. 666	Soubiran fr. ii
TD 3.76	Cic. trans. Aesch. *PV* 377–380	Soubiran fr. i
TD 4.3	ref. to *carmina conuiualia*	*FPL* p2
TD 4.4	ref. to Appius Claudius Caecus' *carmen*	*FPL* p12
TD 4.18-19	Ennius' *Alcmeo*	*TrRF* II 12c
TD 4.25	ref. to Atilius' *Misogynos*	
TD 4.35	Trabea: unknown comedy	Ribbeck 6
TD 4.35	Unknown tragedy	*TrRF* I 60
TD 4.45	Afranius: unknown comedy	Ribbeck 411
TD 4.48	Lucilius' *Saturae*	Warmington 176-181
TD 4.49	ref. to Homer	
TD 4.52	Ennius: unknown work	Goldberg-Manuwald F4
TD 4.52	ref. to Homer	
TD 4.52	Unknown tragedy	*TrRF* I 61
TD 4.55	Accius' *Atreus*	Dangel 64
TD 4.55	Afranius: unknown comedy	Ribbeck 411
TD 4.63	Cic. trans. Eur. *Or.* 1–3	Soubiran fr. iii
TD 4.67	Naevius' *Hector Proficiscens*	*TrRF* I 14
TD 4.67	Trabea: unknown comedy	Ribbeck 1–5
TD 4.68	Caecilius: unknown comedy	Ribbeck 259–263
TD 4.69	Ennius' *Medea*	*TrRF* II 92
TD 4.69	Pacuvius' *Medus?*	Schierl fr. 185/*TrRF* I 62
TD 4.70	Ennius: unknown tragedy	*TrRF* II 158
TD 4.72–73	Turpilius' *Leucadia*	Ribbeck 115–120
TD 4.76	Terence's *Eunuchus*	59–63
TD 4.77	Unknown tragedy	*TrRF* I 63
TD 4.77	Accius' *Atreus*	Dangel 58–59
TD 5.7	ref. to Homer	
TD 5.25	Cic. trans. Chaeremon Nauck fr. 2	Soubiran fr. v

(*cont.*)

TD 5.46	Pacuvius' *Niptra*	Schierl fr. 191
TD 5.49	Ennius: epigram	Goldberg-Manuwald F3a
TD 5.52	Unknown tragedy	*TrRF* I 65
TD 5.101	Cic. trans. epitaph of Sardanapallus	Soubiran fr. x
TD 5.114	ref. to Homer	
TD 5.108	Pacuvius' *Teucer?*	Schierl fr. 250/ *TrRF* I 66
ND 1.13	Caecilius' *Synephebi*	Ribbeck 211–212, 213–214
ND 1.41	ref. to Hesiod	
ND 1.41	ref. to Homer	
ND 1.63	Lucilius' *Saturae*	Warmington 1138–1141
ND 1.79	Catulus epigram	Courtney fr. 2
ND 1.97	Ennius' *Saturae*	Goldberg-Manuwald F17
ND 1.107	ref. to Homer	
ND 1.107	ref. to Archilochus	
ND 1.119	ref. to Ennius' *Euhemerus*	*TrRF* II T 31
ND 1.119	Unknown tragedy	*TrRF* I 69
ND 1.119	Unknown tragedy	*TrRF* I 70
ND 2.4	Ennius' *Thyestes*	*TrRF* II 134a
ND 2.4	Ennius' *Annales*	Skutsch 592
ND 2.25	Unknown verse?	Mayor 1883: 112
ND 2.49	Ennius: unknown tragedy	*TrRF* II 204
ND 2.60	Terence's *Eunuchus*	732
ND 2.64	Ennius' *Annales*	Skutsch 592
ND 2.65	Ennius' *Thyestes*	*TrRF* II 134b
ND 2.65	Ennius: unknown tragedy	*TrRF* II 159
ND 2.65	Cic. trans. Eur. Nauck fr. 941	Soubiran fr. ix
ND 2.70	ref. to Homer	
ND 2.89	Accius' *Medea*	Dangel 467–478
ND 2.89	Accius' *Medea*	Dangel 479–480
ND 2.89	Accius' *Medea*	Dangel 481–482
ND 2.91	Pacuvius' *Chryses*	Schierl fr. 79
ND 2.91	Pacuvius: unknown tragedy	Schierl fr. 266
ND 2.93	ref. to Ennius' *Annales*	
ND 2.104	Cicero's *Aratea*	Soubiran fr. iii
ND 2.105	Cicero's *Aratea*	Soubiran fr. iv
ND 2.105	Cicero's *Aratea*	Soubiran fr. v
ND 2.105	Cicero's *Aratea*	Soubiran fr. vi
ND 2.106	Cicero's *Aratea*	Soubiran fr. vii
ND 2.106	Cicero's *Aratea*	Soubiran fr. viii
ND 2.107	Cicero's *Aratea*	Soubiran fr. ix
ND 2.108	Cicero's *Aratea*	Soubiran fr. x
ND 2.108	Cicero's *Aratea*	Soubiran fr. xi
ND 2.108	Cicero's *Aratea*	Soubiran fr. xii
ND 2.108	Cicero's *Aratea*	Soubiran fr. xiii

(cont.)

ND 2.109	Cicero's *Aratea*	Soubiran fr. xiv
ND 2.109	Cicero's *Aratea*	Soubiran fr. xv
ND 2.109–110	Cicero's *Aratea*	Soubiran fr. xvi
ND 2.110	Cicero's *Aratea*	Soubiran fr. xxii
ND 2.110	Cicero's *Aratea*	Soubiran fr. xxv
ND 2.110	Cicero's *Aratea*	Soubiran fr. xxvi
ND 2.110	Cicero's *Aratea*	Soubiran fr. xxvii
ND 2.111	Cicero's *Aratea*	Soubiran fr. xxviii
ND 2.111	Cicero's *Aratea*	Soubiran fr. xxix
ND 2.111	Cicero's *Aratea*	Soubiran fr. xxx
ND 2.111	Cicero's *Aratea*	Soubiran fr. xxxi
ND 2.111	Cicero's *Aratea*	Soubiran fr. xxxii
ND 2.111	Cicero's *Aratea*	Soubiran fr. xxxiii
ND 2.111	Cicero's *Aratea*	Soubiran 12–13
ND 2.111	Cicero's *Aratea*	Soubiran 20–21
ND 2.112	Cicero's *Aratea*	Soubiran 22
ND 2.112	Cicero's *Aratea*	Soubiran 27–28
ND 2.112	Cicero's *Aratea*	Soubiran 42
ND 2.112	Cicero's *Aratea*	Soubiran 47
ND 2.112	Cicero's *Aratea*	Soubiran 56
ND 2.112	Cicero's *Aratea*	Soubiran 58–61
ND 2.113	Cicero's *Aratea*	Soubiran 77–78
ND 2.113	Cicero's *Aratea*	Soubiran 85
ND 2.113	Cicero's *Aratea*	Soubiran 87
ND 2.113	Cicero's *Aratea*	Soubiran 91–101
ND 2.113	Cicero's *Aratea*	Soubiran 102
ND 2.114	Cicero's *Aratea*	Soubiran 108
ND 2.114	Cicero's *Aratea*	Soubiran 125–126
ND 2.114	Cicero's *Aratea*	Soubiran 143–144
ND 2.114	Cicero's *Aratea*	Soubiran 150
ND 2.114	Cicero's *Aratea*	Soubiran 151
ND 2.114	Cicero's *Aratea*	Soubiran 183–184
ND 2.114	Cicero's *Aratea*	Soubiran 207
ND 2.114	Cicero's *Aratea*	Soubiran 210–211
ND 2.114	Cicero's *Aratea*	Soubiran 213–214
ND 2.114	Cicero's *Aratea*	Soubiran 219–222
ND 2.116	ref. to Homer	
ND 2.151	Unknown tragedy	*TrRF* II p250 (= *TrRF* I 81)
ND 2.159	Cicero's *Aratea*	Soubiran fr. xviii
ND 3.10	Ennius' *Thyestes*	*TrRF* II 134c
ND 3.11	ref. to Homer	
ND 3.24	Ennius' *Annales*	Skutsch 302
ND 3.40	Ennius' *Thyestes*	*TrRF* II 134d
ND 3.40	ref. to Ennius' *Iphigenia*	*TrRF* II p169
ND 3.41	ref. to Accius: unknown tragedy	Dangel 709–710
ND 3.41	ref. to Homer	

(cont.)

ND 3.48	ref. to Pacuvius' *Medus*	Schierl T 59
ND 3.65	Ennius' *Medea?*	Jocelyn 225–227/ *TrRF* I 71
ND 3.66	Ennius' *Medea?*	Jocelyn 228/ *TrRF* I 72
ND 3.66	Ennius' *Medea?*	Jocelyn 229–231/ *TrRF* I 73
ND 3.67	Unknown tragedy	*TrRF* I 74
ND 3.68	Accius' *Atreus*	Dangel 31–32
ND 3.68	Accius' *Atreus*	Dangel 33
ND 3.68	Accius' *Atreus*	Dangel 34–36
ND 3.68	Accius' *Atreus*	Dangel 37–41
ND 3.71	ref. to Ennius' *Medea?*	Jocelyn 225–227/ *TrRF* I 71
ND 3.72	Terence's *Eunuchus*	46
ND 3.72	Terence's *Eunuchus*	49
ND 3.72	Caecilius' *Synephebi*	Ribbeck 199
ND 3.73	Caecilius' *Synephebi*	Ribbeck 200–201
ND 3.73	Caecilius' *Synephebi*	Ribbeck 202–205
ND 3.73	Terence's *Phormio*	321
ND 3.75	Ennius' *Medea*	*TrRF* II 89f
ND 3.79	Ennius' *Telamo*	*TrRF* II 117a
ND 3.90	Accius: unknown tragedy	Warmington 19–21
De Sen. 1	Ennius' *Annales*	Skutsch 335, 336, 337–339
De Sen. 10	Ennius' *Annales*	Skutsch 363–365
De Sen. 14	Ennius' *Annales*	Skutsch 522–523
De Sen. 14	ref. to Ennius	
De Sen. 16	Ennius' *Annales*	Skutsch 199–200
De Sen. 20	Naevius' *Ludus/Lupus/ Lydus*	Powell 1988: 145–146
De Sen. 23	ref. to Homer	
De Sen. 23	ref. to Hesiod	
De Sen. 23	ref. to Simonides	
De Sen. 23	ref. to Stesichorus	
De Sen. 24	Caecilius' *Synephebi*	Ribbeck 210
De Sen. 25	Caecilius' *Plocium*	Ribbeck 173–175
De Sen. 25	Caecilius' *Ephesio*	Ribbeck 28–29
De Sen. 31	ref. to Homer	
De Sen. 36	Caecilius: unknown comedy	Ribbeck 243
De Sen. 50	ref. to Naevius' *Bellum Punicum*	
De Sen. 50	ref. to Plautus' *Truculentus*	
De Sen. 50	ref. to Plautus' *Pseudolus*	
De Sen. 50	ref. to Livius Andronicus	
De Sen. 50	Ennius' *Annales*	Skutsch 308
De Sen. 54	ref. to Homer	
De Sen. 61	epitaph of A. Atilius Calatinus	*FPL* pp13–14

(*cont.*)

De Sen. 65	ref. to Terence's *Adelphoe*	
De Sen. 73	Ennius: epigram	Goldberg-Manuwald F2b
Div. 1.13-14	Cicero's *Prognostica*	Soubiran fr. iii
Div. 1.14–15	Cicero's *Prognostica*	Soubiran fr. iv
Div. 1.15	Cicero's *Prognostica*	Soubiran fr. v
Div. 1.17–22	Cicero's *De Consulatu Suo*	Soubiran fr. ii
Div. 1.23	ref. to Ennius' *Andromacha*	*TrRF* II T 33
Div. 1.24	Pacuvius' *Teucer*	Schierl fr. 239
Div. 1.29	Unknown tragedy	*TrRF* I 75
Div. 1.40-41	Ennius' *Annales*	Skutsch 34–50
Div. 1.42	Ennius' *Alexander*	Jocelyn 50–61
Div. 1.44	Accius' *Brutus*	Dangel 657–662
Div. 1.45	Accius' *Brutus*	Dangel 663–672
Div. 1.52	Cic. trans. *Iliad* 9.363	Soubiran fr. v
Div. 1.65	ref. to Homer	
Div. 1.65	Plautus' *Aulularia*	178
Div. 1.66–67	Ennius: unknown tragedy	*TrRF* II 151c
Div. 1.72	ref. to Homer	
Div. 1.80	Pacuvius' *Teucer*	Schierl fr. 251
Div. 1.81	Cic. trans. Pythian oracle to Brennus	Soubiran fr. ix
Div. 1.87	ref. to Homer	
Div. 1.88	Ennius: unknown tragedy	*TrRF* II 160
Div. 1.88	ref. to Homer	
Div. 1.89	ref. to oracles of the Marcii	*FPL* p15
Div. 1.89	ref. to Homer	
Div. 1.106	Cicero's *Marius*	Soubiran fr. iii
Div. 1.107–108	Ennius' *Annales*	Skutsch 72–91
Div. 1.114	Ennius: unknown tragedy	*TrRF* II 151d
Div. 1.114	Ennius' *Annales*	Skutsch 207
Div. 1.115	ref. to oracles of Marcius and Publicius	*FPL* p15
Div. 1.131	Pacuvius' *Chryses*	Schierl fr. 77
Div. 1.131	Pacuvius' *Chryses*	Schierl fr. 80
Div. 1.132	Ennius' *Telamo*	*TrRF* II 117b
Div. 2.12	Cic. trans. Eur. Nauck fr. 973	Soubiran fr. x
Div. 2.25	Cic. trans. unknown Greek verse	Soubiran fr. vii
Div. 2.25	ref. to Homer	
Div. 2.25	ref. to Atellan farce	
Div. 2.30	Ennius' *Iphigenia*	*TrRF* II 82b
Div. 2.45	Cicero's *De Consulatu Suo*	Soubiran fr. ii
Div. 2.57	Ennius: unknown tragedy	*TrRF* II 161
Div. 2.63–64	Cic. trans. *Iliad* 2.299-330	Soubiran fr. i

(cont.)

Div. 2.82	Ennius' *Annales*	Skutsch 541
Div. 2.82	Cic. trans. *Iliad* 9.236	Soubiran fr. iv
Div. 2.97	ref. to Homer	
Div. 2.104	Ennius' *Telamo*	*TrRF* II 117c
Div. 2.111	ref. to Ennius	
Div. 2.112	Ennius: unknown tragedy	*TrRF* II 151e
Div. 2.113	ref. to oracles of Marcius	*FPL* p15
Div. 2.115	Unknown tragedy	*TrRF* I 77a
Div. 2.115	Cic. trans. Pythian oracle	Soubiran fr. viii
Div. 2.116	Ennius' *Annales*	Skutsch 167, 197–198
Div. 2.127	Ennius: unknown tragedy	*TrRF* II 205
Div. 2.133	ref. to Euphorion	
Div. 2.133	ref. to Homer	
Div. 2.133	Lucilius' *Saturae?*/	Marx 1377/
	Cic. trans. Greek poet?	Soubiran fr. ii
Div. 2.133	Pacuvius' *Antiopa*	Schierl fr. 3
Div. 2.139	ref. to Homer	
De Fato fr. 3[16]	Cic. trans. *Ody.* 18.136–137	Soubiran fr. ix
De Fato 5	ref. to Antipater	
De Fato 34–35	Ennius' *Medea*	*TrRF* II 89g
De Am. 22	Ennius: unknown work	Skutsch *op. inc.* 18
De Am. 24	ref. to Pacuvius' *Chryses*	Schierl T 52
De Am. 63	Lucilius' *Saturae*	Warmington 1249
De Am. 64	Ennius: unknown tragedy	*TrRF* II 166
De Am. 89	Terence's *Andria*	68
De Am. 93	Terence's *Eunuchus*	252–253
De Am. 98	Terence's *Eunuchus*	391–392
De Am. 99	Caecilius: unknown comedy	Ribbeck 243
De Off. 1.26	Ennius: unknown tragedy	*TrRF* II 150b
De Off. 1.30	Terence's *Heaut.*	77
De Off. 1.38	Ennius' *Annales*	Skutsch 183–190
De Off. 1.48	Hesiod's *Works and Days*	350
De Off. 1.51–52	Ennius: unknown tragedy	*TrRF* II 145b
De Off. 1.61	Unknown tragedy	*TrRF* I 79
De Off. 1.61	Ennius: unknown tragedy	*TrRF* II 162
De Off. 1.77	Cicero's *De Consulatu Suo*	Soubiran fr. vi
De Off. 1.84	Ennius' *Annales*	Skutsch 363–365
De Off. 1.97	Accius' *Atreus*	Dangel 47
De Off. 1.104	ref. to Plautus	
De Off. 1.114	ref. to Accius' *Epigoni*	
De Off. 1.114	ref. to Pacuvius' *Medus*	
De Off. 1.114	ref. to Ennius' *Melanippa*	

[16] *De Fato* fr. 3 = Aug. *Civ. Dei* 5.8.

(*cont.*)

De Off. 1.114	ref. to Accius' *Clytemestra*	
De Off. 1.114	ref. to Pacuvius' *Antiopa*	
De Off. 1.114	ref. to Ennius' *Ajax*	
De Off. 1.114	ref. to D. Laberius?	Panayotakis 2010: 459
De Off. 1.139	Unknown tragedy	*TrRF* I 80a
De Off. 1.150	Terence's *Eunuchus*	257
De Off. 2.13	Unknown tragedy	*TrRF* I 81
De Off. 2.23	Ennius: unknown tragedy	*TrRF* II 163
De Off. 2.62	Ennius: unknown tragedy	*TrRF* II 164
De Off. 3.62	Ennius' *Medea*	*TrRF* II 90b
De Off. 3.82	Cic. trans. Eur. *Phoen.* 524–525	Soubiran fr. ii
De Off. 3.84	Accius: unknown tragedy	Dangel *inc.* i
De Off. 3.97	ref. to Homer	
De Off. 3.98	Unknown tragedy	*TrRF* I 82
De Off. 3.102	Accius' *Atreus*	Dangel 60–61
De Off. 3.104	Ennius: unknown tragedy	*TrRF* II 165
De Off. 3.106	Accius' *Atreus*	Dangel 61
De Off. 3.108	Cic. trans. Eur. *Hipp.* 612	Soubiran fr. i

Appendix II   By Latin Poet

(*cont.*)

TD 1.105	Accius' *Epinausimache*	Dangel 160
Pro Sestio 120	Accius' *Eurysaces*	Dangel 360–361, 362–363
Pro Sestio 121	Accius' *Eurysaces*	Dangel 364
Pro Sestio 122	Accius' *Eurysaces*	Dangel 366
ND 2.89	Accius' *Medea*	Dangel 467–478, 479–480, 481–482
TD 3.20	Accius' *Melanippus*	Dangel 536
TD 2.23	Accius' *Philocteta*	Dangel 208–211
TD 2.33	Accius' *Philocteta*	Dangel 214–216
Fin. 2.94	Accius' *Philocteta*	Dangel 215–216
Fin. 5.32	Accius' *Philocteta*	Dangel 217–219
Fam. 7.33.1	Accius' *Philocteta*	Dangel 221–222
Fin. 2.94	Accius' *Philocteta*	Dangel 235–236
TD 2.19	Accius' *Philocteta*	Dangel 235–236, 237–240
TD 1.68	Accius' *Philocteta*	Dangel 242–243
Verr. 2.5.94	ref. to Accius: unknown tragedy	Dangel 700
ND 3.41	ref. to Accius: unknown tragedy	Dangel 709–710
De Off. 3.84	Accius: unknown tragedy	Dangel 692
TD 3.62	Accius: unknown tragedy	Dangel 696
Or. 156	Accius: unknown tragedy	Dangel 700
Or. 156	Accius: unknown tragedy	Dangel 701
Fin. 4.68	Accius: unknown tragedy	Dangel 724
ND 3.90	Accius: unknown tragedy	Warmington 19–21

Accius' *praetextae*

Att. 16.5.1	ref. to Accius' *Brutus*	
Div. 1.44	Accius' *Brutus*	Dangel 657–662
Div. 1.45	Accius' *Brutus*	Dangel 663–672
Pro Sestio 123	Accius' *Brutus*	Dangel 674

Reference to L. Afranius

Brut. 167	ref. to L. Afranius	
Fin. 1.7	ref. to L. Afranius	

L. Afranius' comedies (togatae)

Pro Sestio 118	Afranius' *Simulans*	Ribbeck 304–305
TD 4.45	Afranius: unknown comedy	Ribbeck 411
TD 4.55	Afranius: unknown comedy	Ribbeck 411
Att. 16.2.3	Afranius: unknown comedy	Ribbeck 411

Reference to Livius Andronicus

TD 1.3	ref. to Livius Andronicus	

(cont.)

De Leg. 2.39	ref. to Livius Andronicus	
De Sen. 50	ref. to Livius Andronicus	
Brut. 71	ref. to Livius Andronicus' *Odyssia*	
Brut. 71	ref. to Livius Andronicus' *fabulae*	
Brut. 72	ref. to Livius Andronicus	
Atilius' tragedies		
Fin. 1.5	ref. to Atilius' *Electra*	
Atilius' comedies (palliatae)		
TD 4.25	ref. to Atilius' *Misogynos*	
Att. 14.20.3	Atilius: unknown comedy	Ribbeck 1–2
Reference to Caecilius Statius		
Att. 1.16.15	ref. to Caecilius Statius	
Brut. 258	ref. to Caecilius Statius	
De opt. gen. 2	ref. to Caecilius Statius	
Rep. 4.11	ref. to Caecilius Statius	
Caecilius Statius' comedies (palliatae)		
Pro S. Roscio 46–47	ref. to Caecilius Statius' *Hypobolimaeus*	
Fin. 1.4	ref. to Caecilius' *Synephebi*	
De opt. gen. 18	ref. to Caecilius' *Synephebi*	
De Sen. 25	Caecilius' *Ephesio*	Ribbeck 28–29
Fin. 2.22	Caecilius' *Hymnis*	Ribbeck 70
De Sen. 25	Caecilius' *Plocium*	Ribbeck 173–175
ND 3.72	Caecilius' *Synephebi*	Ribbeck 199
ND 3.73	Caecilius' *Synephebi*	Ribbeck 200–201
ND 3.73	Caecilius' *Synephebi*	Ribbeck 202–205
TD 1.31	Caecilius' *Synephebi*	Ribbeck 210
De Sen. 24	Caecilius' *Synephebi*	Ribbeck 210
ND 1.13	Caecilius' *Synephebi*	Ribbeck 211–212, 213–214
Fin. 2.14	Caecilius: unknown comedy	Ribbeck 230
Pro Caelio 37	Caecilius: unknown comedy	Ribbeck 230, 231, 232–233, 237–238, 241–242
De Am. 99	Caecilius: unknown comedy	Ribbeck 243
De Sen. 36	Caecilius: unknown comedy	Ribbeck 243
De Or. 2.257	Caecilius: unknown comedy	Ribbeck 245–246
Fam. 2.9.2	Caecilius: unknown comedy	Ribbeck 252

(cont.)

Fin. 2.13	Caecilius: unknown comedy	Ribbeck 252
Att. 7.3.10	Caecilius: unknown comedy	Ribbeck 258
TD 4.68	Caecilius: unknown comedy	Ribbeck 259–263
TD 3.56	Caecilius: unknown comedy	Ribbeck 266
De Or. 2.40	Caecilius: unknown comedy	Ribbeck fr. xxv

Reference to Ennius

Ac. post. 1.10	ref. to Ennius
Ac. pr. 2.51	ref. to Ennius
Fin. 1.7	ref. to Ennius
TD 1.3	ref. to Ennius
Or. 109	ref. to Ennius
De Or. 2.276	ref. to Ennius
Pro Archia 22	ref. to Ennius
Pro Archia 27	ref. to Ennius
De Sen. 14	ref. to Ennius
De Or. 1.154	ref. to Ennius
De Or. 3.27	ref. to Ennius
Div. 2.111	ref. to Ennius
Brut. 72	ref. to Ennius
Brut. 73	ref. to Ennius
Brut. 79	ref. to Ennius
De opt. gen. 2	ref. to Ennius

Ennius' Annales

ND 2.93	ref. to Ennius' *Annales*	
Rep. 6.10	ref. to Ennius' *Annales*	Skutsch 1985: 151
De Prov. Cons. 20	ref. to Ennius' *Annales*	Skutsch 1985: 106
De Leg. 1.4	ref. to Ennius' *Annales*?	Zillinger 1911: 102
Ac. pr. 2.51	Ennius' *Annales*	Skutsch 3
Ac. pr. 2.88	ref. to Ennius' *Annales*	Skutsch 3
Ac. pr. 2.88	Ennius' *Annales*	Skutsch 4
TD 1.27	Ennius' *Annales*	Skutsch 22
Div. 1.40–41	Ennius' *Annales*	Skutsch 34–50
Or. 161	Ennius' *Annales*	Skutsch 63
Div. 1.107–108	Ennius' *Annales*	Skutsch 72–91
Rep. 1.64	Ennius' *Annales*	Skutsch 105–109
De Or. 3.154	Ennius' *Annales*	Skutsch 110
TD 1.28	Ennius' *Annales*	Skutsch 110–111
Rep. 1.25	Ennius' *Annales*	Skutsch 153
Rep. 5.1	Ennius' *Annales*	Skutsch 156
Div. 2.116	Ennius' *Annales*	Skutsch 167

(*cont.*)

De Off. 1.38	Ennius' *Annales*	Skutsch 183–190
Div. 2.116	Ennius' *Annales*	Skutsch 197–198
De Sen. 16	Ennius' *Annales*	Skutsch 199–200
Or. 157	Ennius' *Annales*	Skutsch 206
Brut. 76	Ennius' *Annales*	Skutsch 206–207
Div. 1.114	Ennius' *Annales*	Skutsch 207
Brut. 71	Ennius' *Annales*	Skutsch 207–209
Or. 171	Ennius' *Annales*	Skutsch 207, 210
De Inv. 1.27	Ennius' *Annales*	Skutsch 216
Pro Balb. 51	Ennius' *Annales*	Skutsch 234–235
Pro Murena 30	Ennius' *Annales*	Skutsch 248, 248–249, 249, 252, 253
Att. 15.7.1	Ennius' *Annales*	Skutsch 252
Fam. 7.13.2	Ennius' *Annales*	Skutsch 252–253
Att. 12.5.1	Ennius' *Annales*	Skutsch 290
TD 1.45	Ennius' *Annales*	Skutsch 302
ND 3.24	Ennius' *Annales*	Skutsch 302
Brut. 58	Ennius' *Annales*	Skutsch 304–306
Brut. 59	Ennius' *Annales*	Skutsch 306–308
Brut. 59	Ennius' *Annales*	Skutsch 308
De Sen. 50	Ennius' *Annales*	Skutsch 308
Fam. 9.7.2	Ennius' *Annales*	Skutsch 309
De Or. 3.167	Ennius' *Annales*	Skutsch 309
Or. 93	Ennius' *Annales*	Skutsch 309
Rep. 1.30	Ennius' *Annales*	Skutsch 329
TD 1.18	Ennius' *Annales*	Skutsch 329
De Or. 1.198	Ennius' *Annales*	Skutsch 329
De Sen. 1	Ennius'*Annales*	Skutsch 335, 336, 337–339
Att. 16.3.1	ref. to Ennius' *Annales*/ Cicero's *De Senectute*	Skutsch 337
Att. 2.19.2	Ennius' *Annales*	Skutsch 363
De Off. 1.84	Ennius' *Annales*	Skutsch 363–365
De Sen. 10	Ennius' *Annales*	Skutsch 363–365
Rep. 3.6	Ennius' *Annales*	Skutsch 456
Or. 157	Ennius' *Annales*	Skutsch 504
De Sen. 14	Ennius' *Annales*	Skutsch 522–523
De Or. 3.168	Ennius' *Annales*	Skutsch 525
Div. 2.82	Ennius' *Annales*	Skutsch 541
De Or. 3.168	Ennius' *Annales*	Skusch 560–561
Rep. 1.3	Ennius' *Annales*	Skutsch 590
ND 2.4	Ennius' *Annales*	Skutsch 592
ND 2.64	Ennius' *Annales*	Skutsch 592
Att. 6.2.8	Ennius' *Annales*?	Skutsch 589
Pro Archia 18	Ennius' *Annales*?	Skutsch 1985: 131; xvi
Pro Archia 31	Ennius' *Annales*?	Skutsch 1985: 131; xvi
Fin. 1.51	Ennius' *Annales*	Zillinger 1911: 105
Pro Plancio 20	Ennius' *Annales*?	Zillinger 1911: 107

(*cont.*)

Att. 2.15.3	Ennius' *Annales?*/	Skutsch *dub.* 5/
	Cicero: unknown work?	Soubiran 1972: 300
TD 1.10	Ennius' *Annales?*/	Skutsch (*dubia*) 3–4
	Lucilius' *Saturae?*	Marx 1375–1376
Ennius' tragedies		
Verr. 2.1.46	Ennius' *Achilles*	*TrRF* II 1a
De Off. 1.114	ref. to Ennius' *Ajax*	
Pro S. Roscio 67	ref. to Ennius' *Alcmeo?*	Zillinger 1911: 109
De Leg. 1.40	ref. to Ennius' *Alcmeo?*	Zillinger 1911: 109
In Pisonem 46	ref. to Ennius' *Alcmeo?*	Zillinger 1911: 109
De Or. 3.154	Ennius' *Alcmeo*	*TrRF* II 12a
De Or. 3.218	Ennius' *Alcmeo*	*TrRF* II 12b
TD 4.18–19	Ennius' *Alcmeo*	*TrRF* II 12c
Fin. 4.62	Ennius' *Alcmeo*	*TrRF* II 12d
Fin. 5.31	Ennius' *Alcmeo*	*TrRF* II 12e
Hortensius fr. 102 Grilli	Ennius' *Alcmeo*	*TrRF* II 12f
Ac. pr. 2.52	Ennius' *Alcmeo*	*TrRF* II 13a
Ac. pr. 2.88–89	Ennius' *Alcmeo*	*TrRF* II 13b
Or. 153	Ennius' *Alcmeo*	*TrRF* II p55
Div. 1.42	Ennius' *Alexander*	Jocelyn 50–61
De opt. gen. 18	ref. to Ennius' *Andromacha*	
Att. 4.15.6	ref. to Ennius' *Andromacha*	*TrRF* II T 18
Ac. pr. 2.20	ref. to Ennius' *Andromacha*	*TrRF* II T 28
Div. 1.23	ref. to Ennius' *Andromacha*	*TrRF* II T 33
Pro Sestio 121	Ennius' *Andromacha*	*TrRF* II 23a
De Or. 3.102	Ennius' *Andromacha*	*TrRF* II 23b
De Or. 3.183	Ennius' *Andromacha*	*TrRF* II 23c
De Or. 3.217	Ennius' *Andromacha*	*TrRF* II 23d
Or. 93	Ennius' *Andromacha*	*TrRF* II 23e
TD 1.85	Ennius' *Andromacha*	*TrRF* II 23f
TD 1.105	Ennius' *Andromacha*	*TrRF* II 23g
TD 3.44–46	Ennius' *Andromacha*	*TrRF* II 23h
TD 3.53	Ennius' *Andromacha*	*TrRF* II 23i
Att. 2.1.5	Ennius' *Andromacha?*	*TrRF* II p86
TD 1.48	Ennius' *Andromacha?*	Ribbeck 70–72
Pro Milone 8	ref. to Ennius' *Eumenides?*	Jocelyn 1969a: 284
ND 3.40	ref. to Ennius' *Iphigenia*	*TrRF* II p169
Rep. 1.30	Ennius' *Iphigenia*	*TrRF* II 82a
Div. 2.30	Ennius' *Iphigenia*	*TrRF* II 82b
Fin. 1.4	ref to. Ennius' *Medea*	*TrRF* II T 29
De Inv. 1.91	Ennius' *Medea*	*TrRF* II 89b
Pro Caelio 18	Ennius' *Medea*	*TrRF* II 89c
Fin. 1.5	Ennius' *Medea*	*TrRF* II 89d
TD 1.45	Ennius' *Medea*	*TrRF* II 89e
ND 3.75	Ennius' *Medea*	*TrRF* II 89f
De Fato 34–35	Ennius' *Medea*	*TrRF* II 89g

(cont.)

Top. 61	Ennius' *Medea*	*TrRF* II 89h
Fam. 7.6.1–2	Ennius' *Medea*	*TrRF* II 90a
De Off. 3.62	Ennius' *Medea*	*TrRF* II 90b
TD 3.63	Ennius' *Medea*	*TrRF* II 91
TD 4.69	Ennius' *Medea*	*TrRF* II 92
ND 3.71	ref. to Ennius' *Medea?*	Jocelyn 225–227/TrRF I 71
ND 3.65	Ennius' *Medea?*	Jocelyn 225–227/*TrRF* I 71
ND 3.66	Ennius' *Medea?*	Jocelyn 228/*TrRF* I 72
ND 3.66	Ennius' *Medea?*	Jocelyn 229–231/*TrRF* I 73
Pro Murena 88	ref. to Gaius Gracchus/ Ennius' *Medea?*	Jocelyn 217–218/*TrRF* I 25
De Or. 3.214	ref. to Gaius Gracchus/ Ennius' *Medea*	Jocelyn 217–218/*TrRF* I 25
De Or. 3.217	Ennius' *Medea?*	Jocelyn 217–218/*TrRF* I 25
Att. 10.12.1	Ennius' *Medea?*	Jocelyn 217–218/*TrRF* I 25
De Off. 1.114	ref. to Ennius' *Melanippa*	
ND 3.79	Ennius' *Telamo*	*TrRF* II 117a
Div. 1.132	Ennius' *Telamo*	*TrRF* II 117b
Div. 2.104	Ennius' *Telamo*	*TrRF* II 117c
Brut. 78	ref. to Ennius' *Thyestes*	
In Pisonem 43	Ennius' *Thyestes*	*TrRF* II 132a
TD 1.107	Ennius' *Thyestes*	*TrRF* II 132b
Or. 184	Ennius' *Thyestes*	*TrRF* II 133
ND 2.4	Ennius' *Thyestes*	*TrRF* II 134a
ND 2.65	Ennius' *Thyestes*	*TrRF* II 134b
ND 3.10	Ennius' *Thyestes*	*TrRF* II 134c
ND 3.40	Ennius' *Thyestes*	*TrRF* II 134d
De Or. 3.164	Ennius' *Thyestes?*	Jocelyn 290/*TrRF* I 22
De Or. 3.164	Ennius' *Thyestes?*	Jocelyn 293–294/*TrRF* I 56b
Verr. 2.1.81	Ennius' *Thyestes?*	Jocelyn 295/*TrRF* II p227
De Inv. 1.91	Ennius: unknown tragedy	*TrRF* II 143b
Pro S. Roscio 90	Ennius: unknown tragedy	*TrRF* II 144a
Pro Balb. 36	Ennius: unknown tragedy	*TrRF* II 145a
De Off. 1.51–52	Ennius: unknown tragedy	*TrRF* II 145b
De Or. 1.199	Ennius: unknown tragedy	*TrRF* II 146
De Or. 2.155–156	Ennius: unknown tragedy	*TrRF* II 147a
Rep. 1.30	Ennius: unknown tragedy	*TrRF* II 147b
TD 2.1–2	Ennius: unknown tragedy	*TrRF* II 147c
De Or. 2.222	Ennius: unknown tragedy	*TrRF* II 148
De Or. 3.162	Ennius: unknown tragedy	*TrRF* II 149a
Rep. 1.49	Ennius: unknown tragedy	*TrRF* II 150a
Off. 1.26	Ennius: unknown tragedy	*TrRF* II 150b
Att. 8.11.3	Ennius: unknown tragedy	*TrRF* II 151a
Or. 155	Ennius: unknown tragedy	*TrRF* II 151b
Div. 1.66–67	Ennius: unknown tragedy	*TrRF* II 151c

(cont.)

Div. 1.114	Ennius: unknown tragedy	*TrRF* II 151d
Div. 2.112	Ennius: unknown tragedy	*TrRF* II 151e
Or. 155	Ennius: unknown tragedy	*TrRF* II 152
Or. 155	Ennius: unknown tragedy	*TrRF* II 153a
TD 2.38–39	Ennius: unknown tragedy	*TrRF* II 153b
Or. 160	Ennius: unknown tragedy	*TrRF* II 154
Fin. 2.41	Ennius: unknown tragedy	*TrRF* II 155
TD 3.5	Ennius: unknown tragedy	*TrRF* II 156
TD 3.44	Ennius: unknown tragedy	*TrRF* II 157
TD 4.70	Ennius: unknown tragedy	*TrRF* II 158
ND 2.65	Ennius: unknown tragedy	*TrRF* II 159
Div. 1.88	Ennius: unknown tragedy	*TrRF* II 160
Div. 2.57	Ennius: unknown tragedy	*TrRF* II 161
De Off. 1.61	Ennius: unknown tragedy	*TrRF* II 162
De Off. 2.23	Ennius: unknown tragedy	*TrRF* II 163
De Off. 2.62	Ennius: unknown tragedy	*TrRF* II 164
De Off. 3.104	Ennius: unknown tragedy	*TrRF* II 165
De Am. 64	Ennius: unknown tragedy	*TrRF* II 166
ND 2.49	Ennius: unknown tragedy	*TrRF* II 204
Div. 2.127	Ennius: unknown tragedy	*TrRF* II 205
Ennius' epigrams		
De Leg. 2.57	Ennius: epigram	Goldberg-Manuwald F1a
Rep. fr. 1 Powell	Ennius: epigram	Goldberg-Manuwald F1b
TD 1.34	Ennius: epigram	Goldberg-Manuwald F2a
TD 1.117	Ennius: epigram	Goldberg-Manuwald F2b
De Sen. 73	Ennius: epigram	Goldberg-Manuwald F2b
TD 5.49	Ennius: epigram	Goldberg-Manuwald F3a
Rep. fr. 2 Powell	Ennius: epigram	Goldberg-Manuwald F3b
Other works by Ennius		
ND 1.119	ref. to Ennius' *Euhemerus*	*TrRF* II T 31
Ac. 2.51	Ennius' *Epicharmus*	Goldberg-Manuwald F1
ND 1.97	Ennius' *Saturae*	Goldberg-Manuwald F17
De Or. 3.167	Ennius' *Scipio*	Goldberg-Manuwald F1
Fin. 2.106	Ennius' *Scipio*	Goldberg-Manuwald F1
De Or. 3.167	Ennius' *Scipio*	Goldberg-Manuwald F2
Or. 152	Ennius' *Scipio*	Goldberg-Manuwald F3
De Leg. 2.68	Ennius: unknown work	Goldberg-Manuwald F3a
TD 4.52	Ennius: unknown work	Goldberg-Manuwald F4
De Am. 22	Ennius: unknown work	Skutsch *op. inc.* 18
Reference to Lucilius		
Ac. pr. 2.102	ref. to Lucilius	
Fam. 9.15.2	ref. to Lucilius	
Lucilius' *Satires*		
De Or. 3.171	Lucilius' *Saturae*	Warmington 84–85, 86

(*cont.*)

Or. 149	Lucilius' *Saturae*	Warmington 84–85
Brut. 274	Lucilius' *Saturae*	Warmington 85
Fin. 1.9	Lucilius' *Saturae*	Warmington 87–93
Or. 161	Lucilius' *Saturae*	Warmington 173
TD 2.41	Lucilius' *Saturae*	Warmington 173
De opt. gen. 17	Lucilius' *Saturae*	Warmington 172–175
TD 4.48	Lucilius' *Saturae*	Warmington 176–181
Phil. 13.15	ref. to Lucilius' *Saturae*	Warmington 176–181
De Or. 3.86	Lucilius' *Saturae*	Warmington 182–183
Fin. 2.24	Lucilius' *Saturae*	Warmington 200–205
Fin. 2.25	Lucilius' *Saturae*	Warmington 206–207
Att. 13.52.1	Lucilius' *Saturae*	Warmington 206–207
Brut. 172	ref. to Lucilius' *Saturae*	Warmington 448–449
Att. 6.3.7	Lucilius' *Saturae*	Warmington 609–610
Att. 2.8.1	Lucilius' *Saturae*	Warmington 610
Rep. 1 fr. 1	Lucilius' *Saturae*	Warmington 632–634
De Or. 2.25	Lucilius' *Saturae*	Warmington 635
Fin. 1.7	Lucilius' *Saturae*	Warmington 635
Brut. 99	ref. to Lucilius' *Saturae*	Warmington 635
De Or. 2.253	Lucilius' *Saturae*	Warmington 1135
ND 1.63	Lucilius' *Saturae*	Warmington 1138–1141
Fin. 2.23	Lucilius' *Saturae*	Warmington 1226–1227
Ac. pr. 2.94	Lucilius' *Saturae*	Warmington 1249
Att. 13.21.3	Lucilius' *Saturae*	Warmington 1249
De Am. 63	Lucilius' *Saturae*	Warmington 1249
De Or. 2.262	Lucilius' *Saturae*?	Marx 173
De Or. 2.268	Lucilius' *Saturae*?	Marx 396
De Or. 2.277	Lucilius' *Saturae*?	Marx 421
Fin. 5.92	Lucilius' *Saturae*?	Marx 1300
TD 3.31	Lucilius' *Saturae*?	Marx 1300
ad Q. fr. 3.4.2	ref. to Lucilius' *Saturae*	Marx 1300
Fam. 2.8.2	Lucilius' *Saturae*?	Marx 1372
De Or. 1.72	ref. to Lucilius' *Saturae*?	Marx 1241
Brut. 160	ref. to Lucilius' *Saturae*	Marx 1180
Pro Plancio 33–34	ref. to Lucilius' *Saturae*?	Marx 1181
De Or. 2.224	ref. to Lucilius' *Saturae*?	Marx 1181
De Or. 2.254	ref. to Lucilius' *Saturae*?	Marx 1181
De Or. 2.281	ref. to Lucilius' *Saturae*?	Marx 1181
Att. 16.11.1	ref. to Lucilius' *Saturae*?	Marx 1317
De Or. 2.22	ref. to Lucilius' *Saturae*?	Zillinger 1911: 167
De Or. 3.164	ref. to Lucilius' *Saturae*?	Zillinger 1911: 167
De Or. 2.284	Lucilius' *Saturae*?	Zillinger 1911: 161
De Or. 2.267	Lucilius' *Saturae*?	Zillinger 1911: 162
De Or. 2.263	Lucilius' *Saturae*?	Zillinger 1911: 167
Fin. 2.15	Lucilius' *Saturae*?	Zillinger 1911: 167

(*cont.*)

TD 1.10	Lucilius' *Saturae?*/	Marx 1375–1376
	Ennius' *Annales?*	Skutsch (*dubia* 3–4)
Div. 2.133	Lucilius' *Saturae?*/	Marx 1377/
	Cic. trans. Greek poet?	Soubiran fr. ii
Reference to Naevius		
Verr. 1.29	ref. to Naevius?	*TrRF* I T7
Rep. 4.11	ref. to Naevius	
TD 1.3	ref. to Naevius	
De Leg. 2.39	ref. to Naevius	
De Or. 3.45	ref. to Naevius	
Brut. 60	ref. to Naevius	
Brut. 73	ref. to Naevius	
Naevius' works		
De Sen. 50	ref. to Naevius' *Bellum*	
	Punicum	
Brut. 76	ref. to Naevius' *Bellum*	
	Punicum	
TD 4.67	Naevius' *Hector Proficiscens*	*TrRF* I 14
Fam. 5.12.7	Naevius' *Hector Proficiscens*	*TrRF* I 14
Fam. 15.6.1	Naevius' *Hector Proficiscens*	*TrRF* I 14
De Sen. 20	Naevius' *Ludus/Lupus/*	Powell 1988: 145–146
	Lydus	
Or. 152	Naevius: unknown tragedy	*TrRF* I 41
Or. 152	Naevius: unknown tragedy	*TrRF* I 42
Phil. 2.65	Naevius: unknown tragedy	*TrRF* I 46
Reference to Pacuvius		
Ac. post. 1.10	ref. to Pacuvius	Schierl T 24
De Or. 3.27	ref. to Pacuvius	
Brut. 229	ref. to Pacuvius	
Brut. 258	ref. to Pacuvius	
Or. 36	ref. to Pacuvius	
De opt. gen. 2	ref. to Pacuvius	
Pacuvius' tragedies		
De opt. gen. 18	ref. to Pacuvius' *Antiopa*	
De Off. 1.114	ref. to Pacuvius' *Antiopa*	
Fin. 1.4	ref. to Pacuvius' *Antiopa*	Schierl T 25
Ac. pr. 2.20	ref. to Pacuvius' *Antiopa*	Schierl T 40
De Inv. 1.94	ref. to Pacuvius' *Antiopa*	Schierl T 46
De Or. 2.155	ref. to Pacuvius' *Antiopa*	Schierl T 47
Rep. 1.30	ref. to Pacuvius' *Antiopa*	Schierl T 48
Div. 2.133	Pacuvius' *Antiopa*	Schierl fr. 3
Fin. 2.79	ref. to Pacuvius' *Chryses*	Schierl T 51
De Am. 24	ref. to Pacuvius' *Chryses*	Schierl T 52
De Or. 3.167	Pacuvius' *Chryses*	Schierl fr. 63

(*cont.*)

Fin. 5.63	Pacuvius' *Chryses?*	Schierl fr. 69/*TrRF* I 48
ND 2.91	Pacuvius' *Chryses*	Schierl fr. 79
Or. 155	Pacuvius' *Chryses*	Schierl fr. 76
Div. 1.131	Pacuvius' *Chryses*	Schierl fr. 77
Div. 1.131	Pacuvius' *Chryses*	Schierl fr. 80
TD 2.47	ref. to Pacuvius' *Hermiona*	Schierl fr. 139
De Or. 2.187	Pacuvius' *Hermiona*	Schierl fr. 139
Pro Sestio 126	Pacuvius' *Iliona*	Schierl fr. 146/T 55
Ac. pr. 2.88	Pacuvius' *Iliona*	Schierl fr. 146/T 56
TD 1.106	Pacuvius' *Iliona*	Schierl fr. 146
Ac. pr. 2.88	Pacuvius' *Iliona*	Schierl fr. 147
TD 2.44	Pacuvius' *Iliona*	Schierl fr. 147
Att. 14.14.1	Pacuvius' *Iliona*	Schierl fr. 147
De Or. 3.219	Pacuvius' *Iliona?*	Schierl fr. 150/*TrRF* I 26a
De Off. 1.114	ref. to Pacuvius' *Medus*	
Rep. 3.14	ref. to Pacuvius' *Medus*	Schierl T 61
ND 3.48	ref. to Pacuvius' *Medus*	Schierl T 59
De Inv. 1.27	Pacuvius' *Medus*	Schierl fr. 171
De Inv. 1.90	Pacuvius' *Medus*	Schierl fr. 186
TD 4.69	Pacuvius' *Medus?*	Schierl fr. 185/*TrRF* I 62
TD 5.46	Pacuvius' *Niptra*	Schierl fr. 191
TD 2.48–50	Pacuvius' *Niptra*	Schierl fr. 199
TD 2.50	Pacuvius' *Niptra*	Schierl fr. 200
De Or. 1.246	ref. to Pacuvius' *Teucer*	
De Or. 3.157	Pacuvius' *Teucer*	Schierl fr. 239
Div. 1.24	Pacuvius' *Teucer*	Schierl fr. 239
De Or. 2.193	Pacuvius' *Teucer*	Schierl fr. 243
De Or. 3.217	Pacuvius' *Teucer*	Schierl fr. 243
TD 5.108	Pacuvius' *Teucer?*	Schierl fr. 250/*TrRF* I 66
Div. 1.80	Pacuvius' *Teucer*	Schierl fr. 251
Fam. 8.2.1	Pacuvius: unknown tragedy	Schierl fr. 263
Or. 155	Pacuvius: unknown tragedy	Schierl fr. 264
Fin. 5.31	Pacuvius: unknown tragedy	Schierl fr. 265
ND 2.91	Pacuvius: unknown tragedy	Schierl fr. 266

Reference to Plautus

Rep. 4.11	ref. to Plautus
TD 1.3	ref. to Plautus
Fam. 9.16.4	ref. to Plautus
De Off. 1.104	ref. to Plautus
De Or. 3.45	ref. to Plautus
Brut. 60	ref. to Plautus
Brut. 73	ref. to Plautus

(cont.)

Plautus' comedies		
Div. 1.65	Plautus' *Aulularia*	178
Pro Q. Roscio 20	ref. to Plautus' *Pseudolus*	
De Sen. 50	ref. to Plautus' *Pseudolus*	
Phil. 2.15	ref. to Plautus' *Pseudolus*	
De Inv. 1.95	Plautus' *Trinummus*	23–26
ad Brut. 1.2.3 (2a.1)	Plautus' *Trinummus*	319
In Pisonem 61	Plautus' *Trinummus*	419
De Or. 2.39	Plautus' *Trinummus*	705
De Sen. 50	ref. to Plautus' *Truculentus*	
Reference to Terence		
De opt. gen. 3	ref. to Terence	
Terence's comedies		
De Sen. 65	ref. to Terence's *Adelphoe*	
De Inv. 1.27	Terence's *Adelphoe*	60–64
Pro Caelio 38	Terence's *Adelphoe*	120–121
Fin. 1.4	ref. to Terence's *Andria*	
De opt. gen. 18	ref. to Terence's *Andria*	
De Inv. 1.33	Terence's *Andria*	49–50
De Inv. 1.27	Terence's *Andria*	51
De Inv. 1.33	Terence's *Andria*	51
De Or. 2.326	Terence's *Andria*	51
De Am. 89	Terence's *Andria*	68
De Or. 2.172	Terence's *Andria*	110–112
Fam. 9.7.1	Terence's *Andria*	112
De Or. 2.327	Terence's *Andria*	117, 128–129
Pro Caelio 61	Terence's *Andria*	126
De Inv. 1.33	Terence's *Andria*	157
De Inv. 1.33	Terence's *Andria*	168
Att. 13.34	Terence's *Andria*	185
Fam. 12.25.5	Terence's *Andria*	189
Phil. 2.15	ref. to Terence's *Eunuchus*	
ND 3.72	Terence's *Eunuchus*	46
ND 3.72	Terence's *Eunuchus*	49
TD 4.76	Terence's *Eunuchus*	59–63
Att. 7.3.10	Terence's *Eunuchus*	114–115
De Am. 93	Terence's *Eunuchus*	252–253
De Off. 1.150	Terence's *Eunuchus*	257
De Am. 98	Terence's *Eunuchus*	391–392
Fam. 1.9.19	Terence's *Eunuchus*	440–445
Att. 7.3.10	Terence's *Eunuchus*	539
ND 2.60	Terence's *Eunuchus*	732
Fin. 1.3	Terence's *Heaut.*	69
Fin. 2.14	Terence's *Heaut.*	53
Att. 12.6.3(6a.1)	Terence's *Heaut.*	75

(cont.)

De Leg. 1.33	Terence's *Heaut.*	77
De Off. 1.30	Terence's *Heaut.*	77
Fin. 5.29	Terence's *Heaut.*	80
Fam. 7.10.4	Terence's *Heaut.*	86
Att. 9.6.5	Terence's *Heaut.*	86
TD 3.65	Terence's *Heaut.*	135
Fin. 5.28	Terence's *Heaut.*	147, 148
TD 3.65	Terence's *Heaut.*	147–148
Phil. 2.15	ref. to Terence's *Phormio*	
Pro Caecina 27	Terence's *Phormio*	123
Att. 2.19.1	Terence's *Phormio*	232–233
TD 3.30	Terence's *Phormio*	241–246
ND 3.73	Terence's *Phormio*	321
Or. 157	Terence's *Phormio*	384, 390

Trabea's comedies (palliatae)

Fam. 9.21.1	ref. to Trabea	Ribbeck fr. iii
TD 4.67	Trabea: unknown comedy	Ribbeck 1–5
Fam. 2.9.2	Trabea: unknown comedy	Ribbeck 6
Fin. 2.13	Trabea: unknown comedy	Ribbeck 6
TD 4.35	Trabea: unknown comedy	Ribbeck 6

Sextus Turpilius' comedies (palliatae)

Fam. 9.22.1	Turpilius' *Demiurgus*	Ribbeck 43–44
TD 4.72–73	Turpilius' *Leucadia*	Ribbeck 115–120

Atellan farce (fabula Atellana)

Fam. 9.16.7	ref. to Atellan farce	
Div. 2.25	ref. to Atellan farce	
De Or. 2.255	Novius: unknown *Atellana*	Ribbeck 115
De Or. 2.279	Novius: unknown *Atellana*	Ribbeck 113–114
De Or. 2.285	Novius: unknown *Atellana*	Ribbeck 116
Fam. 7.31.2	Pomponius: unknown *Atellana*	Ribbeck 191

Mime

Att. 1.16.13	ref. to *Faba* (mime)	Zillinger 1911: 157
De Or. 2.259	ref. to *Tutor* (mime)	Ribbeck 1855: 311
Fam. 7.11.2	ref. to D. Laberius	
Fam. 12.18.2	ref. to D. Laberius	
De Off. 1.114	ref. to D. Laberius?	Panayotakis 2010: 459
Phil. 11.13	ref. to Nucula	
Fam. 12.18.2	ref. to Publilius Syrus	
Att. 14.2.1	ref. to Publilius Syrus	
Fam. 7.11.2	ref. to Valerius	
Fam. 9.16.7	ref. to mime	
Phil. 2.65	ref. to mime	
Pro Caelio 65	ref. to mime	

(cont.)

Pro Q. Gallio fr. 2	ref. to mime	
De Or. 2.274	Unknown mime	Ribbeck 1–2
De Or. 2.274	Unknown mime	Ribbeck 3–4
De Or. 2.274	Unknown mime	Ribbeck 5
Plays without authors		
Fam. 7.1.2	ref. to *Equus Troianus*	*TrRF* I p85
Fam. 7.16.1	*Equus Troianus*	*TrRF* I *adesp.* 29a
TD 1.116	ref. to *Iphigenia*	
Unknown tragedies		
De Inv. 1.83	Unknown tragedy	*TrRF* I 9
Pro Murena 60	Unknown tragedy	*TrRF* I 13a
Att. 1.18.1	Unknown tragedy	*TrRF* I 14
Att. 2.19.3	Unknown tragedy	*TrRF* I 15a
Pro Sestio 45	Unknown tragedy	*TrRF* I 16
Har. resp. 39	Unknown tragedy	*TrRF* I 17
De Or. 3.102	Unknown tragedy	*TrRF* I 18
De Or. 3.154	Unknown tragedy	*TrRF* I 19a
Or. 164	Unknown tragedy	*TrRF* I 19b
De Or. 3.158	Unknown tragedy	*TrRF* I 20
De Or. 3.162	Unknown tragedy	*TrRF* I 21a
Ac. pr. 2.89	Unknown tragedy	*TrRF* I 21b
De Or. 3.166	Unknown tragedy	*TrRF* I 23a
De Or. 3.166	Unknown tragedy	*TrRF* I 24a
Or. 164	Unknown tragedy	*TrRF* I 26b
Fam. 7.1.2	Unknown tragedy	*TrRF* I 27
ad Q. fr. 2.11.3	Unknown tragedy	*TrRF* I 28
Fam. 7.16.1	Unknown tragedy	*TrRF* I 30
Pro Rab. Post. 28	Unknown tragedy	*TrRF* I 31
Pro Rab. Post. 29	Unknown tragedy	*TrRF* I 32
Pro Rab. Post. 29	Unknown tragedy	*TrRF* I 33
Pro Rab. Post. 29	Unknown tragedy	*TrRF* I 34a
Att. 7.26.1	Unknown tragedy	*TrRF* I 34b
Pro Scauro 3	Unknown tragedy	*TrRF* I 35
Att. 6.9.5	Unknown tragedy	*TrRF* I 36
Or. 153	Unknown tragedy	*TrRF* I 37
Or. 153	Unknown tragedy	*TrRF* I 38
Or. 153	Unknown tragedy	*TrRF* I 39
Or. 157	Unknown tragedy	*TrRF* I 40
Or. 163–164	Unknown tragedy	*TrRF* I 41
Or. 164	Unknown tragedy	*TrRF* I 42
Or. 166	Unknown tragedy	*TrRF* I 43a
Top. 55	Unknown tragedy	*TrRF* I 43b
Fam. 6.6.6	Unknown tragedy	*TrRF* I 44
Pro Reg. Deiot. 25	Unknown tragedy	*TrRF* I 45
Fin. 2.18	Unknown tragedy	*TrRF* I 46

(*cont.*)

Fin. 2.71	Unknown tragedy	*TrRF* I 47
TD 1.10	Unknown tragedy	*TrRF* I 49
TD 1.37	Unknown tragedy	*TrRF* I 50
TD 1.37	Unknown tragedy	*TrRF* I 51
TD 1.69	Unknown tragedy	*TrRF* I 52a
De Or. 3.154	Unknown tragedy	*TrRF* I 52b
TD 2.34	Unknown tragedy	*TrRF* I 53
TD 2.36	Unknown tragedy	*TrRF* I 54
TD 3.26	Unknown tragedy	*TrRF* I 55
TD 3.26	Unknown tragedy	*TrRF* I 56a
Att. 9.9.2	Unknown tragedy	*TrRF* I 56, 3
TD 3.26	Unknown tragedy	*TrRF* I 57
TD 3.39	ref. to unknown tragedy	*TrRF* I 57
TD 3.28	Unknown tragedy	*TrRF* I 58
TD 3.39	Unknown tragedy	*TrRF* I 59a
Fam. 9.26.2	Unknown tragedy	*TrRF* I 59b
TD 3.58	Unknown tragedy	*TrRF* I 58
TD 4.35	Unknown tragedy	*TrRF* I 60
TD 4.52	Unknown tragedy	*TrRF* I 61
TD 4.77	Unknown tragedy	*TrRF* I 63
TD 5.52	Unknown tragedy	*TrRF* I 65
Att. 12.51.3	Unknown tragedy	*TrRF* I 67a
Att. 14.21.3	Unknown tragedy	*TrRF* I 67b
Top. 55	Unknown tragedy	*TrRF* I 67c
Att. 13.47.1	Unknown tragedy	*TrRF* I 68a
ND 1.119	Unknown tragedy	*TrRF* I 69
ND 1.119	Unknown tragedy	*TrRF* I 70
ND 3.67	Unknown tragedy	*TrRF* I 74
Div. 1.29	Unknown tragedy	*TrRF* I 75
Div. 2.115	Unknown tragedy	*TrRF* I 77a
Top. 61	Unknown tragedy	*TrRF* I 78
De Off. 1.61	Unknown tragedy	*TrRF* I 79
De Off. 1.139	Unknown tragedy	*TrRF* I 80a
Phil. 2.104	Unknown tragedy	*TrRF* I 80b
De Off. 2.13	Unknown tragedy	*TrRF* I 81
De Off. 3.98	Unknown tragedy	*TrRF* I 82
Att. 14.12.2	Unknown tragedy	*TrRF* I 83a
Att. 15.11.3	Unknown tragedy	*TrRF* I 83b
Fam. 7.30.1	Unknown tragedy	*TrRF* I 83c
Fam. 7.28.2	Unknown tragedy	*TrRF* I 83d
Phil. 13.49	Unknown tragedy	*TrRF* I 83e
Fam. 9.22.1	Unknown tragedy	*TrRF* I 84
Fam. 9.22.1	Unknown tragedy	*TrRF* I 85
Fam. 9.22.1	Unknown tragedy	*TrRF* I 86
Phil. 13.49	Unknown tragedy	*TrRF* I 87
Att. 4.1.8	Unknown tragedy	*TrRF* I 160a

(cont.)

Att. 4.2.1	Unknown tragedy	*TrRF* I 160b
ad Brut. 1.10.2	Unknown tragedy	*TrRF* I 160c
Pro Sestio 48	Unknown tragedy	*TrRF* I 161
TD 2.67	Unknown tragedy	*TrRF* I 162
TD 1.48	Unknown tragedy	Jocelyn 1969a: 255
Pro Marcello 14	Unknown tragedy	*TrRF* I p215
ND 2.151	Unknown tragedy	*TrRF* II p250 (= *TrRF* I 81)
Unknown comedies		
De Or. 2.242	Unknown comedy	Ribbeck 1
Att. 10.2.2	Unknown comedy	Ribbeck 28–29
Fam. 5.10.2	Unknown comedy	Ribbeck 30
De Or. 3.219	Unknown comedy	Ribbeck 32–34
Fin. 2.14	Unknown comedy	Ribbeck 37
Fam. 2.9.2	Unknown comedy	Ribbeck 38
Fam. 2.9.2	Unknown comedy	Ribbeck 39
Fam. 2.9.2	Unknown comedy	Ribbeck 40
TD 1.94	Unknown comedy	Ribbeck 43–44
De Or. 2.257	Unknown comedy	Ribbeck 45
Fam. 3.8.8	Unknown comedy	Ribbeck 49
Att. 1.16.1	Unknown comedy	Ribbeck 63
Att. 5.15.3	Unknown comedy	Ribbeck 66–67
Att. 4.3.3	Unknown comedy	Ribbeck 71
Pro Caelio 36	Unknown comedy	Ribbeck 72
Par. Stoic. 34	Unknown comedy	Ribbeck 75
Fam. 7.3.4	Unknown comedy	Ribbeck 90–91
In Clod. et C.		
fr. 21 Crawford	Unknown comedy	Zillinger 1911: 160
Or. 147	Unknown comedy?	Ribbeck 30[1]
Att. 15.1.4	Unknown comedy?	Palmer 1883: 446
Other Latin Verse		
TD 4.4	ref. to Appius Claudius Caecus' *carmen*	*FPL* p12
Fin. 2.116	epitaph of A. Atilius Calatinus	*FPL* pp13–14
De Sen. 61	epitaph of A. Atilius Calatinus	*FPL* pp13–14
Brut. 75	ref. to *carmina conuiualia*	*FPL* p2
TD 1.3	ref. to *carmina conuiualia*	*FPL* p2
TD 4.3	ref. to *carmina conuiualia*	*FPL* p2
De Or. 3.197	ref. to *epulae solemnes* (ceremonial banquets)	

---

[1] Ribbeck (1852: xix) initially assigned this fragment to tragedy, later (1873: xxii) to comedy.

(cont.)

De Or. 3.197	ref. to Hymn of the Salii	*FPL* p3
Div. 1.89	ref. to oracles of Marcii	*FPL* p15
Div. 1.115	ref. to oracles of Marcius and Publicius	*FPL* p15
Div. 2.113	ref. to oracles of Marcius	*FPL* p15
De Leg. 2.62	ref. to *neniae* (funeral dirges)	
Contemporary poets		
Brut. 132	ref. to Furius Antias	
ND 1.79	Catulus epigram	Courtney fr. 2
Q. fr. 2.9.3	ref. to Lucretius	
Or. 161	ref. to *poetae noui*	
De Or. 3.225	ref. to Porcius Licinius	
Fin. 1.5	Porcius Licinius	*FPL* fr. 5
De Or. 3.43	ref. to Q. Valerius Soranus	
Brut. 169	ref. to Q. Valerius Soranus	
Brut. 167	ref. to C. Titius	
Brut. 177	ref. to Julius Caesar Strabo Vopiscus	
Q. fr. 3.1.13	ref. to Quintus' *Erigona*	Courtney 2003: 181
Q. fr. 3.5.7	ref. to Quintus' *Erigona*	Courtney 2003: 181
Q. fr. 3.5.7	ref. to Quintus' tragedies	Courtney 2003: 181
Q. fr. 3.7.6	ref. to Quintus' *Erigona*	Courtney 2003: 181
Cicero's poetry		
Rep. 1.56	ref. to Cicero's *Aratea*	Soubiran fr. i
Q. fr. 3.7.6	ref. to Cicero's epic for Caesar	Courtney 2003: 181
De Leg. 2.7	Cicero's *Aratea*	Soubiran fr. i
ND 2.104	Cicero's *Aratea*	Soubiran fr. iii
ND 2.105	Cicero's *Aratea*	Soubiran fr. iv
ND 2.105	Cicero's *Aratea*	Soubiran fr. v
ND 2.105	Cicero's *Aratea*	Soubiran fr. vi
ND 2.106	Cicero's *Aratea*	Soubiran fr. vii
Ac. pr. 2.66	Cicero's *Aratea*	Soubiran fr. vii
ND 2.106	Cicero's *Aratea*	Soubiran fr. viii
ND 2.107	Cicero's *Aratea*	Soubiran fr. ix
ND 2.108	Cicero's *Aratea*	Soubiran fr. x
ND 2.108	Cicero's *Aratea*	Soubiran fr. xi
ND 2.108	Cicero's *Aratea*	Soubiran fr. xii
ND 2.108	Cicero's *Aratea*	Soubiran fr. xiii
ND 2.109	Cicero's *Aratea*	Soubiran fr. xiv
ND 2.109	Cicero's *Aratea*	Soubiran fr. xv
ND 2.109–110	Cicero's *Aratea*	Soubiran fr. xvi
ND 2.159	Cicero's *Aratea*	Soubiran fr. xviii
ND 2.110	Cicero's *Aratea*	Soubiran fr. xxii

(cont.)

Or. 152	Cicero's *Aratea*	Soubiran fr. xxiii
ND 2.110	Cicero's *Aratea*	Soubiran fr. xxv
ND 2.110	Cicero's *Aratea*	Soubiran fr. xxvi
ND 2.110	Cicero's *Aratea*	Soubiran fr. xxvii
ND 2.111	Cicero's *Aratea*	Soubiran 12–13
ND 2.111	Cicero's *Aratea*	Soubiran 20–21
ND 2.112	Cicero's *Aratea*	Soubiran 22
ND 2.112	Cicero's *Aratea*	Soubiran 27–28
ND 2.112	Cicero's *Aratea*	Soubiran 42
ND 2.112	Cicero's *Aratea*	Soubiran 47
ND 2.112	Cicero's *Aratea*	Soubiran 56
ND 2.112	Cicero's *Aratea*	Soubiran 58–61
ND 2.113	Cicero's *Aratea*	Soubiran 77–78
ND 2.113	Cicero's *Aratea*	Soubiran 85
ND 2.113	Cicero's *Aratea*	Soubiran 87
ND 2.113	Cicero's *Aratea*	Soubiran 91–101
ND 2.113	Cicero's *Aratea*	Soubiran 102
ND 2.114	Cicero's *Aratea*	Soubiran 108
ND 2.114	Cicero's *Aratea*	Soubiran 125–126
ND 2.114	Cicero's *Aratea*	Soubiran 143–144
ND 2.114	Cicero's *Aratea*	Soubiran 150
ND 2.114	Cicero's *Aratea*	Soubiran 151
ND 2.114	Cicero's *Aratea*	Soubiran 183–184
ND 2.114	Cicero's *Aratea*	Soubiran 207
ND 2.114	Cicero's *Aratea*	Soubiran 210–211
ND 2.114	Cicero's *Aratea*	Soubiran 213–214
ND 2.114	Cicero's *Aratea*	Soubiran 219–222
Div. 1.13–14	Cicero's *Prognostica*	Soubiran fr. iii
Div. 1.14–15	Cicero's *Prognostica*	Soubiran fr. iv
Div. 1.15	Cicero's *Prognostica*	Soubiran fr. v
Div. 1.17–22	Cicero's *De Consulatu Suo*	Soubiran fr. ii
Div. 2.45	Cicero's *De Consulatu Suo*	Soubiran fr. ii
De Off. 1.77	Cicero's *De Consulatu Suo*	Soubiran fr. vi
In Pis. 72–74	Cicero's *De Consulatu Suo*	Soubiran fr. vi
Ph. 2.20	Cicero's *De Consulatu Suo*	Soubiran fr. vi
Att. 2.3.4	Cicero's *De Consulatu Suo*	Soubiran fr. viii
ad Q. fr. 3.1.24	ref. to Cicero's *De Temp.*	Soubiran ii
ad Q. fr. 2.(7).8.1	ref. to Cicero's *De Temp.*	Soubiran iii
De Leg. 1.2	Cicero's *Marius*	Soubiran fr. i
De Leg. 1.2	Cicero's *Marius*	Soubiran fr. ii
Div. 1.106	Cicero's *Marius*	Soubiran fr. iii
Spuria/dubia		
ND 2.25	Unknown verse?	Mayor 1883: 112
Att. 2.15.3	Ennius' *Annales*?/	Skutsch *dub.* 5/
	Cicero: unknown work?	Soubiran 1972: 300

Appendix III   By Greek Poet

(*cont.*)

Rep. 2.19	ref. to Homer
Rep. 4.5	ref. to Homer
Rep. 6.10	ref. to Homer
De Leg. 1.2	ref. to Homer
Fin. 1.7	ref. to Homer
Fin. 2.115	ref. to Homer
Fin. 2.116	ref. to Homer
Fin. 5.49	ref. to Homer
TD 1.3	ref. to Homer
TD 1.37	ref. to Homer
TD 1.65	ref. to Homer
TD 1.79	ref. to Homer
TD 1.98	ref. to Homer
TD 4.49	ref. to Homer
TD 4.52	ref. to Homer
TD 5.7	ref. to Homer
TD 5.115	ref. to Homer
ND 1.41	ref. to Homer
ND 1.107	ref. to Homer
ND 2.70	ref. to Homer
ND 2.116	ref. to Homer
ND 3.11	ref. to Homer
ND 3.41	ref. to Homer
De Sen. 23	ref. to Homer
De Sen. 31	ref. to Homer
De Sen. 54	ref. to Homer
Div. 1.65	ref. to Homer
Div. 1.72	ref. to Homer
Div. 1.87	ref. to Homer
Div. 1.88	ref. to Homer
Div. 1.89	ref. to Homer
Div. 2.25	ref. to Homer
Div. 2.97	ref. to Homer
Div. 2.133	ref. to Homer
Div. 2.139	ref. to Homer
Div. 3.97	ref. to Homer
Fam. 3.11.5	ref. to Homer
Fam. 5.12.7	ref. to Homer
Fam. 10.13.2	ref. to Homer
De opt. gen. 6	ref. to Menander
Fin. 1.4	ref. to Menander
Fin. 1.7	ref. to Menander
Fin. 2.115	ref. to Pindar
De Sen. 23	ref. to Simonides
De Sen. 23	ref. to Stesichorus
Or. 4	ref. to Sophocles
Fin. 1.5	ref. to Sophocles' *Electra*

(*cont.*)

Q. fr. 2.16.3	ref. to Sophocles' *Syndeipnoi*	

Greek poets quoted in Latin

TD 3.76	Aeschylus' *PV* 377–380	Soubiran fr i.
TD 2.23–25	Aeschylus' *Prometheus Unbound* Nauck fr. 193	Soubiran fr. ii
TD 1.41	Aristophanes' *Wasps?*	1431
TD 5.25	Chaeremon Nauck fr. 2	Soubiran fr. v
Fin. 2.105	Euripides' *Andromeda* Nauck fr. 133	Soubiran fr. iv
TD 1.115	Euripides' *Cresphontes* Nauck fr. 449	Soubiran fr. vi
De Off. 3.108	Euripides' *Hippolytus* 612	Soubiran fr. i
TD 3.59	Euripides' *Hypsipyle* Nauck fr. 757	Soubiran fr. vii
TD 4.63	Euripides' *Orestes* 1–3	Soubiran fr. iii
De Or. 3.141	ref. to Euripides *Philoctetes*	Nauck fr. 796
De Off. 3.82	Euripides' *Phoenissae* 524–525	Soubiran fr. ii
TD 3.67	Euripides' *Phrixos* Nauck fr. 821	Soubiran fr. viii
Div. 2.12	Euripides Nauck fr. 973	Soubiran fr. x
TD 3.29	Euripides Nauck fr. 964	Soubiran fr. v
TD 3.58	Euripides Nauck fr. 964	Soubiran fr. v
Brut. 15	Hesiod's *Works and Days*	350
Off. 1.48	Hesiod's *Works and Days*	350
Div. 2.63–64	Homer's *Iliad* 2.299–330	Soubiran fr. i
TD 3.63	Homer's *Iliad* 6.201–202	Soubiran fr. ii
Div. 2.82	Homer's *Iliad* 9.236	Soubiran fr. iv
Div. 1.52	Homer's *Iliad* 9.363	Soubiran fr. v
TD 3.18	Homer's *Iliad* 9.646–647	Soubiran fr. vi
TD 3.65	Homer's *Iliad* 19.226–229	Soubiran fr. vii
Fin. 5.49	Homer's *Odyssey* 12.184–191	Soubiran fr. viii
De Gloria fr. 2[1]	Homer's *Iliad* 7.89–91	Soubiran fr. iii
De Fato fr. 3[2]	Homer's *Odyssey* 18.136–137	Soubiran fr. ix

[1] Gellius *NA* 15.6.1. [2] Aug. *Civ. Dei* 5.8.

(cont.)

TD 1.101	Simonides	Soubiran fr. ii	
De Sen. 73	ref. to Solon	Campbell fr. 22.5–6	
TD 1.117	Solon	Campbell fr. 22.5–6	
TD 2.20–22	Sophocles' *Trachiniae*	1046–1102	Soubiran fr. i
TD 3.71	Sophocles Nauck fr. 666	Soubiran fr. ii	
Fin. 3.64	Unknown Greek poet	Nauck fr. 513	
ND 1.79	ref. to Alcaeus	Campbell fr. 431	
Div. 2.25	Unknown Greek verse	Soubiran fr. vii	
Div. 2.133	Unknown Greek verse?/ Lucilius' *Saturae?*	Soubiran fr. ii/ Marx 1377	
Div. 2.115	Pythian oracle	to Croesus	Soubiran fr. viii
Div. 1.81	Pythian oracle	to Brennus	Soubiran fr. ix
Fin. 2.106	ref. to epitaph of Sardanapallus	Soubiran fr. x	
TD 5.101	epitaph of Sardanapallus	Soubiran fr. x	

Greek poets quoted in Greek

Att. 14.10.1	Aeschylus' *PV*	682
Q. fr. 1.2.13	Aeschylus' *PV*	750
Att. 5.12.1	Archilochus	Diehl fr. 56.2
Att. 5.10.3	Aristophanes' *Wasps?*	1431
Att. 6.9.3	Callimachus' *Epigrams*	32.2
Att. 8.5.1	Callimachus	Pfeiffer fr. 732
Att. 2.25.1	Euripides' *Andromache*	448
Att. 13.11.1	Euripides' *Ion*	585
Att. 2.25.1	Euripides' *Phoenissae*	393
Att. 7.11.1	Euripides' *Phoenissae*	506
Q. fr. 2.14.5	Euripides' *Suppliants*	119
Att. 7.3.5	Euripides' *Troades*	455
Att. 6.8.5	Euripides' *Philoctetes*	Nauck fr. 796
Att. 1.20.3	Euripides' *Telephus*/ Greek proverb	Nauck fr. 723/ *CPG* I p307
Att. 4.6.2	Euripides' *Telephus* Greek proverb	Nauck fr. 723/ *CPG* I p307
Fam. 13.15.2	Euripides: unknown tragedy	Nauck fr. 905
Fam. 16.8.2	Euripides: unknown tragedy	Nauck fr. 906
Att. 8.8.2	Euripides: unknown tragedy	Nauck fr. 918.1–3
Att. 6.1.8	Euripides: unknown tragedy	Nauck fr. 918.3
Att. 9.2a.2	Euripides: unknown tragedy	Nauck fr. 958
Att. 7.13.4	Euripides: unknown tragedy	Nauck fr. 973

(cont.)

Fam. 6.18.5	Hesiod's *Works and Days*	289
Att. 13.12.3	Hesiod's *Works and Days*	350
Fam. 3.7.6	Homer's *Iliad*	1.174–175
Fam. 13.15.2	Homer's *Iliad*	1.343
Q. fr. 3.7.1	Homer's *Iliad*	4.182/8.150
Att. 14.13.2	Homer's *Iliad*	5.428–429
Att. 2.16.4	Homer's *Iliad*	6.181
Fam. 13.15.2	Homer's *Iliad*	6.208/11.784
Q. fr. 3.5.4	Homer's *Iliad*	6.208/11.874
Att. 6.1.22	Homer's *Iliad*	6.236
Att. 6.1.23	Homer's *Iliad*	7.93
Att. 16.11.6	Homer's *Iliad*	7.93
Q. fr. 3.7.2	Homer's *Iliad*	8.355
Att. 14.13.1	Homer's *Iliad*	9.228–230
De Or. 3.57	ref. to Homer's *Iliad*	9.443
Att. 7.11.3	Homer's *Iliad*	9.524
Att. 9.6.4	Homer's *Iliad*	10.93–94
Att. 9.6.6	Homer's *Iliad*	10.244
Fam. 9.7.1	Homer's *Iliad*	10.224
Att. 13.25.3	Homer's *Iliad*	11.654
Att. 2.3.4	Homer's *Iliad*	12.243
Att. 1.16.5	Homer's *Iliad*	16.112–113
Q. fr. 3.5.8	Homer's *Iliad*	16.385–386, 387–388
Att. 16.5.5	Homer's *Iliad*	17.280
Att. 9.5.3	Homer's *Iliad*	18.96, 98–99
Att. 7.1.9	Homer's *Iliad*	18.112/19.65
Att. 10.12a.1	Homer's *Iliad*	18.112/19.65
Att. 7.8.4	Homer's *Iliad*	18.309
Att. 2.5.1	Homer's *Iliad*	22.100
Att. 7.1.4	Homer's *Iliad*	22.100
Att. 2.5.1	Homer's *Iliad*	22.105/6.442
Att. 7.1.4	Homer's *Iliad*	22.105/6.442
Att. 7.12.3	Homer's *Iliad*	22.105/6.442
Att. 8.16.2	Homer's *Iliad*	22.105/6.442
Att. 13.13(14).2	Homer's *Iliad*	22.105/6.442
Att. 13.24.1	Homer's *Iliad*	22.105/6.442
Att. 1.1.4	Homer's *Iliad*	22.159
Att. 1.15.1	Homer's *Iliad*	22.268
Att. 10.1.1	Homer's *Iliad*	22.304–305
Fam. 13.15.2	Homer's *Iliad*	22.304–305
Att. 16.11.1	Homer's *Iliad*	22.308
Att. 2.9.3	Homer's *Iliad*	24.369
Fam. 13.15.1	Homer's *Odyssey*	1.302/3.200
Att. 9.8.2	Homer's *Odyssey*	3.22
Att. 9.15.4	Homer's *Odyssey*	3.26–27
Att. 16.6.1	Homer's *Odyssey*	3.169

(cont.)

Att. 16.13.1–2	Homer's *Odyssey*	3.169, 172, 171
Fam. 13.15.1	Homer's *Odyssey*	7.258
Att. 7.1.2	Homer's *Odyssey*	7.258/9.33
Att. 2.11.2	Homer's *Odyssey*	9.27–28
Fam. 10.13	Homer's *Odyssey*	9.504
Q. fr. 1.2.1	Homer's *Odyssey*	9.513
Att. 2.13.2	Homer's *Odyssey*	10.82
Att. 9.7.3	Homer's *Odyssey*	11.634
Att. 7.6.2	Homer's *Odyssey*	12.209
Att. 4.7.3	Homer's *Odyssey*	17.488/20.384
Att. 9.15.3	Homer's *Odyssey*	20.18
Att. 4.7.2	Homer's *Odyssey*	22.412
Fam. 13.15.1	Homer's *Iliad*/ *Odyssey*	17.591/ 24.315
Att. 4.15.7	Homer's *Iliad*/ *Odyssey*	23.326/ 11.126
Att. 9.7.5	Leonidas	*Ath. Pal.* 10.1.1
Att. 9.18.3	Leonidas	*Ath. Pal.* 10.1.1
Att. 10.2.1	Leonidas	*Ath. Pal.* 10.1.1–2
Att. 4.11.2	Menander's *Epitrepontes*	fr. 2
Att. 1.12.1	Menander's *Monostichoi*	726
Att. 12.5.1	Pindar's *Nemeans*	1.1
Att. 13.38.2	Pindar	Snell fr. 213.1–2, 4
Att. 1.20.3	Rhinthon?	Kaibel 1899: 189
Att. 2.7.4	Sophocles' *Tympanistai*	Nauck fr. 579
Att. 4.8.1	Sophocles' *Tyro*	Nauck fr. 601
Att. 2.16.2	Sophocles: unknown tragedy	Nauck fr. 701
Q. fr. 2.9.2	Sophocles: unknown tragedy	Nauck fr. 877
Att. 9.13.1	Stesichorus	Diehl fr. 11.1
Att. 4.8a.2	Unknown Greek comedy	Kock fr. 189
Att. 14.22.2	Unknown Greek tragedy	Nauck fr. 105
Att. 15.11.3	Unknown Greek tragedy	Nauck fr. 106
Att. 16.6.2	Unknown Greek tragedy	Nauck fr. 106
Fam. 9.7.2	Unknown Greek tragedy	Nauck fr. 107
Fam. 12.14.7	Unknown Greek tragedy	Nauck fr. 411
Att. 13.21a.1	Greek proverb	*CPG* I p116
Att. 10.5.2	Greek proverb	*CPG* I p207
Att. 1.19.10	Greek proverb	*CPG* I p314
Att. 5.11.5	Greek proverb	*CPG* II p44
Att. 7.18.4	Greek proverb	*CPG* II p759

Bibliography

Albrecht, M. von. 1997. *A History of Roman Literature: From Livius Andronicus to Boethius*. Leiden: Brill.

Albrecht, M. von. 2003. *Cicero's Style*. Leiden: Brill.

Alexander, M. C. 1990. *Trials in the Late Roman Republic, 149 BC to 50 BC*. Toronto: University of Toronto Press.

Alexander, M. C. 2002. *The Case for the Prosecution in the Ciceronian Era*. Ann Arbor: University of Michigan Press.

Allen, J. 2005. "The Stoics on the Origin of Language and the Foundations of Etymology." In D. Frede and B. Inwood (eds.), *Language and Learning. Philosophy of Language in the Hellenistic Age*. Cambridge: Cambridge University Press. 14–35.

Anderson, W. D. 1966. *Ethos and Education in Greek Music*. Cambridge, MA: Harvard University Press (London: Oxford University Press).

Arnim, H. von. (ed.) 1903–1924. *Stoicorum veterum fragmenta*. Leipzig: Teubner.

Artigas, E. 2009. *Marc Pacuvi, Tragèdies. Fragments*. Barcelona: Fundació Bernat Metge.

Astin, A. E. 1978. *Cato the Censor*. Oxford: Clarendon Press.

Atzert, C. 1908. *De Cicerone interprete Graecorum*, dissertation. Göttingen: Acad. Huthiana.

Austin, R. G. 1960. *Cicero Pro Caelio*. Oxford: The Clarendon Press.

Badian, E. 1972. "Ennius and His Friends." In O. Skutsch (ed.), *Ennius. Entretiens sur l'antiquité classique* 17. Geneva: Fondation Hardt. 151–208.

Baehrens, A. 1886. *Fragmenta Poetarum Romanorum*. Leipzig: Teubner.

Baker, N. 1991. *U and I: A True Story*. New York: Random House.

Bakola, E. 2019. "Metallurgical Imagination: the *Prometheus Triology*." In D. Braund, E. Hall, R. Wyles (eds.), *Ancient Theatre and Performance Culture around the Black Sea*. Cambridge: Cambridge University Press. 225–251.

Baldwin, B. 1992. "Greek in Cicero's Letters." *Acta Classica* 35: 1–17.

Barrile, A. R. 1969. *Frammenti. Dalle tragedie e dalle preteste*. Bologna: Zanichelli.

Bauman, R. A. 1983. *Lawyers in Roman Republican Politics. A Study of the Roman Jurists in their Political Setting, 316–82 BC*. Münchener Beiträge zur Papyrusforschung und antiken Rechtsgeschichte 75. Munich: C H Beck.

Beare, W. 1955. "*Scaenicorum Romanorum Fragmenta* edidit Alfredus Klotz." *Classical Review* 5.2: 170–171.

Beare, W. 1964. *The Roman Stage.* London: Methuen.

Behrendt, A. 2013. *Mit Zitaten kommunizieren: Untersuchungen zur Zitierweise in der Korrespondenz des Marcus Tullius Cicero.* Litora classica, 6. Rahden, Westphalia: VML Verlag Marie Leidorf.

Bergson, H. 1912. *Laughter. An Essay on the Meaning of the Comic.* New York: The MacMillan Company.

Bishop, C. 2018. "Pessimus omnium poeta: Canonization and the Ancient Reception of Cicero's Poetry." *ICS* 43.1: 137–159.

Bishop, C. 2019. *Cicero, Greek Learning, and the Making of a Roman Classic.* Oxford, New York: Oxford University Press.

Blanchot, M. 1995. *The Writing of the Disaster.* Translated by A. Smock. Lincoln, London: University of Nebraska Press.

Blänsdorf, J. 1995. *Fragmenta poetarum Latinorum epicorum et lyricorum praeter Ennium et Lucilium.* Post W. Morel novis curis adhibitis ed. C. Büchner. Leipzig: Teubner.

Blom, H. van der. 2010. *Cicero's Role Models: the Political Strategy of a Newcomer.* Oxford: Oxford University Press.

Blom, H. van der. 2016. *Oratory and Political Career in the Late Roman Republic.* Cambridge: Cambridge University Press.

Bloom, H. 1973. *The Anxiety of Influence.* Oxford; New York: Oxford University Press.

Bloomer, W. M. 2011. *The School of Rome: Latin Studies and the origins of Liberal Education.* Berkeley: University of California Press.

Bonaria, M. 1965. *Romani Mimi.* Rome: Athenae.

Bonner, S. F. 1977. *Education in Ancient Rome.* Berkeley: University of California Press.

Bosak-Schroeder, C. 2020. *Other Natures: Environmental Encounters with Ancient Greek.* Berkeley: University of California Press.

Boyle, A. J. 2006. *An Introduction to Roman Tragedy.* London: Routledge.

Boyle, A. J. 2017. *Seneca: Thyestes.* Oxford: Oxford University Press.

Brandwood, L. 1976. *A Word Index to Plato.* Leeds: W. S. Maney and Son.

Broughton, T. R. S. 1951. *The Magistrates of the Roman Republic, Vol. 1.* American Philological Association Philological Monographs. New York: American Philological Association.

Brunt, P. A. 1965. "*Amicitia* in the Late Roman Republic." *PCPS* 191: 1–20.

Brunt, P. A. 1979. "Cicero and Historiography." In *Miscellanea di studi classici in onore di Eugenio Manni*, 1.311–40. Rome: Bretschneider.

Büchner, K. 1982. *Fragmenta poetarum Latinorum epicorum et lyricorum praeter Ennium et Lucilium.* Leipzig: Teubner.

Butler, J. 1993. *Bodies That Matter.* London; New York: Routledge.

Butler, S. 2002. *The Hand of Cicero.* London; New York: Routledge.

Cameron, A. 1976. *Circus Factions. Blues and Greens at Rome and Byzantium.* Oxford: Clarendon Press.

Cappello, O. 2019. *The School of Doubt. Skepticism, History and Politics in Cicero's Academica.* Leiden; Boston: Brill.

Carson, A. 1992. "How Not to Read a Poem: Unmixing Simonides from Protagoras." *CP* 87.2: 110–130.

Casali, S. 2018. "Caesar's Poetry in its Context." In L. Grillo and C. B. Krebs (eds.), *The Cambridge Companion to the Writings of Julius Caesar*. Cambridge: Cambridge University Press. 206–214.

Chahoud, A. 2004. "The Roman Satirist Speaks Greek." *Classics Ireland* 11: 1–46.

Chahoud, A. 2010. "Verbal Mosaics: Speech Patterns and Generic Stylization." In B. W. Breed, E. Keitel, R. Wallace (eds.), *Lucilius and Satire in Second-Century BC Rome*. Cambridge: Cambridge University Press. 132–161.

Charpin, F. 1978–1991. *Lucilius Satires*. 3 vols. Paris: Belles Lettres.

Christenson, D. M. 2000. Plautus' *Amphitryo*. Cambridge: Cambridge University Press.

Christes, J. and Garbugino, G. 2015. *Satiren: lateinisch und deutsch*. Darmstadt: WBG (Wissenschaftliche Buchgesellschaft).

Coffey, M. 1976. *Roman Satire*. London: Methuen.

Collins, R. 1998. *The Sociologies of Philosophies: A Global Theory of Intellectual Change*. Cambridge, MA: Harvard University Press.

Colonna, H. 1590 (F. Hesselio reprint, 1707). *Q. Ennii poetae vetustissimi quae supersunt fragmenta*. Amsterdam: Wetstein.

Comotti, G. 1991. *Music in Greek and Roman Culture*. Translated by R. V. Munson. Baltimore: Johns Hopkins University Press.

Connerton, P. 1989. *How Societies Remember*. Cambridge: Cambridge University Press.

Cornell, T. J. 2001. "Cicero on the Origins of Rome." In J. G. F. Powell and J. A. North (eds.), *Cicero's Republic* (Bulletin of the Institute of Classical Studies, Supp. 76). London: Institute of Classical Studies, University of London. 41–56.

Corpet, E. F. 1845. *Satires de C. Lucilius*. Paris: Panckoucke.

Courtney, E. 2003. *The Fragmentary Latin Poets*. Oxford: Oxford University Press.

Craig, C. P. 1990. "Cicero's Strategy of Embarrassment in the Speech for Plancius." *AJP* 111: 75–81.

Crawford, J. 1994. *M. Tullius Cicero. The Fragmentary Speeches: an Edition with Commentary*. Atlanta: Scholars Press.

Cribiore, R. 1996. *Writing, Teachers, and Students in Greco-Roman Egypt*. Atlanta: Scholars Press.

Csapo, E. 2004. "The Politics of the New Music." In P. Murray and P. Wilson (eds.), *Music and the Muses: The Culture of 'Mousike' in the Classical Athenian City*. Oxford: Oxford University Press. 207–248.

Čulík-Baird, H. 2018. "Stoicism in the Stars: Cicero's *Aratea* in the De Natura Deorum," *Latomus* 77: 646–670.

Čulík-Baird, H. 2019. "Staging Roman Slavery in the 2nd Century BCE." *Ramus* 48.2: 174–197.

Čulík-Baird, H. 2020. "Archias the Good Immigrant." *Rhetorica* 38.4: 382–410.

Čulík-Baird, H. 2021. "Fragments of 'Anonymous' Latin Verse in Cicero." In B. Kayachev (ed.), *Poems Without Poets: Approaches to Anonymous Ancient Poetry*. Cambridge: Cambridge Classical Journal Supplement 43. 105–119.

D'Anna, G. 1967. *M. Pacuvi Fragmenta*. Rome: Aedibus Athenaei.

D'Antò, A. 1980. *Accius: I frammenti delle tragedie*. Lecce: Milella.

Dahlmann, H. 1932. *Varro und die hellenistische Sprachtheorie*. Berlin; Zürich: Weidmannsche Verlagsbuchhandlung.

Damen, M. 1990. "Electra's Monody and the Role of the Chorus in Euripides' *Orestes* 960–1012." *TAPA* 120: 133–45.

Dangel, J. 2001. "Varron et les citations poetiques dans le De Lingua Latina." In Calboli (ed.), *Papers on Grammar 6*: 97–122. Bologna: Clueb.

Dangel, J. 2002. *Accius. Oeuvres, Fragments*. Paris: Les Belles Lettres.

De Graff, T. B. 1940. "Plato in Cicero." *CP* 35.2: 143–153.

Della Corte, F. 1970. *Varrone: il terzo gran lume romano*. Florence. La nuova Italia.

Delrius, M. A. 1593. *Syntagma Tragoediae Latinae*. Antwerp: Moretus.

Deufert, M. 2002. *Textgeschichte und Rezeption der plautinischen Komödien im Altertum*. Berlin: De Gruyter.

Dickey, E. 2016. *Learning Latin the Ancient Way: Latin Textbooks from the Ancient World*. Cambridge: Cambridge University Press.

Diehl, E. 1911 (6th edition: 1967). *Poetarum romanorum veterum reliquiae*. Berlin: Walter de Gruyter.

Diehl, E. 1936/1942. *Anthologia Lyrica Graeca*. Leipzig: Teubner.

Dionisotti, A. C. 1997. "On Fragments in Classical Scholarship." In G. W. Most (ed.), *Collecting Fragments – Fragmente Sammeln*. Göttingen: Vandenhoeck & Ruprecht. 1–33.

Dix, T. K. 2004. "Aristotle's Peripatetic Library." In J. Raven (ed.), *Lost Libraries: The Destruction of Great Book Collections Since Antiquity*. Basingstoke: Palgrave Macmillan.

Dix, T. K. 2013. "'Beware of Promising Your Library to Anyone': Assembling a Private Library at Rome." In J. König, K. Oikonomopoulou, G. Woolf (eds.), *Ancient Libraries*. Cambridge: Cambridge University Press. 209–236.

Dougan, T. W. 1905–1907. *M. Tulli Ciceronis Tusculanarum disputationum libri quinque*. Cambridge: Cambridge University Press.

Dousa, F. 1597. *Satyrarum quae supersunt reliquiae*. Lugdunum Batavorum: Franciscus Raphelengius.

DuBois, P. 1995. *Sappho is Burning*. Chicago; London: The University of Chicago Press.

Dué, C. 2006. *The Captive Woman's Lament in Greek Tragedy*. Cambridge, MA: Harvard University Press.

Dufallo, B. 2001. "Appius' Indignation: Gossip, Tradition, and Performance in Republican Rome." *TAPA* 131: 119–142.

Dufallo, B. 2007. *The Ghosts of the Past: Latin Literature, the Dead, and Rome's Transition to a Principate*. Columbus, OH: The Ohio State University Press.

Dugan, J. 2005. *Making a New Man: Ciceronian Self-Fashioning in the Rhetorical Works*. Oxford: Oxford University Press.

Dugan, J. 2012. "*Scriptum* and *Voluntas* in Cicero's *Brutus*." In M. Citroni (ed.), *Letteratura e civitas: transizioni dalla repubblica all'impero, in ricordo di Emanuele Narducci*. Pisa: Edizioni ETS. 117–128.

Dugan, J. 2013. "Cicero and the Politics of Ambiguity: Interpreting the *Pro Marcello*." In C. Steel, H. van der Blom (eds.), *Community and Communication: Oratory and Politics in Republican Rome*. Oxford: Oxford University Press.

Duncan, A. 2006. *Performance and Identity in the Classical World*. Cambridge: Cambridge University Press.

Durante, G. de. 1966. *Le fabulae praetextae*. Rome: Fratelli Palombi.

Dutsch, D. M. 2008. *Feminine Discourse in Roman Comedy*. Oxford: Oxford University Press.

Dyck, A. 1996. *A Commentary on Cicero, De Officiis*. Ann Arbor: The University of Michigan Press.

Dyck, A. 2003. *Cicero: De Natura Deorum. Liber I*. Cambridge; New York: Cambridge University Press.

Dyck, A. 2004. *A Commentary on Cicero, De Legibus*. Ann Arbor: The University of Michigan Press.

Dyck, A. 2008. *Cicero: Catilinarians*. Cambridge: Cambridge University Press.

Dyck, A. 2010. *Cicero. Pro Sexto Roscio*. Cambridge: Cambridge University Press.

Dyck, A. 2013. *Cicero: Pro Marco Caelio*. Cambridge: Cambridge University Press.

Edwards, C. 1993. *The Politics of Immorality in Ancient Rome*. Cambridge: Cambridge University Press.

Elliott, J. 2013. *Ennius and the Architecture of the Annales*. Cambridge: Cambridge University Press.

Emerson, R. W. 1971. "Quotation and Originality." In A. R. Ferguson, R. E. Spiller (eds.), *The Collected Works of Ralph Waldo Emerson, VIII: Letters and Social Aims*. Cambridge, MA: Harvard University Press. 93–107.

Ernout, A. 1916 (4th edition: 1973). *Recueil de textes latins archaïques*. Paris: Klincksieck.

Estienne, H. 1564. *Fragmenta Poetarum Veterum Latinorum*. Geneva: H Stephanus.

Ewbank, W. W. 1933. *The Poems of Cicero*. New York and London: Garland Publishing, Inc.

Fantham, E. 1984. "Roman Experience of Menander in the Late Republic and Early Empire." *TAPA* 114, 299–309.

Fantham, E. 2002. "Orator and/et actor." In P. Easterling and E. Hall (eds.), *Greek and Roman Actors. Aspects of an Ancient Profession*. Cambridge: Cambridge University Press. 362–376.

Fantham, E. 2004. *Roman World of Cicero's De Oratore*. Oxford: Oxford University Press.

Feeney, D. 1991. *The Gods in Epic*. Oxford: Oxford University Press.

Feeney, D. 2016. *Beyond Greek*. Cambridge, MA: Harvard University Press.

Ferri, R. 2014. "The Reception of Plautus in Antiquity." In M. Fontaine and A. C. Scafuro (eds.), *Oxford Handbook of Greek and Roman Comedy*. Oxford: Oxford University Press. 767–81.

Flores, E. (ed.) 2000–2009. *Quinto Ennio. Annali*. Naples: Liguori.

Flower, H. I. 1996. *Ancestor Masks and Aristocratic Power in Roman Culture.* Oxford: Clarendon Press.

Fornara, C. W. 1983. *The Nature of History in Ancient Greece and Rome.* Berkeley, University of California Press.

Fox, M. 2007. *Cicero's Philosophy of History.* Oxford: Oxford University Press.

Fraenkel, E. 2007. *Plautine Elements in Plautus.* Translated by T. Drevikovsky and F. Muecke. Oxford: Oxford University Press.

Frahm, E. 2003. "Images of Ashurbanipal in Later Tradition." *Eretz Israel* 27: 37–48.

Frampton, S. A. 2016. "What to Do with Books in the *De Finibus.*" *TAPA* 146.1:117–147.

Frampton, S. A. 2019. *Empire of Letters. Writing in Roman Literature and Thought from Lucretius to Ovid.* Oxford: Oxford University Press.

Franchella, Q. 1968. *Lucii Accii tragoediarum fragmenta.* Bologna: Compositori.

Frier, B. W. 1985. *The Rise of the Roman Jurists. Studies in Cicero's Pro Caecina.* Princeton, NJ: Princeton University Press.

Gärtner, U. 2001. "Lucilius und die Freundschaft." In G. Manuwald (ed.), *Der Satiriker Lucilius und Seine Zeit.* Munich: Zetemata. 90–110

Gee, E. 2000. *Ovid, Aratus and Augustus.* Cambridge: Cambridge University Press.

Gee, E. 2001. "Cicero's Astronomy." *CQ* 51. 2: 520–36.

Gee, E. 2013a "Cicero's Poetry." In C. Steel (ed.), *The Cambridge Companion to Cicero.* Cambridge: Cambridge University Press. 88–106.

Gee, E. 2013b. *Aratus and the Astronomical Tradition.* New York; Oxford: Oxford University Press.

Geffcken, K. 1973. *Comedy in the Pro Caelio.* Leiden: Brill.

Gellar-Goad, T. H. M. 2018. "Lucretius' Personified *Natura Rerum*, Satire, and Ennius' *Saturae.*" *Phoenix* 71.1/2: 143–160.

Gerlach, F. D. 1846. *C. Lucili Saturarum Reliquiae.* Zurich: Meyer et Zeller.

Gigon, O. 1959. "Cicero und Aristoteles." *Hermes* 87: 143–62

Gildenhard, I. 2007. "Greek Auxiliaries: Tragedy and Philosophy in Ciceronian Invective." In J. Booth (ed.) *Cicero on the Attack: Invective and Subversion in the Orations and Beyond.* Swansea: Classical Press of Wales. 149–182.

Goh, I. 2016. "Of Cabbages and Kin: Traces of Lucilius in the First Half of Horace's *Epodes.*" In P. Bather and C. Stocks (eds.), *Horace's Epodes: Contexts, Intertexts, and Reception.* Oxford: Oxford University Press. 63–83.

Goh, I. 2018. "Scepticism at the Birth of Satire: Carneades in Lucilius' *Concilium Deorum.*" *CQ* 68.1: 128–142.

Goldberg, S. 1989. "Poetry, Politics, and Ennius." *TAPA* 119: 247–261.

Goldberg, S. 1995. *Epic in Republican Rome.* New York: Oxford University Press.

Goldberg, S. 1996. "The Fall and Rise of Roman Tragedy." *TAPA* 126: 265–286.

Goldberg, S. 2005. *Constructing Literature in the Roman Republic.* Cambridge: Cambridge University Press.

Goldberg, S. 2013. *Terence: Hecyra.* Cambridge: Cambridge University Press.

Goldberg, S. and G. Manuwald. 2018. *Fragmentary Republican Latin, Vol. I: Ennius, Testimonia. Epic Fragments.* Cambridge, MA: Harvard University Press.

Goldberg, S. and G. Manuwald. 2018. *Fragmentary Republican Latin, Vol. II: Ennius, Dramatic Fragments. Minor Works.* Cambridge, MA: Harvard University Press.

Goldschmidt, N. 2012. "Absent Presence: *pater Ennius* in Renaissance Europe." *Classical Receptions Journal* 4.1: 1–19.

Goldschmidt, N. 2013. *Shaggy Crowns: Ennius' Annales and Virgil's Aeneid.* Oxford: Oxford University Press.

Graver, M. 2002. *Cicero on the Emotions: Tusculan Disputations 3 and 4.* Chicago: University of Chicago Press.

Grimal, P. 1984. "Sénèque juge de Cicéron." *MEFRA* 96.2: 655–70.

Gronewald, M. 1980. "P. Köln III 131 adespotum: Euripides, *Orestes* 134–142." *ZPE* 39: 35–6.

Gruen, E. 1968. *Roman Politics and the Criminal Courts, 149–78 BC.* Cambridge, MA: Harvard University Press.

Gruen, E. 1990. *Studies in Greek Culture and Roman Policy.* Leiden; New York: Brill.

Gruen, E. 1992. *Culture and National Identity in Republican Rome.* Ithaca, New York: Cornell University Press.

Guastella, G. 2017. *Word of Mouth. Fama and its Personifications in Art and Literature from Ancient Rome to the Middle Ages.* Oxford: Oxford University Press.

Gumbrecht, H. U. 2003. *The Powers of Philology.* Urbana, Ill.: University of Illinois Press.

Gurd, S. 2012. *Work in Progress: Literary Revision as Social Performance in Ancient Rome.* Oxford; New York: Oxford University Press

Gutzwiller, K. J. 1998. *Poetic Garlands.* Berkeley and Los Angeles, CA: University of California Press.

Habinek, T. N. 2005. *The World of Roman Song.* Baltimore: The Johns Hopkins University Press.

Hall, E. 2002. "The Singing Actors of Antiquity." In P. Easterling and E. Hall (eds.), *Greek and Roman Actors: Aspects of an Ancient Profession.* Cambridge: Cambridge University Press. 3–38.

Hall, J. 2009. *Politeness and Politics in Cicero's Letters.* Oxford; New York: Oxford University Press.

Halliwell, S. 2000. "The Subjection of Mythos to Logos: Plato's Citations of the Poets." *CQ* 50: 94–112.

Halliwell, S. 2012. *Between Ecstasy and Truth: Interpretations of Greek Poetics from Homer to Longinus.* Oxford: Oxford University Press.

Hammond, N. G. L. 1966. "The Opening Campaigns and the Battle of the Aoi Stena in the Second Macedonian War." *JRS* 56: 39–54.

Hanses, M. 2020. *The Life of Comedy after the Death of Plautus and Terence.* Ann Arbor, MI: University of Michigan Press.

Harries, B. 2007. "Acting the Part: Techniques of the Comic Stage in Cicero's Early Speeches." In J. Booth (ed.) *Cicero on the attack: invective and subversion in the orations and beyond.* Swansea: Classical Press of Wales. 129–147.

Harrison, S. J. 1990. "Cicero's *de Temporibus Suis.* The Evidence Reconsidered." *Hermes* 118: 455–463.

Henderson, J. 2004a. *Morals and Villas in Seneca's Letters: Places to Dwell.* Cambridge; New York: Cambridge University Press.

Henderson, J. 2004b. "Terence's Selbstaussöhnung: Payback Time for the Self (*Hautontimorumenus*)." *Ramus* 33.1–2: 53–81.

Henderson, J. 2016. "Cicero's Letters to Cicero, *ad QFr*: Big Brothers Keepers." *Arethusa* 49.3: 439–461.

Hinds, S. 1998. *Allusion and Intertext: Dyamics of Appropriation in Roman Poetry.* Cambridge: Cambridge University Press.

Højte, J. M. (ed.) 2002. *Images of Ancestors.* Aarhus, Oxford, and Oakville, CT: Aarhus University Press.

Hollis, A. S. 1998. "A Tragic Fragment in Cicero, *Pro Caelio* 67?" *CQ* 48: 561–564.

Hollywood, A. 2002. "Performativity, Citationality, Ritualization." *History of Religions* 42.2: 93–115.

Hostis, A. 1874. *Scritti Inediti di Francesco Petrarca.* Trieste: Tipografia del Lloyd Austro-Ungarico.

Houston, G. W. 2013. "The non-Philodemus book collection in the Villa of the Papyri." In J. König, K. Oikonomoupoulou, G. Woolf (eds.), *Ancient Libraries.* Cambridge: Cambridge University Press. 183–208.

Houston, K. 2013. *Shady Characters: the Secret Life of Punctuation, Symbols, and Other Typographical Marks.* New York; London: W.W. Norton & Company.

Howley, J. A. 2018. *Aulus Gellius and Roman Reading Culture.* Cambridge: Cambridge University Press.

Huby, P. M. 1989. "Cicero's *Topics* and its Peripatetic Sources." In W. W. Fortenbaugh and P. Steinmetz (eds.) *Cicero's Knowledge of the Peripatos.* London: Routledge. 61–76.

Hughes, J. J. 1998. "Invective and Comedic Allusion: Cicero, *In Pisonem,* Fragment 9 (Nisbet)." *Latomus* 57: 570–577.

Hutchinson, G. O. 1998. *Cicero's Correspondence.* Oxford: Oxford University Press.

Hutchinson, D. S. and M. R. Johnson. 2017. *Aristotle. Protrepticus or Exhortation to Philosophy.* www.protrepticus.info

Inwood, B. 2005. *Reading Seneca: Stoic Philosophy at Rome.* Oxford; New York: Oxford University Press.

Janko, R. 1995. "Reconstructing Philodemus' *On Poems.*" In D. Obbink (ed.), *Philodemus and Poetry: Poetic Theory and Practice in Lucretius, Philodemus, and Horace.* Oxford; New York: Oxford University Press. 69–96.

Jocelyn, H. D. 1969a. *The Tragedies of Ennius.* Cambridge: Cambridge University Press.

Jocelyn, H. D. 1969b. "The Fragments of Ennius' Scenic Scripts." *L'Antiquité Classique,* T. 38, Fasc. 1. 181–217.

Jocelyn, H. D. 1973a. "Greek Poetry in Cicero's Prose Writing." *YCS* 23: 61–111.

Jocelyn, H. D. 1973b. "*Homo sum: humani nil a me alienum puto* (Terence, *Heauton timoumenos* 77)." *Antichthon* 7: 14–46.

Jones, D. M. 1959. "Cicero as a Translator." *BICS* 6: 22–34.

Kaibel, G. 1899. *Comicorum Graecorum Fragmenta*. Berlin: Weidman.

Karamanou, I. 2017. *Euripides' Alexandros: Introduction, Text and Commentary*. Berlin, Boston: De Gruyter.

Kaster, R. 1995. *Suetonius: De grammaticis et rhetoribus*. Oxford: Clarendon Press.

Kaster, R. 2006. *Cicero: Speech on Behalf of Publius Sestius*. Oxford: Clarendon Press.

Kennedy, G. 1972. *The Art of Rhetoric in the Roman World 300 BC–AD 300*. Princeton, NJ: Princeton University Press.

Kennedy, G. 2002. "Cicero's Oratorical and Rhetorical Legacy." In J. M. May (ed.), *Brill's Companion to Cicero*. Leiden: Brill. 481–501.

Klotz, A. 1953. *Scaenicorum Romanorum Fragmenta*. Munich: R. Oldenbourg.

Knapp, C. 1911. "Vahlen's Ennius." *AJP* 32.1: 1–35.

Knox, P. 2011. "Cicero as a Hellenistic Poet." *CQ* 61: 192–204.

Kock, T. 1880–1888. *Comicorum Atticorum Fragmenta*. Leipzig: Teubner.

Konstan, D. 2011. "Excerpting as a Reading Practice." In G. Reydams-Schils (ed.), *Thinking through Excerpts: Studies on Stobaeus*. Turnhout: Brepols. 9–22.

Krenkel, W. 1970. *Lucilius, Satiren*. 2 vols. Leiden: Brill.

Kronenberg, L. 2009. *Allegories of Farming from Greece and Rome: Philosophical Satire in Xenophon, Varro, and Virgil*. Cambridge: Cambridge University Press.

Krostenko, B. 2000. "Beyond (Dis)belief: Rhetorical Form and Religious Symbol in Cicero's *de Divinatione*." *TAPA* 130: 353–391.

Kubiak, D. P. 1989. "Piso's Madness," *AJP* 110: 237–45.

Lachmann, C. 1876. *C. Lucili Saturarum Reliquiae*. Berlin: Reimer.

Landels, J. G. 1999. *Music in Ancient Greece and Rome*. London: Routledge.

Lehmann, L. 1997. *Varron: Théologien et philosophe romain*. Brussels: Latomus.

Leigh, M. 2004. "The *Pro Caelio* and Comedy." *CP* 99.4: 300–335.

Lerner, G. 1986. *The Creation of Patriarchy*. New York, Oxford: Oxford University Press.

Lindsay, W. M. 1904. *The Ancient Editions of Plautus*. Oxford: J. Parker and Co.

Lintott, A. 1990. "Electoral Bribery in the Roman Republic." *JRS* 80: 1–16.

Lintott, A. 2008. *Cicero as Evidence: A Historian's Companion*. Oxford; New York: Oxford University Press.

Long, A. A. 1992. "Stoic Readers of Homer." In R. Lamberton and J. J. Keaney (eds.), *Homer's Ancient Readers*. Princeton: Princeton University Press. 41–66.

Long, A. A. 2005. "Stoic Linguistics, Plato's *Cratylus*, and Augustine's *De dialectica*." In D. Frede and B. Inwood (eds.), *Language and Learning. Philosophy of Language in the Hellenistic Age*. Cambridge: Cambridge University Press. 36–55.

Long, A. A. 2006. *From Epicurus to Epictetus: Studies in Hellenistic and Roman Philosophy*. Clarendon Press: Oxford. 285–306.

Long, A. A, and D. N Sedley. 1987. *The Hellenistic Philosophers*. Cambridge: Cambridge University Press.

Malcovati, E. 1943. *Cicerone e la poesia*. Pavia: Annali della Facoltà di lettere e di filosofia della Università di Cagliari.

Maltby, R. 2012. *Terence: Phormio. Edited with Introduction, Translation and Commentary*. Oxford: Aris & Phillips Classical Texts.

Mankin, D. 2011. *Cicero: De Oratore Book III*. Cambridge: Cambridge University Press.

Manuwald, G. 2011. *Roman Republican Theatre*. Cambridge: Cambridge University Press.

Marinone, N. 1997. *Cronologia Ciceroniana*. Rome: Centro di Studi Ciceroniani.

Marlowe, E. 2013. *Shaky Ground: Context, Connoisseurship and the History of Roman Art*. London, New York: Bloomsbury.

Marrou, H. I. 1964. *A History of Education in Antiquity*. New York: New American Library.

Marshall, C. W. 2006. *The Stagecraft and Performance of Roman Comedy*. Cambridge: Cambridge University Press.

May, J. 1988. *Trials of Character. The Eloquence of Ciceronian Ethos*. Chapel Hill: The University of North Carolina Press.

May, J. M and J. Wisse, 2001. *Cicero. On the Ideal Orator*. Oxford: Oxford University Press.

May, J. M. 2002. "Ciceronian Oratory in Context." In J. M. May (ed.), *Brill's Companion to Cicero: Oratory and Rhetoric*. Leiden: Brill. 49–70.

Mayor, J. B. 1883. *M. Tulli Ciceronis De Natura Deorum Libri Tres*. Cambridge: Cambridge University Press.

McElduff, S. 2013. *Roman Theories of Translation: Surpassing the Source*. New York; London: Routledge.

McNamee, K. 2007. *Annotations in Greek and Latin Texts from Egypt*. New Haven: American Society of Papyrologists. Vol. 45.

Merula, P. 1595. *Q. Enni, poetae cum primis censendi, annalium libb. XIIX: quae apud varios Auctores superant, fragmenta*. Leiden: Joannis Paetsij & Ludovici Elzeverij.

Milnor, K. 2014. *Graffiti and the Literary Landscape in Roman Pompeii*. Oxford: Oxford University Press.

Monda, S. 1998. "Le citazioni di Cecilio Stazio nella *Pro Caelio* di Cicerone." *Giornale italiano di filologia* 50: 23–39.

Monda, S. 2004. *Titus Maccius Plautus. Vidularia et deperditarum fabularum fragmenta*. Sarsina: QuattroVenti.

Monda, S. 2015. "Terence Quotations in Latin Grammarians: Shared and Distinguishing Features." In A. Turner and G. Torello-Hill (eds.), *Terence between Late Antiquity and the Age of Printing: Illustration, Commentary and Performance*. Leiden: Brill. 105–137.

Moore, T. J. 1998. *The Theatre of Plautus: Playing to the Audience*. Austin: University of Texas Press.

Moore, T. J. 2012. *Music in Roman Comedy*. Cambridge: Cambridge University Press.

Morel, W. 1927. *Fragmenta poetarum Latinorum epicorum et lyricorum praeter Ennium et Lucilium, post Aemilium Baehrens iterum*. Leipzig: Teubner.

Müller, L. 1872. *C. Lucili Saturarum Reliquiae*. Leipzig: Teubner.

Murray, G. 1897. *A History of Ancient Greek Literature*. London: D. Appleton and Company.

Narducci, E. 1981. "Cicerone, Crasso e un verso di Ennio. Nota a *Pro Caelio* 18." *Maia* 33: 145–146.

Nethercut, J. 2021. *Ennius Noster. Lucretius and the* Annales. Oxford: Oxford University Press.

Neubecker, A. J. 1986. *Philodemus. Über Die Musik IV. Buch*. Naples: Bibliopolis.

North, H. 1952. "The Use of Poetry in the Training of the Ancient Orator." *Traditio* 8: 1–33.

Nosarti, L. 1993. "Medo, Medea, e il 'doctus' Pacuvio." In G. Aricò (ed.), *Atti del V seminario di studi sulla tragedia romana*. Palermo: Università degli Studi di Palermo. 21–43.

Nosarti, L. 1999. *Filologia in frammenti. Contributi esegetici e testuali ai frammenti dei poeti latini*. Bologna: Pàtron.

Otto, A. 1890 (Reprint: 1971). *Die Sprichwörter und Sprichwörtlichen Redensarten der Römer*. Hildesheim, New York: Georg Olms Verlag.

Padilla Peralta, D. 2017. "Slave Religiosity in the Roman Middle Republic." *Classical Antiquity* 36.2: 317–369.

Palmer, A. 1883. "Emendations." *Hermathena* 4.9: 446–452.

Panayotakis, C. 2010. *Decimus Laberius: The Fragments*. Cambridge: Cambridge Unviersity Press.

Pedroli, L. 1953. *Fabularum Praetextarum Quae Extant*. Genova: Universita di Genova.

Pfeiffer, R. 1949–1953. *Callimachus*. Oxford: Clarendon Press.

Piras, G. 1998. *Varrone e i poetica verba: studio sul settimo libro del De lingua latina*. Bologna: Pàtron.

Piras, G. 2015. "*Cum poeticis multis verbis magis delecter quam utar*: Poetic Citations and Etymological Enquiry in Varro's *De Lingua Latina*." In D. J. Butterfield (ed.), *Varro Varius: The Polymath of the Roman World*. Cambridge: Cambridge Philological Society. 51–72.

Pocetti, P. 2018. "Another Image of Literary Latin," in B. W. Breed, E. Keitel, R. Wallace (eds.) *Lucilius and Satire in Second-Century BC Rome*, pp81–131.

Pociña, A. 1984. *El tragediógrafo latino Lucio Acio*. Granada: Universidad de Granada.

Pöhlmann, E. 1960. *Griechische Musikfragmente*. Nuremberg: H. Carl.

Pöhlmann, E. 1970. *Denkmäler Altgriechischer Musik*. Nuremberg: H. Carl.

Pöhlmann, E. and M. L West. 2001. *Documents of Ancient Greek Music*. Oxford: Clarendon Press.

Polt, C. 2021. *Catullus and Roman Comedy. Theatricality and Personal Drama in the Late Republic*. Cambridge: Cambridge University Press.

Poncelet, R. 1957. *Cicéron, traducteur de Platon; l'expression de la pensée complexe en latin classique*. Paris: E. de Boccard.

Powell, J. G. F. and J. Paterson (eds.). 2004. *Cicero the Advocate*. Oxford; New York: Oxford University Press.

Powell, J. G. F. 1988. *Cicero: Cato Maior De Senectute*. Cambridge: Cambridge University Press.
Powell, J. G. F. 1995. *Cicero the Philosopher: Twelve Papers*. Oxford; New York: Clarendon Press.
Prauscello, L. 2006. *Singing Alexandria*. Leiden: Brill.
Rambaud, M. 1953. *Cicéron et L'Histoire Romaine*. Paris: Les Belles Lettres.
Raschke, W. 1987. "*Arma pro amico*. Lucilian Satire at the Crisis of the Roman Republic." *Hermes* 115.3: 299–318.
Rawson, E. 1972. "Cicero the Historian and Cicero the Antiquarian." *JRS* 62: 33–45.
Rawson, E. 1985. *Intellectual Life in the late Roman Republic*. Baltimore: Johns Hopkins University Press.
Rawson, E. 1991. *Roman Culture and Society: Collected Papers*. Oxford: Clarendon Press.
Reeve, M. D. 1996. "Classical Scholarship." In J. Kraye (ed.), *The Cambridge Companion to Renaissance Humanism*. Cambridge: Cambridge University Press. 20–46.
Regali, M. 2015. "Amicus Homerus: Allusive Art in Plato's Incipit to Book X of the Republic (595a–c)." In G. Cornelli (ed.), *Plato's Styles and Characters: Between Literature and Philosophy*. Berlin; Boston: De Gruyter. 173–186.
Reynolds, L. D., P. K. Marshall, and R. A. B. Mynors (eds.). 1983. *Texts and Transmission: a Survey of the Latin Classics*. Oxford: Clarendon Press.
Ribbeck, O. ¹1852/ ²1871/ ³1897. *Scaenicae Romanorum poesis fragmenta: Vol. I. Tragicorum Romanorum fragmenta*. Leipzig: Teubner.
Ribbeck, O. ¹1855/ ²1873/ ³1898. *Scaenicae Romanorum poesis fragmenta: Vol. II. Comicorum Romanorum praeter Plautum et Terentium fragmenta*. Leipzig:Teubner.
Ribbeck, O. 1875. *Die römische Tragödie im Zeitalter der Republik*. Leipzig: Teubner.
Richlin, A. 1992. *The Garden of Priapus: Sexuality and Aggression in Roman Humor*. New York; Oxford: Oxford University Press.
Richlin, A. 2017. *Slave Theater in the Roman Republic: Plautus and Popular Comedy*. Cambridge; New York: Cambridge University Press.
Riggsby, A. 1999. *Crime and Community in Ciceronian Rome*. Austin: University of Texas Press.
Rollinger, R. 2017. "Assyria in Classical Sources." In E. Frahm (ed.), *A Companion to Assyria*. Hoboken, NJ: Wiley-Blackwell. 570–582.
Rosenmeyer, P. A. 1997. "Ovid's *Heroides* and *Tristia*: Voices from Exile." *Ramus* 26.1: 29–56.
Rouse, R. H. and M. A. Rouse. 1979. *Preachers, Florilegia and Sermons: Studies on the Manipulus Florum of Thomas of Ireland*. (Studies and Texts, number 47.) Toronto: Pontifical Institute of Mediaeval Studies.
Saller, R. P. 1997. *Patriarchy, Property and Death in the Roman Family*. Cambridge: Cambridge University Press.
Salzman, M. R. 1982. "Cicero, the *Megalenses* and the Defense of Caelius." *AJP* 103: 199–304.

Schierl, P. 2006. *Die Tragödien des Pacuvius: ein Kommentar zu den Fragmenten mit Einleitung, Text und Übersetzung.* Berlin; New York: De Gruyter.

Sciarrino, E. 2011. *Cato the Censor and the Beginnings of Latin Prose.* Columbus: Ohio State University Press.

Scriverius, P. 1620. *Collectanea veterum tragicorum fragmenta cum notis G. I. Vossii.* Leiden: J Maire.

Shackleton Bailey, D. R. 1965–70. *Cicero's Letters to Atticus.* Cambridge Classical Texts and Commentaries 3–9. Cambridge: Cambridge University Press.

Shackleton Bailey, D. R. 1977. *Cicero: Epistulae ad Familiares.* Cambridge Classical Texts and Commentaries 16–17. Cambridge: Cambridge University Press.

Shackleton Bailey, D. R. 1983. "Cicero and Early Latin Poetry." *ICS* 8.2: 239–249.

Shackleton Bailey, D. R. 1995. *Onomasticon to Cicero's Letters.* Stuttgart: Teubner.

Shackleton Bailey, D. R. 1996. *Onomasticon to Cicero's Treatises.* Stuttgart: Teubner.

Skinner, M. 2011. *Clodia Metelli: The Tribune's Sister.* Oxford; New York: Oxford University Press.

Skutsch, O. 1968. *Studia Enniana.* London: Athlone Press.

Skutsch, O. 1985. *The Annals of Q. Ennius.* Oxford: Oxford University Press.

Smith, D. 1983. "Mosaics." In M. Henig (ed.), *A Handbook of Roman Art.* London: Phaidon Press. 116–138.

Snell, B. 1953. *Pindari Carmina cum Fragmentis.* Leipzig: Teubner.

Soubiran, J. 1972. *Aratea: fragments poétiques.* Paris: Les Belles Lettres.

Spahlinger, L. 2005. *Tulliana Simplicitas.* Göttingen: Vandenhoeck & Ruprecht.

Spaltenstein, F. 2008. *Commentaire des fragments dramatiques de Livius Andronicus.* Brussels: Latomus.

Spencer, D. 2011. "Movement and the Linguistic Turn: Reading Varro's *De Lingua Latina.*" In R. Laurence and D. K. Newsome (eds.), *Rome, Ostia, Pompeii. Movement and Space.* Oxford: Oxford University Press. 57–80.

Spencer, D. 2015. "Varro's Romespeak: *De lingua Latina.*" In D. J. Butterfield (ed.), *Varro Varius.* Cambridge: Cambridge Philological Society. 73–92.

Spencer, D. 2019. *Language and Authority in De Lingua Latina: Varro's Guide to Being Roman.* Madison, WI: Wisconsin Studies in Classics.

Stark, R. 1957. "Sapphoreminiszenzen." *Hermes* 85: 325–326.

Starr, R. J. 1991. "Reading Aloud: *Lectores* and Roman Reading." *CJ.* 86.4: 337–43.

Steel, C. 2001. *Cicero, Rhetoric, and Empire.* Oxford: Oxford University Press.

Steel, C. 2002. "Cicero's *Brutus*: the End of Oratory and the Beginning of History?" *BICS* 46: 195–211.

Steele, R. B. 1900. "The Greek in Cicero's Epistles." *AJP* 21.4: 387–410.

Stein, P. 1978. "The Place of Servius Sulpicius Rufus in the Development of Roman Legal Science." In O. Behrends, M. Disselhorst, H. Lange, D. Liebs, G. Wolff, and C. Wollschläger (eds.), *Festschrift für Franz Wieacker zum 70. Geburtstag.* Göttingen: Vandenhoeck and Ruprecht. 175–184.

Stem, R. 2006. "Cicero as Orator and Philosopher: The Value of the *Pro Murena* for Ciceronian Political Thought." *The Review of Politics* 68.2: 206–231.

Steuart, E. M. "The Earliest Narrative Poetry of Rome." *CQ* 15.1: 31–37.

Stroup, C. S. 2010. *Catullus, Cicero, and a Society of Patrons.* Cambridge: Cambridge University Press.

Suerbaum, W. 1968. *Untersuchungen zur Selbstdarstellung aelterer roemischer Dichter : Livius Andronicus Naevius, Ennius.* Hildesheim: G. Olms Verlag.

Sumner, G. V. 1973. *The Orators in Cicero's Brutus: Prosopography and Chronology.* Toronto: University of Toronto Press.

Syme, R. 1961. "Who Was Vedius Pollio?" *JRS* 51: 23–30.

Terzaghi, N. 1934 (2nd edition: 1966). *Lucilio.* Turin: L'Erma.

Thomson, R. M. 1987. *William of Malmesbury.* Woodbridge: The Boydell Press.

Timpanaro, S. 1949. "Note a Livio Andronico, Ennio, Varrone, Virgilio." *Annali della Scuola Normale Superiore di Pisa* 18: 186–204.

Traglia, A. 1962. *Cicerone, I frammenti poetici.* Milan: A. Mondadori.

Traglia, A. 1986. *Poeti latini arcaici.* Turin: Unione Tipografico-Editrice Torinese.

Treggiari, S. 1969. *Roman Freedmen During the Late Republic.* Oxford: Oxford University Press.

Tronzo, W. (ed.) 2009. *The Fragment: An Incomplete History.* Los Angeles: Getty Research Institute.

Uden, J. 2006. "Embracing the Young Man in Love: Catullus 75 and the Comic *adulescens.*" *Antichthon* 40: 19–34.

Vahlen, J. 1854. *Ennianae Poesis Reliquiae, recensuit.* Leipzig: Teubner.

Vahlen, J. 1903. *Ennianae Poesis Reliquiae, iteratis curis recensuit.* Leipzig: Teubner.

Vanderbroeck, P. J. J. 1987. *Popular Leadership and Collective Behaviour in the late Roman Republic (80–50 BC).* Amsterdam: Gieben.

Vasaly, A. 1985. "The Masks of Rhetoric: Cicero's *Pro Roscio Amerino.*" *Rhetorica* 3: 1–20.

Vasaly, A. 1996. *Representations. Images of the World in Ciceronian Oratory.* Berkeley: University of California Press.

Vasaly, A. 2002. "Cicero's Early Speeches." In J. M. May (ed.), *Brill's Companion to Cicero.* Leiden: Brill. 71–111.

Vaughn, J. W. 1985. "Law and Rhetoric in the *Causa Curiana.*" *CA* 4: 208–222.

Victor, B. 2013. "History of the Text and the Scholia." In A. Augoustakis and A. Traill (eds.), *A Companion to Terence.* Chichester, West Sussex; Malden, MA: Wiley-Blackwell. 343–362.

Victor, B. 2014. "The Transmission of Terence." In M. Fontaine and A. C. Scafuro (eds.), *Oxford Handbook of Greek and Roman Comedy.* Oxford: Oxford University Press. 699–716.

Volk, K. 2013. "The Genre of Cicero's *De consulatu suo.*" In S. A. Franoulidis, S. J. Harrison, T. D. Papanghelis (eds.), *Generic interfaces in Latin literature: encounters, interactions, and transformations.* Berlin; Boston: De Gruyter.

Walbank, F. W. 1955. "Tragic History: a Reconsideration." *BICS* 2: 4–14.

Wallace, R. 2015. *Reconstructing Damon: Music, Wisdom Teaching, and Politics in Perikles' Athens*. Oxford: Oxford University Press.

Ward, J. O. 2015. "What the Middle Ages Missed of Cicero." In W. H. F. Altman (ed.), *Brill's Companion to the Reception of Cicero*. Leiden: Brill.

Welsh, J. T. 2011. "Accius, Porcius Licinus, and the Beginning of Latin Literature." *JRS* 101: 31–50.

West, M. L. 1992. *Ancient Greek Music*. Oxford: Clarendon Press.

Wheeler, A. L. 1934/1974. *Catullus and the Traditions of Ancient Poetry*. Berkeley: University of California Press.

White, H. 1990. *The Content of the Form. Narrative Discourse and Historical Representation*. Baltimore: The Johns Hopkins University Press.

White, P. 2010. *Cicero in Letters*. New York: Oxford University Press.

Wille, G. 1967. *Musica Romana*. Amsterdam: P. Schippers.

Wiseman, T. P. 1974. *Cinna the Poet, and other Roman essays*. Leicester: Leicester University Press.

Wiseman, T. P. 1979. *Clio's Cosmetics*. Leicester: Leicester University Press.

Wiseman, T. P. 1985. *Catullus and his World: A Reappraisal*. Cambridge: Cambridge University Press.

Wiseman, T. P. 1999. *Historiography and Imagination. Eight Essays on Roman Culture*. Exeter: University of Exeter Press.

Wiseman, T. P. 2002. "History, Poetry, and *Annales*." In D. S. Levene and D. P. Nelis (eds.), *Clio and the Poets: Augustan Poetry and the Traditions of Ancient Historiography*. Leiden: Brill. 331–362.

Woodman, A. J. 1988. *Rhetoric in Classical Historiography: Four Studies*. Portland, OR: Areopagitica Press.

Woolf, V. 1929 (1989). *A Room of One's Own*. San Diego, New York, London: Harcourt, Inc.

Wooten, C. W. 2011. *Hermogenes' 'On Types of Style.'* Chapel Hill: The University of North Carolina Press.

Wright, F. W. 1931. *Cicero and the Theater*. Northampton, MA: Smith College Classical Studies. No. 11.

Yakobson, A. 1992. "*Petitio* and *Largitio*: Popular Participation in the Centuriate Assembly of the Late Republic." *JRS* 82: 32–52.

Young, E. M. 2015. *Translation as Muse. Poetic Translation in Catullus' Rome*. Chicago: The University of Chicago Press.

Zetzel, J. E. G. 1972. "Cicero and the Scipionic Circle." *HSCP* 76: 173–179.

Zetzel, J. E. G. 1995. *Cicero, De Republica. Selections*. Cambridge: Cambridge University Press.

Zetzel, J. E. G. 2007. "The Influence of Cicero on Ennius." In W. Fitzgerald and E. Gowers, (eds.), *Ennius Perennis: the* Annals *and beyond*. Cambridge: Cambridge Philological Society. 1–16.

Zetzel, J. E. G. 2018. *Critics, Compilers, and Commentators. An introduction to Roman Philology, 200 BCE – 800 CE*. Oxford: Oxford University Press.

Zillinger, W. 1911. *Cicero Und Die Altrömischen Dichter*. Würzberg: Staudenraus.

Zinn, E. 1959. "Fragment über Fragmente." In J. A. Schmoll gen. Eisenwerth (ed.), *Das Unvollendete als künstlerische Form*. Bern: Francke.

Ziolokowski, J. 2000. "*Nota bene*: why the classics were neumed in the Middle Ages." *The Journal of Medieval Latin* 10: 74–114.

Zoll, G. 1962. *Cicero Platonis Aemulus*. Zurich: Juris.

Index of Passages Discussed

General Index

within textual embrace, 11, 20
within void, 20
freedmen, 58, 164
Freud, Sigmund, 5, 6
Fulvius Nobilior, M. (pr. 93 BCE), 32, 49
funeral dirges, 48, 183
Furies, 111–116
Furius Antias, A., 55

Geffcken, Katherine, 133
gemitus, 73, 179–180, 182, 183, 187, 195
genres of Latin poetry
  comedy, 20, 21, 24, 27, 39, 51, 95, 98–99, 101,
    103, 108–111, 123, 129, 136–141, 142, 146–149,
    155–172, 216
  epic, 30–35, 39, 46–49, 50–51, 98–99, 100–101,
    103, 116–119, 210–225
  fabula Atellana, 53, 141
  fabula praetexta, 20, 27, 104, 105, 130
  fabula togata, 51, 128, 160, 163
  mime, 24, 53, 99, 103, 104, 105, 106, 125, 133,
    146, 149
  satire, 20, 22–23, 39, 52, 151–152, 158–159,
    202–210
  tragedy, 19, 21, 24, 28, 39, 49, 50–51, 54, 95,
    98–99, 103, 111–116, 127, 129–132, 134–136,
    143–144, 146, 149–150, 152–154, 158–159,
    166–167, 173–176, 178–196, 215
glosses, 76, 79, 158, 161, 163
Goldschmidt, Nora, 9, 16, 17, 18
Gorgias, 34
Gracchus, C. (tr. pl. 123–122 BCE), 93, 120,
  189
Granius (herald), 202
Greek Anthology, 20, 27, 88, 89
Greek poets
  quoted in Greek, 27, 58–66, 87, 146, 148,
    160
  quoted in Latin, 23, 28, 60–61, 64, 65, 66–76,
    87, 88, 89, 90, 91, 184
Gumbrecht
  Hans Ulrich, 12

Habinek, Thomas, 6–7, 47, 48
Halliwell, Stephen, 80
Hannibal, 32, 118, 211
Hermogenes of Tarsus, 107
Herodotus, 213–214, 216
Hesiod, 59–61, 62, 75, 84, 91, 92, 141
hiatus, 57, 208, 217
historicity, 33, 38, 40, 49, 99, 200, 210–217
historiography, 199, 216, 222, 224
Hollywood, Amy, 7
Homer, 5, 10, 16, 27, 46–47, 61, 62–66, 77, 79, 80,
  91, 109, 113–114, 212

Iliad, 27, 58–59, 60, 62, 64, 65, 66, 67, 71, 74,
  77, 81, 83, 106, 148, 160, 215
Odyssey, 25, 46, 59, 62, 63–64, 67, 218
homo sum, 25, 147
Horace, 10, 50, 52, 95, 176, 183, 209
Hortensius Hortalus, Q. (cos. 69 BCE), 13, 42–43,
  124, 141, 199–201, 210, 212
humour, 53, 58, 100–101, 133, 136, 144, 202, 207
Hymn of the Salii, 48, 157, 160
Hyperbolus, 126

illud, 15, 21, 24, 41, 55, 60, 85, 102, 130, 131, 145, 151,
  209, 219, 220, 228
imagines, 6, 36
immortality, 5, 11, 33, 36, 125, 219
inquit, 21, 47, 67, 68, 73, 88, 117, 121, 122, 153, 186,
  188, 228
Isidore of Seville, 185
Isocrates, 34, 87
Iuventius, 171

Jocelyn, Henry, 9, 15, 16, 17, 18, 19, 21, 25, 58, 66,
  67, 71, 74, 78, 100, 104, 112, 113, 114, 115, 120,
  124, 130, 136, 141, 144, 145, 176, 190
jurists, 15, 17, 116–119, 144, 146, 203

Laberius, D. (writer of mime), 53, 146
Laelia (daughter of C. Laelius cos. 140 BCE),
  52, 166
Laelius, C. (cos. 140 BCE), 33, 34, 52, 119, 165, 200,
  204, 206, 208, 209, 211, 212, 221
laetari, 153, 171, 172
laetitia, 168, 169
lamentor, 27, 36, 120, 179, 180, 186, 189, 192, 196
Latinity
  bad, 50, 52, 163, 165
  good, 52, 69, 94, 163, 165
Leigh, Matthew, 133, 134, 139
Lentulus Spinther, P. Cornelius (cos. 57 BCE), 39,
  58, 105
Leonidas of Tarentum, 61, 62, 64
Lepta, Q. (praef. fab. 51 BCE), 58, 61, 84, 141
Lerner, Gerda, 197
lessus, 182–185
Lex Cincia, 32
Lex Licinia Mucia, 101
Lex Plautia, 133
Lex Roscia, 42, 131
Lex Seruilia, 203
Lex Voconia, 212
Libo, L. (annalist), 200
Licinia (Vestal Virgin), 203
Licinius Macer, C. (annalist), 199
Livius Andronicus, 19, 34, 47, 48, 175, 212
  Aegisthus, 112

For EU product safety concerns, contact us at Calle de José Abascal, 56–1°,
28003 Madrid, Spain or eugpsr@cambridge.org.